THE PHENOMENO-LOGIC OF THE I

Hector-Neri Castañeda.
Indiana University, 1985.

The Phenomeno-Logic of the I

Essays on Self-Consciousness

Hector-Neri Castañeda

Edited by

James G. Hart and Tomis Kapitan

INDIANA UNIVERSITY PRESS

Bloomington and Indianapolis

This book is a publication of

Indiana University Press

601 North Morton Street

Bloomington, Indiana 47404-3797 USA

www.indiana.edu/~iupress

Telephone orders 800-842-6796

Fax orders 812-855-7931

Orders by e-mail iuporder@indiana.edu

The paper used in this publication
meets the minimum requirements of American National Standard
for Information Sciences—Permanence of Paper
for Printed Library Materials,
ANSI Z39.48-1984.

Manufactured in the United States of America

Library of Congress Cataloging-in-Publication Data

Castañeda, Hector-Neri, date
The phenomeno-logic of the I : essays on self-consciousness /
Hector-Neri Castañeda ; edited by James G. Hart and Tomis Kapitan.
p.   cm.
Includes bibliographical references and index.
ISBN 0-253-33506-X (hardcover : alk. paper)
1. Self (Philosophy)   2. Self-consciousness.   I. Hart, James G.,
date.   II. Kapitan, Tomis, date.   III. Title.
B945.C251C37   1999
191—dc21   98-50153

1 2 3 4 5   04 03 02 01 00 99

Contents

Preface: A Note on the Essays

Hector-Neri Castañeda (1924–1991) was one of the most original philosophers in the last half-century of American philosophy. Born and raised in Guatemala, he attended the University of Minnesota, where he received a Ph.D in philosophy and wrote a dissertation under the direction of Wilfrid Sellars. He studied at Oxford University in 1955–1956, and in 1957–1969 taught philosophy at Wayne State University, where he founded the journal *Noûs* in 1967. From 1969 to 1991 he taught at Indiana University, where he was the Mahlon Powell Professor of Philosophy. He also held numerous visiting positions at different universities. He edited or authored several books and published over 200 articles during his philosophical career. In 1990 he was named to the American Academy of Arts and Sciences, and in the last month of his life he received the Presidential Medal of Honor from the Government of Guatemala.

These essays constitute Castañeda's most original work on the topics of self-reference and self-consciousness. They are chronologically arranged, though this is not necessarily the best order in which to study them. The pioneering papers, " 'He': A Study in the Logic of Self-Consciousness" (chapter 1) and "Indicators and Quasi-Indicators" (chapter 2) are wonderfully detailed studies of indexicals, attributions of indexical reference, and the irreducibility of indicators and quasi-indicators as mechanisms of reference. However, both are technical studies that contributed to Castañeda's reputation as a difficult and demanding writer (as he soon realized). Three sequels (Castañeda 1967c, 1968a, 1970) were written to introduce readers to his ideas, but while each begins simply enough, it quickly develops into a discussion of fine points within the logic of belief and knowledge. For those unfamiliar with Castañeda's work, it is advisable to begin with "On the Phenomeno-Logic of the 'I' " (chapter 3) which summarizes his early work on self-reference and foreshadows his subsequent views on the self. For an excellent summary of his overall views on indexical reference, the reader might look at chapter 4 of Castañeda 1989a.

Chapters 4–10 focus on broader philosophical issues surrounding the notion of self and the phenomenon of self-consciousness. In some of them, Castañeda developed his initial insights within the framework of his so-called *guise theory* (see Castañeda 1974, 1977a, 1983c), but much of the material is independent of that framework. Chapters 4 and 5 relate Castañeda's earlier discoveries to concerns about self-reference raised by Roderick Chisholm (in 1976 and 1981). Of chapter 5, Chisholm, in a lecture entitled "The I of Castañeda," given at Indiana University in September 1990, stated that "of all the epoch-making contributions that Hector has made to philosophy, that paper, it seems to me, is the most brilliant." Chapters 6–8 develop Castañeda's views in relation to those of Kant and Frege, while chapter 5 also contains a reply to Stephen Böer's and William Lycan's critique of the claim that first-person reference is irreducible. Chapters 9 and 10 are in many ways the most sustained, original, and philosophically relevant studies of self-consciousness. Each of chapters 4–10 can be understood without mastery of the earlier papers and, for the most part, each can be studied independently. Those who would like to understand how the views developed therein fit into Castañeda's general philosophical scheme are advised to read his "*De Dicto*: My Philosophical Search" in the *Profiles* volume (Tomberlin 1986, 77–140).

Castañeda's references to other works have been adjusted to the name-date system of citation correlated to a single bibliography for the entire volume. Beyond this change and minor typographical corrections, the essays are reprinted as they originally appeared, with one exception. In 1989 Castañeda published an essay entitled "The Reflexivity of Self-Consciousness: Sameness/Identity, Data for Artificial Intelligence" followed by "Self-Consciousness, *I*-Structures, and Physiology" in 1990. That these essays are manifestations of a single philosophical work is evidenced by the fact that the 1990 essay contains *verbatim* most of the material of the 1989 essay. To avoid repetition, we have used the 1990 essay as a base text and inserted into it those portions of the 1989 essay it does not contain. Where this is done, brackets indicate the inserted material. The result is that both papers are included in their entirety within chapter 10, and the overall product is a more complete and unified narrative than either offers singly.

Having two introductions to an edited volume is unusual. The purpose of Tomis Kapitan's introduction is to show how Castañeda's reflections on self-consciousness are anchored in his theory of indexical reference. James G. Hart's introduction points out the surprising linkages between Castañeda's views and theories of self-consciousness developed within Continental philosophy since Husserl. Together, they illustrate how Castañeda's reflections on the self and the first-person are both systematic yet relevant to a broad range of contemporary philosophical concerns.

A word of advice to the reader. Besides the conceptual challenges Castañeda's essays pose, they are burdened by cumbersome notations, particularly by unwieldy labels for main principles and by the ubiquitous asterisk. It would be unfortunate if these were allowed to become barriers to understanding. We believe that, collectively, these papers contain novel insights into some of the most intriguing issues connected with the Cartesian *cogito*, namely, the nature and implications of self-consciousness. Though challenging, they are conceptually rich, imaginative, and like their author, interspersed with measures of humor, elegance, and generosity.

Acknowledgments

The editors would like to thank George Nakhnikian, Myles Brand, Michael Dunn, Oscar Marti, James Tomberlin, William Rapaport, and Christopher Crockett, who have helped us at various stages in this project. We are indebted to Kicab Castañeda for access to Castañeda's computer files and for permission to reprint chapter 7; to members of the Lilly Library staff whose assistance was necessary to determine whether anything in Castañeda's unpublished work merited inclusion in this volume; to the Indiana University Office of Publications for permission to reprint the photograph of Castañeda; and to the editors and publishing houses of the original texts for their kind permission to republish the material included herein. Finally, we would like to express our gratitude to those philosophers, unknown to us, who expressed support for this project to Indiana University Press.

INTRODUCTION

First-Person Reference

Tomis Kapitan

A self is what is referred to in the first person: what the first person pronoun denotes in its proper and correct use. Hence, the structure of the mechanisms of self-reference reveal at least part of the structure of the self.
—Hector-Neri Castañeda, "Attributions of Self-Reference"
(*Nachlass*)

Castañeda's writings on self-consciousness and first-person reference span nearly three decades, and until his final days, these topics continued to be at the forefront of his philosophical attention. Building upon his early work on practical thinking and the private language arguments, he was among the first to locate an indispensable element of self-reference in the genesis of action and to investigate the logic of attributions of self-regarding attitudes. Convinced that philosophical questions concerning the *self* are rooted in the use of first-person pronouns, he went on to develop his initial insights within a philosophical system designed to resolve a wide array of problems in metaphysics, epistemology, and ethics. Yet many of his proposals concerning self-reference and self-consciousness are adaptable to other frameworks and deserve separate attention in their own right.

The Irreducibility of First-Person Reference

One of Castañeda's best-known observations was that replacements of first-person pronouns by coreferring expressions, such as names, definite descriptions, and demonstratives, commonly fail to preserve truth and meaning. A woman might use the sentence, 'The one who wrote that letter lacks subtlety,' to express a belief that she would not express with 'I lack subtlety' even though, unbeknownst to her, she is the one who wrote the letter. Conversely, she might assert 'I am a clever writer' yet reject 'The one who wrote that letter is a clever writer.' Other substitutions disrupt modal status, for instance, 'I am uttering nothing' is contingently false, but 'The person uttering this token is uttering nothing' is self-contradictory. This substitution also imputes conceptual abilities—e.g., concepts of *person*, *token*, or *utterance*—that cannot be expected of all users such as small children. As such, the meaning of 'I' is not that of 'the person uttering this token.'

Related difficulties arise in the attempt to accurately report or ascribe first-person usage. For example, if I want to report what the Editor of *Soul* said with the words,

(1) I am a millionaire.

it would be inappropriate to use,

(2) The Editor of *Soul* believes that I am a millionaire.

since 'I' invariably expresses the speaker's self-reference—in this case, my own—not the attributee's, unless I know that I am the attributee. Instead, I must indicate that it is the Editor of *Soul* who is believed to be a millionaire. By whom? Well, by himself, the very man I refer to with 'the Editor of *Soul*,' and his belief is true just in case this referent is a millionaire. However, the report,

(3) The Editor of *Soul* believes that the Editor of *Soul* is a millionaire.

is misleading if it ascribes to the Editor the belief,

(4) The Editor of *Soul* is a millionaire.

The Editor might not realize that he is the Editor of *Soul* and, consequently, might not believe what he would report with (4) despite his affirmation of (1). Similar difficulties arise by substituting other coreferring descriptions, names, or demonstratives for the occurrence of 'the Editor of *Soul*' within attitudindal scope in (3). Even if the Editor of *Soul* takes 'the Editor of *Soul*' to designate himself, it is doubtful that (3) captures what is affirmed with (1). If it did, then

(5) I am an editor.

as uttered by the Editor of *Soul*, and

(6) The Editor of *Soul* is an editor.

should have the same significance. Yet (5) seems contingent and informative in a way that (6) does not.

A more promising candidate for recording the Editor's belief is,

(7) The Editor of *Soul* believes that he himself is a millionaire.

The reflexive 'he himself' serves as a proxy for the first-person pronoun by depicting a first-person reference that someone makes or is disposed to make. It too cannot be replaced by coreferring descriptions, names, or demonstratives, even when these are its antecedents. Nor does it behave as a typical bound variable as in,

(8) $(\exists x)(x=$The Editor of *Soul* and the Editor of *Soul* believes that x is a millionaire).

This statement is true if (3) is, but since (3) can be true without the Editor believing that he himself is a millionaire, (7) cannot be parsed as (8). More generally, insofar as 'he himself' is used to attribute belief in what a person would normally express by using the first-person pronoun, it cannot be replaced by the standard variables of quantification.

Although 'he himself' represents or depicts someone's first-person reference, it is not itself an indexical. It is a *quasi-indicator*—a linguistic device for attributing indexical reference—whose proper abode is within *oratio obliqua* constructions. Like the first-person pronoun, it cannot be eliminated from the language of propositional attitudes without loss of content and change of truth-value. This fact constitutes further evidence for the *irreducibility* of first-person reference, though the order of explanation is exactly the reverse: quasi-indicators like 'he himself' and 'she herself' are ineliminable because they represent what is essentially first-person usage.[1]

At first sight, the claim that first-person pronouns constitute irreplaceable, ineliminable referring expressions is odd. It seems obvious that my 'I' tokens designate the very same person picked out by the name 'Tomis Kapitan,' or by various descriptions or demonstratives available to others as well as to me. So what does the irreducibility of first-person reference come to? What is its source? What is its significance?

These questions motivated Castañeda's subsequent studies of self-consciousness. He addressed the source of irreducibility from the outset when he spoke of first-person pronouns as unique *mechanisms of reference* or *ways of referring* through which one refers to oneself. But this raises only further questions: what are these referential "mechanisms" or "ways," and in what sense are they irreducible? To answer them we must examine what reference is for Castañeda and how indexical reference is distinguished from other forms.

Thinking Reference

The term 'refers' and its cognates are multifaceted. We are familiar with talk about the reference of singular terms, but, for Castañeda, referring is first and foremost something we *do* intentionally, for example, when we direct someone's attention to a thing. Since we cannot purposely direct attention upon what we ourselves do not attend to, there must be a psychological process of consciously "picking out" an item to be talked about. This, too, is a kind of reference—*thinking reference*—wherein one focuses upon one item to the exclusion of others for the purposes of thinking or saying something about it.[2] Linguistic "mechanisms of reference" play a causal role in producing and communicating references, and the irreducibility of any such mechanism is a function of the peculiar semantic or conceptual resources that guide its use. Indexicals, in particular, are irreducible to non-indexical mechanisms since they embody a unique access to referents. Let us expand upon this more carefully.

To thinkingly refer to something requires some means of distinguishing it from other things of which one is aware. These means—modes of presentation or identifying properties of the referent—constitute the conceptual mechanisms underlying reference. If I report that *the Louvre is in Paris,* for example, I must have some way of picking out the Louvre, say, as the largest art gallery in France or *qua* that huge building over there across the Seine. Each description corresponds to a mode through which the referent is distinguished, even if this mode is not itself articulated in my report. Several modes of presentation might be operative within a single act, as when one says; "Look at that one, the statue to the left, the only Michelangelo in the room," and while some modes may be generic, at least one must permit the user to identify or individuate the referent.

It is tempting to say that a mode of presentation cannot guide reference unless it corresponds to a genuine status or property of the referent, but this is not quite right. If the one I pick out with 'the man drinking a martini in the corner' is neither a man nor drinking a martini then the expressed mode is not satisfied. Since I have referred, however, I have utilized some identifying mechanism even if best conveyed through demonstratives, e.g., 'that person,' or, simply, 'that.' If one of these does not hit the mark, then I have not succeeded in referring to anything. We must recognize the following *satisfaction principle*:

> One thinkingly refers to an item only by distinguishing it through a mode of presentation uniquely satisfied by it.

While it is another matter to characterize precisely the act of distinguishing, we can allow that a mode is operative in reference only if it is either satisfied by the referent or *implies* a mode that is so satisfied.[3]

Indexical Execution Is
Not Indexical Interpretation

Indexicals offer a simple means of making, expressing, and communicating thinking references. They are particularly useful when proper names or descriptions are either cumbersome or unavailable, say, when demonstratives like *that* or *that thing over there* represent the only way of picking out what suddenly looms into vision. Or, a kidnapped heiress locked in a trunk of a car might think: *It is quiet here now*, without having any other means of locating herself. In such cases indexicals provide *autonomous* mechanisms for executing a reference that do not depend upon the user's possession of other ways of referring to the same items.

How is indexical reference explained? The context-sensitivity of indexicals precludes both a causal chain account and a solution in terms of the reference-fixing meanings, senses, or *characters* of linguistic types.[4] One popular solution takes character in combination with context of usage to do the trick. That is, by (i) grasping rules specifying the relations between tokens of a given indexical type to their referents, and (ii) understanding relevant features of context, one is able to understand what indexically expressed thoughts are about. For instance, the relation of a 'now' token to a duration is that of being the time of the token's utterance, while that of an 'I' token to its referent is given in a rule such as:

(I) A token of the first-personal indexical pronoun 'I' refers to the speaker of the utterance in which it occurs.

Hearing you say, 'I am now going to throw the ball over there,' for example, then my grasping the characters of 'I,' 'now,' and 'there'—as displayed in rules like (I)—and knowing that you uttered the sentence, when you uttered it, and what region you demonstrated, enable me to determine what your referents are.

To so account for my interpretation of your indexical utterance, however, is not to explain your indexical reference. In fact, if all indexical references were guided by token-reflexive rules, then none would be *autonomous*.[5] Obviously, to *interpret* what another person is referring to indexically one must have a separate access to the referent—for which reason quasi-indicators have antecedents—but this does not explain the speaker's *production* of first-person pronouns. One who uses 'I am hungry' to demand food is referring with 'I,' but not by first apprehending that very 'I' token and then determining its referent by recourse to context. Otherwise we would be at a loss to explain how 'I' references are initiated.[6] The speaker's production of a first-person pronoun is not guided by a rule suitable only for its interpretation and, therefore, the mechanisms for executing a first-person reference must be distinguised from those used in its interpretation.[7]

How Indexical Identification Is Achieved

If token-reflexive accounts cannot explain the execution of a first-person reference, what will? Castañeda's solution exploits the idea that reference is *indexical* because it originates in and reflects a thinker's experience of objects from a particular point of view or *perspective*: "indexicality is simply the general involvement with experience that indicators denote" (Castañeda 1990m, 68). Accordingly, each indexical referent is singled out through a unique perspectival mode of presentation or, as Castañeda preferred to say, a *particularized* perspectival property, a relational attribute that the referent has in virtue of being experienced by the user. There are two central features of such a property; an indexical *form* of experience and a *position* within a perspective. Let us look at each in turn.

I. *The Indexical Form.* Part of the productive meaning of any indexical token is the manner in which the speaker encounters the referent, as evidenced by the information values of indexical types. If I say, *You will be more comfortable in this chair*, then I am addressing someone I take to be within my present communicational reach. Similarly, my saying, *It was hot here yesterday* expresses something about my perspective on a place and time designated in a way that *It was hot in Chicago on July 13, 1997* does not. No indexical is a mere label; each informs the audience of how items are experienced, whether as immediately presented, e.g., pure demonstratives such as 'this' or 'there,' or as vicariously confronted through a relation to present experience, as in 'that building [pointing to a photo of the Dome of the Rock] is in Jerusalem.' The temporal demonstratives 'now' and 'then' not only designate intervals of time, but intervals *as* related to a present experience, the former to the actual time of that experience, the latter to some preceding interval. Similarly, 'this' and 'that' represent items as *present to* consciousness, respectively, in the foreground and background. Each indexical type is associated with a unique *manner* or *form of encounter* through which the user is related experientially to a referent.[8]

What, then, is the form of encounter associated with the production of first-person pronouns? It cannot be what is offered by rule (I), and the irreducibility arguments block the simple rule of reflexivity:

(I′) A token of the first-personal indexical 'I' is used by the speaker to refer to himself (herself).

Referring to oneself is necessary for a first-person use of 'I' but not sufficient. Instead, Castañeda offered,

(I*) A token of the first-personal indexical 'I' is used (by the speaker) to refer to oneself *qua* self.

That is, to refer with a first-person token is to be aware of oneself *internally*, through an irreducible *self* mode, and this differs from any variety of *external* awareness of oneself through non-first-person forms of encounter. While Castañeda spoke of the self-concept as unique, primitive, and inexplicable, chapter 10 below attempts to deepen our understanding of this form of personal encounter.

Still, generic indexical forms of encounter like that specified in (I*) do not perform the identifying tasks associated with the production of indexical tokens. What does? It is not enough to relativize forms to persons or utterances since tokens of the same indexical type belonging to a single utterance can differ in reference, e.g., 'This is larger than this' or 'You, you, you, and you leave, but you stay here.' Nor is the user's *perspective* enough, whether we understand this to be the user's spatio-temporal vantage point or a spatio-temporal ordering of contents determined by that vantage point. As long as the temporal component of a perspective has the temporal thickness of an utterance, then tokens of 'this' or of 'you' in these examples issue from one and the same perspective yet are connected to distinct mechanisms of identification. Perspective alone does not do the job.

II. *The Position within a Perspective*. Particularized indexical properties or modes also embody the orientations or *positions* that referents occupy within a given perspective. In the example above, each of the 'you' referents is individuated through a different place in a field of awareness vis-à-vis the speaker's unique vantage point identified with 'here' and 'now.' The referent itself occupies the position if reference is immediate, whereas a distinct content does when reference is vicarious, e.g., the photo in the Dome of the Rock case. For dynamic thoughts like, *This is moving fast*, where the referent retains its identity as a *this* though not its spatio-temporal locale, we can speak of an ordering of positions. For 'I' tokens, the position is always that of the perspective's point of origin.

Thus, indexical individuation exploits a unique blend of three factors: (i) a generic form of encounter (an *I*, a *you*, a *this*, etc.), (ii) a perspective, and (iii) a position or ordering of positions within that perspective. An item is an indexical referent by having a *particularized* indexical status, that is, by being encountered *through* a form of encounter *at* a position *within* a perspective.[9] Such a finely grained status is *ephemeral*, but, as indicated above, a token-solipsism that posits a special individuating mode for each indexical token can be avoided, thereby allowing instances of 'I am I' or 'this is this' to be trivially true.

Some Corollaries of This Analysis

With this account other properties of indexicals are readily derivable. First, indexicals are multiply *irreducible*. Since non-indexical mechanisms of reference fail to express the essential involvement with immediate experience, none can serve as an analysandum of an indexical mode. Nor can the various indexical types be reduced to another, since each differs in associated form of encounter. Further, each individuating mode or property differs from others of the same type because of a difference either in perspective or in position within perspective.

Second, there is an essential *subjectivity* of individuating indexical modes. One person's 'I,' 'this,' or 'over there' expresses, in part, what is unique to his or her perspective at the time of utterance, making it impossible for another to gain a cognitive fix on the very same item in precisely the same way (see chapter 10). For this reason, interpreting indexicals is not to replicate indexical production. Nor do quasi-indicators reproduce someone's indexical references but, at best, only approximate them.[10]

Third, because of the essential involvement with experience, indexical status is a relational or an *extrinsic* property of the referent. Just as something is not a *you* unless encountered as an addressee, so too, no one is an *I* apart from internal self-awareness. Of course, a referent of 'I' is something intrinsically, namely, a "subject of experience" (see chapter 9), but its status as an *I* is possessed only *qua* object of experience, specifically, as the object of an episode of internal self-awareness.

From Indexical Mechanisms to Indexical Contents

It is tempting to conclude that first-person pronouns have no special ontological significance, that the irreducibility of 'I' and other indexicals is rooted in their indispensible psychological roles, not in reference to unique sort of entities.[11] But this is not Castañeda's view. While he did not follow Descartes in concluding that the first-person referent is a non-physical substance—preferring to leave this question open—he resisted attempts to confine irreducibility to statements about the psychological roles of referential mechanisms. Let us see why.

The conjunction of the satisfaction principle (above) with Castañeda's understanding of the irreducibility thesis implies that there are first-person *properties* possessed by the referents of first-person pronouns. I am an *I*, and so are you and any other internally self-aware being. But while we are the same to this extent, my particular *I*-ness differs from yours. Moreover, my *I*-ness now differs from that of last year, yesterday, or an hour ago. Some philosophers balk at this point; indexical mechanisms are just that, mechanisms or modes of apprehension—properties of the thinker, not of the contents apprehended—and it is only a "sloppy thinker" who confuses a "privileged perspective" on ourselves with a "privileged picture" of what is seen (Kaplan 1989, 533–534).

Castañeda leaned towards a direct reference account of indexicals in his early writings (chapters 1 and 2) but abandoned it when he realized that by acknowledging indexical elements within attitudinal contents various properties of those contents can be explained. Specifically, first-person elements are integral not only to their motivational force of intentions but also to their inferential powers. Suppose I believe,

(9) I am obliged to award the Medal of Efficiency to Henry at 10 A.M.

To comply with this self-avowed obligation, I must be able to pick out the appropriate items and link them to the appropriate elements in my commitment. How is this achieved? Indexically, of course. I see a small round object on the table and think that *This medallion is the Medal of Efficiency*; my attention is directed to the candidates seated in a row of chairs and I realize that *That man is Henry*; I glance at my watch and conclude that *Now it is 10 A.M., the time to act*. In each case, I accept observational statements of the form: *i is the same as a*, where *i* is an indexical and *a* is a non-indexical. By their means I infer from (9),

(10) I am obliged, all things considered, to give this medal to that man now.

and from this, I infer the proximal intention,

(11) I shall now give this medal to that man.

My action is explained by my acceptance of (11) and this, in turn, by my acceptance of (10). The inference from (9) to (11) could not be made if the sameness propositions I accept are of the form: *a is the same as a*. Were (10) the very same proposition as (9), then (9) alone should be sufficient for my inferring (11) and explaining my action. Since it is *not* sufficient, (10) must differ from (9), and the difference lies with the modes associated with the referring expressions.[12]

If content is indexical, then the subjective, privileged status of indexical reference is as much a property of what is apprehended as it is of an apprehending. The mere claim that experience is real does not imply this since non-perspectival descriptions of particular experiences are possible. But if there are truths expressible *only* in indexical language, as the irreducibility arguments imply, then perspectivity and subjectivity demand special ontological attention. Castañeda was not among the reductive naturalists at this point. Instead, he followed in the footsteps of Leibniz and Whitehead by taking perspective as an irreducible aspect of experience.

The Metaphysics of First-Person Reference: The Empirical Self

First-person modes of presentation enter into content because they are constitutive of first-person *referents*, for when we thinkingly refer we immediately grasp referents—individuals, logical subjects—not just Fregean *Sinn*. However, like Frege, Castañeda did not think that these graspable individuals are the distant, massive, physical objects posited to account for the unity of one's experience: "the *total* physical object is never before the consciousness of the perceiver, nor before his belief-rehearsing consciousness" (Castañeda 1977a, 300; 1989a, 16–17). Instead, each individuating mode of presentation determines a distinct object of referential consciousness, a *strict* thinking referent. Each time I think about the Washington Monument, for example, I confront what I express with tokens of 'the Washington Monument' or 'that big obelisk'. I might also *believe* that there is an external enduring physical structure, but that massive continuant is not what I am directly aware of. At best, it is my *doxastic referent*, what I believe to be the semantic value of the type 'the Washington Monument' in my idiolect. Similarly, while I might believe that 'I' is correlated to a person, a disembodied soul, or an organic physical system, the enduring me, that continuant is not immediately confronted. What is confronted is a more finely individuated strict referent of a first-person token.

Castañeda analyzed strict referents by means of his theory of guises. Each guise is a concrete entity of the form $c\{F_1, \ldots, F_n\}$, where $\{F_1, \ldots, F_n\}$ is a set of properties constitutive of, or internal to, it and by which it is differentiated. The operator 'c' expresses the transformation of a set of properties into a distinct concrete individual.[13] Indexical thinking referents are distinguished by having a particularized indexical property within its core properties. Not being cognitive contents, alleged substrates find no place within thinking semantics, nor are the strict thinking referents massive external objects. All predication of external properties—those not included in the guise core—is analyzed in terms of various *sameness* relations among guises (Castañeda 1974, 1983c).

The first-person strict referent is an *I-guise* whose core internal property is a particularized self-property or first-person mode. Every first-person reference posits an *I*-guise as fully present (chapter 9); there are no past selves or future selves since past and future perspectives cannot be accessed (chapter 6). Nor is there a substrate underlying the history of a self; immediate consciousness is confined to properties and groupings of properties that make up individuals. There is no enduring *I*, and insofar as we speak of a "self" or "person," we are speaking either of the *empirical self*—a set of contemporaneous consubstantiated I-guises—or a temporally ordered series of empirical selves (chapters 6, 8). Of course, there is a sense in which I am the same as the person who wrote a dissertation under Hector-Neri Castañeda's direction over twenty years ago. *I* wrote that dissertation. Which *I*? Well this *I*, the same one who is now writing this introduction. Yet on Castañeda's view, there is no genuine identity here, only a very tight sameness relation—*transubstantiation*—between present *I*-guises and previous *I*-guises that I can now refer to only vicariously.[14]

The Metaphysics of First-Person Reference: The Transcendent Subject

If the *I* exists only as an object of first-person awareness, then a metaphysics of first-person consciousness should begin and end with a theory of the empirical selves, hence, with *I*-guises. However, Castañeda also accepted the Kantian view that an *I think* must be capable of accompanying all conscious states. He referred to the "I think" as a *transcendental prefix* but went beyond Kant in expanding it to include the *here* and *now* as well. The 'I' of the prefix designates a *transcendental I-guise*, yet its full significance is not exhausted by a guise-theoretic analysis since it also *points*—not *refers*—to a transcendent self or subject existing beyond immediate thinking content (Castañeda 1986a, 106). This subject cannot be an *I* given his account of indexical status, yet it can be the "same" as various empirical and transcendental I-guises (Castañeda 1986a, 109–110). A similar point can be made for the 'here' and 'now' of the transcendental prefix.

The presence of 'thinks' in the prefix provided Castañeda an opening to a metaphysical examination of the structures underlying self-consciousness. Not everything real can be an *I*. Since the pointed-to reality—the transcendent self—is something that *thinks,* then only thinking things are capable of being first-person referents, whatever else they might be. Unlike the ontologically promiscuous 'this' and 'that,' an 'I' is appropriately applied only to subjects of experience, more exactly, to subjects capable of internal reflexive awareness: "the essence and substance of an I is just to conceive itself as subject *qua* subject" (chapter 6). The interesting metaphysical questions include these: What it is about an entity that makes it capable not only of internal reflexive awareness, but of self-awareness over time? What properties must an experiencing subject have that allow it to be an entity capable of self-consciousness and self-reference?

This last question is of special interest since, on Castañeda's view, the internal self-awareness that underlies first-person reference is not a universal feature of consciousness,[15] and he thought that blindsight is a type of visual consciousness without self-consciousness. Accordingly, there must be some account of how internal self-consciousness arises within the broader domain of experiences, including those episodes of self-consciousness that are merely external. Like Kant, Castañeda was very much concerned with the unity of self within a single episode of consciousness composed of several experiences; thus, while the subject "pointed" to by the *I* of the transcendental prefix is not an internally self-aware being, it does correspond to a maximal unity of the experiences that are "internally unified into one total experience by virtue of the being co-conscious of a manifold of contents." A detailed examination of this unification is the concern of chapters 9 and 10.

There is no polished finalized theory in these last papers. Instead, we are left with a series of probings into the nature of the consciousness that makes self-reference and first-person thinking possible. On this score, Castañeda followed in the footsteps of Hume, Kant, and Whitehead, who also endeavored to give a metaphysics of experiential processes. There are many interesting features of his treatment, and the reader is encouraged to examine them directly. The purpose of this introduction has been to indicate their genesis in Castañeda's novel account of first-person reference.

Notes

1. Castañeda noted that some occurrences of both 'he himself' and 'I' within *oratio obliqua* are replaceable, but the replacement sentences must contain other occurrences of those expressions. Quasi-indicators within the scope of a single operator are ineliminable. He extended the notion of a *quasi-indicator* to cover expressions that can be used to repre-

sent other types of indexical usage, for example, 'there' and 'then' in 'Yesterday, in the trunk, the heiress thought that it was quiet there then' to report a thought that a kidnapped heiress formulates with 'It is quiet here now.'

2. To thinkingly refer to something is to "pick it up in thought as a subject of properties and as an object of a propositional attitude" (chapter 10). Castañeda also spoke of *singular reference* as "reference to individuals *insofar as* they are thought of as individuals" and as "a fundamental phenomenon lying at the root of every exercise of our thinking powers" (Castañeda 1989a, 3). Yet, reference does not exhaust consciousness. To think referringly to an item is to think it *qua* logical subject, whereas we think *predicatively* of a property in attributing it to a logical subject (chapter 5). One can also think of things in a *classificatory* way, as when I think of blueness in thinking that *the blue tie is expensive*.

3. The linkage of identifying to referring is similar to what Evans called "Russell's Principle" (Evans 1982, 74, 89), namely that in order to think about a particular object one must be able to "discriminate the object from all other things" (89). That Castañeda was committed to what I here call the satisfaction principle is evident in Castañeda 1989a: " . . . thinking in (perceptual) absence can reach its objects only if it segregates them from other objects by means of a set of uniquely possessed traits" (77). This principle should not be taken as requiring an ability to *re*identify the same item in another context; in one setting I might distinguish a square box by means of its color and location, but I may be unable to reidentify that same box if the background is altered.

4. Context-sensitivity does not distinguish indexical reference since proper names are similarly context-sensitive (Castañeda 1989a, chapter 2). Nor is it enough to say that indexicals express the speaker's point of view. For Castañeda, every thinking reference is from the thinker's "point of view," never from an external or absolute point of view; there is no direct word-to-world connection that does not go through the thinker(s) to whom the words belong. This is the kernel of Kant's Copernican Revolution (see chapter 10 and Castañeda 1981, 285–286).

5. This conclusion is explicitly favored by some who offer token–reflexive rules like (I). For instance, Ruth Millikan writes: " . . . a token of 'I' does not tell me who the originator of that token is, that it is, say, Alvin. Rather, if I am to understand a token of 'I', I must *already know* who the speaker is" (Millikan 1993, 270–271).

6. This point is overlooked by Carol Rovane, who writes that one who uses 'I' needs to know that she is the speaker, since one speaks with the intention of getting the interpreter to recognize that its referent is identical to the speaker (Rovane 1987, 161, 166). This view is inimical to Castañeda's insistence that thinking reference is different from communicational reference, and it fails to distinguish between *referring with 'I'* and *knowing that one refers with 'I.'* The latter requires knowing that the referent of 'I' is also the speaker, but the former does not.

7. This argument is presented in Castañeda 1983b, 323. See also Evans 1985, 320, and Recanati 1993, chapter 4. Castañeda's emphasis upon the creative or executive role of indexical usage (1989a, chapter 4; 1983b; and 1989c) suggests a limitation to the view that our use of language is primarily that of *consumers* (as advocated in Kaplan 1989, 602–603, and Millikan 1993, 86). To be sure, we are first exposed to language as consumers; the words we consume come with prepackaged meaning and our use of indexicals illustrates this as much as anything else. Yet the speaker produces the tokens, and with indexicals— perhaps more so than with descriptions and names—the speaker invests the tokens with content.

8. Indexical forms of encounter are ways that thinkers cognize referents, e.g., as an *I*, a *you*, or a *now*. While distinct from the interpretive forms of being the speaker, being the

addressee, and being simultaneous with the time of utterance, they are equally public. Since each corresponds to a relational property of the referent, then we can understand how indexical expressions can be coupled with determiners, e.g., "an I", "a this", "her that," "*qua* you," and so forth. The common noun usage of indexicals helps explain quasi-indicators: when we say that 'Yesterday at noon, Marlo thought that she herself was then happy,' the quasi-indicator 'she herself' is a proxy for Marlo's 'I' because it expresses, for the attributor, 'Marlo, thought of by Marlo *qua* I.' Similarly, 'then' expresses 'Yesterday noon, thought of by Marlo *qua* now.'

9. See chapter 2, which speaks of *perspectival properties*, and Castañeda 1990d, 303, where a contrast is drawn between determinable and determinate indexical properties. The situation is more complex for the modes associated with indexical descriptions like 'the man in the corner' which include an additional sortal factor. Also, for vicarious reference it is not the position of the *referent* that enters the mode but that of the *immediate content*— the photograph in the example of the Dome of the Rock—to which the referent bears a special relation.

10. This is a matter on which Castañeda's views changed. In the 1980s he gave up his earlier view that the quasi-indexical *that*-clause in an attribution like (5) expresses the very same proposition expressed by the attributee's (1) (see Castañeda 1983a, 307). Lacking the essential perspectivity and subjectivity of indexicals, 'he himself' does not express the full content of 'I.' This consequence came to Castañeda "embarrassingly slowly" as he once put it, but it is a natural consequence of the fine-grained distinctions made in response to the puzzles surrounding thinking reference. In Kapitan 1998b I argue that quasi-indica-tors are abstractive devices, best construed as variables bound by implicit quantifiers. Al-though quasi-indicators do not capture the exact content of what the attributee thinks indexically, they do tell us *what* is being referred to (*qua* anaphors) and *how* the reference is being made.

11. See, for example, Lycan 1996, which urges that the failures of substitutivity for 'I' can be "rendered unsurprising and ontologically harmless" (56). Lycan argues that con-cepts can have the same extension but differ functionally by playing different roles in the guidance of behavior given various stimuli. Also, concepts can have similar functional profiles but differ in extension. Now a *self* concept or mental *I* is one which functions as an *I*, has its owner as the sole member of its extension, and no one else could use a com-putationally parallel concept of their own to designate the original owner. But this dis-tinctness of the self-concept "reveals no ontological specialness of the self" (58), and there is no warrant for positing "intrinsically subjective or perspectival facts" that serve as the objects of self-regarding attitudes (68).

12. See chapters 6 and 10 of Castañeda 1975a, and also 1989c. Castañeda's account differs from direct reference views of indexicals that regard only the *referents* of indexicals as significant for semantic evaluations, not their mediating senses, concepts, or modes (see Kaplan 1989). To be sure, these accounts do not share Castañeda's concern with immedi-ate thinking reference, and in their view of indexical referents as enduring external objects it is understandable that they take indexicality as negligible in semantic content.

13. See Rosenberg 1986a, 157–161, and Kapitan 1990b, 478–479 for more extended discussions of the concretizing operator.

14. See Castañeda 1974 on transubstantiation. Despite the appeal to guises at this juncture, it is important to understand that Castañeda's account of first-person reference is compatible with a variety of ontological schemes, and does not stand or fall with the viability of Guise Theory. There are other accounts of objects *qua* modes that make fine-grained distinctions among thinking referents, for example, Whitehead's, to whose meta-

physics of experience Castañeda's theory is similar. Both thinkers took episodes of experience as fundamental units and explained larger spatio-temporal structures in terms of relationships among experiences, relations that involve not only an integration of experiences but an amalgamation of their contents (see Whitehead 1929, part III). Also, both found experience to be saturated with indexicality; in Whiteheadian terms, this is the *vector* character of experience whereby there is a transmission of content from a particular point to a percipient unification.

15. From 1970 on Castañeda argued for the possibility of an Externus consciousness, one without self-consciousness (see Castañeda 1970). In chapter 5 below he rejects the "Self-Ascription" views of Chisholm 1981 and Lewis 1979. Chisholm has since acknowledged the force of some of Castañeda's criticisms (Hahn 1997, 531). Even if one agrees that not all consciousness involves first-person awareness, it remains open whether a consciousness of perspective—the perspective that happens to be one's own—accompanies every state of perceptual thinking. I have argued for this claim in discussing the views of Castañeda, Manfred Frank, and others in Kapitan 1998a.

Castañeda

A Continental Philosophical Guise

James G. Hart

1. Introduction

This essay presents a continental-philosophical perspective on the thought of Hector-Neri Castañeda, especially his theory of self-consciousness. By "continental philosophy" I shall mean primarily phenomenology, which had its birthplace on "the continent" but now enjoys residence almost everywhere; but I shall also mean the "Heidelberg School," i.e., Dieter Henrich and his students, primarily Manfred Frank. Through the work of these thinkers, along with phenomenology's continued inquiry into self-consciousness, the self, first-person reference, and intersubjectivity, there have been convergences of philosophical interests on the side of analytic and continental philosophies.

Some ("Post-modern" and "deconstructionist") continental philosophers have come to hold that the themes of consciousness and subjectivity have outlived their significance in the disclosure of the foundation of meaning. Indeed, for these philosophers the subject's central position is to be displaced in favor of a play of differences analogous to the de Saussurian displacement of a positive central phonemic sense for, e.g., *b,* in favor of the differences in which it occurs, e.g., *bed, bang, blow, bat, bud, bingo,* etc. These philosophers, often under the influence of Nietzsche and Heidegger, have been busy eliminating consciousness's essential function in the foundations of meaning in favor of the interplay of differences and, at the same time, eliminating or indefinitely postponing (Derrida's *différance*) any essentially determining contexts. At the same time, and quite in contrast, Dieter Henrich and the Heidelberg School had occasion to enter into conversation with the remarkable renascent philosophy of the subject in British and American analytic philosophy, especially in the writings of Castañeda, Geach, Anscombe, Chisholm,

Shoemaker, Nagel, McGinn, *et alii*. The teaching and writings of Dieter Henrich (to whom Castañeda dedicated an essay in this volume) as well as the work of Manfred Frank were the primary forces in seeing that Castañeda's thought has become at least as well known in parts of Europe as in the United States and that "continental philosophy" in Germany now has undergone a transformation so as to include Castañeda *et alii* as major voices.[1] This introduction will sketch some of the issues of this analytic-continental conversation as they pertain to Castañeda's theories of self-consciousness and transcendental philosophy.

2. Castañeda's Transcendental Prefix and the Transcendental Philosophical Standpoint

Post-modern continental philosophy's rejection of the philosophy of consciousness and the subject was in part propelled by the appropriation of the later Wittgenstein in the service of hermeneutics and Heidegger's own displacement of the subject.[2] But for Castañeda the Wittgensteinian critiques are far too drastic to support a semantic socialism, i.e., the project of bestowing authority for meaning on conventional linguistic practices is building on sand. Castañeda believed that the numerous difficulties generated by Wittgenstein's reflections, in fact, pointed in the direction of classical skepticism. The doubts sowed by first considering that a rule is something that we are free to follow, and then the difficulty of applying the rule based on the previous applications when, indeed, we may doubt the reliability of the previous applications of the rules, and, further compounding these difficulties, the questionable reliability of memory, apply not merely to the private individual but also to the other persons set on correcting a fellow speaker's use of a language. In a word, Wittgenstein's skeptical query does not lead to complacency in a semantic socialism but rather to an extreme Protagoreanism or even a Heraclitean chaos where the very notion of a linguistic rule is called into question.[3]

Thus Castañeda sees Wittgenstein's wrestle with the foundations of meaning in the great tradition of those who strove to answer the problems posed by Descartes' supposition of an Evil Demon. And this is the tradition wherein Castañeda locates himself. He holds that the radical skeptic's arguments are indefeasible. All experience might be illusory; I might be a brain in a vat "caused to live those experiences and beliefs by the trains of cosmic waves and rays impinging upon the vat." Such bizarre hypotheses cannot be proven with logical certainty to be false.[4]

Castañeda calls his position "minimal transcendental realism." The totality of what I experience may be illusory and utterly remote from the thing in itself. Yet the Evil Demon cannot deceive me in my first-person experiencing. For Castañeda there is a rock bottom metaphysical realm revealed in two basic assertions, i.e., two minimally realist allegiances: 1) I (here, now) think, and 2) I (here, now) am having such and such experiences. These assertions reveal the ultimate access we have to an otherwise inaccessible noumenal realm. Castañeda proposes that we conceive the possibly illusory totality of what we experience after the convention of portraying the thoughts of characters in the comics with sentences printed in a white bubble or balloon. In "I think that (The Balloon)" the apodictically evident "I think that" (or what Castañeda also calls "the transcendental prefix") points to a noumenal realm in as much as what here is known is incorrigible and indubitable. (See chapter 8.) As far as (content-filled) knowledge of The Balloon (the world or the totality of experience) and ourselves the basic fact, metaphysically speaking, is that there is "NO access to an external point of view." What we take to be real and our articulated world "is the one we have beliefs about and act on"; for us there is no other. (See chapter 10.) To the extent that his metaphysical allegiance to the Kantian thing-in-itself is thereby set aside, Castañeda's philosophical work is phenomenological in the sense that the account of the world is inseparable from the mind's engagement of it; being and its disclosures may be distinguished but not separated. Nevertheless, Castañeda rejects transcendental phenomenology's claim to metaphysical ultimacy in the disclosure of "the absolute sphere" of first-person reference by maintaining that the indubitable evidence of the Transcendental Prefix merely points to, and it itself is not, an underlying noumenal realm.

It is at this point that the symmetry and contrast with Husserl become intriguing. Although I will not pursue the details here, consider how the following quote from Castañeda suggests some of the themes of agreement and difference.

> The self is the geometrical origin of the world, that is the center of the universe as an experienced whole. Yet it is *not* the source, or the root of the world, nor is it the provenience of experience. Origin but no source, that is the fundamental contrast in the structuring of the self and the world. Self-awareness is the linkage in that structuring; awareness of self *qua* self is simply the highest portion of that linkage. (See chapter 4)

Besides the last sentence, to which the greater part of this Introduction as well as the articles in this volume are dedicated, what most obviously reverberates here is Husserl's theme of the *I* as *Leib*, as the null-point of spatial orientation of the world. Clearly also the problem of the phenomenological correlation of what appears to its appearings, and of the appearings to the intentional or referential acts, is touched upon. In contrast Husserl himself (see *Ideas* I, §76) speaks of the world as being rooted in consciousness, suggesting a phenomenological monism which Castañeda clearly wishes to avoid. Getting clear on the phenomenological theme of constitution would seem to involve getting clear on Castañeda's distinction between origin and center, on the one hand, and root and source, on the other. Finally, it is evident that for both thinkers philosophy is phenomenological at least in the sense that its primary focus is the world as engaged by the mind: the world as perceived, as syntactically linked, as indexically signalled, etc.

20

The *basic philosophical situation* of transcendental philosophy is

I think that (The Balloon), or
I think that {I think that (the Balloon)}.

Castañeda maintains that because the thinking I of "I think that" is already a thought-of I, "in a sense the true thinking I is the *unthought of I*" that thinks *the basic philosophical situation.* (See chapters 6 and 8.) Because this process is iterative with no end of "guises" (of reflecting and reflected on I's) the true thinking I which is here "unthought of" is called the transcendental I and "the inexhaustible reservoir." (See chapter 8.) As some philosophers have already noted, there are intriguing connections between Castañeda's "phenomenological ontology" of guises ("guise theory") and Husserl's theory of appearing and noema.[5] Suffice it here to say that Castañedan guises, like Husserlian *Abschattungen*, are the endless myriad aspects in which "macro-objects," like that person or building over there, are presented to us. For Castañeda our "mental states, are thus metaphysical prisms that refract ordinary objects into spectra of ontological guises." (See Castañeda 1975b.) Guise theory, as phenomenological ontology, is a phenomeno-logic, the logic of the transcendental prefix and the Balloon's manifestation.

Some phenomenologists have introduced the notions of the genitive and dative of manifestation.[6] That which appears is manifest through its appearings. Thus appearings of . . . are the genitive of manifestation. But all appearings of . . . are appearings to———, i.e., one to whom they appear. As Castañeda put it, for someone to think, (a) "X refers to Y as Z," it is not enough that there occurs the representational event; rather "that representation event must deliver a *presentation to the thinker of what he is thinking of.*" (See chapter 10.) Therefore (a) also requires (b) "Y is manifest to X as Z." The thinker to whom the presentation is delivered is the "dative of manifestation." A basic philosophical issue is whether the dative referred to here, although grammatically named an indirect *object* of a verb, is an ob-ject, *Gegen-stand*, i.e., something for consciousness, something somehow able to enter into a referential relation after the fashion of the genitive of appearing. Thus a basic issue for phenomenology and guise-theory is whether the transcendental subject, what Castañeda above calls the unthought "true thinking I" which thinks the "I think that" (the transcendental prefix), or that to which or to whom the "I think that" is manifest, is itself manifest, is itself a guise (understood as a genitive of manifestation). Clearly it is "anonymous," but is it unconscious? or is it merely implied? or is it somehow uniquely manifest, i.e., "guiselessly" self-aware?

3. I-Guises and Transcendental Subjectivity

Before wrestling with this matter consider that an *I*, of course, might also say such things as: "I was born a Guatemalan peasant," "I was expelled from a brutal military academy during the reign of the dictator Ubico," "I am being honored by the government of Guatemala." All of these guises insert the "I" in nature and society. Thus we have other guises placing the I in The Balloon and which are other than the more or less disembodied ones of the reflections of the unthought and thought of transcendental I. And, of course, all such Balloon-residing guises may fall under the sweep of the Evil Demon. Although there is a phenomenological certainty that I must be tied down to a kind of foundational residency in The Balloon, still that residency can fall victim to radical skepticism. (See chapter 8.)

Obviously one of the tasks of Guise Theory is establishing the identity or sameness of these various guises and how the transcendental and empirical guises find a connecting point or bridge. Although we must neglect the details for the most part, a key distinction that runs throughout Castañeda's discussions is between external and internal reflexive reference. External reflexive reference differs from simple external reference in that the former one refers not to others but to oneself under a guise through which one appears to oneself or to others in a way other than in the first-person. In external reflexive reference one may refer to oneself and not be aware that it is oneself to which one is referring. Internal reflexive reference is first-person reference; it is a way of referring to oneself as oneself, where, in the referring, one recognizes the referred to as identical with the one referring. (Speakers may refer to others' internal reflexive references by way of quasi-indicators. See Kapitan's introduction as well as the essays in this volume, *passim*.)

When someone, e.g., a young Guatemalan peasant boy by the name of Hector-Neri Castañeda, refers to himself, he refers to a guise or a group of the endless guises to which he has doxastic allegiance as belonging to him and through which he appears to himself and others. But suppose the young man had a dream about a vigorous brilliant philosopher who wrote a famous difficult book called *Thinking and Doing*, and who discovered he himself was ill with a disease which would strike him down before he could finish his lifework. The philosopher in the dream knew that he himself was soon to die of the illness; but the young dreamer of the dream, young Hector Neri-Castañeda, in so referring (externally) to himself, did not know he was dreaming about himself. His circumstance resembles that of Ernst Mach, who, when getting onto a tram, saw coming toward him a "shabby old pedagogue," not knowing that that one was he himself reflected in a mirror. Similarly the young man in recounting the dream refers with "he himself" to the philosopher as internally reflexively referring to himself (this is the famous Castañedian "quasi-indicator"); but in recounting this dream he is referring to himself externally. Later as an older man, when he recalls the dream of his youth, he might have had occasion to make an internal reflexive reference and say, "That philosopher about whom I as a boy dreamed was myself."

The internal reflexive reference is a referring to oneself as oneself. Every internal reflexive act is an external reflexive one in as much as it is reference to oneself, to one of one's guises, and to an aspect under which one appears.[7] But not every external reflexive act is an internal one; one can and does often refer to oneself without referring to oneself as oneself. For example, in shaving oneself, one is attentive through the reflection in the mirror to the contours of the skin, the stroke of the razor, etc. and presumably one could have this kind of intention regardless of whose face it was. Or consider when a coeditor and coauthor of a volume might say, going through the names of the editors and authors: "The contributors to this volume did their best to make this a valuable contribution to the field." The editor, in looking over the contents of the book, may well refer to her own name and contribution (under the aspect of contributor/contribution), but she may look at them from the standpoint of their being ingredients of what, taken together with the other valuable contributions, is a worthwhile project.

For Castañeda what characterizes the I-guise is precisely internal reflexive reference. In saying "I" I refer to myself as myself. Or, in the third-person, when the speaker says "I" he/she "is presented with an *I*" and thereby, in saying "I," "ONE" refers to ONEself qua *oneSELF*." The speaker is presented with himself as himself, and this is "a unique, ephemeral and irreducible presentation." (See chapter 10.) "A necessary and sufficient condition of being a person, or being fully a person, is to be able to think of oneself as *oneself*, in the first-person way" (chapter 9). Referring to oneself as oneself is equated with the I's conceiving itself as a subject: "The essence and substance of an I is just to conceive itself as a subject *qua* subject" (chapter 9).

It is important *not* to take "subject" here as the concrete embodied and enworlded subject of knowing or feeling, especially if the subject becomes the "person" having certain feelings, perceptions, belief-systems, and bodily properties. I can never know myself as the person in this mood, or as the person with this career, or as the person with this family, or as a person having this perception, etc. with the certainty with which I know myself as an I.[8] Further, there is no third-person special characteristic that one has to think that one possesses in order to think of oneself as *I*, e.g., that I am male, or an academic, or the parent of a certain child, etc. Not only does "I" not mean these other specific guises, but the guises of being in this mood, or having these experiences, are contingent and empirical guises within The Balloon and fall under the sweep of the Evil Demon.[9]

The achievement of "I" results in a unique, private, and ephemeral guise or representation. The uniqueness and privacy are found, in part, in the consideration that there is no third-person attribute that one can point to or has to think in order to think of oneself as *I*. And no such worldly third-person property can serve to individuate an *I*. Using such a property "presupposes that one has already, so to speak in one's hands, a constituted subject of predication—an *I*" (chapter 9). Furthermore, no one can refer to anyone else in the first-person way. And, further, a person may refer to him- or herself in myriad third-person guises which in fact are the same as the I of this person but fail, e.g., through amnesia, to know that he himself (she herself) is the same as these guises. (See, e.g., chapter 10.) In contrast (the achievement of) "I" un-failingly "harpoons" its target, i.e., the subject which is "myself as myself."

For Castañeda, "I," like other subjective indexical particulars (e.g., *this*, *that*, *here*, *now*), exists only during the experience of its achievement. Al-though there are essential or logical connections between an *I*, its achieve-ments, and the content of its achievements/acts, nevertheless, because the I exists only in the present of its achieving, and because it has, or is the subject of, experiences with contents, and because there is a contingency between a particular I, its particular experiences, and the contents, the enduring I is nothing but a constructed hypostasis. The enduring I is brought about by the ephemeral I's identifying itself with some of its experiences and contents. All these guises come together to form a persisting unitary entity, i.e., they are "consubstantiated" or "transubstantiated" with some contemporary guises depending on whether the unity they form is co-actual (synchronic) or whether it is a unity formed over time (diachronic). Thus a certain story would have to be told to determine whether certain beliefs, memories, as-sumptions, commitments, and takens-for-granted which make up a world as the framework for one's judgments form consubstantial or transubstantial guises.[10]

Castañeda, who repeatedly differentiates himself in at least one respect from Fichte (see section 4 below), draws near to Fichte's position that self-positing or self-feeling is always a positing or feeling of the Other and of the self as limited.[11] Castañeda makes a distinction between how "I" as a self-ref-erence to oneself as oneself is achieved without it necessarily identifying any objective worldly properties or without any perceptual procedure of identify-ing oneself from among other second- or third-person entities in the world, and how, nevertheless, "I," i.e., the full sense of self-consciousness, involves necessarily a manifold of contrasts and negations, e.g., I-this/that, I-they (ex-ternal objects of the world), I-he/she, I-they (other persons), I-you, and I-we. (See chapter 10.) He acknowledges his debt "for the hyphen" to Martin Buber in this matter. He speaks of this manifold of contrasts and negations both as ways the I is connected to the world ("strands") and as gestalt-like wholes ("schemata"). Although, for Castañeda, these I-strands or I-schemata are wholes of which the I and the other indexicals are parts, the perspective he chooses is less a whole or a manifold of wholes wherein each constitutive part reciprocally determines the other. Rather, it would seem, the considera-tion is one wherein the I is the whole and the non-I contrasts or negations ("strands" or "schemata") are ways in which the "I" as "self-consciousness" is internally modified. Castañeda proposes a list of nine "*I*-schemata" (or "*I*-strands"). Although each of these distinctively negates or contrasts the I in a felt way, this "felt negativity" is further determined by the personality of the person, the context of the experience, etc. For example, a person with a pathological disorder might be able to respond lovingly only in the I-they (nonhuman and human others) schemata and not in the I-you schemata. Although Castañeda holds that there is a logical order in his nine-strand list, an order founded on the nature of perceiving/thinking, he also notes that there is a spiraling and mingling of the strands which enriches one's concept of *I* and the world.

> Animists mingle the I-strands in such a way that everything has its own internal *I*. Solipsists find the total world at large to be merely experiential content of the only accessible *I*. Deists promote the whole of reality to the veridical content of an all-embracing *I*. Pantheists are animist deists. Mystics do all sorts of things; some raise themselves up to the status of partial *I*'s within an all-encompassing one. (Chapter 10)

He believes that these *I*-schemata provide blueprints for egological development "and also furnish a master chart against which to check a person for possible *I*-disturbances" (chapter 10.)

The non-enduring I or self would be a crazy quilt held together by inscrutable forces were it not for Castañeda's theory of the hierarchy of integration within self-consciousness. Self-consciousness is erected on a complex doxastic pedestal which is a hierarchy of powers (for unconscious and conscious activities) and dispositions (e.g., to respond, to be attracted, to attend, etc.) Most of the tiers of the pedestal are unconscious; and the bottommost ones are the deep-seated takens-for-granted, "the hardware," that underlies all thinking episodes. The basic hierarchical structure internal to the reflexivity of self-consciousness has

1) conceptually inarticulated sensory consciousness,
2) egoless or I-less articulated consciousness of objects,
3) unowned consciousness of occurring mental episodes, and
4) I-consciousness, where we have articulated contents owned by an I and awareness of an I as an *I* interacting with *you* and, perhaps, constituting *we*. (Chapters 10 and 8.)

The levels are subsumptive, i.e., the higher include the lower within themselves. Castañeda (echoing themes in Leibniz and Husserl) believes that waking is a case of ontogeny recapitulating phylogeny, i.e., in waking after a deep sleep we go through all the levels of consciousness as different stages of the process of waking up. In falling asleep slowly we have "anti-recapitulation" (chapter 10).

Castañeda claims that at level (2) there is a linking or synthesizing of the contents of a simple experience or sub-experiences in such a way that they form *one* experience. This he calls "co-consciousness." And the systematic integration of low-level instantiations of co-consciousnesses he calls "co-integration." "Meta-integration" is the synthesizing and structuring of unowned reflexive experiences. And when the I or subject subordinates or actively integrates experiences into its plans, goals, etc., we have what Cas-

tañeda calls "subjections." Normally we have a case wherein "every mechanism runs perfectly and all run in marvellous unison" and wherein "the *now*
of the total experience is the hierarchical cumulation of the *nows* of the sub-
experiences" (chapter 9).

Again there are numerous striking parallels with Husserl. Of special interest is the question of whether the various integrations, which "all run in marvellous unison" can be given a first-person phenomenological account, or
whether they are transcendentally deduced, postulated, or are simply hypotheses from third-person observations. Clearly the "subjections" are something we experience in the first-person, but is there a way of talking about
these other anonymous automatic passive integrations and syntheses? And is
our awareness of the temporality of our psychological life of reference and
sensation ("The *now* of the total experience" cumulating "the *nows* of the
sub-experiences") to be connected with this coursing in "marvellous unison?" These, more or less, are the basic Husserlian issues of "inner-time consciousness" and "passive synthesis."[12]

Whether or not Castañeda would have been persuaded by Husserl's way of
accounting for the integration, Husserl's massive and detailed analysis is of
interest because it offers a first-person account of "this marvellous unison."
(For Castañeda, "philosophy, after all, is done in the first-person for the first-
person." See chapter 4.)

4. The Anti-Fichtean Thesis and
Pre-reflexive Consciousness

What Castañeda understands by the "Fichtean Thesis" is that all consciousness is self-consciousness and in being aware of the non-I I am also, in some
way, aware of myself. It was the essay by Dieter Henrich on "Fichte's Original
Insight" which inaugurated an era of research and debate on self-consciousness as well as the beginnings of the fruitful meditations by "the Heidelberg
School" on Castañeda and other analytic philosophers.[13] Recall that for Castañeda self-consciousness is proper to the achievement of "I," as a referring
to myself as myself and that it is the highest tier on the hierarchy of the doxastic pedestal. It is contrasted most decisively with level (1), i.e., both animal
and human sensory consciousness wherein there are no intentional acts or
conceptual articulations of the world. But it is also absent in the feeble conceptual articulations of (2) wherein there is no real focus. And it is also not to
be found in the articulating, focal consciousness of level (3) wherein there is
a perspectival organization of the perceptual field. "What is attended to
reflects the attender's attention. Yet in the absence of *self*-consciousness the
perspective is not apprehended as such." (See chapter 10.)

The "Fichtean Thesis" maintains that all consciousness involves a kind of
inner awareness that accompanies all referential or intentional awareness. The
two versions of the Fichtean Thesis are, on the one hand, that the self-con-

sciousness is an implicit simultaneous referential act which permits one to be aware of oneself and one's act of perception of an external object while at the same time one is perceiving the external object; and, on the other hand, the self-awareness is an utterly non-reflexive, non-referential, non-intentional, non-propositional self-manifestation which belongs to all acts of reference and intentionality as their necessary condition.[14]

Consider how (a) "There are many people in this room" may render a possible, not necessary, sense of (b) "There seem to be many people in this room." Consider also how (c) "There seem to me to be many people in this room" may be regarded as a necessary implication of (b). For most phenomenologists (and Roderick Chisholm from whom the example is taken), (b) and (c) as explications of (a) lead necessarily to (d) "That there seem to me to be many people in the room couldn't possibly obtain without my knowing it" (chapter 4). According to this theory this points to the ubiquity of pre-reflective self-consciousness in all acts of reference and the position that all acts, while not necessarily acts of awareness *of* oneself, are self-aware acts. And (d) is also a way of saying that unless the dative of appearing, that to which what appears appears, enjoys an immediate non-reflective self-presence, the manifestation of the world, (a) and (b) as explicated by (c), could not occur. At the same time it is clear that the pre- or non-reflective self-manifestation of the dative of manifestation cannot itself be a guise if guises are manifestations of . . . , to———.

The essays in this volume offer numerous objections and responses to this position, usually under the rubric of Externus, i.e., a consciousness which is thoroughly diaphanous and in no way pre-reflexively conscious, i.e., in no way knows that it is knowing when it is knowing. (For the time being we will use pre-reflective, pre-reflexive, non-reflective, and non-reflexive synonymously; see our discussion below, in section 5.) An especially intriguing objection is the consideration in connection with experiencing pains, itchings, illusory presentations in the visual field, afterimages, etc. Castañeda holds that these are apodictic *cogitatum* propositions or experiences whose *esse est percipi*, and therefore lie necessarily in the consciousness of the perceiver in relation to whom they exist, and yet these experiences or propositions do not involve that the perceiver think of himself in the first-person way. In being absorbed by a toothache I am not referring to myself as myself. I am completely Externus, even though I am unfailingly directed to something which is necessarily tied to my consciousness. (See chapter 4.)

In the later discussions, Castañeda believed he could illustrate Externus as well as his second-from-the-bottom rung on the hierarchy of consciousness by taking advantage of the datum of the anomalous instance of "blind-sight." Here is a case of people having lost a part of their cerebral cortex related to vision. While declaring that they do not see, e.g., anything in the left field of vision, they are nevertheless able to respond correctly to questions that seem to require clear visual perception. Castañeda sees this datum as eliminating

(d) as a necessary implication of (c): The contents in the left field of the afflicted person's field of vision become accessible to him as if he were seeing, "but they continue being as if they were not seen *by him*" (chapter 10).

Thus is supported Castañeda's view that one could say, (a) "There are many people in this room," and not be able to say that (b) "There seem to be many people in this room." In other words if (b) is not only a possible version of (a) but (a) a possible version of (b), then we may have (c) and (d) for certain kinds of experiences, but surely not all of them. Other arguments he uses even include indexicals wherein, e.g., a young girl is relating everything she is contemplating in a way which is absolutely free of any self-awareness; "That ant is moving faster than this one; the ant over there! coming out of the big hive . . . " (chapter 5).

It is important to note that in spite of both Castañeda's claim that the "I" or self is essentially ephemeral and the claim that there are forms of consciousness in which there is no self-awareness, he does hold that there is a kind of all-encompassing involvement of the self or I in one's acts of reference. But this, he maintains, is a matter of "implicit self-reference of unreflective consciousness." "Singular reference to objects in the world is essentially to objects in *one's* world" (chapter 5). The implicit references to the thinker are not brought out every time the little girl identifies the behavior of the ants, "but are holistically built into the contents of experience. Indexicality and contextuality are, albeit different, closely connected." Here the position seems to be that, as phenomenologists would put it, the I is marginally or horizonally experienced, not inferred. In another place we find similar formulations.

> The I is the point of Origin within each experience. That Origin is certainly revealed. In that sense we are certainly acquainted with the self. But the Origin is revealed as the way experience is organized, hence it is in a sense not empirically discoverable. . . . (chapter 4)

Yet it is not clear from either of these statements whether *this* awareness of the self is the result of the intending of an unexplicated implication or of the elucidating of the context; or whether it is an ongoing pre–reflexive tacitly referential marginal awareness, e.g., an implicit awareness of one's indexical perspective.[15] None of these amount to the I-guise, i.e., the internal reflexive reference of Castañeda. (Recall above the text which noted that in such perspectival thinking "what is attended to reflects the attender's attention" but in the absence of achieving "I," the perspective is not one of self-consciousness as such. (See chapter 10.)

5. Still Dangling Threads in the Conversation

Castañeda believed he found an ally in J.-P. Sartre who held there is an impropriety in inserting an "I" in the typical transcendences of consciousness, as in "a streetcar needing to be caught" or "Peter having to be helped." For Castañeda, Sartre's egoless consciousness was an instance of what he meant by non-reflexive "Externus" consciousness. But what would Castañeda have done with Sartre's insistence on the "interiority of consciousness," i.e., that "to be and to be aware of itself are one and the same thing for consciousness"?[16] One must distinguish the consciousness "of" self that is a result of an act of reflection from the unconditional, unpositional self-awareness that necessarily occurs regardless of how absorbed I am in the contemplated object.[17] Thus, in fact for Sartre, the more basic and prevalent egoless form of consciousness, e.g., "There is a streetcar to be caught," not "I am chasing this streetcar," is immanently self-aware, is still internally, non-reflectively self-aware, even though I-less.

One way of clarifying Sartre's position on this non-positional and immanent self-awarenesss is to distinguish senses of "reflective" and "reflexive." For Castañeda self-reflexivity is a property of a relation, i.e., that of reference to oneself. Pre- or non-reflective self-awareness must enjoy a guise; non-reflexive self-awareness must be bereft of any guise, i.e., any manifestation of . . . , to————. For Sartre, as well as for the continental philosophers who are partners in this discussion, the non- or pre-reflective consciousness they wish to highlight is both non-referential and non-relational. Therefore it enjoys a kind of self-sufficient and radical interiority. Even if othering, alterity, intentionality, and reference are held, as, e.g., Husserl always maintained, to be essential to consciousness, the continental philosophers tend to agree that the self-manifestation of the othering as the condition for the othering's being conscious is immanent and itself does not stand in need of this othering, even the internally reflexive self-othering, for its luminosity.

As non-relational it is not to take its bearings from the pre- and non-reflective which may be thought of as deficient modes of intentional awareness in the way the implicit or marginal intention obscurely and emptily makes present what the explicit focal attending fully and properly makes present. Its being bereft of a guise does not mean that it is without manifestation or is unconscious. In this sense, because of its essential non-relationality and because all reflection is a form of intentional relatedness, the basic awareness they wish to call attention to is non-reflexive rather than non- or pre-reflective. If intentional or referring acts involve a relation to what is other to consciousness, even if it be another act of the same stream of consciousness, then this non-reflexive awareness is an "unothered act" realizing, as Chisholm noted, the Aristotelian *desideratum* of the identity of knower and known.[18]

For Sartre pleasure and the consciousness of pleasure are one and the same thing; in the pre- or non-reflexive self-consciousness there is no distinction between subject and object, dative of manifestation and genitive of manifestation. For Castañeda the example of pleasure is an example of an Externus proposition wherein there is no self-consciousness evident. This is because self-consciousness is revealed only in "I." With "I" there is referred to or "harpooned" myself as myself. And this is the "presentational representation" with which the speaker is presented (chapter 10).

For continental philosophers an infinite regress threatens if "oneself as oneself," i.e., the subject of one's referring which is the unique indubitable first-person reference that is not reducible to or replaceable by any third-person references, is realized through a (referring-relating) presentation to oneself because the presented self must already be acquainted with, indeed, in some strong sense identical with, the presenting self to whom the presentation is made; but if this acquaintance itself is not non-reflexive but is achieved only through a reflecting presentation, this prior acquaintance itself requires a presentation, etc. Or, "the attempt to know the I to which one relates in an act of self-consciousness as the same as the subject of this act of consciousness leads inevitably to a regress"[19] In this view, self-consciousness or "ipseity" or a prior familiarity of the self with itself is either there from the start or it will never be there.

The critique of the position that self-consciousness is a result of acts of reflection and reference has been a central theme of Dieter Henrich and Manfred Frank. In France, Michel Henry has attempted to show in countless ways what he calls the "monist" prejudice of most philosophy, i.e., that manifestation, appearing, etc. requires intentionality or reference. This blinds philosophers to the non-reflexive, non-intentional form in which consciousness is always self-consciousness. Without a self-presence of that (dative of manifestation) to which what appears appears, the genitive of manifestation, the appearings of . . . , could not happen. In this sense all manifestation is self-manifestation.[20]

On the other hand, for Castañeda, "a non-reflexive form of self-consciousness" is a contradiction in terms. Self-consciousness means that the self or I refers back to itself. If there is not the self-reference of the "I" achievement, there is no self-consciousness. To require that one dispense with an act of reference would require that there was a strict and necessary identity between the reflecting-I-pole, the reflected-on I-pole, and what "I" achieves. But in the reflecting reference a sameness, not identity, emerges. The pre-reflective (calling it non-reflexive self-awareness begs the question) guise is not identical with the one emergent in "I," i.e., myself as myself. Whereas most phenomenologists, in contrast to Castañeda, would maintain that there are reasons for distinguishing I-less consciousness and I-less non-reflexively self-aware consciousness, they have not highlighted "I" consciousness with the clarity that we find in Castañeda. If one grants to the continental philosophers that in reflection on a prior unreflected-on act, the I-pole of the reflected-on act appears the same as the I-pole of the reflecting act, this is not the same guise as the "I"-guise—assuming that this is the manifestation of "myself as myself." Whereas in the relation where "ONE refers to ONEself qua *oneself*" there is strict identity and necessity the sameness relations are contingent, "consubstantiational." Castañeda challenges phenomenologists to show that the basic identity syntheses which found the claims for the I's identity (through reflection, memory, passive synthesis, etc.) enjoy the necessity of strict identity and are not mere contingent sameness relations. (See chapter 6, especially sections 15–17.) For Castañeda, if self-consciousness is the presence of myself as myself, then it is patently false that I am always self-conscious; if self-consciousness is something else, then phenomenologists must acknowledge the non-identity and mere sameness of the "I"-guise and this something else, e.g., this unremittant, unbegun, and unceasing "ipseity."

Of special interest to continental philosophers is the way Castañeda makes it clear that although there is apodictic certainty in the achievement of "I" (i.e., the "I"-guise and in this respect *what* I am), as soon as I attempt to say who this I is, there is the element of uncertainty because *who* I am (with its manifold guises) is inserted in the world and therefore lacks this apodicticity. As soon as "myself as myself" takes on contours and becomes an identifiable someone, it loses the complete essential certainty realized with "I."

Furthermore continental philosophers must note that when Castañeda distinguishes multiple layers of I-less and non-reflexive *consciousness* as the doxastic basement upon which the higher-order of reflexive self-consciousness builds, he is talking about consciousness (admittedly guise-less) and not unconsciousness at these levels. (A standard argument among continental philosophers is that if these levels do not contain an original *self*-awareness— and therefore are unconscious—self-reflection would not find its target; for Castañeda this begs the question of whether all consciousness is self-consciousness.)

And, finally, in his examples of both I-less and non-reflexive levels of perspectival consciousness Castañeda allows for forms of implicit marginal awareness of perspectives which imply or reflect the attender's attending. Yet for Castañeda this marginal awareness is not what is meant properly by self-awareness; and for the continental partners to this discussion, it similarly is not what is meant by the basic self-awareness, i.e., the self-manifestation that is utterly non-referential and non-reflexive.

Notes

1. In the case of Castañeda this is greatly facilitated by Helmut Pape's translation of major texts in Castañeda 1982a as well as Jacobi and Pape 1990. This latter work, besides containing essays by Castañeda, resembles the two Castañeda volumes edited by James Tomberlin in that it has critical essays by sixteen, mostly German, philosophers, to which Castañeda responded. Among Dieter Henrich's writings related to the essays in this volume one should consult Henrich 1982a, 1982b, and 1971, and among Manfred Frank's writings are Frank 1991a, 1991b, 1994, and 1995. For Frank's critique of Post-modern or deconstructionist thought, wherein the theory of self-consciousness plays an important role, see Frank 1988. These works of Frank, the work of 1994 having been dedicated to

the memory of Castañeda, are basic research tools for the analytic-continental philosophical dialogue on self-consciousness.

2. See Frank 1991a, 10 ff., where he follows Sartre's critique of Heidegger.

3. For an important summary of his early reflections on private language, his interpretation of Wittgenstein, and a brief statement of his "phenomenological linguistics," see Tomberlin 1986, 91–99.

4. Tomberlin 1986, 98; see also this volume, chapter 8.

5. See Smith 1986 and Küng 1990; cf. also my comments in Hart 1992, 122–126.

6. These distinctions are implicit in Husserl. But for a more explicit use of them, see Prufer 1993, 57, 65, 75–76, 84–89; and Sokolowski 1974, 128, 170–171.

7. For this distinction see especially chapter 10. I was instructed here by Fricke 1991.

8. See Fricke 1991 and Castañeda 1991b.

9. See Fricke 1991 and Castañeda 1991b.

10. On ephemerality, see chapter 9; for the "consubstantiation" of the guises, see, e.g., chapter 9.

11. See Breazeale 1995.

12. See Husserl 1991 and 1996; and Sokolowski 1974, ch. vi.

13. See note 1 above.

14. Although there is debate among Fichte scholars about the unity and consistency of Fichte's theory of self-consciousness, a debate in which the participants usually take positions on Henrich 1966, it is clear that Fichte did on occasion argue for an essentially non-reflective mode of self-awareness as constitutive of consciousness and as foundational for the world's manifestness. Manfred Frank's selections from Fichte, in Frank 1991b, give two good examples of his mighty wrestle with these issues.

15. See Kapitan 1998.

16. See Sartre 1957, 83–84.

17. See Sartre 1948; reprinted in Frank 1991b.

18. See Chisholm 1981, 37; cf. Hart 1998. But Chisholm's theory of "direct attribution" where the knower has for its object itself "self-presentingly" is a case of an "object" presenting itself to a self in such a way that while having this object there is indubitable belief that one is having it. (See Chisholm 1981, 80–81.) Here we see that he too maintains the structure of a genitive of manifestation and dative of manifestation within the self's "direct attribution." The issue of whether the self itself is self-aware apart from its self-presenting objects is neglected.

19. See Fricke 1991 and Castañeda 1991b.

20. Michel Henry 1973; on the monist view of manifestation, see 47 ff. For an excellent discussion of the issues from the continental perspective, see Zahavi, 1999; cf. also Hart 1998. I wish here to express thanks to Tomis Kapitan and Dan Zahavi for comments on earlier drafts of this introduction.

THE PHENOMENO-LOGIC OF THE I

1

'He'

A Study in the Logic of Self-Consciousness

Introduction

The word 'he' is a device for talking about persons, beings who enjoy, even indulge in, self-awareness. The word 'he' and the phrase 'he himself' are sometimes used to refer to the entity known, thought of, by the person who knows, thinks of, himself. We say, e.g., "He believes (knows, says, argues, claims) that he (himself) is healthy (rich, tall, heavy, Napoleon, a victim)." This use of 'he' (to be called the *S-use* of 'he') as a pointer to the object of someone's self-knowledge, self-belief, self-conjecture, is the main topic of this study.[1]

My purpose here is to provide an exhaustive discussion of, and a rigorous treatment of the logic of, the S-used third-person pronoun. My major contentions are: (a) that the S-uses of 'he' are quite different from the other uses of the third-person pronoun; (b) that the S-uses of 'he' constitute the employment of a *unique logical* category, which is not analyzable in terms of any other type of referring mechanism (i.e., the other uses of 'he', other personal pronouns, proper names, demonstratives, and definite descriptions); (c) that in each sentence containing tokens of the S-used 'he' there is at least one such token which is not analyzable, but there may be other tokens which are analyzable in terms of an unanalyzable token of the S-used 'he'; (d) that the complex logic of the S-used 'he' is governed by the principles (H*), (H*1)–(H*3), whose formulation is a high point of the paper; (e) that the first-person pronoun is also an unanalyzable category, even though some tokens of 'I' can be analysed in terms of some unanalyzable token of 'I', in accordance

This essay was first published in *Ratio* 8 (1966), 130–157. Reprinted by permission of the editor.

with principle (P′); (f) that the widely accepted rule of detachment 'From "x knows that p" one is allowed to infer that p′ breaks down when the statement that p is expressible in a sentence containing an S-used 'he'; (g) that a valid substitute for the above rule is (K*).

The results of this investigation have important consequences for the philosophy of mind, which will be discussed in a separate paper. In yet another paper I will defend theses parallel to (a)–(g) for the case of expressions like 'then' and 'there' when used in *oratio obliqua*, for instance, in "At place p and time t x believed that it was then raining there".

1. The 'he' of self-consciousness

Let us, first, demarcate our field of enquiry. We want to study the uses of 'he (him, his)' and 'she (her, hers)' in which the pronoun refers to the object of a person's knowledge, beliefs, thoughts, assertions, about himself. We shall, for simplicity, speak of the 'he' of self-consciousness, or of the S-use of 'he', or of the pronoun 'he*'. We shall put an asterisk after a form of the third-person pronoun to indicate that it exemplifies an S-use. The 'he*' pronoun appears, for instance, in sentences like 'Arthur believes that he* is happy' and 'Mary claims that she* knows that Paul loves her*'. For simplicity we shall concentrate our discussion mainly on statements about cognitive attitudes or acts, but our investigation also applies to linguistic acts which attribute a self-reference to someone. We shall speak of *cognitive verbs* to refer to verbs expressing cognitive acts or attitudes or dispositions ('think', 'believe', 'know', 'suppose', 'infer') as well as to linguistic acts of the assertive or quasi-assertive kind ('claim', 'hold', 'state', 'say', 'deny', 'argue', etc.).

It is only a linguistic freak that 'he' in the sense of 'he*' looks exactly like the third-person pronoun 'he', which occurs, for instance, in 'Arthur came, but he knew nobody he saw; he left early'. This can be seen simply by glancing at the other uses of the third-person pronoun. But before taking this glance we shall introduce other simplifying conventions.

(1) Single quotes will be used to form names of sentences or expressions.

(2) Indentation of, as well as double quotes around, a sentence will be employed to form a name of some statement that has, or could have, been made by means of a normal utterance (in normal contexts and with its ordinary meaning) of a token of the sentence indented, or quoted. We shall assume that the name so produced names the same statement throughout the present investigation, but we shall assume nothing about the method for picking out the statement in question.

(3) Numerals prefixed to indented sentences will sometimes refer to the indented sentence and sometimes to the statement formulated with that sentence; the context will make clear which one is meant.

(4) We shall sometimes speak of 'he' [or 'I'] as short for 'a pronominal expression used to formulate third-person [or firstperson] reference'.

(5) We shall use '$token_n$,' and '*token in the narrow sense*' to refer to each of the tokens of each form of a pronoun or verb; e.g., the $tokens_n$ of 'I' are not, but contrasts with, the $tokens_n$ of 'me'; similarly, a $token_n$ of 'runs' is not, but contrasts with, a $token_n$ of 'run' or 'ran'.

(6) We shall call all $tokens_n$ of a pronoun or verb, regardless of inflection, $tokens_w$ or *tokens in the wider sense* of the pronoun in question. Thus, each $token_n$ of 'I', each $token_n$ of 'me', each $token_n$ of 'my', each $token_n$ of 'mine', and each $token_n$ of 'myself' are all $tokens_w$ of the pronoun 'I (me, my, mine, myself)' or simply, 'I'.

It seems that, aside from its S-uses, the pronoun 'he (him, his, she, her, hers)' is normally used in a way that falls in one or other of the following categories:

(A) The third-person pronoun is sometimes a *proxy for the ostensive demonstrative description* 'that (this) man' or 'that (this) woman'. This is probably the case when someone says, e.g. "Look, he is dragging her". The pronoun is sometimes a proxy for a *quasi-ostensive demonstrative description*. This is the case, for instance, when a person sees a picture (photograph, bust, replica) of another person and asserts, e.g., "She is beautiful!" Here the uttered token of 'she' simply stands for the description 'the woman whose picture (photograph, bust, replica) this is'.

(B) 'He' is perhaps used sometimes as an *(ostensive) demonstrative pronoun*, i.e., as a substitute for no definite description, but merely to point to a person singled out from the remaining objects present in one's current experience. In this use the third-person pronoun is merely a colorful proxy for 'this (that)'.

(C) 'He' is used sometimes as a mere part of a *universal quantifier*, as, e.g., when one says "He who marries young . . . " The pronoun 'he' is also used as a mere *variable* bound by a universal, or existential, quantifier to which it refers back. Examples of these uses are, respectively, found in normal utterances of sentences of the form 'Anyone who marries young is such that he . . . ' and 'Somebody came when I was out and he returned my book'.

(D) The third-person pronoun is frequently employed as a *relative pronoun*, i.e., as a proxy for a name or description which precedes or follows it. An example is furnished by the assertion "If Arthur comes late, he (i.e., Arthur) will call." Clearly, this statement is the same as the statement that one would make, in the same circumstances, by asserting "If Arthur comes late, Arthur will call" or by asserting "If he (Arthur) comes late, Arthur will call."

(E) 'He' is, perhaps occasionally, a proxy for the definite ostensive description 'that (this) body'. This would be the case if the sentence 'He weighs 185 pounds', for instance, were used to formulate the statement "That (this) body [pointing to the body of some person] weighs 185 pounds."

(F) 'He' is often employed as a place-holder for some *unspecified* description which refers to a previously mentioned object. This is typical of constructions in *oratio obliqua*, i.e., clauses subordinated to cognitive verbs in the sense characterized above. Examples are "Paul said (believes, knows) of (someone who in point of fact is[2]) Mary that she is happy." These statements must be distinguished from the statements "Paul said (believes, knows) that Mary is happy." The former are (nearly) the same as the statements: "There is a property ϕ such that Mary is the only person who is ϕ and Paul said (believes, knows) that the only person who is ϕ is happy." The most 'I' characteristic pattern of the (F)-'he' is " . . . believes (knows, thinks, asserts, holds) of y that . . . he (she) . . . ", as just illustrated. But Helen Cartwright[3] has furnished an example which deviates from this pattern, viz., "Paul saw Mary and believes that she is happy."

(G) The pronoun 'he' is often used to indicate what Russell called the larger scope of a description. For instance, "If the author of *Principia Mathematica* remembers it, he will write to you about it" is analyzable (as Russell thought) as, or merely presupposes (as Strawson wants it), "There is just one author of *Principia Mathematica* such that: if he remembers it, he will write you about it" (where the new occurrences of 'he' are variables of quantification). On the other hand, "If the author of *Principia Mathematica* remembers it, the author of *Principia Mathematica* will write you about it" seems to be analyzable as, or to presuppose, "If there is just one author of *Principia Mathematica* and he remembers it, then there is just one author of *Principia Mathematica* and he will write you about it" (where again the new occurrences of 'he' are variables of quantification).

Here we are not claiming that these six uses of 'he' are really all distinct and non-overlapping. We are simply not interested in examining them for their own sakes. We want to show only that they are quite different from the S-uses of 'he'.

Suppose that a man called Privatus informs his friend Gaskon that

(1) The Editor of *Soul* knows that he* is a millionaire.

It is immediately clear that Privatus' use of 'he himself' or of 'he*' is not a quantifier or a variable referring back to a quantifier. Hence, Privatus' use of 'he*' is not an instance of use (C). But as P. T. Geach pointed out to me, 'he*' can *also* be an instance of use (C). It plays this role in "Someone thinks that he* is a genius."

It is extremely doubtful that the Editor of *Soul* or Privatus or Gaskon think of a mere body as a millionaire. But even if they all did, we may suppose that in this case they all think of persons. Thus, Privatus' use of 'he*' is not a proxy for 'this (that) body'. We can, thus, disregard uses (C) and (E) entirely.

The token$_n$ of 'he*' in (1) is not a proxy for 'the Editor of *Soul*'. If it were, statement (1) would be the same statement as:

(2) The Editor of *Soul* *knows* that the Editor of *Soul* *is* a millionaire.

But (2) is not the same statement as (1). For (1) does not entail (2). The Editor of *Soul* may know that he himself is a millionaire while failing to know that he himself is the Editor of *Soul*, because, say, he believes that the Editor of *Soul* *is* poverty-stricken Richard Penniless. Indeed, (2) also fails to entail (1). To see this suppose that on January 15, 1965, the man just appointed to the Editorship of *Soul* does not yet know of his appointment, and that he has read a probated will by which an eccentric businessman bequeathed several millions to the man who happens to be the Editor of *Soul* on that day. Thus, Privatus' use of 'he himself' or 'he*' just cannot be a proxy for 'the Editor of *Soul*'.

Clearly, the same considerations apply to any name or description that replaces 'the Editor of *Soul*' as well as to any token$_w$ of 'he*'. Hence we conclude that a use of a token$_w$ of 'he*' is not an instance of use (D).

We can discuss uses (A) and (B) together. If 'he*' were used demonstratively meaning 'this (that) man' or simply 'this (that)', the demonstrative reference would have to be made by the speaker. But Privatus can truly and correctly say to Gaskon "The Editor of *Soul* knows (believes, thinks) that he* is a millionaire", even when the Editor of *Soul is* wholly outside Privatus' and Gaskon's experience, e.g., when the Editor is locked up alone inside a spaceship travelling near the end of the Milky Way. Hence, the pronoun 'he*' is not simply the strictly third-person pronoun 'he' used demonstratively.

Use (F) of 'he' does resemble the use of 'he*' in important respects. For simplicity we shall speak of *the (F)-'he'* to refer to the tokens of 'he' which are instances of use (F). To start with, the (F)-'he' and 'he*' can appear only in a construction having a clause in *oratio obliqua*. In the second place, each token of 'he*' or of the (F)-'he' must have an antecedent description or name or pronoun, which determines to whom the token refers. Thirdly, in neither case is the token in question a proxy for its antecedent. Clearly,

(3) Paul believes of (someone who is in point of fact) Mary that she is happy

is not the same statement as

(4) Paul believes that Mary is happy.

Likewise, the statement:

(5) Mary believes that she* is happy

is not the same as

(6) Mary believes that Mary is happy.

Yet there are crucial differences between 'he*' and the (F)-'he'. In the first place, (4) and "Mary exists" together entail (3); but neither (5) and "Mary exists" together entail (6), nor (6) and "Mary exists" together entail (5). In the second place, the (F)-'he' can always be analyzed away, while 'he*' can never be analyzed away, as we shall establish in sections 2 and 4 below.

Consider (3) again. Clearly (3) entails that what Paul believes is expressible in a sentence of the form "Z is happy", where "Z" stands for some unspecified way of referring to Mary that Paul employs. (Obviously, the way in question may very well be the name "Mary" itself.) If Paul were to express his belief, he would employ some name or demonstrative or description referring to Mary. But (3) does not decide this point. Statement (3) is merely the statement that for some person Paul refers to as Z. Paul believes that Z is happy, while we refer to that person as Mary.

This matter of referring to someone as Z, or as Mary, or as the man next door, is a murky business which we shall not clarify in this paper. Here we shall take the concept *way of univocally referring to X as Z as primitive*. We do not commit ourselves here to any of the following natural ways of analyzing this concept. *Way 1:* We abandon the idea of a universe of discourse constituted by particulars, and make our variables of quantification range over guises (or guised particulars, i.e., particulars *qua* satisfying some condition). Then we analyze, e.g., (3) as "There is a guise, call it x, such that x = (the guise) Mary, and (the guise) Paul believes that x is happy." *Way 2:* We keep our individual variables ranging over particulars *qua* particulars, but analyze 'ways of referring' in terms of Russellian descriptions. Then, (3), for instance, becomes analyzed as "There is a property ϕ such that just Mary is ϕ and Paul believes that the only thing which is ϕ is happy." *Way 3*: With Frege we distinguish sense and denotation for names, demonstratives, etc., and introduce variables ranging over individual senses; we form a term denoting a particular by underscoring an expression denoting an individual sense. Then (3) can be analyzed as "There is an individual sense Z such that Z = Mary and Paul believes that Z is happy."[4]

Likewise, we shall not analyze here the perplexing phrases 'believes (knows, thinks, says, etc.) that Z is . . . ' where 'Z' is a variable. It makes no difference at this juncture whether 'Z' is a variable ranging over particulars, guises, or individual senses. The natural temptation is to analyze such phrases in terms of quantification over propositions or statements. For instance, "Paul believes that Z is happy" would be treated as an abbreviation of "There is a proposition which is the object of Paul's belief and which is constituted by the entity Z (whatever it may be, individual sense, guise, or whatnot) as subject and the property happiness as predicate." Other philosophers and logicians would prefer an analysis in terms of sentences. But in this essay we do not have to decide this issue.

The problems we are dealing with in this essay are essentially independent of one's ultimate views on reference to particulars and on the role of variables inside cognitive contexts. We want here to formulate an analysis of the (F)-'he' as well as partial analyses of *some* special uses of 'I' and of 'he*' in terms of our primitive 'ways of univocally referring to X as Z'. We grant, of course, that our analyses are rightly regarded as incomplete inasmuch as our present primitive needs to be analyzed.

Let '$\phi(he_y)$' be a sentence containing one or more tokens$_w$ of the (F)-'he', which refer to a person Y; let '$\phi(Z)$' be the result of replacing each of these tokens$_w$ by tokens$_w$ of 'Z'; let 'E' stand for any of the cognitive verbs (in the sense explained above). Then:

(P)   A statement of the form "X E's of Y that $\phi(he_y)$" is the same statement as the corresponding one (i.e., the one that has the same variables standing for the same terms where these terms have the same
references and meanings and logical positions) (i) "There is a way of
referring univocally to Y as Z and X E's that Z is $\phi(Z)$", or alternatively, the statement corresponding in the same way, (ii) "There is a
way of referring univocally to Y as Z which is different from each of
the ways of referring to Y as W_1 W_2, . . . , as W_n, and X E's that
$\phi(Z)$", where for each 'W_i' the clause represented by '$\phi(he_y)$' contains some subclause of the form '(. . . = W_i)'.

Alternative (ii) is included in principle (P) in order to meet a counter example
proposed by Nuel Belnap and developed by Charles Chihara against alternatives (i)[5]. The counter-example is this: consider the case of Jaakko Hintikka[6]
and Nuel Belnap[7] who believe that every statement of the form "a = a" is
(analytically) true. Suppose that, say, Hintikka believes that the morning star
= the morning star and that he has no other belief about the morning star.
Since the morning star is in fact identical with the evening star, there is a way
of referring univocally to the evening star as Z and Hintikka believes that Z
is identical with the morning star. Yet it would be false in ordinary language
that Hintikka believes of (some object which in point of fact is) the evening
star that it is identical with the morning star. It seems to me that this case
conforms to alternative (ii). On the other hand, there are people[8] who would
say in the case of Hintikka as just described that Hintikka does believe of
something, which is in point of fact identical with the evening star, that it is
identical with the morning star. For these persons alternative (i) suffices.

Now, my central point here is that the (F)-'he' is fully analyzable along the
lines of principle (P). Whether alternative (i) suffices or whether other alternatives besides (i) and (ii) are required is immaterial here. Alternative (ii)
merely introduces conditions on the way of referring to an entity that is attributed to a person. And I can easily conceive of ordinary statements expressed
through sentences with tokens$_w$ of the (F)-'he' in which other restrictions on
a way of referring to an entity are implicit. Yet my primary contention stands
unaffected: The (F)-'he' can be analyzed away.

To sum up, the S-uses of 'he' are logically different from the uses (A)–(F)
of the third-person pronoun.

2. 'He*', Descriptions, Names, and Demonstrative Reference

We have seen that when Privatus asserts "The Editor of *Soul* believes that he*
is a millionaire", Privatus' token$_w$ of 'he*' is not a proxy for the description
'The Editor of *Soul*'. More generally, Privatus' token$_w$ of 'he*' is not replaceable by any other description or name of the Editor of *Soul* (or of any other

person or things), which does not include another token$_w$ of 'he*'.[9] Suppose that 'the person ϕ' is a definite description, with no tokens$_w$ of 'he*', of the Editor of *Soul*. Clearly the statement "The Editor of *Soul* believes that the person ϕ is a millionaire" does not entail "The Editor of *Soul* believes that he* is a millionaire." Since there are no tokens$_w$ of 'he*' in "The Editor of *Soul* believes that the person ϕ is a millionaire", this sentence does not make an assertion of self-belief. The same holds for names. But more importantly, when Privatus asserts "The Editor of *Soul* believes that he* is a millionaire", Privatus does not attribute to the Editor the possession of any way of referring to himself aside from his ability to use the pronoun 'I' or his ability to be conscious of himself. The latter ability is the only way of referring to himself that Privatus must attribute to the Editor for his statement to be true. Hence, the statement "The Editor of *Soul* believes that he* is a millionaire" does not entail any statement of the form "The Editor *of Soul* believes that ϕ is a millionaire", where 'ϕ' stands for a name or description not containing tokens$_w$ of 'he*'.

It is also apparent that Privatus' token of 'he*' is not a proxy for a token$_w$ of 'I' or 'You'. On the one hand, Privatus' statement "The Editor of *Soul* believes that I am a millionaire" is obviously quite different from his statement "The Editor of *Soul* believes that he* is a millionaire." On the other hand, Privatus' statement "The Editor of *Soul* believes that you are a millionaire" does not entail, and *a fortiori is* different from, his statement "The Editor of *Soul* believes that he* is a millionaire," even if Privatus uses the word 'you' to talk and refer to the Editor of *Soul*. The latter may simply be ignorant that he* is the Editor of *Soul*.

Now, all the above considerations apply to any token$_w$ of 'he' regardless of what name or description happens to be its logical and grammatical antecedent. Thus, we conclude that *the pronoun 'he*' is never replaceable by a name or a description not containing tokens$_w$ of 'he*'*. This suggests that 'he*' is a purely referential word. But demonstrative pronouns seem to be purely referential: they, it is often said, seize the objects they refer to directly, without attributing to these objects any feature or characteristic relation. They have denotation, but not sense, it is said; they, indeed, seem like the closest approximation to the logician's ideal of logical names. One is tempted to think that, although 'he*' is not always a demonstrative pronoun, nevertheless it must be analyzed, or understood, in terms of the demonstrative uses, (A) and (B), of 'he'. In particular it might be thought that the analysis of 'he*' could be worked out of four related prongs:

(i)   'he*' in sentences of the form 'X E's (e.g., believes, knows, thinks) that he* is ϕ', used assertively, corresponds to some use of the demonstrative 'he' by the person X;

(ii) if one asserts "X believes (knows, thinks) that he is ϕ" [or "X believes (knows, thinks) of him that he is ϕ] and uses 'he' [or 'him'] demonstratively to refer to the person X, then one has asserted "X believes (knows, thinks) that he* is ϕ";

(iii) if one asserts truly "X believes (knows, thinks) that he is ϕ" using 'he' demonstratively to refer to the person X and the person X is in a position to take one's use of 'he' as a demonstrative use, then believes (knows, thinks) that he* is ϕ;

(iv) if a person X asserts "he is ϕ," using 'he' purely demonstratively to refer to X, then X believes that he* is ϕ.

    Claim (i) is false. To begin with, it is not uncommon that a man, say Privatus, asserts truly something like "The Editor of *Soul* believes (claims, knows) that he* is a millionaire", in spite of the fact that the Editor of *Soul* may have never expressed his belief through any sentence so that he has never used the word 'he' demonstratively in a sentence that would have to correspond to Privatus' use of 'he*'. Nevertheless, suppose that the Editor of *Soul* has just asserted what, according to Privatus, he believes (claims, knows). Most likely he said "I am a millionaire." Thus, Privatus' use of 'he*' may correspond to the Editor of *Soul's* use of 'I', and need not correspond to this Editor's use of the demonstrative 'he'. That it can never correspond to a demonstrative use of 'he' will be established with the refutation of (iv).

    Claim (ii) is also false. Suppose that Privatus says to Gaskon:

(7) The Editor of *Soul* believes of *him* [using this word purely demonstratively, with a pointing to the Editor of *Soul*, as a proxy for 'this'] that he is a millionaire.

[Here the occurrence of 'he' is an instance of use (F).] By asserting (7) Privatus does not tell Gaskon *what* exactly it is that the Editor of *Soul* believes to be the case, i.e., the proposition or statement that the Editor takes to be true. Privatus just informs Gaskon that under some way or other of referring to the man he is pointing to, the Editor of *Soul* believes that man to be a millionaire. Hence, the truth of (7) does not require that the Editor of *Soul* thinks of the man Privatus is pointing to as the same as he* (the Editor himself). Thus, (7) may be true because the Editor believes, e.g., that a man with a unique scar on his back is a millionaire and this man happens to be the one Privatus is pointing to. But the Editor of *Soul* need not realize that he* is the man with the unique scar, or that he* is a millionaire. He may not even know of Privatus' statement.

    Suppose that Privatus says to Gaskon:

(8) The Editor of *Soul* believes that he [using this word purely demonstratively, with a pointing to the Editor of *Soul*] *is* a millionaire.

Suppose now: (a) that Privatus has never before seen the Editor of *Soul* and that he cannot recognize him, (b) that Privatus knows of the Editor's belief because he has just talked with him on the telephone, (c) that the Editor informed Privatus that a man with a unique scar on his forehead is a million-aire, (d) that such a man is the one Privatus is pointing to when he asserts (8), and (e) that Privatus does not know that the Editor is the man with that unique scar. Clearly, from (a)–(e) it follows that Privatus' statement (8) is not the same as his statement "The Editor of *Soul* believes that he* is a millionaire."

Claim (iii) is equally false, in spite of its greater plausibility. Consider once again Privatus' statement (8) to Gaskon. As above, suppose (a)–(e). However, suppose now: (f) that the Editor of *Soul* is near Privatus and overhears his statement (8), and (g) that the Editor is in a position to identify the man Privatus is pointing to. In short, the Editor is in a position to take Privatus' demonstrative use of 'he' as a demonstrative use of 'he'. Can the Editor fail to realize that he* is the one being pointed to by Privatus? It seems to me that he can. This is very unlikely, I grant, but not impossible. For suppose (h) that Privatus knows that the man he talked to on the telephone is the new Editor of *Soul*, while this man does not know of his* own appointment yet, and (i) that there is a set of mirrors arranged with the right kind of angulation, so that the Editor of *Soul* sees, in a mirror, Privatus pointing to the man with the unique scar. Suppose further, as we may, (j) that the Editor does not real-ize that he* is seeing himself* in the mirror, so that when he himself points to the man with the unique scar (by pointing to his own mirror image), he may say "He is a millionaire", without realizing that he is pointing to him-self* (or his* own mirror image). Thus, Privatus' assertion of (8) may be both true and understood by the Editor of *Soul* without the Editor of *Soul* believ-ing that he* is a millionaire. Hence, (a)–(j) yield the falsity of claim (iii).

It might be replied that in the preceding fantasy Privatus uses 'he' demon-stratively to refer to the Editor of *Soul*, while this Editor uses 'he' demonstra-tively to refer to his mirror image, so that the Editor does not really take Privatus' use of 'he' in exactly the same way, i.e., to refer exactly to the same entity. This reply is unsound. No doubt, the Editor of *Soul* points to his mir-ror image, but only because in this case he is primarily pointing to the Editor of *Soul*. Surely he is not referring to a mirror image, but to the man he sees, even if he only sees the man indirectly via the mirror image. (Ordinary usage is against the reply. We do say things like: "The sheriff saw the outlaw in the mirror and shot first.")

At any rate, it is only an empirical, though perhaps physiologically neces-sary, fact that one sees the physical world from the top of one's nose as the focus of the perspective one finds in one's visual perceptions. We can easily imagine a universe in which one's focus of perspective is located several feet away from one's nose. We can also imagine this focus changing from time to time, according, perhaps, to certain happenings in one's brain. In such a uni-verse one's focus of perspective might be on the left of one's body, say at one moment, and later it might be in front with one's own body among the objects one sees. Of course, one would know that a certain body is one*'s body in the usual way, namely, by feeling kinesthetic sensations, pains, itches, etc., in the body. But at moments in which all his bodily sensations were non-existing, or dull and he were not attending to them, one identical twin, for instance, would sometimes be momentarily in doubt as to which of two similar bodies was his*. He could get out his doubt, for instance, by walking or trying to grab something: the body in which he felt the sensations of effort, pressure, etc. would be his body. Now, in a world of this sort nothing need impede Privatus, Gaskon, and the other people talking with them from being very similar to the Editor of *Soul* in both bodily and vestiary appearance. Let us call all this (k).

Here again we may suppose (a)–(h) as the background of facts behind Privatus' statement (8). Suppose (I) that while asleep the Editor has been carried to a chair near Privatus, so that his body is surrounded by very similar bodies. Suppose (m) that the Editor and Privatus both know that the unique mark on the forehead of the new millionaire is to be produced suddenly as a remote effect of some drug, or food, or drink. Thus, we may imagine (n) that the Editor wakes up at the very moment the mark appears, (o) that he and Privatus both see the mark at once and (p) that Privatus points to the body with the mark, in *order* to point to the person whose body it is and says to Gaskon "The Editor of *Soul* believes that he is a millionaire." Now if (q) the Editor of *Soul* dies of a heart attack before he has any kinesthetic sensation through which he can identify the body pointed to by Privatus as his*, he will never come to believe that he* is a millionaire. Thus, (a)–(h), and (k)–(q) establish the falsity of claim (iii).

The two situations that yield the falsity of claim (iii) also yield the falsity of claim (iv). In the first situation, the Editor of *Soul* may see his body (via his mirror image) and say "He is a millionaire" without realizing at the time that he is pointing to himself through pointing to his body (via his mirror image). In the second situation, the Editor may say "He is a millionaire" on seeing the mark on his forehead, and if he does not point and is not aware of any bodily sensation at that very moment, he may die, by (q), without realizing that he was talking of himself.

The crucial weapon in the refutation of claim (iii) is the fact, which philosophers (especially Hume and Kant) have known all along, that there is no object of experience that one could perceive as the self that is doing the perceiving. However it is that one identifies an object of experience as oneself, whenever one does, one identifies an object of experience with a thing which is not part of the experience, and this thing is the one to which the person in question will refer to by 'I' (or its translation in other languages), and another person will refer to by 'he*', or 'he himself' in the special S-use.

Carl Ginet has proposed[10] an ingenious analysis of 'he*' in terms of the pronoun 'I', which seems to preserve the directly referring role of 'he*' by dumping it, so to speak, on the demonstrative reference of the first-person pronoun. Ginet writes:

for any sentence of the form "X believes that he* is H" [there is] a corresponding sentence that contains no form of "he*" but that would in most circumstances make the same statement. The corresponding sentence that will do the job, I suggest, is the one of the form "X believes (to be true) the proposition that X would express if X were to say, "I am H" or, perhaps more clearly, "If X were to say 'I am H' he would express what he (X) believes."

This suggestion looks very plausible at first sight. But it faces some serious difficulties.

Merely saying 'I am H' does not guarantee that any proposition is expressed. We must, then, construe Ginet's "saying 'I am H'" as something like "assertively uttering 'I am H' and nothing else." But this does not suffice. For one can express many different propositions by assertively uttering 'I am H'. What Ginet's formula lacks is a precise specification of the proposition that X believes when he believes that he* is H. That is to say, Ginet's "saying 'I am H'" must be understood as "assertively uttering 'I am H' and nothing else, when the sentence 'I am H' means what it normally means." But the analysis requires that we unpack the clause 'what it normally means'. Evidently, when this is done we are going to come out with something like "assertively uttering 'I am H' and nothing else, when the word 'I' is used by X to refer to himself*." Thus, this analysis of 'he*' in terms of 'I' is at bottom circular.

On the other hand, suppose that Ginet's formula is sufficient to specify propositions without circularity. Then there is the crucial trouble, pointed out to me by Robert C. Sleigh, that the subjunctive proposition "If X were to say 'I am H' he would express a true proposition" is true if X is a truth-telling person, even if in fact X does not believe that he* is H. The analysis is, then, too broad.

There is also the fact that "X believes that he* is H" does not entail that there are any sentences or that 'I am H' is a sentence in some language, or that 'I' is a word. But Ginet's analysans does require that 'I am H' be a sentence and 'I' be a word in some language.

In sum, the S-uses of 'he' or 'he himself', that is, *the uses of the pronoun 'he** *cannot be analyzed in terms of the demonstrative reference of the strictly third-person pronoun 'he'.* The only demonstrative reference of 'he*' is bound up with that pertaining to the first-person pronoun 'I'.

3. 'I'

In order to analyze in detail the connection between a use of 'he*' and an implicit use of 'I', we need some grasp of the logic of 'I'. For our purpose it suffices here to discuss just a few of the most general features of the logic of 'I'. We consider first the use of 'I' in *oratio recta*, i.e., in clauses which are neither subordinated to cognitive verbs (in the sense we gave this term in section 1) nor enclosed within quotation marks.[11] This use of 'I' is characterized by the following properties.

(I) Like all other demonstratively used pronouns, be they called demonstratives, be they called personal pronouns, 'I' has a *referential priority* over all names and descriptions of objects. A name, or a description, correctly used may fail to refer to the object to which it purports to refer because there may be not one, but many objects, which have the name in question, or the properties mentioned in the description. A demonstrative, however, cannot fail to refer because of a multiplicity of candidates for reference. Once the demonstrative is correctly tendered, there is for its user at most one candidate for reference by it.

(II) The pronoun 'I' has an *ontological priority* over all names and descriptions. A correct use of 'I' cannot fail to refer to the object it purports to refer. Some philosophers would argue that every demonstratively used pronoun has this priority over all names and descriptions. They could claim that if a token of a demonstrative is correctly used in *oratio recta*, of necessity, the token in question would succeed in referring to something in the speaker's current experience. They would argue that even in the case of a delusion, if, e.g., a man honestly asserts "That is a dog", his token of 'that' successfully picks out a complex of sense-data, or a region of physical (or psychological) space, or a set of features, or what not. Here, however, we do not have to go into this matter. Whether 'I' alone or all demonstratively used pronouns have this ontological priority is of no consequence for the present investigation. What matters to us here is that 'I' does have this priority over names and descriptions.

(III) The pronoun 'I' and all descriptions and, to a certain extent, names have an *epistemological priority* over all the other demonstratively used pronouns. In order to keep knowledge or belief, or in order merely to rethink, of the objects originally apprehended by means of demonstratives one must reformulate one's knowledge or belief, or thought, of those objects. One must replace each purely demonstrative reference by a reference in terms of descriptions or names, or in terms of the demonstrative 'I'. If Privatus asserts "This is blue", perhaps with a pointing, he seems both to single out an object in his experience and to attribute to it nothing but blueness. Let this be as it may. The crucial thing, however, is that later on, when the object is no longer in his presence, the pronoun 'this' has to yield to a name or description of the object Privatus called "this". Demonstratives are necessarily *eliminable for their users*. The only exception is the demonstrative 'I'. Nobody can at all keep knowledge or belief of whatever information about himself he receives, unless he manages to replace every single reference to himself in terms of descriptions or names, or in terms of other demonstratives (like 'you', 'he', 'this'), by a reference in terms of 'I (me, my, mine, myself)'. This does not mean, of course, that whenever, e.g., Privatus hears "Privatus is ϕ," he is to perform a physically, or psychologically, distinguishable act of translation: "That is, I am ϕ." The point is a logical one. Privatus cannot remember, or merely consider later on, that he* is ϕ, unless he remembers, or considers, what he would formulate by saying "I am ϕ" or "Privatus is ϕ and I am Privatus." At least the statements of identity "I am Privatus" or "I am the one who . . . " must include an ineliminable use of 'I' for Privatus. If he only entertains or thinks the statements, without actually making any assertion, we shall speak of his making an implicit use of 'I'.

(IV) But the epistemological priority of the demonstrative 'I' is only partial. Everybody else must replace a person's references to himself in terms of 'I (me, my, mine, myself)' by references in terms of some description or name of the person in question.

These are all trivial features of 'I', names, descriptions and the other demonstrative pronouns. But they have some important consequences. For instance, even though a demonstrative seems merely to denote an object, it has a *sense* for its user, which consists in its being a place-holder for some description or other, to which, by (III), it must yield.

Some philosophers may be tempted to claim that every demonstrative has as its sense a set of descriptions, namely, the descriptions to which it can, or must, yield in future references to the same entity the demonstrative denotes. They may be tempted to this claim by the natural principle that every statement can be repeated, i.e., reasserted or at least re-thought. Thus, if Privatus says "This is ϕ" he can be supposed to be capable of making this very same statement any time he wishes to. But since when the objects of his experience have changed, he can no longer call 'this' the same object he called 'this' before, he must employ some description, and this description, one is tempted to think, is part of the sense of his original token$_w$ of 'this'. This seems an extreme view which we need neither attack nor defend here. Indeed, we need not even take issue here with the weaker view that the sense of a token$_w$ of a demonstrative is given by some descriptions pinpointing the object as one experienced at the time or place it was referred to demonstratively. Descriptions of this type are, e.g., "The cow I saw yesterday" and "The man I touched just a little while ago." The view in question need not object to the sense of a token$_w$ of a demonstrative being given in terms of other tokens$_w$ of the same or other demonstratives. This view does not have to include the thesis that demonstratives can be analyzed away in terms of descriptions.

Let us move on to *oratio obliqua*. In the case of tokens$_w$ of the pronoun 'I' occurring in clauses subordinated to cognitive verbs (in the sense of 'cognitive verb' explained in section I), we must distinguish two types.

(Ii) There are (F)-uses of 'I'. These are found in statements of the form "X believes (thinks, knows, asserts, argues, etc.) of me that I (me, my, mine, myself) . . . ", here the second token$_w$ of 'I' is characterized both by having a logical and grammatical antecedent, which is a token$_n$ of 'me', and by being a place-holder for some unspecified description or name of the person to whom 'me' refers.

(Iii) There are directly self-referring uses of 'I'. These are found in statements of the form "X believes (thinks, knows, argues, etc.) that . . . I (me, my, mine, myself) . . . ", where at least some tokens$_w$ of 'I' have no grammatical or logical antecedent, and, thus, refer directly to the speaker, instead of referring to the person referred to by a first-person antecedent. Let us consider type (Ii). By analogy with the (F)-uses of 'he' we may expect the (F)-uses of 'I' to be eliminable for the speaker in essentially the same way. This is in fact what happens. But in the case of 'I' there is a new reason to suspect that an (F)-token$_w$ must be eliminable. By (IV) above, nobody can refer to another person by means of 'I'. Thus, when someone, call him Y, asserts (or thinks), e.g., "X believes of me that I am ϕ", the token$_w$ of 'I' here cannot represent in and by itself the sort of reference to Y that the person X can make.[12] It must, perforce, stand for some way of referring to Y that is available to X. In general, let 'E' stand for a cognitive verb; let '$\phi(I)$' stand for a sentence containing some (F)-tokens$_w$ T of 'I' whose antecedent is a token of 'me' not occurring in '$\phi(I)$', and let '$\phi(Z)$' be obtained by replacing in 'f(I)' every token$_w$ T by a token$_w$ of 'Z'. Then:

(P′) A statement of the form "X E's of me that $\phi(I)$" is the same as the statement of the corresponding form "There is a way of referring to a certain person as Z, I am that person and X E's that $\phi(Z)$."

Suppose, for example, that Privatus asserts:

(3) Paul believes of Mary that she is happy.

Here Privatus' token$_n$ of 'she' is an instance of the (F)-use of 'he'. Suppose further that Mary wants to say about herself* what Privatus has said about her. She will say:

(9) Paul believes of me that I am happy.

Here Mary's second token$_w$ of 'I' corresponds to Privatus' token$_n$ of 'she'. It is an instance of the (F)-use of 'I'. It is at bottom not an authentic first-person use of 'I'. Its first-person role is wholly derivative: it consists merely in having as its logical and grammatical antecedent Mary's token$_n$ of the authentically first-person 'me'. 'I' in 'that I am happy' does not refer by itself to the speaker. Just as (3) does not ascribe to Paul the belief *that* Mary is happy, likewise (9) does not ascribe to Paul the belief *that* "I (Mary) am happy" is true.

When Mary utters (9), her tokens of 'I' functions simply as a place-holder for some unspecified name or description which refers to the person referred to by Mary's token$_n$ of 'me'. This is the complete analysis of this (F)-use of 'I'. Hence Mary's (F)-used token$_n$ of 'I' is eliminable for Mary by principle (P′). Mary's statement (9) is the statement she would have made had she said:

(9a) There is a way of referring univocally to a certain person as Z, I am that person, and Paul believes that Z is happy.

For contrast, note that Mary's token of 'me' in (9) is not in *oratio obliqua*. Mary cannot eliminate this token$_w$ of 'I' from (9): it reappears in (9a) in the clause 'I am that person'.

Let us proceed to type (Iii). The main features of a use of 'I' of type (Iii) are determined by (III) and (IV). In the first place, since by (III) a person's uses of 'I' in *oratio recta* are for him ineliminable, these uses are also ineliminable when they are preceded by a cognitive prefix of the form 'I (believe, know, think, claim, argue, assert, etc.)'. The person who is said to do the believing (knowing, thinking, arguing, asserting, etc.) must make genuine self-references by means of 'I'. In the second place, by (IV) a person must replace somebody else's, say Y's, uses of 'I' by descriptions. Hence, every token$_w$ of 'I' in a clause subordinated to a prefix of the form 'X believes (knows, thinks, says, etc.)', where 'X' is not the pronoun 'I', can only be a place-holder for a way of referring to Y which is available to X.

To simplify let us define a *cognitive prefix* as a clause containing a cognitive verb and ending in 'that'.[13] For instance, 'While staring at Mary, in the kitchen, John told Irene that he would love her forever' has as its cognitive prefix 'while staring at Mary, in the kitchen, John told Irene that'. Thus, we have that:

(V) If a token$_w$ of 'I' of type (Iii) occurs *oratio obliqua* immediately subordinated to a cognitive prefix containing a token$_w$ of 'I', then the former is eliminable for the person it refers to if the latter is also eliminable for the same person.

(VI) A token$_w$ of 'I' of type (Iii) is eliminable for the person it refers to, provided that the *oratio obliqua* in which it occurs is subordinated to a cognitive prefix containing no tokens$_w$ of 'I'.

That (VI) cannot be strengthened to a statement about a sufficient and necessary condition was shown to me by Geach. In "I believe that I am a millionaire, and Gaskon believes that he* is a millionaire" the second token$_w$ of 'I' is eliminable, even though subordinated to an ineliminable token$_w$ of 'I', inasmuch as the statement is, as Geach pointed out, equivalent to "Each of two persons, Gaskon and me, believes that he* is a millionaire." Since in this case a token$_w$ of 'I' is eliminable for a token$_w$ of 'he*' we shall distinguish it from *strict eliminability* which consists in being eliminable, *salva propositione*, by something other than tokens of the S-pronoun 'he*', whatever these may be. Thus, strict eliminability implies eliminability *simpliciter*. Similarly, for 'he*' strict eliminability is eliminability in terms other than tokens$_w$ of 'I'.

Concerning the elimination procedure we must note that there are two cases of tokens$_w$ of 'I' eliminable for their users: (a) tokens$_w$ which are not subordinated to cognitive prefixes with eliminable tokens$_w$ of 'I', and (b) tokens$_w$ which are subordinated to cognitive prefixes with eliminable tokens$_w$ of 'I'. The procedure of elimination for case (b) involves the procedure for case (a). Suppose, for instance, that Privatus asserts "Jones believes that I know that I am happy." The first token of 'I' is a place-holder for some description or name of Privatus known to Jones; let it be 'Z'. But the second token of 'I' is not a place-holder for 'Z'. For Privatus has not asserted something like "There is a way of referring to me as Z, and Jones believes that Z knows that Z is happy." Surely, the man known to Jones as Z may fail to know himself* as Z, and this is something which Jones may be expected to know, and Privatus may also know that Jones knows it. But, more importantly, Privatus' statement makes the claim that Jones ascribes self-knowledge to Privatus, i.e., a knowledge in terms of the purely referential first-person way. Privatus' assertion is, at bottom, "There is a way of univocally referring to a person as Z, I am Z, Jones can identify Z in the relevant respect, and Jones believes that Z knows that he* is happy." The main point is that the elimination of tokens of 'I' in *oratio obliqua*, is in case (b), to be made in terms of fresh tokens of 'he*'.

Let us formulate the general principle of elimination for cases (a) and (b) at once. Let 'E' stand for a cognitive verb; let '$\phi(I)$' stand for a sentence or clause containing tokens$_w$ of 'I' which are not subordinated to any cognitive verb in '$\phi(I)$'; let '$\phi(Z)$' stand for the result obtained from '$\phi(I)$' by: (1) replacing all tokens$_w$ of 'I' not subordinated to any cognitive verb in '$\phi(I)$' by tokens of Z, (2) replacing all tokens$_w$ of 'I' subordinated in '$\phi(I)$' only to cognitive prefixes containing tokens$_w$ of 'I' by tokens$_w$ of 'he*' whose antecedent is Z, and (3) by replacing nothing else. Then:

(P″)   A statement of the form of "X E's that $\phi(I)$" is the same as the corresponding statement of the form "There is a way of referring to a certain person as Z, X can identify Z (in the relevant respect, or knows who Z is), I am Z, and X E's that $\phi(Z)$."

There is a serious obscurity about (P″), namely, the obscurity surrounding the notion of identification. What counts as identifying a person is something that cries out for analysis. However, this analysis lies too far afield from us here. All we can say at this juncture is that there seem to be different criteria for identifying a person, depending on the circumstances of the persons involved, in particular the circumstances linking the identifier and the identified person. Thus, suppose that a certain crime has been committed. In this case in order to know who the criminal is, a detective must be able to know at least how to bring the criminal to jail or to court. On the other hand, for a high-school student to know who the President of the United States is he needs only to be able to answer certain questions that his teacher may put to him.

Consider Mary's statement:

(10)   Paul believes that I am happy.

Clearly, the reference to Mary by means of 'I' is one that Paul just cannot make (assuming ordinary meanings, of course). By (III) and (IV), whatever Paul believes of Mary, he has to believe it by thinking that a certain person Z is happy. The claim that Z is (the same as) Mary is one that Paul need not make, nor is it one that Mary's statement (10) attributes to him. Indeed, the claim that Mary is Z is one that Mary herself need, or does, not make when she asserts (10). Thus, we have to analyze (10) very much in the same way that we analyze statements made by means of sentences containing tokens of the (F)-'he'. But not quite. Mary's statement (10) is not identical with her statement (9), "Paul believes of me that I am happy"; hence, we are not to analyze (10) as (9a) above.

The difference between (9) and (10) is very intriguing. But we do not have to dwell upon it here. We need note only that it lies in the claim, made by (10) but not by (9), that Paul's way of referring to Mary as Z enables him to pick out, or identify, Mary as the person whom he believes to be happy. This is precisely what principle (P″) asserts.

Now, by (V)–(VI) a token$_w$ T of 'I' subordinated to a cognitive verb whose subject is not a token of 'I' is eliminable for the person referred to by the token$_w$ T, even if T is subordinated to a cognitive verb whose subject is another token$_w$ T′ of 'I'. For example, suppose that Privatus asserts:

(11) I believe that the Editor of *Soul knows* that Mary believes that I am a millionaire.

Here the first token$_n$ of 'I' is in *oratio recta*, and by (III) it is ineliminable for Privatus. The second token$_n$ of 'I' is, by (VI), eliminable even for Privatus. By applying (P″) to (11) Privatus could eliminate the latter token$_n$ of 'I' in favour of a new token$_w$ of 'I' that would be subordinated to the prefix 'I believe that'. Hence, this new token$_n$ would also be ineliminable for Privatus, by (V). But all these tokens$_w$ of 'I' would be eliminable for Privatus if he were to subordinate (11) or its equivalent, by (P″), to a prefix of the form 'X E's that'. Yet, again, the eliminable tokens$_w$ of 'I' would give rise to ineliminable tokens$_w$ of 'I' by virtue of (P″). The whole thing is simply that the only ineliminable tokens of 'I' for the user of 'I' are (1) those occurring in *oratio recta* and (2) those in *oratio obliqua* subordinated only to prefixes of the form 'I E that'.

4. 'He*' and 'I'

We must now discuss the eliminability of tokens$_w$ of 'I' for a person who, instead of making them, hears them. By (IV) above, the tokens$_w$ of 'I' in *oratio recta* are necessarily eliminable for anyone who does not make them. But the tokens$_w$ of 'I' in *oratio obliqua* that are ineliminable for the person whom the tokens$_w$ refer to are not, for another person, eliminable in terms of descriptions or names of the former persons. For instance, suppose that Privatus asserts "I believe that I am a millionaire." For everybody else Privatus' first tokens of 'I' must yield to some description or name of Privatus, e.g., 'Privatus'. But his second token$_n$ of 'I' must be replaced by a token$_w$ of 'he*'. His statement would yield for us the statement "Privatus believes that he* is a millionaire." In general, the precise correspondence between 'he*' and 'I' is simply this:

(H*) A use of 'I' in *oratio obliqua* that is ineliminable for the person it refers to, who uses it, corresponds to, in the sense that it must yield to, another person's ineliminable use of 'he*' in *oratio obliqua*.

At this juncture the question arises: Can the pronoun 'he*' appear in *oratio recta?* It might seem obvious that the answer to this question is in the affirmative. There are in fact three general considerations which might at first sight seem to support an affirmative answer. *First,* when a person formulates what he believes (knows, thinks, etc.) he says "I . . . ," and other persons say "He . . . "; *second,* in a sentence of the form 'X believes (knows, thinks, says, etc.) that he* . . . ' the person X is precisely the one 'he*' refers to; *third,* what one knows is true, thus if X knows that he* is ϕ, it seems, *simpliciter,* that he* is ϕ.

To be sure, when a person X hears Y say "I am ϕ", X will understand what he heard as "He is ϕ." But from this it does not follow that this token of 'he' is a token of 'he*'. Indeed, there is a good reason for suspecting that here we do not have a token of 'he*'. X's token of 'he' must be a demonstrative if it is to refer to Y univocally and without describing him. But we saw in section 2 that the pronoun he*' is not demonstrative. Thus, the first reason for the claim that 'he*' appears in *oratio recta* provides, rather, evidence against this claim.

Doubtless, in the sentence 'X believes that he* is ϕ' the token of 'he*' does refer to the person X. This suggests both that we could have statements of the form "he* is X" and that whoever believed I or asserted "X believes (knows, thinks, says, etc.) that he* is ϕ" should certainly know the truth of the corresponding statement "he is X". It would seem, then, that tokens of 'he*' can appear in *oratio recta*. However, if there were complete statements of the form "he* is X", these statements could be known to be true by the person X himself. But suppose that X, who does not know that he* is X, does assert (or just thinks, for that matter) "X believes (knows, thinks, says, etc.) that he* is X". That is, X could come to know that he* is X simply by thinking that the man X has some property or other. For instance, the heaviest man of Europe could come to know that he* weighs more than anybody else without resorting at all to scales and comparison of weights! This absurdity arises simply from allowing the tokens$_w$ of 'he*' to function as independent symbols, i.e., as referring devices in their own right, without the need of a grammatical and logical antecedent. Hence, we must conclude that there are no complete statements of the form "he* is X". That is, a sentence containing a token$_w$ of 'he*' can, given ordinary meanings, formulate a statement only if the token$_w$ in question has an antecedent in the same sentence.

Let us turn now to the third reason for supposing that 'he*' can appear in *oratio recta*. Doubtlessly, the following principle is true:

(K) A statement of the form "X knows that . . . " entails that the statement denoted by the sentence filling the blank ' . . . ' is true.

Thus, the statement "The Editor of *Soul* knows that he* is a millionaire" entails that the statement (or proposition) denoted by the clause he* is a millionaire' is true. But (K) must be distinguished from two rules of inference, which seem to follow immediately from (K). They are:

(K.1)   From a statement of the form "X knows that *p*" you may infer the corresponding statement that *p*.

(K.2)   If a sentence of the form 'X knows that *p*' formulates a statement you accept, then you may detach the sentence (or clause) S represented by '*p*' and use S by itself to make the statement which S formulates as part of the larger sentence 'X knows that *p*', provided that S contains no tokens$_w$ or either first or second-person pronouns.

Clearly, neither principle (K) nor rule (K.1) says anything about the kind of sentence through which the proposition *p* is to be formulated. Only (K.2), of the three, establishes a condition about sentences that could support the claim that tokens$_w$ of 'he*' can appear, correctly in *oratio recta*. But I want to argue that rule (K.2) is invalid: it leads to contradictions. Moreover, I want to argue that rule (K.1) is also in need of revision.

Let us consider (K.2) first. It is a fact that in ordinary life one often draws, or can draw anyway, *valid* inferences like:

(11) The Editor of *Soul knows* that he himself [i.e., he*] is a millionaire.

hence,

(12) he is a millionaire.

This inference seems validated by (K.2). One feels tempted to say that the token of 'he' in (12) is simply an instance of the pronoun 'he*' which appears in (11). Indeed, since the above inference is valid, the token of 'he' in any token of sentence (12) is a token of 'he*' if and only if the above inference is validated by (K.2). If the inference is validated by (K.2), then (12) contains an independent use of 'he*' in *oratio recta*.

The validity of the inference "(11), hence (12)" does not, of course, depend at all on who draws it. Thus, the role of (K.2) and the character of the token of 'he' in (12) remain unaltered if Privatus draws the inference, even though

(13) It is not the case that Privatus believes that he* is a millionaire.

Suppose further that Privatus believes that (11) and draws out loud, or in writing, the inference from (11) to (12). Clearly, while drawing the inference Privatus believes both the premise and the conclusion to be true. Make now the assumption that the occurrence of 'he' in (12) is an instance of 'he*'. Then while drawing the inference from (11) and (12), Privatus believes that both (11) the Editor of *Soul* knows that he himself is a millionaire and (12) he* is a millionaire. But then the latter 'he*' refers back to 'Privatus', so that we can infer that Privatus believes that he* is a millionaire. Since this result contradicts (13), the assumption is false. The use of 'he' in (12), as part of the inference from (11), is the same regardless of whether or not the Editor of *Soul* believes (or knows) that he* is the Editor of *Soul*. Hence, we may conclude that in no case is the token of 'he' in (12) a token of 'he*'. This being the case, the inference "(11), hence (12)" is not validated by rule (K.2).

Evidently, the same arguments apply to any statement of the form "X E's that ϕ(he*)." Thus, we may regard as established that

(H*1)   The pronoun 'he*' is strictly a subordinate pronoun: it is by itself an incomplete, or syncategorematic, symbol, and *every* sentence or clause containing a token$_w$ of 'he*' which is not in *oratio obliqua*, is also an incomplete or syncategorematic sentence or clause.

Let us return to the inference "(11), hence (12)". The inference is palpably valid. But what kind of 'he' is, then, the one appearing in (10) to me that (12) has a token of 'he' which is an instance of use (D), i.e., a relative pronoun which is here a proxy for the definite description "The Editor of *Soul*." In other words, the conclusion of the inference "(11), hence (12)" is the statement "(He =) The Editor of *Soul is* a millionaire." But then, the inference "(11), hence (12)" is *not* validated by rule (K.1)! By the arguments of section 2 above, the token$_w$ of 'he*' in (11) does not have a sense that can be given by any other use of the third-person pronoun, or any name, or any definite description. Thus, the question arises: Is there a way at all of formulating the proposition which, by (11), the Editor of *Soul* knows to be true, so that we can apply rule (K.1) to (11)?

The proposition that the Editor of *Soul knows* to be true, if (11) is true, is one which the Editor can formulate by saying: "I am a millionaire." But even though the Editor of *Soul* would not be inferring a false conclusion from a true premise, the inference "The Editor of *Soul* knows that he* is a millionaire, hence I am a millionaire" is even for him not validated by an application of rule (K.1). On the other hand, the inference "I am the Editor of *Soul*, the Editor of *Soul knows* that he* is a millionaire, hence I am a millionaire" is valid, but it is, obviously, not validated by rule (K.1).[14]

There is just one other referring expression that has to be considered: the pronoun 'you'. Let us assume that any of us can formulate the statement that, according to (11), the Editor of *Soul* knows to be true by uttering the sentence "You are a millionaire." But the inference the Editor of *Soul* knows that he* is a millionaire, hence you are a millionaire" is not valid, and, *a fortiori*, not an application of rule (K.1). On the other hand, "The Editor of *Soul* knows that he* is a millionaire, and you are the Editor of *Soul*, hence, you are a millionaire" is a valid reference, but it is not validated by (K.1). Actually, I doubt very much that it is always possible to formulate the very same proposition denoted by a clause of the form 'he* is ϕ' in *oratio obliqua* by means of the corresponding *oratio recta* sentence of the form 'You are ϕ'. Consider, for instance, the statement "Just before his death Caesar thought that he* was to be crowned king." It seems to me that the statement "Caesar, you were to be crowned king" is not precisely the one Caesar thought to be true. For one thing, the latter statement entails or implies or presupposes that somebody is talking to Caesar, while the statement (or proposition) that Caesar thought to be true does not carry that implication or presupposition or entailment.

At any rate, even if the proposition that, by (11), the Editor of *Soul* knows to be true can be formulated by sentences in *oratio recta* containing the pronoun 'you', we have seen that rule (K.1) cannot apply to (11). Obviously, similar considerations hold for any other third-person statement ascribing self-consciousness to someone. Hence

(H*2)   The generally accepted rule (K.1) is invalid: it fails for statements p expressible in sentences containing tokens$_w$ of 'he*'.

(H*2) raises a serious task, namely, that of formulating a set of true principles which are to replace the widely accepted (K.1).

By (H*) and by (V) and (VI) of section 3, we should expect the tokens$_w$ of 'he*' that are ineliminable in a sentence S to become eliminable when S is concatenated to a prefix of the form 'X thinks (believes, knows, says, etc.)'. As we shall see in the sequel, this is precisely the case even when the occurrence of 'X' in this prefix-form stands for another token of the expression which is the antecedent of a token$_w$ of 'he*' in S. To say it at once, the principle governing the ineliminability of 'he*' is:

(H*3)   A token$_w$ T of 'he*' is strictly ineliminable for its user in two types of cases, and only in these two types of cases: (1) T occurs in an *oratio obliqua* subordinated to just one cognitive prefix containing the antecedent of T; (2) T occurs in an *oratio obliqua* subordinated to $n + 1$ cognitive prefixes such that the very first one, from the left, has the antecedent A of T, and the other n verbs have tokens$_w$ of 'he*' whose antecedent is also A.

By (H*3) the following tokens$_w$ of 'he*' are ineliminable for their users: "Privatus believes that he* is happy", and "Alexander believed that he* knew that he* once thought that he* was a god." (H*3) separates the tokens$_w$ of 'he*' that are eliminable for their users from those which are not; but it does not furnish the elimination procedures. By (H*)–(H*3), these procedures are similar to those employed for the elimination of 'I', but there is the important difference already noted in section 3 that many a token$_w$ of 'I' has to be eliminated in favor of a token$_w$ of 'he*'. We shall discuss the general principles for the elimination of 'he*' by considering some simple examples with 'he*'. As in the case of 'I', there are two cases: (a) some tokens$_w$ of 'he*' are eliminable from a subordinate clause at the cost of introducing another token$_w$ of 'he*' in the main clause and (b) some tokens$_w$ of 'he*' are eliminable in the sense that they are replaced by tokens$_w$ of 'he*' in the very same subordinate clause but with a different antecedent.

A simple example of case (a) is this. Suppose that Privatus asserts:

(14) The Editor of *Soul* believes that the Editor of *Soul* believes that he* is a millionaire.

It is not evident what exactly it is that Privatus has asserted. His utterance has an interesting ambiguity. Imagine the Editor of *Soul* himself making the same, or very similar, statement. He has a choice between

(15) I believe that the Editor of *Soul* believes that I am a millionaire.

and

(16) I believe that the Editor of *Soul* believes that he* is a millionaire.

Of course, he can also say:

(17) I believe that I believe that I am a millionaire.

What interests us now is the contrast between (15) and (16). The occurrence of 'he*' in (16) stands for an occurrence of 'I', as it were, two steps removed: it stands for a token$_w$ of 'I' that the Editor of *Soul* mentioned by the Editor of *Soul* could produce to say "I am a millionaire." Thus, in the case of (14), we must distinguish two cases. On the one hand, the token$_w$ of 'he*' occurring in (14) may have as its antecedent the second occurrence, from it to the left, of the phrase 'the Editor of *Soul*'. This is the syntax of the sentence that Privatus meant to utter, if he meant to make the statement, (18), below, analogous to the Editor of *Soul's* statement (15). On the other hand the occurrence of 'he*' in (14) may have as its antecedent the first occurrence, from it to the left, of 'the Editor of *Soul*'. This is the syntax of the sentence Privatus meant to utter, if he meant to make the statement, (19) below, analogous to (16). Let us affix numerals to a token$_w$ of 'he*', in such a way that we can determine which expression is the antecedent of the token$_w$ in question by counting to the left of it, the cognitive verbs to which it is subordinated. Thus, our two interpretations of (14) can be written as follows:

(18) The Editor of *Soul* believes that the Editor of *Soul* believes that he*$_2$ is a millionaire.
(19) The Editor of *Soul* believes that the Editor of *Soul* believes that he*$_1$ is a millionaire.[15]

By principle (P″) above, the second occurrence of 'I' in (15) is eliminable. Hence, by (H*) the token$_w$ of 'he*' in (18) should also be eliminable in a similar way. Thus, (18) is the same as the statement:

(18a) The Editor of *Soul* believes that there is a way of univocally referring to a certain person as Z, that he* is Z, and that the Editor of *Soul* both can identify Z in the relevant respect and believes that Z is a millionaire.

On the other hand, by (H*3), neither (19) nor (18a) has occurrences of 'he*' that are eliminable for their users. Note, incidentally, that a first cousin of

(18), 'The Editor of *Soul* believes that the Editor of *Soul* believes of him$^*_1$ that he is a millionaire' also has an ineliminable occurrence of 'he*': the antecedent of 'him$^*_1$' is the very first occurrence of 'the Editor of *Soul*' (the last token$_n$ of 'he' is an instance of the (F)-use).

An example of case (b) appears in

(20) The Editor of *Soul* believes that Privatus believes that he$^*_2$ knows that he$^*_3$ is the Editor of *Soul*.

Given our convention on subscripts, the two tokens$_w$ of 'he*' in (20) have 'the Editor of *Soul*' as their antecedent. Statement (20) is the same as the statement

(20a) The Editor of *Soul* believes: that there is a way of referring to a certain person as Z, that he$^*_1$ is Z, and that Privatus can both identify Z in the relevant respect and believe that Z knows that he$^*_1$ is the Editor of *Soul*.

By our convention, in (20a) the first occurrence of 'he$^*_1$' has 'the Editor of *Soul*' as antecedent, while the second occurrence has 'Z' as antecedent. By (H*3) neither occurrence is eliminable for the speaker.

Notes

This essay was concluded while the author was doing research supported by the National Science Foundation, Grant No. G.S. 828.

1. The main topic of this essay is almost brand new. My first glimpse of its complexity occurred when I was trying to formulate what I called "Meaning postulates of 'pain'" in Castañeda 1963a. But I am deeply indebted to Jaakko Hintikka for having fully awakened me to this topic. For my critical review of Hintikka 1962 (Castañeda 1964b), I had to study his formal treatment of statements expressed in sentences of the form "The man who is in fact *a* knows that he is *a*." Hintikka points out that "Ka(a=a)" is not a symbolization of that sentence form. He proposes to symbolize it as "(Ex)(Ka(x=a))" (1962, 159). This symbolization is satisfactory inasmuch as Hintikka has very ingeniously taken the free but bindable individual variables occurring in contexts of the form 'Ka(...)' to range over objects or persons known to *a*. Thus, '(Ex)(Ka(x=a))' can be read as "There is a person known to *a* such that *a* knows that such a person is *a*." There is, surely, a sense of 'knowing a person' in which for *a* to know the person who is in fact *a* is to know himself.

Yet Hintikka's very reading makes his calculus inadequate to handle several important statements. It cannot handle, e.g., contingent statements expressed in sentences of the form 'There is an object such that *a* does not know that it exists.' Here the individual variable 'it' occurs free in the clause 'such that *a* does not know that it exists.' Hence, by Hintikka's reading, that 'it' must refer to an object known to *a*, such statements would be self-contradictory. For another difficulty let '*a*' stand for 'The Editor of *Soul*'. Suppose now that Smith has never seen his image or pictures in photographs, mirrors, ponds, etc. Suppose that at time *t* Smith does not know that he has been appointed the Editor of *Soul* and that at t he comes to know that the man whose photograph lies on a certain table is the new Editor of *Soul*, without Smith realizing that he himself is the man in the photograph. In this situation, "There is a person such that the Editor of *Soul* knows that that person is the Editor of *Soul*, without the Editor knowing that he himself is that person" is true. This statement cannot, however, be symbolized in Hintikka's calculus. The obvious candidate '(Ex)(Ka(x=a) & ~Ka(x=a))' is strictly a formal contradiction. What is needed is something like '(Ex)(Ka(x=a) & ~Ka(x=himself))' where the expression 'himself' has 'a' as its logical antecedent. This is precisely the initial insight into the peculiar syncategorematic character of the pronoun 'he*' that led to the claims and principles put forward in sections 4 and 5 below.

Hintikka's calculus (together with his ingenious reading of free variables) is, furthermore, inadequate to handle the complexities of the pronoun 'he*.' See note 15 below.

Some time after I had finished this paper I came across Geach 1957. Here Geach formulates three important things. First, "$a=b$ and b believes that b is ϕ" entails "a believes that b is ϕ". Second, "$a=b$ and b believes that b is ϕ" does not entail "a believes that a is ϕ". Third, "$a=b$ and b believes that he himself is ϕ" does entail "a believes that he himself is ϕ". Thus, Geach should be credited (as far as I know) with having posed the problem of the logic of the pronoun 'he*' for the first time.

My greatest debt is to P. T. Geach who saved me from several errors and suggested objections and corrections.

2. This parenthetical clause was inserted on the suggestion of Professor Wilfrid Sellars. I hope that it makes it clear that I do not claim that the sentence "Paul believes of Mary that she is happy," is never used in ordinary speech to make the same statement that is more properly made with the sentence "Paul believes that Mary is happy". I claim only that the former sometimes is used, or can at any rate be used to make a statement such that (1) it does not imply that the proposition Paul takes to be true is "Mary is happy", and (2) it implies that Paul takes as true some proposition of the form "Z is happy", where 'Z' stands for some way he uses to refer to a certain person, who happens to be Mary.

3. At the October 13th, 1964, Wayne State University Colloquium, at which the earlier version of this paper was discussed.

4. I am indebted to Edmund Gettier and Wilfrid Sellars for pointing out the need for saying something about my primitive *way of referring* so that it would not be wholly obscure. I hope that with this promissory note I may be allowed to continue using an apparent quantification over ways of referring. Sellars was very helpful in emphasizing the need for mentioning way 3.

5. During the discussion of the earlier version of the paper at the University of Pittsburgh Philosophy Colloquium, on November 20th, 1964.

6. See Hintikka 1958.

7. See Belnap's review of Hintikka 1958 in Belnap 1960.

8. For example, Wilfrid Sellars and Bruce Aune during the discussion mentioned in note 5.

9. I am indebted to Richard Cartwright for the following example of a description that can replace a token$_w$ of 'he*': 'the person (or entity) identical with himself*'. Clearly, there is an infinite chain of descriptions generated from this: 'the entity identical with the entity identical with . . . the entity identical with himself*'.

10. In his comments on this paper when it was presented at the meeting of the Michigan Academy in March 1965.

11. Here I am not regarding modal contexts as *oratio obliqua*. For our discussion of 'I' and 'he*' there is no difference between, e.g., "X loves me" or "It is possible that X loves me." In neither case there is an appearance of attributing to X a first-personal way of referring to another person, as there is, e.g., in "Peter believes that I love him."†

12. I am indebted to Norman Kretzmann for the following teasing use of 'I' which looks like a counter-example to this claim. Suppose that there is a play about Privatus and that Privatus is in the audience. Suppose further that the actor representing Privatus is losing his moustache and that Privatus referring to the actor says "I am losing my moustache."

13. This shift from cognitive verbs to cognitive prefixes was required to meet an objection of Geach's to principle (P″) below.

14. I am very grateful to both Richard Cartwright and Robert Sleigh, Jr. for having impressed upon me during the discussion mentioned in footnote 3 the need for distinguishing between principles (K.1) and (K.2). They also pointed out some errors in my confused discussion of (K.1) and (K.2), e.g., that I had not discussed the case of 'you" as I do below in this version. However, neither Cartwright nor Sleigh are responsible for the present formulation of (K.1) or (K.2).

15. The distinction between (18) and (19) cannot be formulated in Hintikka's calculus mentioned in note 1. There is nothing in this calculus that corresponds to the criss-crossing references mirrored by our subscript notation. Yet the possibility of criss-crossing is central to the pronoun 'he*'.

---

†In the last sentence of this note, the order of 'there' and 'is' should be reversed.—Eds.

2

Indicators and Quasi-Indicators[1]

1. Purpose, Problem, and Conventions

Crucial to many problems in the philosophy of mind, epistemology, and meta-physics are: (A) a clear understanding of the roles and interrelations of the types of words we employ to refer to the entities we encounter, and (B) a clear understanding of the logic of cognitive and linguistic verbs (like 'think,' 'sup-pose,' and 'infer,' on the one hand, and 'say,' 'inform,' 'argue,' and 'show,' on the other). My ultimate purpose here is to make a contribution towards both (A) and (B).[2]

My contribution toward (A) consists mainly in showing, via principles (Q.7)–(Q.10) below, that a certain mechanism of reference to particulars, which is indispensable to a conceptual scheme that allows for the possibility of other persons or selves, is a unique logical category of reference not reduc-ible to the better-studied mechanisms of reference namely, demonstrative pro-nouns or adverbs, proper names, singular descriptions, and ordinary variables of quantification. This irreducible mechanism is constituted by what I call quasi-indicators. Following Goodman,[3] I call *indicators* personal and demon-strative pronouns and adverbs like 'this,' 'that,' 'I,' 'you,' 'here,' 'there,' 'now,' when they are used to make a strictly demonstrative reference, i.e., when they are used purely referentially either to single out an item present in the speaker's current experience or to pinpoint a self that is a relatum in the cog-nitive relation evinced by the speaker. I call *quasi-indicators* the expressions which in *oratio obliqua* represent uses, perhaps only implicit, of indicators,

This essay first appeared in *American Philosophical Quarterly* 4 (1967), 85–100, and is reprinted here with the permission of the editor. It also appeared as chapter 12 in Castañeda 1989a with two minor adjustments (indicated in editorial notes below). A German translation occurs in Castañeda 1982a, 160–201, together with an introduction written for that volume (148–159).

i.e., uses which are ascribed to some person or persons by means of a cognitive or linguistic verb. For example, suppose that at a certain place p and time t, A says to B: (1) "I am going to kill you here now." Suppose that C reports this by asserting: (2) "A said to B at p that he was going to kill him there then." Sentence (2) contains the quasi-indicators 'he,' 'him,' 'there,' and 'then,' which represent uses, ascribed to A, of the indicators 'I,' 'you,' 'here,' and 'now,' respectively. We shall see that the very same marks or noises 'I,' 'you,' 'here,' 'there,' 'he,' 'this,' function as either indicators, quasi-indicators, or something else. It is a mere accident of grammar that the same physical objects are used in different logical roles. The underlying rationale is this: indicators are a primary means of referring to particulars, but the references made with them are personal and ephemeral; quasi-indicators are the derivative means of making an indexical reference both interpersonal and enduring, yet preserving it intact.

My contribution toward both (A) and (B) together consists of the formulation, with as much precision as I can here, of the fundmental principles of the logic of both indicators and quasi-indicators in *oratio obliqua*. In this regard principles (I.5), (I.12)–(I.14), (Q.2), (Q.11), and (Q.12) are the most important of the lot.

I have aimed at an exhaustive treatment of the basic logic of singular indicators and quasi-indicators in *oratio obliqua*, except for the treatment of the obvious indicators and quasi-indicators included in verbal tenses.[4]

To simplify the discussion I shall abide by the following conventions: (1) single quotes will be used to form names of sentences or expressions; (2) double quotes will be used to form names of statements made or that can be made by uttering the quoted sentences on given occasions; (3) numerals within parentheses will be used as either names of sentences or names of statements, the context indicating which one is meant; (4) the phrase 'statement of the form " . . . "' will be short for 'statement made by the sentence of the form " . . . " (if assertively used by a certain person on a certain occasion)'; (5) an asterisk '*' after a word or phrase indicates that the word or phrase functions in a given sentence as a quasi-indicator; (6) 'statement' and 'proposition' will be used interchangeably in the sense these words have been used by Strawson and others.[5]

2. Indicators

Let us start our investigation by listing some well-known properties of indicators. These properties determine the special roles of indicators in *oratio obliqua*.

(I.1) Indicators formulate a personal reference to a single entity made primarily by the speaker, made derivatively by the hearers, and not made at all by other persons. Here we shall be concerned with primary reference only.

(I.2) Reference to an entity by means of an indicator is purely referential, i.e., it is a reference that attributes no property to the entity in question. Since an indicator expresses an act of placing an item in a person's experience or expresses an act of pinpointing the person who enters in a current cognitive relation, it can at most be said that the use of an indicator indirectly, or implicitly, attributes to an entity the property of being a thinker or the property of being placed in a thinker's (or speaker's) experience at the time of thinking or speaking.

(I.3) Reference by means of an indicator is neither identical with, nor equivalent to, reference by means of descriptions that contain no indicators. By (I.2) reference by means of an indicator could at most be equivalent to reference by means of a description that has no indicators but attributes to the referred entity just the property of being a thinker or of being placed in a thinker's (or speaker's) experience at the time of thinking (or speaking). But this is, of course, false. On the one hand, this attribution by being direct goes beyond what a mere indicator can accomplish. On the other hand, such a description would have to have a word that refers to the thinker (or speaker) in question without in the least attributing to him any property at all, and similarly for the time of thinking. But since the description under consideration has no indicators, there is no way for it merely to refer to the thinker or to the time of his thinking. Thus, at least one sentence S containing an indicator I formulates or can formulate, as uttered on a certain occasion, a statement not equivalent to the statement formulated by any other sentence that differs from S by having descriptions with no indicators instead of I.

(I.4) Indicators have a *referential priority* over all names and descriptions. A person may use a name or description correctly, and yet fail to refer to the object to which he purports to refer because there may be not one, but many, objects which have the name in question, or the properties mentioned in the description. However, a man who uses an indicator correctly cannot, because of a multiplicity of candidates for reference, fail to refer to the object he purports to refer to.

(I.5) The first-person pronoun has a strong *ontological priority* over all names, contingent descriptions, and other indicators. A correct use of 'I' cannot fail to refer to the entity it purports to refer; moreover, a correct use of 'I' cannot fail to pick up the category of the entity to which it is meant to refer. The first-person pronoun, without predicating selfhood, purports to pick out a self *qua* self, and when it is correctly tendered it invariably succeeds. On the other hand, correctly used names, contingent descriptions, and non-first-person indicators may fail either to even pick out a referent or to pick out the intended category. The time- and space-indicators, e.g., 'now' and 'here,' have a weak ontological priority over names, descriptions, and other categories of third-person indicator. They succeed in always picking out a time or a place, although they may in principle fail to pick out the category of physical or external time and space as in a dream. (These ontological priorities are one of the fundamental facts underlying Descartes' *Cogito* and

Kant's theses on the transcendental self and on space and time as forms of perception.)

It might be induced that this contrast between 'I' and the other indicators is misguided, on the ground that 'I' is analyzable in terms of 'this' or 'here now.' Reichenbach, for instance, claims that "the word 'I' means the same as 'the person who utters this token'."[6] This claim is, however, false. A statement formulated through a normal use of the sentence 'I am uttering nothing' is contingent: if a person utters this sentence he falsifies the corresponding statement, but surely the statement *might*, even in such a case, have been true. On the other hand, the statements formulated by 'The person uttering this token is uttering nothing' are self-contradictory: even if no one asserts them, they simply cannot be true.

The first-person indicator is unanalyzable. On the one hand, if 'ϕ' stands for an analytic predicate, i.e., a predicate such that the statement of the form "Everything is ϕ" is analytic or necessarily true, then, obviously, the first-person indicator 'I' cannot be defined as 'the only person who is ϕ.' On the other hand, if 'ϕ' stands for a contingent predicate, then the normal singular statements of the form "I am ϕ" assertable by human beings are contingent. This is so, because all such statements entail the corresponding singular statements of the form "I exist," which are contingent, since they can be false, i.e., since the corresponding singular statements of the form "I might have not existed" are true. Hence, the corresponding singular statements of the form "I am not-ϕ" are also contingent. Yet the corresponding statements of the form "The only person who is ϕ is not-ϕ," are self-contradictory. Hence, the first-person indicator cannot be analyzed in terms of any other expressions whatever; *a fortiori*, it cannot be analyzed in terms of the other indicators. In particular, 'I' cannot be analyzed as 'this self' or 'the self here now': a person's statements of the form "I am not-a-self" are contingent, while his statements of the form "This self (or the self here now) is not-a-self" are self-contradictory. (The unanalyzability of 'I,' especially its unanalyzability in terms of [third-person] demonstratives, is another fundamental fact underlying the idea of the transcendental self.)

Evidently, parallel arguments hold for the second-person indicators, the third-person indicators referring to persons or objects, and the time- and space-indicators. For instance, the object-indicator 'this' cannot be defined in terms of any description, since the indicator attributes no property at all to the object it refers to; and it cannot be defined merely indexically as 'here now,' for statements of the form "This [meaning an object] is not here now" are contingent, while statements of the form "What is here now is not here now" are self-contradictory, if the two occurrences of 'here now' have the same reference.

It must be noted that the words 'now' and 'here' are sometimes replaced by 'this,' as e.g., in "Here (this) is a good place to park." But this in no way argues against the unanalyzability of the time- and space-indicators. What we have here are two interesting features of ordinary language: (i) the grammatical fact that 'here,' 'there,' and 'now' are primarily adverbs, and lack, therefore, the syntactical flexibility of substantival pronouns, so that in certain constructions they are replaceable by some other expression; (ii) the words 'this' and 'that' have two indexical uses: (a) as general signs of third-person indexical reference, and (b) as categorical indicators of third-person indexical reference to objects. It is in their use (a) that 'this' can replace 'now' and 'here,' and 'that' can replace 'there.' Obviously, 'here,' 'there,' and 'now' are not definable in terms of use (b) of 'this' or 'that.' For instance, 'here' is not analyzable as '(at) the place occupied by this object,' since "Nothing is here" is contingent, while "Nothing is at the place occupied by this object" is self-contradictory. In sum,

(I.6) There are five irreducible indexical roles, whatever noises or marks we may employ to discharge them: first-person, second-person, third-person, (specious) present-time, and (speciously) presented place. [(I.6) is supplemented by (I.15) below, after (Q.5).]

(I.7) The pronoun 'I' and all descriptions primarily, and all names derivatively, have an *epistemological priority* over all other indicators. A person's own uses of the first-person pronoun differ radically from his uses of the other indicators. One's knowledge or belief about oneself must be in the first-person form for it to be really self-knowledge or self-belief. On the other hand, to retain knowledge or belief, or merely to re-think, of the objects or persons originally apprehended by means of indicators, one must reformulate one's knowledge or belief, or thought, of those objects in terms of names or descriptions, or in terms of 'I.' *The references made by an indicator other than 'I' are ephemeral, and necessarily eliminable for those who make them.* Of course, the elimination of an indicator may very well introduce another one, as, for instance, when a man thinks something of the form "This is blue," and later on re-thinks it as, e.g., "The object I saw *there* an hour ago was blue." Elimination is here a process of preserving information, not a process of analysis or of literal translation. By (I.6) we already know that there is no analysis of the indexical role.[7]

(I.8) A person's uses of indicators are first-personal and eliminable for every other person.

3. oo-Prefixes

Now we shall discuss some general properties of *oratio obliqua* to which we shall continuously refer in the ensuing investigation.

Cognitive acts or attitudes or dispositions are second-order tetradic relations involving a subject (person or self), a place, a time, and a proposition. Linguistic acts are second-order relations involving typically five or more relata: a speaker, one or more addressees, a place, a time, and a proposition. (I call them all second-order relations because one of the relata is a proposition.)

In a sentence formulating a proposition to the effect that a cognitive or linguistic relation obtains, we shall distinguish two parts: (i) an *oratio obliqua*, and (ii) an *oratio obliqua* prefix. *Oratio obliqua* is the clause that formulates or represents the propositional relatum of the cognitive or linguistic relation. *A strict oratio obliqua prefix*, or simply *strict oo-prefix*, is a clause that contains: (a) a cognitive or linguistic verb, (b) expressions denoting the non-propositional relata, and (c) the word 'that' at the right-hand end. For example, in

(1) Grabbing the knife on the table Peter told Mary in the kitchen at 3:00 P.M. yesterday that he would kill her with it there,

the strict oo-prefix is 'Peter told Mary in the kitchen at 3:00 P.M. yesterday that.' In (1) 'Grabbing the knife on the table' is not part of the strict oo-prefix. Clearly, (1) is really the conjunction "Peter grabbed the knife on the table at 3:00 P.M. yesterday, and (he) said to Mary in the kitchen at 3:00 P.M. yesterday that he would kill her with it there." Now, a clause containing a strict oo-prefix and other expressions will be called an *extended oo-prefix*.

For the sake of brevity we shall sometimes represent an oo-prefix by the schema

$$L[x, y_1, \ldots, y_n, p, t] \ (\text{------}),$$

where x is the speaker or thinker (arguer, knower, etc.), $y_1, \ldots, y_n$ are the addressees, p the place, and t the time involved in the linguistic or cognitive relation. If the relation is cognitive, 'y_1', . . . ,'y_n' vanish. Here '------' indicates the place of the *oratio obliqua* involved.

Linguistic acts of the assertive kind, i.e., whose objects are propositions, not sentences or noises, are dependent on cognitive acts. For example, to state or say or claim is at once to have the thought that something is the case. It is clear that a noise or mark by itself is not an indicator: it is one if and only if it carries with itself an indexical reference. Likewise, a word is not a name or description unless it carries within itself a nominal or descriptive reference that some speaker means it to carry. Thus, the roles which words or phrases or clauses discharge as vehicles of components of a proposition depend on the structural relations of these components *qua* components of the proposition in question. The structure of what is thought, the proposition, is the fundamental structure, and in principle one could think without using a language as a means of thinking.[8] Nevertheless, by the same token, even if one can think without using a language at all, the propositions one deals with in mere non-linguistic thinking have a structure which parallel certain structures of the complete sentences in which one would formulate one's thoughts, if one had a language.[9] We may suppose that in the case of a being who performs a non-communicating cognitive act, e.g., the having of the silent thought that it is raining, the object of his act is structurally analogous to the sentence 'It is raining.'[10] In particular, in silent cognitive acts that include references to particulars, these references can be put in one-to-one correspondence with the types and kinds of singular-referring expressions. Thus,

(I.9) To attribute a cognitive or linguistic propositional act to a person may very well be to attribute to the person in question purely indexical references.

Some cognitive relations are dispositional. A sleeping man, for example, may believe or know that the Earth is not flat. Here the disposition consists of a propensity to perform acts whose objects are analogous to sentences. We shall say that attributing a cognitive disposition to a person is to attribute to him *implicit* uses of sentences or words of certain types (without this implying a reduction of cognitive acts to linguistic acts). Now, a cognitive disposition may be exercised through different cognitive acts at very different times and places. Hence, to attribute a cognitive disposition to a person P is to attribute to P implicit uses of an indicator D, if and only if every possible exercise of P's disposition is unavoidably a use of D by P. By (I.5) and (I.6), this is wholly the case for P's use of the first-person pronoun. In brief,

(I.10) To attribute a cognitive disposition to a *person P* is to attribute to P implicit uses of an indicator D, only if D refers to a relatum, or place related to the place which is a relatum, of the cognitive acts through which the disposition is exercisable.

4. Indicators in *Oratio Obliqua*

By (I.1)–(I.2) a use of a genuine indicator refers directly to an entity, and does not depend for its reference on another expression. For example, the word 'he' is genuinely an indicator when it is used demonstratively in place of 'this' or 'that,' and it is an indexical description when it is short for 'this (that) man,' or something like 'that man with a beard.' 'He' is not indexical at all in the sentence 'Anthony came, after he called'; for here the word 'he' refers back to 'Anthony' and does not directly and by itself refer to Anthony. Similarly, the word 'I' is not an indicator in 'Mary told me that I am next in line.' With this sentence the speaker refers directly to himself by means of 'me'; the word 'I' in this case refers back to 'me.' Let us say that an *antecedent* of a pronoun or adverb in a sentence or clause is an expression of the sentence or clause to which the pronoun or adverb refers back. Hence,

(I.11) Whether in *oratio recta* or in *oratio obliqua*, (genuine) indicators have no antecedents.

Suppose now that Privatus asserts of a dead friend of his:

(2) Once it occurred to Jones that I buried a letter here.

Privatus' statement is philosophically perplexing. It seems to attribute to Jones demonstrative references by means of 'I,' and 'here'; yet, quite palpably, neither could Jones ever refer to Privatus in the first-person way nor was he at the time of Privatus' assertions in a position to make any demonstrative reference at all. By (I.1), the demonstrative references of (2) are Privatus', not Jones's. Thus, we have a philosophical question: What exactly is the proposition that, according to Privatus, Jones once took to be true? That is, what exactly are the types of the references that, according to Privatus, Jones made to Privatus and to the place in question?

One thing is clear. In spite of their misleading position in the *oratio obliqua* of (2), the indicators of (2) serve to mark the positions occupied by some unspecified referring expressions in the sentence formulating the unspecified proposition that, according to (2), Jones once took to be true. Those referring expressions that Jones used were, of course, either

(a) single indicators; or
(b) names; or
(c) indexical descriptions, like 'this man,' 'my friend,' or 'five years ago today (now)'; or
(d) Leibnizian descriptions, i.e., descriptions that contain no indicators.

The actual proposition that, by (2), Jones once took to be true can be one of eight different types, depending on which sort of reference Jones made to Privatus and the place in question. And now we must raise another question: Is Privatus' statement (2) definite enough on this point? And the answer seems to be that it is not: Privatus' statement (2) is simply the statement to the effect that one of the eight types of propositions allowed by the two positions occupied by indicators was taken by Jones to be true. That is, Privatus' statement (2) is to be conceived of as a disjunction of certain statements which we proceed to identify.[11]

So far, we know that the indicators of (2) are in a sense misplaced, and that in their positions Jones's references must be represented. This suggests that the preliminary scheme of the analysis of (2) is this:

(2′) Once it occurred to Jones about me and about this place
      that —— buried a letter in —— ——,
        me   this place

where the subscripts indicate the antecedents of the expressions in the blanks.

Suppose that Privatus wanted to attribute to Jones purely indexical references. Hence, what we should put in the blank of (2′) are precisely the quasi-indicators corresponding to the first-person and the place indicators. Thus, Privatus' statement would be more perspicuously put as

(3) Once it occurred to Jones about me and about this place that I* buried a letter here*.

Since we are mainly concerned with the typical logic of indexical reference, we may here lump together names and descriptions. Now, if Privatus wanted to attribute to Jones references by means of either names or descriptions, he would have had a hard time finding an appropriate idiom or locution in ordinary language. We shall, however, introduce a counterpart to quasi-indicators by means of a subscripted 'd'. Thus Privatus' statement analogous to (2), except that through it Privatus attributes to Jones references by means of names or descriptions, can be formulated as

(4) Once it occurred to Jones about me and about this place that I_d had buried a letter here$_d$.

Thus, the first step in the analysis of (2) is to take it as the disjunction of (3), (4), and the two other statements "Once it occurred . . . that I* here$_d$," and "Once it occurred . . . that I_d . . . here*."

Since names and descriptions, Leibnizian or indexical, attribute properties to the entities they refer to, it is natural to think that (4) is analyzable as

(4N) There are properties ϕ-ness and ψ-ness such that: I am the only ϕ, this place (here) is the only ψ, and once it occurred to Jones that the only ϕ buried a letter in the only ψ.

There is a general way in which (4N) is the analysis of (4), namely, the general way in which when a man says "I am ill" other people transmit his information by saying "He is ill" or even "The man . . . is ill." This is the way in which there is one and the same property that both Smith and Jones attribute to Privatus when Jones identifies Privatus by the description 'the man I met three days ago' and Smith identifies Privatus by the description 'the man Jones met three days ago.' On the one hand these descriptions identify Privatus by means of the same property, considered in itself, independently of the ways it is conceived of by Jones or Smith or anybody else. On the other hand, each of these descriptions ascribes to Privatus that property, not merely as it is in itself, but as it appears to either Jones or Smith: 'the man I met three days ago' ascribes to Privatus that property from Privatus' first-person perspective, whereas 'the man Jones met three days ago' ascribes to Privatus the same property from a third-person perspective. By (I.5)-(I.7) we know that a first-person way of considering a certain property is irreducible to a third-person way of considering it, and clearly the latter is irreducible to the former. Since each of the descriptions explicitly mentions the perspective from which the given property is attributed, each description really attributes a *property-cum-perspective*. Thus, in the general sense that a predicate denotes an attributed property, we can, and must, distinguish between a *neutral*, or *non-perspectival*, property and the *perspectival* properties through which the former is presented. (I owe this terminology to W. Sellars.) I will use the italicized word '*properties*' to refer to perspectival properties, and I will indicate with subscripts the person to whose perspective of the world a given *property* belongs. The unitalicized word 'property' will be used to refer to neutral properties, or to neutral and perspectival properties indeterminately.

Since a person has to consider (neutral) properties in some way or other, we are never really dealing with properties naked, so to speak, of their perspectives. But as long as we deal with so-called extensional contexts only, we can enjoy the illusion that we are intellectually manipulating bare neutral properties. However, as soon as we move to the level of discourse about cognitive land linguistic relations, we must face up to the fact that we are in a partial egocentric predicament of properties.

This predicament creates the fundamental problem of the logic of communication: how to correlate another person's *properties* with our own and pass information across these correlations. The fundamental assumption regarding the possibility of communication is simply that such correlations can be achieved. And the exercise we are engaged in, viz., to determine the type of proposition that, according to Privatus, Jones once took to be true, is precisely an exercise in formulating some of the principles that allow the achievement of the communicating correlations.

In short, (4N) is, correctly, the *non-perspectival analysis* of (4). But since (4) is a non-extensional context, (4N) does not allow us to get hold of the precise statement that, according to Privatus, Jones once took to be true. The characteristic feature of (4N) is that one may know what properties ϕ-ness and ψ-ness one should instantiate the quantifier of (4N) into, without being in a position to produce the instance of (4N) that would be the straight report of it having occurred to Jones that such and such. To illustrate, suppose that

ϕ-ness = man-met-by-Jones-on-July-1-1965-ness
ψ-ness = flowerbed-dug-by-Jones-ness

That is, let Privatus know that:

(5) There are properties ϕ-ness and ψ-ness such: ϕ-ness = man-met-by-Jones-on-July-1-1965-ness, ψ-ness = flowerbed-dug-by-Jones-ness, I am the only person who is ϕ, this place is the only one which is ψ, and once it occurred to Jones that the only person who is ϕ buried a letter in the only place which is ψ.

From (5) Privatus cannot conclude that:

(6) I am the only man met by Jones on July 1, 1965, this place is the only flowerbed dug by Jones, and once it occurred to Jones that the only man met by Jones on July 1, 1965 buried a letter in the only flowerbed dug by Jones.

The difficulty lies in the last conjunct "once it occurred to Jones that the only man met by Jones on July 1, 1965 buried a letter in the only flowerbed dug by Jones." Obviously, this may be false even though Jones did refer to Privatus and the place in question as possessors of these properties ϕ-ness and ψ-ness when it occurred to him what occurred to him according to Privatus' statement (2).† For instance, it may have occurred to Jones what he would have reported by saying "The only man met by me on July 1, 1965 buried a letter in the only flowerbed dug by me." The crux of the matter is that in a proposition that a person takes to be true, or simply entertains, a property enters not merely as a neutral property, but as a property determined by the way in which the person in question grasps it or conceives of it. Thus, while Privatus' statement (5) presents the above properties ϕ-ness and ψ-ness as they are grasped by Privatus, his statement (6) presents ϕ-ness and ψ-ness both as grasped by Privatus, in the prefix, and as grasped by Jones, in the *oratio obliqua*. This is why the inference from (5) to (6) is invalid.

Let us turn, then, to *properties*. Consider an expression containing no indicators or quasi-indicators that formulates a property. Clearly, there are four ways of considering or predicating the property in question:

(i)   the first-person way;
(ii) the second-person way;
(iii) the third-person way involving third-person indicators;
(iv) the third-person way formulated by the given expression.

Let us use subscripts to signal these ways of considering properties, as follows: '$_1$' for (i), '$_2$' for (ii), '$_i$' for (iii), and '$_o$' for (iv). Thus, the property being-met-by-Jones-5-days-before-July-1-1965 determines the following *properties* from Jones's perspective, to be called *properties$_J$*:

(a) being a person met by Jones$_1$ 5 days before (July 1, 1965)i;
(b) being met by Jones$_1$ 5 days before (July 1, 1965)o;
(c) being met by Jones$_o$ 5 days before (July 1, 1965)i; and
(d) being met by Jones$_o$ 5 days before (July 1, 1965)o.

On the other hand, for Privatus it determines the *properties$_p$*:

(d) as above;
(e) being a person met by Jones$_2$ 5 days before (July 1, 1965)i;
(f) being a person met by Jones$_1$ 5 days before (July 1, 1965)o;
(g) being a person met by Jones$_o$ 5 days before (July 1, 1965)i; etc.

Note that, by (I.1) and (I.8), *properties* (c) and (g) are quite different.‡

By our definition of quasi-indicators we know that quasi-indicators represent the uses of indicators in *oratio obliqua*. Thus, when a *property* ϕ_x-ness appears in *oratio obliqua*, we can represent it by means of an expression which

---

†In the original, 'it' occurs between 'what' and 'occurred' in the last clause of this sentence. We believe that this is a misprint, and this was also the opinion of the German translator, Dr. Helmut Pape (see Castañeda 1982a, 177). —Eds.

‡ A small point of clarification is in order. The reason that properties (c) and (g) are different is that they are indexed to different perspectives, Jones's on the one hand, Privatus' on the other. —Eds.

results by putting quasi-indicators instead of the indicators in the expression denoting ϕ_x-ness. The result expression does not, of course, represent ϕ_x-ness *simpliciter*, but as it is considered by the one who makes the statement, and even perhaps as it is considered by a few other persons as well.

In general, let $P(i_1, \ldots, i_n)$ be a phrase that Jones uses (or can use) on a certain occasion O to formulate a *property$_J$*, where $i_1, \ldots, i_n$ are indicators that Jones uses (or can use) on O to refer to entities $E_1, E_2, \ldots, E_n$. Let $P(i_1/e_1, \ldots, i_n/e_n)$ be the phrase that results from $P(i_1, \ldots, i_n)$ by replacing each indicator i_k by the corresponding expression e_k, which is an expression that a man X uses (or can use) on O to refer to entity E_k. Clearly, $P(i_1/e_1, \ldots, i_n/e_n)$ formulates a *property$_x$*, and to indicate its correspondence with the *property$_j$* formulated by $P(i_1, \ldots, i_n)$, we shall call it a *property$_{J/x}$*.† Similarly, let $P(i_1/q_1, \ldots, i_n/q_n)$ be the expression that results from $P(i_1, \ldots, i_n)$ by replacing each i_k by its corresponding third-person quasi-indicator q_k. In the next section we shall discuss this correspondence between indicators and quasi-indicators in detail. That there is such a correspondence is obvious from the fact that Privatus' statements (2) and (4) are not addressed to Jones, but are about Jones having taken a certain statement to be true, so that Privatus must have some technique (namely, the use of quasi-indicators) for representing in a third-person way Jones's uses of indicators (if any). We shall say that $P(i_1/q_1, \ldots, i_n/q_n)$ formulates a *property$_{*J}$*, i.e., formulates someone's, here Privatus', *oratio-obliqua* way of considering the *property$_J$* in question. Since the quasi-indicators q_k have nothing to do with Privatus, the *property$_{*J}$* is really an inter-personal or intersubjective version of the corresponding *property$_J$*, and while by (I.7) most *properties$_J$* must yield even for Jones to other *properties$_J$*, the corresponding *properties$_{*J}$* are permanent: anybody can refer to them at any time, as we shall see in detail later on.

With this machinery we can give a deeper analysis of Privatus' statement (4):

(4) Once it occurred to Jones about me and about this place that I_d buried a letter here$_d$.

A perspectival analysis in terms of *properties* is as follows:

(4P) There are *properties* ϕ_J-ness and ψ_J-ness that: I am the only person who is $\phi_{J/I}$, this place is the only place which is $\psi_{J/I}$ and once it occurred to Jones that the only person who is ϕ_{*J} buried a letter in the only place which is ψ_{*J}.

Note that since Privatus is in (4) referring to himself in the first-person way, the *property$_P$* related to ϕ_J-ness and ψ_J-ness must yield the first-person sche-

---

† The original has an occurrence of 'E' in place of the first 'P' in this sentence. This must be a misprint since 'E' is undefined and 'P' is the only predicate schema introduced. —Eds.

matic symbols '$\phi_{j/l}$' and '$\psi_{j/l}$' representing properties and having adjectives as substituends.

Consider now Privatus' statement

(7) Jones believed that I buried a letter here.

By (7) Privatus attributes to Jones a cognitive disposition and, hence, only implicit references to him and to the place in question. These references are not indexical, even if Privatus' statement (7) reports what Jones believed at a single instant. Indeed, suppose that at a certain instant t it occurred to Jones out loud: "He [pointing to Privatus] buried a letter here [pointing to the place in question]," and suppose that Jones died at that very instant. In this case, Jones never exercised the disposition which is his belief in anything but thoughts containing indexical references. Yet, since these references are by (I.7) eliminable for Jones, the onsetting of his belief is precisely the onsetting of procedures of elimination, which were never exercised, but were nevertheless acquired. Furthermore, even at instant t Jones had, dispositionally, i.e., as part of his belief, ways of referring to the place and to Privatus other than by the use of single indicators. For instance, he could have referred to Privatus by means of an indexical description such as 'this man,' 'the man over there,' 'the person I see on my right,' etc. Thus, I submit that in the case of (7) the non-perspectival and the perspectival analyses are non-disjunctive, as follows:

(7N) There are properties ϕ-ness and ψ-ness such that: I am the only person who is ϕ, this place is the only place which is ψ, and Jones believed that the only person who is ϕ buried a letter in the only place which is ψ
(7P) There are *properties* ϕ_j-ness, ψ_j-ness, $\phi_{j/l}$-ness and $\psi_{j/l}$-ness such that: I am the only person who is $\phi_{j/l}$, this place is only place which is $\psi_{j/l}$, and Jones believed that the only person who is ϕ_{*j} buried a letter in the only place which is ψ_{*j}.

Evidently, the discussion of Privatus' statements (2)–(7) is applicable, *mutatis mutandis*, not only to other statements by Privatus, but to any statement made by any other person. Thus, we shall regard as established that:

(I.12) Indicators in *oratio obliqua* are eliminable for their users in terms of indicators in *oratio recta;*

(I.13) Indicators in *oratio obliqua* representing the propositional relata of cognitive or linguistic acts are analyzable non-perspectivally as well as perspectivally. The procedures of analysis can be carried out one step at a time for each oo-prefix, as illustrated by (4N) and (4P), respectively;

(I.14) Indicators in *oratio obliqua* representing propositional relata of cognitive dispositions are analyzable non-perspectivally and perspectivally. The procedures of analysis can be carried out one step at a time for each oo-prefix, as is illustrated by the analysis of (7) as (7N) and as (7P), respectively.

5. Quasi-Indicators

The preceding discussion of indicators is not only a good background for, but has to be complemented by, the study of quasi-indicators.

(Q.1) Quasi-indicators do not make demonstrative references. They may even fail to make reference to single entities, for *they can play the role of variables of quantification*. For instance, in "Always everywhere a boy tells a girl that he* will love her* from then* on" the quasi-indicators 'he*,' 'her*,' and 'then*' are (also) variables bound, respectively, by the quantifiers 'a boy,' 'a girl,' and 'always.'

(Q.2) Quasi-indicators have necessarily an anteedent to which they refer back, but they are not replaceable by their antecedents. Quasi-indicators are both referentially and syntactically dependent: they are syncategorematic expressions. And the sentences (clauses) that contain quasi-indicators without containing the latter's antecedents are also syncategorematic. An interesting example is provided by the following inference:

(8) While in Brown's office Jones knew that Smith was killed there*

hence,

(9) Smith was killed there.

It is obviously valid, and sentence (9) expresses a complete statement in *oratio recta*, in which its 'there' can be replaced by its antecedent 'in Brown's office.' Hence, by (Q.2) 'there' in (9) is not an instance of the quasi-indicator 'there*.'

It might be thought that 'there' in (9) is precisely another occurrence of the word 'there*' of the premiss. It has to be the same quasi-indicator, it might be argued, since the above inference is validated by the rule.

(K.1) From a statement of the form "X knows that p" you may infer that p.

This argument is, however, invalid: (K.1) says nothing about detaching the sentence to the right of 'knows that.' (I have shown in He^{12} that (K.1) itself is a rule that cannot always be applied.) What the argument needs is a rule like

(K.2) If a sentence of the form 'X knows that p' formulates a statement that you accept, then you may detach the sentence (or clause) represented by 'p' and use it by itself, with no change of meaning or sense, to make the very same statement which it formulates as a part of the longer sentence 'X knows that p.'

The word 'there' in (9) is, of course, an instance of the quasi-indicator 'there*,' which does appear in (8), if the inference "(8), hence (9)" is validated by (K.2).

Suppose, then, that Privatus believed (8) to be true, that while he himself was in Brown's office he made out loud that inference, and that

(10) While in Brown's office Privatus did not believe that Brown's office was there*.

While drawing the inference from (8) to (9) Privatus believed that both (8) and (9), i.e., he believed that (while in Brown's office Jones knew that Smith was killed there* and Smith was killed there). Make now the assumption that the word 'there' in the conclusion (9) is the quasi-indicator 'there*.' Then since "X believes that p and q" entails "X believes that q."

(10′) While in Brown's office Privatus believed that Brown's office was there*.

Since (10′) contradicts (10), the assumption is false. Since the use of 'there' in (9) as part of the inference "(8), hence (9)" is the same regardless of the truth of (10), we conclude that in no case is 'there' in (9) the quasi-indicator 'there*.' Therefore, the inference "(8), hence (9)" is not validated by rule (K.2), and (K.2) is *not* a universally valid rule.[13]

(Q.3) Quasi-indicators have an epistemological priority over indicators and indexical descriptions: a person's uses of indicators are not only eliminable for another person in terms of quasi-indicators, but the latter are the only linguistic expressions that preserve the full force of the former. This is clear from the discussion in section 4 above.

(Q.4) There are two types of quasi-indicators: (A) those, to be called *primary quasi-indicators*, whose antecedents belong in a strict oo-prefix to which they are subordinated, and (B) those, to be called *secondary quasi-indicators*, whose antecedents lie in no strict, but only in an extended oo-prefix. The former's antecedents denote structural elements of cognitive or linguistic acts, while the latter's antecedents denote entities external to cognitive or linguistic relations. The distinction is epistemologically important, as we shall see in (Q.8)–(Q.10). For example, suppose that Jones grabbed at time 'I' the sharpest knife in the kitchen and said to Mary:

(11) I am going to kill you with this here now!

Privatus can naturally report the proceedings by asserting:

(12) Jones grabbed at t the sharpest knife in the kitchen and said to Mary that he was going to kill her with it there then.

From (11) and (12) we see that the word 'it' in (12) represents an actual use of the indicator 'this' by Jones, and it has as antecedent the occurrence of the phrase 'the sharpest knife in the kitchen' in (12); it is the quasi-indicator 'it*.' But the antecedent of 'it' is not a part of, while the antecedents of the quasi-indicators 'he,' 'her,' 'there,' and 'then' are parts of, the strict oo-prefix of (12).

Sentence (12) by itself contains a subtle ambiguity, analogous to the one we found in sentence (2) above. It can be used to make three different kinds of statement, depending on whether its 'it' is used to attribute to Jones a reference to the sharpest knife in question, which is (i) purely indexical, or (ii) descriptive, or (iii) one or the other, indeterminately. With the notation already introduced we can formulate these distinctions perspicuously as follows, where the dots indicate that the remaining parts of the sentence (12) are preserved:

(12.i)   ... it$_{*J}$ ...;
(12.ii)   ... it$_d$ ...;
(12.iii) Either (12.i) or (12.ii).

With the background furnished by statement (11) we know that statement (12) is the same as statement (12.i). As we shall see later on, (Q.8)–(Q.10), the quasi-indicator 'it*,' hence 'it$_{*J}$,' is unanalyzable. On the other hand, (12.ii) and (12.iii) are analyzable along the lines of the procedures illustrated in section 4 for the analysis of indicators in *oratio obliqua*.

By definition, 'it$_d$' in (12.ii) expresses that by means of some description, indexical or otherwise, Jones referred to the knife referred to by Privatus as the sharpest one in a certain kitchen. Jones's description may, of course, be entirely different from Privatus'. In brief, we have here very much the same situation as we had in section 4 for the case of indicators. Thus, we also have a non-perspectival and a perspectival analysis of Privatus' statement (12.ii) as follows:

(12.iiN) Jones grabbed the sharpest knife in the kitchen, and there is a property ϕ-ness such that: that knife is the only thing which is ϕ, and Jones said to Mary that he* was going to kill her* with the only thing which is ϕ there* then*;

(12.iiP) Jones grabbed the sharpest knife in the kitchen, and there is a *property ϕ_J-ness* such that: that knife is the only thing which is $\phi_{J/I}$ and Jones said to Mary that he* was going to kill her* with the only thing which is ϕ_{*J} there* then*.

I have put the asterisks signaling the quasi-indexical role of the pronouns they attach to, in conformity with the definition of quasi-indicators and principles (I.9) and (I.10).

(Q.5) The chart below both establishes the third-person correlation between indicators and quasi-indicators appealed to in (2P), (4P), (7P), and (12.iiP), and summarizes previous results, like (I.7), (I.9), (I.10). The columns contain the following:

1.   the type of entity X a person P refers to;
2.   the indicator I by means of which P refers to X;

3. the type of second-order relation R that has as its relata P and the statement constituted by P's mentioned reference to X by means of I;
4. the eventual type of relation, i.e., disposition or occurrence, of R;
5. the third-person quasi-indicator Q that corresponds to I; and
6. the type of oo-prefix containing the antecedent of Q.

We use the following abbreviations:

C-cognitive relation; L-linguistic relation;
O-occurrence; D-disposition;
S-strict oo-prefix; E-extended oo-prefix

1	2	3	4	5	6
I. Self	first-person pronoun: 'I'	C, L	O, D	'he*'	S
II. Time	adverb of time 'now' (mainly)	C, L	$O, \frac{1}{2}D$	'then*'	S
III. Space					
(a) near	adverb of place 'here' (mainly)	C, L	$O, \frac{1}{2}D$	'there*' 'here*'	S
(b) far	adverb of place 'there' (mainly)	C, L	O	'there*'	E
IV. Other Selves					
(a) addressed to	second-person pronoun: 'you'	L	O	'he*'	E
(b) others	third-person pronoun: 'he'	C, L	O	'he*'	E
V. Objects	demonstrative	C, L	O	'it*'	E

In this table, we use $\frac{1}{2}D$ (half disposition) because implicit references to indicators are limited as required by (I.10). Moreover, it should be noted that the quasi-indicator 'now*' has as antecedent the indicator 'now,' and similarly the quasi-indicator 'here*' has as antecedent the indicator 'here.'

By putting 'I*' instead of 'he*' in the next to the last column we can produce the first-person correlation between indicators and quasi-indicators, where 'I*' has the indicator 'I' as antecedent. Similarly, by putting 'you*' in place of 'he*' we obtain the second-person correlation, where, again, 'you*' has the indicator 'you' as antecedent.

The above table makes it apparent how the five (or seven) types of indicators compare with one another. It shows that each type of indicator is fully characterized by pairing a category mentioned in the first column with a pattern yielded by third, fourth, and last columns. For example, type V of indicator is fully determined by the pair (object: C-L-O-E); the first-person indicator[14] is fully determined by the pair (self: C-L-O-D-S). In these pairs, the category determines the only amount of classifying that indicators perform, and this by implication only, indirectly, so to speak, not by attribution. The pattern, on the other hand, merely indicates how wide is the range of use of an indicator. From this we may see immediately that the first-person indicator cannot be defined in terms of the other indicators: no combination of the latter has the wide range of the former. At any rate, it is clear that

(I.15) The pairs of categories and patterns are both adequate conditions for defining the several types of indicator, and criteria for ascertaining the type of indicator to which a certain word of a given language belongs.

Let $S(E)$ be a sentence containing an occurrence O of an expression E, and let $S(E/E')$ be the sentence that results from $S(E)$ just by replacing O with an occurrence of E'. I shall say that O is *a proxy for E' in $S(E)$*, if and only if one and the same person using $S(E)$ assertively on a given occasion would make the very same statement that he would formulate by using $S(E/E')$ assertively on that occasion. I shall say that *O is a substitute for E' in $S(E)$*, if and only if the statement any person would formulate on a certain occasion by using $S(E)$ assertively is logically equivalent to the statement the same person would formulate by using $S(E/E')$ assertively on the very same occasion.

Quasi-indicators are substitutes for other referring expressions in some trivial cases, namely, in sentences formulating self-contradictions, necessary truths, or certain redundant statements. For instance, "—— & Peter believes that he* is ϕ, or ——" is tautologically equivalent to "——"; and replacing the explicit occurrence of 'he*' with any other referring expression does not destroy the equivalence.

(Q.6) An occurrence of a quasi-indicator is not a proxy or a substitute for an indicator or indexical description in some sentence of the form '$L[x,y_1, \ldots ,y_n,p,t]$ (——)' or '$\sim L[x,y_1, \ldots ,y_n,p,t]$ (——)'. This is obvious from our discussion of indicators in *oratio obliqua*.[15]

(Q.7) An occurrence of a quasi-indicator is not a proxy or a substitute for a name or a description containing no quasi-indicators, in some sentence of the form '$L[x,y_1, \ldots ,y_n,p,t]$(——)', or the form '$\sim L[x,y_1, \ldots ,y_n,p,t]$ (——)'.

We can assimilate reference by means of names to reference by means of descriptions. On the one hand, many names apply to several objects, so that to guarantee uniqueness of reference they must be supplemented with a description. On the other hand, one acquires (or learns) a name for an entity either through a description or through a personal confrontation that gives a descriptional support to the name. (This assimilation is not necessary, but it simplifies the argument. The important thing is that reference by means of a name is not equivalent to reference by an indicator.) By (Q.6) we need not consider the case of descriptions containing indicators.

The following statement verifies (Q.7):

(13) On May 15, 1911, the German Emperor believed that it was raining then*.

Clearly, the German Emperor may have had no idea at all as to the date on which it was raining then*, and he may have also failed to have any other non–indexical description that uniquely characterized May 15, 1911. I cannot, however, muster a formal argument to show this. But a general argument for (Q.7) can be framed with the help of (I.3).

Let I be an indicator. Then by (I.3), there is at least one sentence $S(I)$ such that for no description D containing neither indicators nor quasi-indicators, the statement "$S(I)$" formulated by $S(I)$, if $S(I)$ is used assertively in circumstances C by some person X to refer to an object O, is not equivalent to the statement "$S(I/D)$" that $S(I/D)$ would formulate if assertively used by X in C to refer to O. Thus the statements "$S(I/D)$" and "$S(I)$" are both self-consistent. Now, let Q be the quasi-indicator that represents uses of I in *oratio obliqua*. Then by (Q.9), the clause $S(I/Q)$ is syncategorematic and expresses the statement "$S(I)$" only in a context of the form '$L[x,y_1, \ldots ,y_n,p,t]\,(S(I/Q))$' or even a more inclusive one. Consider one of the statements formulated by a sentence of this form and call it "$OS(I/Q)$." This is a statement to the effect that the person X stands at some place p and time t in some cognitive (or linguistic) relation R to (some addressees and) the statement "$S(I)$." On the other hand, the corresponding sentence of the form '$L[x,y_1, \ldots ,y_n,p,t]\,(S(I/D))$' formulates the statement, "$OS(I/D)$," that X stands at the same place p and time t in the same relation R to (the same addressees and) the statement "$S(I/D)$." Obviously, we can choose a name or some self-consistent description of the person X to put in the place of 'x' in the oo-prefix of the above sentences. Thus, we can choose statements "$OS(I/D)$" and "$OS(I/Q)$," which are contingent. Hence, by the principle (P) below it follows that the statement "$OS(I/Q)$" is not equivalent to the statement "$OS(I/D)$," for whatever description D that contains neither quasi-indicators nor indicators:

(P)   If a statement formulated by a sentence of the form '$L[x,y_1, \ldots , y_n, p,t](\text{———})$' is contingent, then if it is equivalent to the corresponding statement of the form '$L[x,y_1, \ldots ,y_n,p,t](\ldots)$', then the statement formulated by what fills the blank '———' is equivalent to the statement formulated by what fills the blank '$\ldots$' provided both are self-consistent.

By (P), to believe that a certain proposition S is true is equivalent to believing that a certain proposition S′ is true, only if S and S′ are themselves logically equivalent. For example, believing that it is both raining and hailing is equivalent to believing that it is both hailing and raining, and, clearly, "it is raining and hailing" is equivalent to "it is hailing and raining."

It should be noted that if in the above reasoning the sentence expressing "$OS(I/Q)$" is categorematic, then Q is a primary quasi-indicator. On the other hand, if the sentence in question is syncategorematic, i.e., it formulates "$OS(I/Q)$" only by being concatenated with another clause, with which it forms a larger context C, then Q may be a primary or a secondary quasi-indicator. In the latter case (as we shall see later on) Q may be a substitute for some description variable in Q. But this in no way affects its being a substitute for no description containing no quasi-indicators in the smaller context that formulates "$OS(I/Q)$."

If "$OS(I/Q)$" is not equivalent to "$OS(I/D)$," then "$\sim OS(I/Q)$" is not equivalent to "$\sim OS(I/D)$." And since being a proxy entails being a substitute for the same expression in the same sentence, (Q.7) is fully established by the preceding argument.

6. Unanalyzability of Strict Quasi-Indicators

Variables of quantification are unanalyzable referring expressions. Thus, inasmuch as quasi-indicators sometimes function as variables of quantification, they cannot be analyzed in terms of names, indicators, or descriptions containing no quasi-indicators. But from (Q.6) and (Q.7) the stronger result follows that no quasi-indicator referring to a single entity is analyzable solely in terms of indicators, names, or descriptions (indexical or Leibnizian) that do not contain quasi-indicators. Furthermore the procedures discussed in section 4 for the analysis of indicators in *oratio obliqua* cannot produce an analysis of quasi-indicators. Consider, for example, Privatus' statement

(14) Jones thought at 3 P.M. yesterday that Paul was then* sick.

If we apply to (14) the procedure for non-perspectival analysis we find

(14N) There is a property ϕ-ness such that: the (time) ϕ = 3 P.M. yesterday and Jones thought at 3 P.M. yesterday that Paul was sick at the (time) ϕ.

But (14N) and (14) can have different truth-values. For while (14) attributes to Jones a purely indexical reference to the time of his thinking, (14N) attributes to him a descriptive reference.

If we apply the procedure for a perspectival analysis we obtain:

(14P) There is a *property* ϕ_j-ness such that: the time which is the only ϕ_j = 3 P.M. yesterday, and Jones thought at 3 P.M. yesterday that Paul was sick at the only time which is ϕ_{*j}.

Again, (14) and (14P) can have different truth-values: it is possible that when Jones thought what Privatus reports, he just made either a purely indexical or a descriptive reference to the time of his thinking, but not both. In the case of (14P) there is the additional point that even if it were an analysis of the singular quasi-indicator 'then*' of (14), it would be an analysis in terms of the quasi-indexical variables 'ϕ_{*j}' Thus, the perspectival procedures would constitute at best an analysis of singular quasi-indicators.

Now, a language or conceptual scheme through which the only self or person that can be conceived is the one who uses the scheme, obviously, does not allow for the conception of the contrast between two persons. Such a language does not allow for the contrast between first- and other-person statements, or between second- and other-person statements. Thus, whatever verbal and whatever pronominal forms are part of that language, they will simply fail to express the distinction among grammatical persons. Thus, we may suppose, for concreteness, that in such a language we only have what appears to be first-person statements of the form "I am ϕ." Yet the pronoun 'I' cannot refer in such statements to an entity which has general mental properties, i.e., properties that do not necessarily have just one instance. For a language to have predicates that formulate such general properties is for it to allow the framing of statements which formulate the possibility that these properties be exemplified by several entities. Thus, the pronoun 'I' in the seemingly first-person statements of the type of language we are discussing has to refer to an entity of a category, namely, self, for which the language does not allow other members. Hence, I submit that the seeming first-person statements in question are really either (i) disguised strictly impersonal statements (like "There is a pain here," "There was a thought that it will rain," and "There was a belief that it would rain now"), or (ii) statements in which the entity the word 'I' refers to is simply the totality (and hence the only entity of its sort) of all the experiences, thoughts, etc., that constitute the user of the conceptual scheme in question.[16] I shall assume that perceptual thinking necessarily involves demonstrative reference.

On the other hand, a conceptual scheme that allows for the mere possibility of other thinking beings, which have perceptions but need not be aware of themselves, allows necessarily for the contrast either between first- and other-person statements, or between third-person statements about one entity and third-person statements about another entity. That is, the user of the scheme can at least consider statements like "This is a cow and X thinks that it* is pregnant," which attribute to the other thinking beings experiences and experiential judgments that involve the use of demonstrative reference. In brief,

(Q.8) A conceptual scheme that allows for the possibility of other perceiving thinking beings (even though their reality isn't affirmed in the scheme) is characterized by the possession of the unique and unanalyzable referring mechanism constituted by the secondary quasi-indicators discussed in (Q.4).

A person is not only a center of consciousness or a factory of thoughts and reasonings. A person is a center of self-consciousness. Thus, a conceptual scheme that allows even for the mere possibility of several persons (or self-aware selves) necessarily allows for: (i) the formulation of the contrast between first- and third-person statements, and (ii) the formulation of statements of the form "X thinks at place p at time t that he* is —— there* then*" and of the form "I think that I* am ——." Therefore

(I.16) A conceptual scheme that allows for the mere possibility of several persons (or self-aware selves) is characterized by the possession of the unana-lyzable referring mechanism constituted by the first-person indicator, and

(Q.9) by the possession of the unanalyzable referring mechanism consti-tuted by the primary first- and third-person quasi-indicators.

Finally, a conceptual scheme that allows for the possibility of communica-tion necessarily allows for: (i) the formulation of the contrast between first- and second-person statements, and (ii) the formulation of second-person statements of the form "You believe that you* are ——". Hence,

(I.17) A conceptual scheme that allows for the possibility of communica-tion is characterized by the possession of the unanalyzable referring mecha-nism constituted by the second-person indicator, and

(Q.10) by the possession of the unanalyzable referring mechanism consti-tuted by the primary second-person quasi-indicator.

7. Quasi-Indicators in n-fold *Oratio Obliqua*

We proceed to discuss the quasi-indicators' counterpart of indicators in *oratio obliqua*, namely, the case of quasi-indicators subordinated to oo-prefixes which themselves occur in *oratio obliqua*. To start with, suppose that Privatus asserts

(15) In Brown's office Smith thought that in Brown's office Jones thought that a treasure was hidden there*.

Then we have a problem: to ascertain what exactly was Privatus' statement. His utterance has a noteworthy ambiguity. It may be brought out neatly by imagining Smith to be in Brown's office making the first-person statement corresponding to (15). He has a choice among:

(16) Here I thought that in Brown's office Jones thought that a treasure was hidden here;

(17) Here I thought that in Brown's office Jones thought that a treasure was hidden there*;

and

(18) Here I thought that here Jones thought that a treasure was hidden here.

In short, the ambiguity lies in that the quasi-indicator 'there*' in (15) may have as its antecedent either the second occurrence of 'in Brown's office' to the left of 'there,' which is in *oratio recta*, or the other occurrence, which is in *oratio obliqua*. In the former case Privatus' statement is the counterpart of (16), while in the latter it is the counterpart of (17). But there seems to be no natural way of expressing this distinction in English. It can be expressed, however, by means of some artificial improvement upon English, e.g., by at-taching to 'there*' a subscript that indicates the distance between it and its antecedent. Either the antecedent, as in the case of (15), lies in a strict oo-prefix P, or it lies in an extended oo-prefix P; thus, we can measure the dis-

tance between an occurrence of a quasi-indicator and its antecedent by counting the strict oo-prefixes up to P to which that occurrence is subordinated.
For instance, Privatus' counterpart of (16) is, then:

(19) In Brown's office Smith thought that in Brown's office Jones thought
that a treasure was hidden there$*_2$.

Privatus' statement which is the counterpart of (17) is:

(20) In Brown's office Smith thought that in Brown's office Jones thought
that a treasure was hidden there$*_1$.

By (Q.2)–(Q.9), the 'there$*_1$' in (20) is not analyzable. But by (I.12) the indicator 'here' at the end of (16) is eliminable for the speaker, and by (I.10)–
(I.11) the elimination conforms to the procedures illustrated in section 4.
Since 'there$*_2$' in (19) represents the use of 'here' in (16), then 'there$*_2$' is
eliminable for the speaker by the same procedures illustrated in section 4.
Thus, Privatus' statement (19) is more perspicuously formulated as the perspectival statement:

(19P) In Brown's office Smith thought that there is a *property* ϕ_J-ness such
that: the only place which is $\phi_{J/P}$ = Brown's office, and in Brown's
office Jones thought that a treasure was hidden at the only place which
is ϕ_{*J1}.

Here I have put 'ϕ_{*J1}' instead of merely 'ϕ_{*J}' to indicate that the quasi-indicators in the description which occupies the place of 'ϕ_{*J1}' have as antecedents
items in the description that occupies the place of 'ϕ_J.'† It is easy to see that
at this stage subscript notation allows of a simplification (hereafter adopted)
without diminishing its power to dissolve ambiguity. An expression of the
form 'ϕ_{*Jn}' is a quasi-indicator such that (i) its antecedent lies n units to the
left of it, in an oo-prefix P, and (ii) it represents J's uses of indicators, where
'J' stands for an expression both referring to person J and being the subject
of the verb in the same oo-prefix P. Thus, we can drop the subscript 'J' from
'ϕ_{*Jn}' since by looking at the nth prefix to its right we can find both its antecedent and the expression 'J' stands for.

Now, it is a trivial exercise to construct parallel distinctions for each of the
other quasi-indicators.[17] And if we regard the subscript notation as a characteristic feature of quasi-indicators, we can, then, conclude that

(Q.11) Quasi-indicators that are more than one unit removed from their
antecedents are eliminable. That is, quasi-indicators of distance 1 are unanalyzable, but all others are analyzable in terms of those of distance 1.

Our subscript notation is, however, not yet fully adequate to eliminate the
ambiguities of some sentences containing quasi-indicators. Consider, for example, Privatus' statement:

† This sentence is missing in the version that appears in Castañeda 1989a, 227. —Eds.

(21) In Brown's office Jones thought that Smith claimed there* that a treasure was hidden there*.

Clearly, the first 'there*' has 'in Brown's office' as its antecedent, and Privatus is not by (21) ascribing to Jones the knowledge or even the idea that the place at which he was when he had the thought in question was precisely Brown's office. But the 'there*' at the end of (21) is ambiguous. No doubt, in some sense it also has 'in Brown's office' as its antecedent. But whose uses of the indicator 'here' does the second 'there*' represent? If it represents Jones', then the second 'there*' has 'in Brown's office' as its direct antecedent. If it represents Smith's, then its *immediate* antecedent is the first 'there*' and 'in Brown's office' is only its *ultimate* antecedent. Yet there is no normal way of expressing this distinction in ordinary language.

At this juncture I want to propose a notation that can be used as an auxiliary to English to make all the necessary distinctions that quasi-indicators in *n*-fold *oratio obliqua* allow. This notation will also serve the theoretical purpose of allowing the precise formulation of a fragment of the logic of quasi-indicators.

8. Notation for Quasi-Indicators

First, we unify the expression of all quasi-indicators by dropping the ordinary pronouns, adverbs, etc., used to express them, and simply indicate the underlying quasi-indexical role by means of '*'. Second, we prefix '*' to an occurrence O of the ultimate antecedent of the quasi-indicator whose expression we are framing. Third, we suffix to such occurrence O a subscript that indicates the distance between the quasi-indicator and its immediate antecedent. (We could drop '*' altogether and express the pure quasi-indexical role by the mere suffixation of the subscript. But we preserve '*' and suggest that it be read as 'he,' 'then,' 'it,' etc., as the case may be.)

With this notation we can unambiguously write the two interpretations of (21) as

(22) In Brown's office Jones thought that Smith claimed *(in' Brown's office)$_1$ that a treasure was hidden *(in Brown's office)$_2$;

and

(23) In Brown's office Jones thought that Smith claimed *(in Brown's office)$_1$ that a treasure was buried *(in Brown's office)$_1$.

This exegesis of (21) satisfies (Q.10). Since the second 'there*' of (22) is at distance 2 from its antecedent, by (Q.10) it is analyzable, and its subscript '2' is an immediate indication of its analyzability. Similarly, the subscripts of (23) clearly convey that none of its quasi-indicators is analyzable.

Parallel examples show that the temporal quasi-indicator 'then*' has parallel ambiguities that can be dissolved by our notation. But the quasi-indicator 'he*,' when it represents a use of the indicator 'I', not, e.g., of the indicator 'this (man),' does not allow the ambiguity parallel to that of (21). Consider, for example

(24) Jones believes that he* believes that he* is sick.

If Jones were to make the first-person counterpart statement, he would say:

(25) I believe that I believe that I am sick.

In short, Privatus' statement (24) attributes to Jones belief in the truth of a first-person statement about somebody's being sick, at the same time that it attributes to Jones belief in the identity of that somebody to himself. Thus, in our notation (24) comes out as

(24A) Jones believes that *Jones$_1$ believes that *Jones$_1$ is sick.

Again, (24.A) palpably shows that by (Q.10) neither occurrence of the quasi-indicator is analyzable. Here we have a distinctive feature of the primary quasi-indicator 'he*' that sets it apart from all the other quasi-indicators.

The secondary quasi-indicator 'he*,' which represents uses of the personal indicator 'this (that),' allows of an ambiguity analogous to the one of (21). For example,

(26) John told of Mary that Brown would think of her* that she* had been appointed.

The occurrence of 'she*' expresses a demonstrative reference either by Brown, in which case it is '*(Mary)$_1$,' or by John, in which case it is '*(Mary)$_2$' with 'her*' as its immediate antecedent. Naturally, 'her*' is '*(Mary)$_1$.'

Our notation is also adequate to dissolve another type of ambiguity proper to linguistic verbs. For example,

(27) John told Paul that he* had been made a full professor.[18]

In this case 'he*' is ambiguous between a use of 'I' or a use of 'you' by John. These interpretations come, respectively, to be:

(28) John told Paul that *(John)$_1$ had been made a full professor,

and

(29) John told Paul that *(Paul)$_1$ had been made a full professor.

For simplicity of the formulation of general principle (P.A) below we shall consider every statement a person X makes or believes to be true, or merely entertains, as subordinated to a tacit strict oo-prefix of the form 'I think here now that.' This conforms with the egocentric characteristic *of properties* above discussed.

The preceding examples suggest that the general principle in operation is the following:

(P*.P) Let $\phi(*_n)$ be an incomplete or syncategorematic clause such that: (i) it contains an occurrence O of $*a_n$, (ii) it does not contain the antecedent A of O, (iii) it is immediately subordinated to the oo-prefix P_n represented by '$L[b, \ldots]$', (iv) P_n is immediately subordinated to the oo-prefix P_{n-1} of the form '$L[c, \ldots]$', and (v) n > 1. Let $\phi(*a_n//*_{n-1})$ be the syncategorematic sentence that results from $\phi(*a_n)$ by replacing: (vi) *all* occurrences Ox of $*a_n$ in $\phi(*a_n)$ whose antecedent is A, and which are subordinated to exactly the same oo-prefixes to which occurrence O of $*a_n$ is subordinated, by occurrences of the description function 'the only thing which is $*\psi_{n-1}$'; and (vii) all occurrences of $*a_m$ in $\phi(*a_n)$ whose antecedent is an occurrence Ox mentioned in (vi) by an occurrence of the description function 'the only thing which is $*\psi_m$.' Then a statement formulated by a sentence of the form

$$\text{——} L[b, \ldots] \, (\phi(*a_n)) \text{ ——}$$

is the same as the statement formulated by the corresponding sentence of the form

there are *properties* μ_b-ness and $\mu_{b/c}$-ness such that: ——(the only thing which is $\mu_{b/c1} = *a_{n-1}$ & $L[b, \ldots] \, (\phi(*a_n//*\mu_{n-1})))$——,

provided that the schematic letter or variable 'μ' does not occur at all in the former sentence.†

---

† In both the original and the German translation, some of the letters in this complex principle are missing, notably, the first two occurrences of 'ψ' and the first occurrence of 'b'. They have been added here. In Castañeda 1989a, a different principle with the same label is given, namely:
 (P*.P) Let $\phi(*_n)$ be an incomplete or syncategorematic clause such that: (i) it contains an occurrence O of $*a_n$, (ii) it does not contain the antecedent A of O, (iii) it is immediately subordinated to the oo-prefix P_n represented by '$L[b, \ldots]$', (iv) P_n is immediately subordinated to the oo-prefix P_{n-1} of the form '$L[c, \ldots]$', and (v) n > 1. Let a formula "$F(u//v)$" denote the result of replacing all the occurrences of the term u under consideration in the formula $F(u)$ with occurrences of the term v not occurring in $F(u)$. Then $L[b, \ldots]\phi(a_n)$ is analyzable as:
  There is a *property* μ-ness such that: $*a_n$ is the only thing that is μ_c and there is a *property* $\mu_{c/b}$-ness such that $L[b, \ldots]\phi(a_n//\mu_{b/c})$. [*Note:* It is our belief that the sole occurrence of '$\mu_{c/b}$-ness' in this principle should be replaced by '$\mu_{b/c}$-ness'. —Eds.]
 Suppose that some of the occurrences Ox of $*a_n$ are the immediate antecedents of occurrences of $*a_1$, in a component of $\phi(*a_n)$ of the form $L[d, \ldots] \, \psi*a_1)$. Then $L[d, \ldots]\psi*a_1$ is analyzable as:
  There is a property $v_{b/d}$-ness such that: $*a_1$ is the only thing that is $v_{b/d}$ and $L[d, \ldots] \, \psi*a_1//v_{b/d})$.

In general, I submit that

(Q.12) By $n-1$ applications of principle (P*.P), we may analyze perspectivally every occurrence of a quasi-indicator $*a_n$ in a sentence $\phi(*a_n)$ in terms of the quasi-indicator $*a_1$.

By dropping the suffixes 'b' and 'b/c' of the predicate variables in (P*.P) we obtain a formulation of the non-perspectival principle (P*.N), and

(Q.13) By $n-1$ applications of (P*.N) we may analyze non-perspectivally every occurrence of a quasi-indicator $*a_n$ in a sentence $\phi(*a_n)$ in terms of the quasi-indicator $*a_1$.

Notes

1. Part of this research was carried out under the National Science Foundation Grant No. GS-828.

2. Some of the main results of this paper are generalizations for all quasi-indicators of previous results obtained, in the terminology of (Q.4) below, for the very special primary quasi-indicator 'he*.' These previous results together with other results are discussed in Castañeda 1966. It will be cited as "*He.*" I owe the initial stimulus for these generalizations to my colleague Robert Sleigh, Jr., who on March 12, 1965, said to me that 'then' in "Jones believed at t that it was raining then" is like (the primary quasi-indicator) 'he*' in not being replaceable by its antecedent 't'. Peter T. Geach has really studied *He* and in correspondence has provided a sustained flow of encouragement, criticisms, and suggestions. George Nakhnikian read the first draft of this paper and pointed out several errors. Wilfrid Sellars read the second draft and pointed out errors and obscurities and suggested improvements.

3. Goodman 1951, 290. However, Goodman's criterion for the selection is different: "a word is an *indicator if* (but, . . . , not necessarily only if) it names something not named by some replica of the word."

4. The latter should offer no major difficulty after both the study of "now" and "then" included here and the study of tenses in Sellars 1957. An important problem open in this area is the examination of difficulties (if any) raised by quasi-indicators for Quine's program of eliminating all singular referring terms in favor of predicates and variables of quantification. See Quine 1960, 163, 170–186. The auxiliary notation introduced here can be easily formalized and, then, adjoined to a calculus of "knows" and "believes," such as Hintikka's in Hintikka 1962. For the need to supplement Hintikka's calculus with some such notation, see Castañeda 1964b.

5. Cf. Strawson 1959 and Cartwright 1962.

6. Reichenbach 1947, 284.

7. For a penetrating defense of the unanalyzability and theoretical indispensability of indexical reference, see Strawson 1959, 117–120. See also the very interesting defense of indicators as singular terms by Manley Thompson in Thompson 1959 against Quine's thesis that all singular terms are eliminable. I hasten to point out that my theses (I.6)–(I.7) do not seem incompatible with Quine's. I am not (here at any rate) laying claim to the necessity of the unanalyzable indexical roles being performed by singular terms in Quine's

sense, and Quine, for his part, does not claim that all indicators can be defined or analyzed away. Quine lets 'now,' 'then,' 'here,' and 'there' to remain uneliminated as general terms (Quine 1960, 185), and he also allows that the attributive use of these indicators as general terms depends on pointing. If Quine's reduction holds, my claims in (I.6) and (I.7) must be construed as claims about the indexical general terms that Quine introduces.

8. I myself have argued for this possibility in Castañeda 1960b, 199–217. I touch on the issue in Castañeda 1967e.

9. This parallelism does not require that there be a component of a proposition P for every word or phrase of a sentence formulating P. The parallelism we need to accept is compatible with certain words or phrases being, e.g., mere grouping devices or scope signals like 'it is the case that.'

10. For theories about thinking based on the structural analogy between a proposition and the sentences expressing it, see Sellars 1956 and Geach 1956, chapters 14, 17, and 22.

11. This analysis of (2) occurred to me after George Nakhnikian pointed out an error in an earlier analysans candidate.

12. Toward the end of section 4.

13. Obviously a similar counter-example against (K.2) can be produced using 'then*' and 'it*.' In *He,* section 4, appears the original argument of this type employing 'he*' *qua* representation of uses of the indicator 'I'.

14. Note that the first-person pronoun, which is also used as a quasi-indicator, is not being characterized here.

15. In *He,* section 2, I examine several natural ways in which it might be thought that the primary indicator 'he*' could be construed as a vehicle for indexical reference.

16. For more details on the impersonal core of first-person statements, see Geach 1956, 117–121 and Castañeda 1967d, sections 9 and 10. Strawson formulates the much stronger principle that "the idea of a predicate is correlative with that of a *range* of *distinguishable* individuals" (Strawson 1959, 99n, my italics in 'distinguishable'), and I have criticized this principle in Castañeda 1960a, 45–50.

17. For the case of the primary indicator 'he*' see *He,* examples (18)–(20).

18. I owe this example to P. T. Geach, and with it the realization that it exhibits a peculiar kind of ambiguity.

3

On the Phenomeno-Logic
of the I

Many mysteries surround the self, but many of them arise from the fact that
a self refers to itself in the first-person way. A self so referred will be called
an I. The I is, thus, the abstraction whose concretions are all the I's just as
the whale is the abstraction whose concretions are all the whales.

My purpose here is to discuss some fundamental features of the I in its
relation to the world. I shall carry out the discussion by means of an examination of the logic of first-person reference, i.e., the logic of the appearance
or phenomen of the I. The large conclusions that will emerge are probably not
all new, but some of them and most of the smaller conclusions and the argument for the larger conclusions are, I think, novel.

Single quotes will be used to form names of expressions. Double quotes
around a sentence will name some given statement or proposition expressed
with that sentence, but we shall not examine the method by means of which
the sentence comes to express the proposition. A numeral within brackets will
name sometimes a sentence it precedes and sometimes a statement expressed
with that sentence. By 'indicator' is meant a personal or demonstrative pronoun, adjective, or adverb used to make a demonstrative reference.

I. "I Exist"

The first-person pronoun has what I have called an ontological priority over
all names, contingent descriptions of objects, and all other indicators: a correct use of I cannot fail to refer to the entity to which it purports to refer;
moreover, a correct use of I cannot fail to pick up the category of the entity

This essay appeared in the Proceedings of the XIV International Congress for Philosophy 3
(1968): 260–266. Reprinted by permission of Herder & Co.

to which it refers. The first-person pronoun, without predicating selfhood, purports to pick out a self *qua* self, and when it is correctly tendered it invariably succeeds. All other mechanisms of singular reference (names, contingent descriptions, and remaining indicators) may be correctly used and yet fail to pick out a referent or to pick up the intended category. Thus, my statement "I don't exist now" is self-contradictory, *internally* inconsistent, regardless of whether it is asserted or not; it is not merely a statement like "I am not uttering anything," which is falsified by an *act* of utterance. The reason many philosophers have not seen the internal inconsistence of negative statements like my "I don't exist now" is that "I am H-N. Castañeda" and "H-N. Castañeda does not exist now" are both contingent statements. But, of course, the contingency of the latter two statements does not establish the contingency of the former. (Witness: "The (constant) number of planets does not exist" and "the (constant) number of planets is 9" are both contingent, and yet "the number 9 does not exist" is necessarily false.) Clearly, the proposition "I exist" assertable by me is different from the proposition "H.-N. Castañeda exists." At any rate we shall establish this difference next.

II. Quasi-Indexical Propositions

Consider the proposition

(1) The Editor of *Soul* believes (at time *t*) that he (himself) is a millionaire.

According to (1), the Editor of *Soul* has a belief whose object is the proposition expressed with the clause in *oratio obliqua* 'he (himself) is a millionaire.' Obviously, that proposition is the one that the Editor would have expressed at *t* by asserting

(2) I am a millionaire.

Thus, we can see, the pronoun 'he (himself)' occurring in sentence (1) has there a very special role: (i) it is not used to make a demonstrative reference by whoever asserts sentence (1); (ii) it refers to the Editor of *Soul*, not directly, but through referring back to the expression 'The Editor of *Soul*', which is, thus, its antecedent; (iii) it appears in *oratio obliqua*, while its antecedent is outside the *oratio obliqua* immediately containing it; (iv) it is used to attribute first-person references to the Editor of *Soul*, though the attributed references are only implicit inasmuch as the Editor need not actually be thinking or asserting what according to the proposition (1) he believes. We shall, from now on, refer to the pronoun 'he' or 'he himself' that has characteristics (i)–(iv) as the *quasi-indicator* 'he*'.

The quasi-indicator 'he*' has some very interesting properties. *First*, it cannot be replaced with its antecedent *salva propositione*. That is, proposition (1) is not equivalent to "The Editor of *Soul* believes at time *t* that the Editor of *Soul* is a millionaire." Clearly, the Editor may very well disbelieve that he* is the Editor of *Soul,* for instance, because his appointment to the editorship has not yet been announced, while both he still believes that the Editor is old poverty-stricken Richard Penniless, and he knows that he* has always been a millionaire. Hence, proposition (2) above is different from the proposition "The Editor of *Soul* is a millionaire."

A moment's reflection suffices to see that if the phrase 'the only one who is ϕ' is a definite description of the Editor of *Soul* not contain occurrences of 'he*' then proposition (2) is also different from the corresponding proposition of the form "The only one who is ϕ is a millonaire." For clearly, the Editor may very well believe that the only one who is ϕ is a millionaire, without believing that he* is the only one who is ϕ, even if he is in fact such a person.

Likewise, if '*a*' is a name of the Editor of *Soul,* proposition (2) above is different from the corresponding proposition of the form "*a* is a millionaire." For the Editor may very well fail to believe that he* is a either because he does not believe that he* is named '*a*' or because he does not believe that he* is the only one who is F, for some property F-ness that supports his being a, i.e., his being referred to by the name '*a*'. (See Searle 1958.)

Finally, 'he*', cannot be replaced in (1), *salva propositione,* with any indicator that refers to the Editor of *Soul.* The reason is the very interesting one that

(I.1) An indexical reference in *oratio obliqua* is made by the thinker (speaker) of the whole proposition (sentence) and is presented by the *oratio obliqua* as being made by him, and not as being made by the person to whom knowledge, belief, conjecture, assertion, etc. is attributed. An indexical reference always has the largest scope in any statement containing it.

For example, consider,

(3) The Editor of *Soul* believes at time *t* that *he* (this man [with a demonstrative pointing to the Editor]) is a millionaire.†

The italics of 'he' are meant to signal that the word is used indexically or demonstratively, not quasi-indexically as an instance of the pronoun 'he*'. Evidently, the Editor may very well fail to believe (realize) that he* is the one being pointed to, or, better, the one being referred to indexically, so that proposition (2) is different from the third-person indexical proposition "He (this man) is a millionaire." In fact, the analysis of (3) is:

---

† In the original text, this example is listed as '(1b)', not as '(3)'. However, there is some confusion with Castañeda's labeling, since first, '(1b)' is also used to label a distinct formula —namely what we have labeled '(4)'; second, there is no statement labeled '(1a)'; and third, '(5)' appears below without '(3)' or '(4)' appearing anywhere. To avoid this confusion, we have used '(3)' to name the first statement labeled with '(1b)' and '(4)' to name the second statement labeled '(1b)'. —Eds.

(4) There is property ϕ-ness such that *he* [indexical] = the one who is ϕ and the Editor of *Soul* believes at time t that the one who is ϕ is a millionaire.

This analysis shows how the indicator '*he*' is only apparently in the scope of 'believes', i.e., that the indexical reference expressed by '*he*' is outside the *propositio obliqua* and has the whole proposition (3) as its scope. This contrasts with the scope of the concept "The King of France" which in "The King of France is-not bald" has as its scope "The King of France is bald" and falls inside the scope of negation.

Obviously, if a name or a description or an indicator does not refer to the Editor of *Soul*, it cannot replace the occurrence of 'he*' in sentence (1), *salva propositione*. Therefore, the singular first-person proposition (2) is different from any third-person proposition in *oratio recta*. Patently, the same considerations hold for any other first-person proposition. Thus, more generally, *no first-person proposition is identical with any third-person proposition, if both are in oratio recta*. (For a comprehensive study of 'he*' see Castañeda 1966, 1968a, Hintikka 1967, and for a general study of all quasi-indicators see Castañeda 1967a.)

Now, it is natural to say that in propositions expressible with sentences of the form 'X believes (knows, assumes, asserts, etc.) that X believes (knows, assumes, asserts, etc.) that ——,' the proposition expressed with the clause occupying the blanks '——' is *an* object of X's belief (knowledge, etc.). We may contrast that object of X's belief (knowledge, etc.) with the *full object* of his belief (knowledge, etc.) which is the proposition expressed with the subordinate clause 'Y believes (knows, etc.) that ——'. Thus, from the preceding discussion we have that

(I.2) Propositions about a given I can be the full objects of belief (knowledge, assumption, assertion, etc.), only if the belief (knowledge, etc.) in question belongs to that same I.

(For the theological relevance of the distinction between full and nonfull object of knowledge see Kretzman 1966 and Castañeda 1967b.)

III. I's and Their Bodies

From the preceding it follows that no proposition expressible with a sentence of the form 'I am ϕ' is identical with the corresponding proposition expressible with the sentence 'My body is ϕ' or 'This body is ϕ'. Thus, it is false that I can *salva propositione* replace the pronoun 'I' in

(5) I weigh 160 pounds

with the expressions 'this body' or 'my body'. It is also false that in (5) 'I' is merely an abbreviation of 'my body'. Undoubtedly, proposition (5) is logically equivalent to the proposition "My body weighs 160 pounds." But from this equivalence it does not follow that I am identical with my body. It does follow, however, that either I am identical with my body, or I am in some relation R to my body such that physical properties, like weighing 160 pounds, that apply to me apply to me derivatively just because I am R to my body and they apply primarily to my body. That relation R is, minimally, membership in a structured pair (my body, x) = I, where for every physical property ϕ-ness I am ϕ whenever body is ϕ. Clearly, relation R may allow me to be an entity logically, though perhaps not causally, independent of my body; that is, R may be, for instance, a relationship like the one that is often expressed with the word 'having' as in "I have a toe." In this case "I weigh 160 pounds" is to be analyzed as "I have a body and it weighs 160 pounds." In any case the first-person pronoun has (*pace* Wittgenstein in Moore 1959 [*Philosophical Papers*], 308–311) exactly the *same* sense regardless of whether it is used to predicate to a person physical properties or whether it is used to predicate mental properties. On the other hand, the so-called physical predicates applied to persons are really ambiguous: they express purely physical properties when applied to bodies, but they express products of the latter properties with the common conjunct having-a-body when applied to selves. (The objection that dictionaries do not report any such ambiguity may be dismissed as frivolous.) But I am not identical with my body, since thinking and my feeling pain and my having sensations are done by me, not by my body. Hence, I, as a possessor of physical properties, am a structured pair of my body and something else.

IV. The Contingency of the I

As we have seen, anyone's "I don't exist now" is a self-contradictory statement. Hence, "I exist now" is necessarily true. Yet this *seems* wrong, for many of us are convinced that the statement one can make by saying "I might have not been existing now" is true. Let us dispel the air of paradox. To begin with, note that all the evidence I normally give for claiming that I might have not been existing now is simply a collection of facts about me that anybody else can also adduce: they are facts about H-N. Castañeda. And we have seen above that those facts can show that H-N. Castañeda might have not been existing now, but from them together with the fact that I am H-N. Castañeda it still does not follow that it is possible that I be not existing, if, as it seems, I am the subject of this denial of existence.

In the second place, I am *not* the subject of that denial of existence. For, as already said in (I.1) above, the reference to an I has as its scope the whole of the statement containing it. Thus, "Anthony believes that I am happy" is deceptive in that it seems to attribute to Anthony first-person references to me, which he certainly cannot make. It is a statement analyzable as either "There is a property ϕ-ness such that I am the one who is ϕ and Anthony believes that the one who is ϕ is happy," or, for some specified name or description to be determined by the context of assertion, and here represented by 'β': "I am

β and Anthony believes that β is happy." Likewise, the statement "I might have not been existing now" is a statement more perspicuously put as "There is a property ϕ-ness such that I am the only one who is ϕ and it is possible that the only one who is ϕ does not exist now." (Compare "The only red thing might have not been red" which is not a self-contradiction when "the only red thing" has the larger scope, in which case it is "there is a property ϕ-ness such that the only ϕ thing is identical with the only red thing and it is possible that the only ϕ thing be not red.") The property ϕ-ness most likely to be used by me is, of course, that of being H-N. Castañeda.

Nevertheless, the fact remains that the statement expressible by the Editor of *Soul* if he were to say "I exist" is constituted by a first-person reference that he is in a position to make. But if the Editor does not exist then such first-person reference cannot enter as a constituent of a proposition. Yet we have said that his proposition "I exist" is necessarily true. Indeed, even if every self is eternal and necessarily existing, if the Editor of *Soul* does not exist then there is no Editor of *Soul's* self, let alone Editor of *Soul's* necessarily existing self.

The answer to this perplexity lies in the following principle which runs counter to the prevailing dogma that all propositions exist necessarily because they are abstract entities:

> *the first-person propositions belonging to a person X have a contingent existence: they exist if and only if X exists.*†

Once they exist, X's proposition "I exist" is, though contingently existing, necessarily true. (Perhaps something like this is what Descartes had in mind when he said as the terminal point of the *cogito:* "cette proposition: *Je suis, j'existe,* est necessairement vraie, toutes les fois que je la prononce, ou que je la conçois en mon esprit.")

V. The I and the World

The fact that the first-person pronoun has always largest scope has as its immediate consequence that certain propositions cannot be asserted by anyone. Propositions attributing modalities *de dicto* to first-person propositions are typical instances. For instance, "It is necessary that I exist" is again of the form "I am β and it is necessary that β exist." No modality can be attributed *de dicto* to "I exist", at least with the present linguistic resources. But this means that the I is never an ordinary object that has properties in quite the same way that all the other objects have them. It means also that each I must be identical with a battery of ordinary entities which have all the properties it has, so that the modalities *de dicto* apply to the corresponding third-person

† On Castañeda's subsequent view that not every conscious agent is capable of first-person reflection, 'if and only if' would here be replaced by 'only if'. —Eds.

propositions. The I is not an entity that can be even thought to be the subject of a fact F such that it is necessary that F, or it is impossible that F, or it is contingent that F. Thus, in a perfectly clear sense, namely that of the modalities *de dicto,* the I is not an entity that either exists contingently or necessarily. It is not, in that sense, an entity *in* the world, but an entity outside the world that must be identifiable in terms of entities in the world.

4

Philosophical Method and Direct Awareness of the Self

The sad fact is that good philosophy is and always has been *hard*, and that it is easier to learn the names of a few philosophers than it is to read their books [or articles].

Hilary Putnam[1]

One ought to theorize taking into account *all* the relevant data available at the time of theorization.

Introduction

The self is the geometrical origin of the world, that is, the center of the universe as an experienced whole. Yet is it *not* the source, or the root of the world, nor is it the provenience of experience. Origin but no source, that is the fundamental contrast in the structuring of the self and the world. Self-awareness is the linkage in that structuring; awareness of self *qua* self is simply the highest portion of that linkage. Thus, any theory of the self and self-awareness has to reveal the nature of the fundamental contrast, and explain the linking roles of the different degrees of self-awareness. (See Sections IX–XI below)

Here my aim is twofold: to provide some valuable data for *any* theory of the self, and to articulate some constraints on the relevant procedures for the construction of such theories. My means are exegetical. My material is Chapter I, "The Direct Awareness of the Self," of Chisholm's treatise *Person and Object: A Metaphysical Study*.[2]

I have always been fascinated by Chisholm's philosophical work. He has always focused on crucial and important problems; his discussion is always insightful; his writing is clear, his philosophical style powerful, and his methodology well structured. Chisholm's ostensive methodology has influenced a

This essay appeared in *Essays on the Philosophy of Roderick M. Chisholm*, edited by Ernest Sosa, published as a special issue of *Grazer Philosophische Studien* 7/8 (1979): 1–58. Reprinted by permission of the editor. In an editorial footnote, Professor Sosa indicated that "the present piece is an excerpt from a longer paper." We have been unable to locate the longer paper, and Sosa informed us in August 1997 that while he must have had the longer paper at some point, he no longer has it. —Eds.

large number of our contemporary practicing philosophers. It is impressive, progressive, and very easy to imitate. But here, as often, the master's practice possesses an evident imponderable quality that can be easily imitated but is hard to attain.

Chisholm claims that we do have direct and immediate awareness of the self. In his characteristic style, his claim is deployed in both a series of definitions and a complementary running commentary. My plan is to scrutinize what he does in order both to determine, first, whether he has succeeded in what seems to be his task and, second, to assess what the success of his task would amount to. I will engage in methodological reflections along the way. There are many important things that we can learn from Chisholm's work.

I have for some time been contemplating writing a thorough study of Chisholm's philosophical work, one of the most important in the second half of our century. This present homage to him has accelerated the writing of my first installment. Perhaps an explanation of my choice of topic may be in order. Chapter I is, of course, a logical starting point. However, on February 16, 1977, Chisholm wrote me the following:

> Since writing to you about your views, I've gone through a kind of philosophical crisis . . . : I've been using the concept of our knowledge of our own individual essences to deal with a lot of philosophical problems, including the one you raise with 'He.*' But I've had all along the gnawing suspicion that we have no such knowledge. So the results of a lot of system building have fallen apart . . . But there is new growth among the debris and the result (including what I'd *now* say about 'he*') is much better and I'm sure much closer to the truth than before.

Thus, in the ensuing discussions I will, as far as Chisholm is concerned, be flogging a dead horse. Why? Well, the horse is not entirely dead. And even if it were totally dead, a careful autopsy of it is the best means I know of to learn about the anatomy of the problems of awareness of self, the physiology of philosophical theorizing, and the nature of the indigestible data that would have caused its death. Moreover, Chisholm has not explained his reasons for his change of mind. And even if he had done so, we must do our own learning through our own detailed examination of his view. (Philosophy is, after all, done ultimately in the first person for the first person.) This examination is bound both to reveal precious elements of Chisholm's views that must be salvaged and to supply suggestions, about either method or subject-matter, that the building of substitute theories had better take into account. Chisholm's book *must* be read and reflected upon.

I. Chisholm's Essay

Chisholm's essay is divided into eight sections that fall into five parts: (i) formulation of the problem; (ii) informal presentation of its solution; (iii) deployment of the formal solution; (iv) rebuttal of Hume and Kant; (v) informal discussion of our awareness of the self. Here I will ignore (iv), although it contains very important discussions.

II. Some Crucial Data about the Self

Chisholm starts his essay (p. 23) with this question:

(Q1) Do we know ourselves directly and immediately?

Patently, this question cannot be answered at all unless we have an idea of what is meant by 'directly and immediately' in (Q1). But the little word 'ourselves' needs equal attention. Chisholm takes care of this by replacing (Q1), without more ado, with

(Q2) Is one ever directly aware of the subject of experience?

This has the merit of dropping the word 'immediately'. But is (Q2) immediately clear? Not by itself; and Chisholm means this question to be understood in the light of the "philosophical data" he has gathered in the introduction to his book. These data are:

(C.D) There are two broad subdivisions in the list and three types of fact in each.

> There are, first, these three types of thing I am justified in believing about myself. '(1) I am now thinking such-and-such. I have such-and-such beliefs, feelings, desires, attitudes. I have such-and-such experiences and such-and-such perceptions. (2) I now have a body of such-and-such a sort. And (3) I am now intentionally bringing about such-and-such things which are such that I could have avoided bringing them about'. (p. 16)
> Let us turn to the second part of our list. To formulate this we have only to look at the first part of the list and then to put similar but different facts in the past tense . . . (p. 17)

It is quite clear what obvious facts Chisholm takes as his starting data. And he can do nothing better than to take them as his point of departure: we think and feel, "we are very much in touch with material things and we know that we are. And . . . we are active beings" (p. 17). Chisholm summarizes this carefully so as not to say that we *are* material things. This does, however, sound prejudicial. It is certainly part of the data, not merely that we "have" a body, but that we *are* in possession of physical properties, e.g., that we are so many kilos heavy, so many meters tall, etc. This is an issue that needs more discussion than Chisholm gives it in the introduction or Chapter I.

Chisholm stresses a point that is clear already in his data (C.D.):

(1) the various items on our list pertain to *one and the same* entity throughout. (p. 17; his italics)

And he puts this emphatically as follows:

(2) If we were to fill out our list, we could formulate one long sentence using a single variable 'x' throughout: 'I am an x such that x thinks so-and-so, x has such-and-such a body, is doing such-and-such things, x formerly thought such-and-such, x formerly had a body of such-and-such a different sort, and x formerly brought about such-and-such other things.' (p. 17)

This prompts one question: Are (1) and (2) merely two formulations of the selfsame *datum*? Given the technical use of formal machinery with its quantifiers and its bound variables, this reader can not suffocate the feeling that (2) is much more than a datum: it is semi-formal formulation that already involves a theoretical commitment. It is definitely true that we *say* and *believe* that it is the same entity that feels pain now as the one who felt pain yesterday, when I say truly "I felt pain yesterday and I feel pain now." But this use of 'same' (or 'identical', for that matter) at the level of data leaves it open that in a *theory* of the self we must distinguish different entities or selves, which are of course, very intimately connected. The ordinary datum statements *establish* a very intimate connection, and the theory must *account* for it. Obviously the strongest account the theory can offer is genuine or strict identity; but one must not limit the theory to this strongest claim in the light of just one datum.

The preceding point is a very important methodological principle. And I am very pleased to find that Chisholm recognizes it fully on p. 105, and proceeds to defend the strict identity of the self through time. This is the topic of his subtle and provoking Chapter III. Undoubtedly, in the background of Chisholm's discussion of direct awareness of the self in Chapter I, lies his conception of the self as a unitary entity that remains strictly identical through time. We shall have occasion to see this. Nevertheless, Chisholm's views in Chapter I can essentially be treated independently of that assumption.

III. Chisholm's Problem and Plan

Chisholm's problem in Chapter I is, as noted above, this:

(Q2) Is one ever directly aware of the subject of experience?

In the light of his data (C.D.) this question must be understood in the sense of the subject of *one's* experiences, and, more specifically, as:

(Q3) Is one ever directly aware of that individual one calls "I" when one describes one's own experiences?

As already noted, Chisholm formulates his data (C.D.) so that he can immediately clarify that

(3) The question (Q3) has nothing to do with perception of one's body.

Now, I agree completely with Chisholm that a person's body is not identical with that person's I, but, whereas Chisholm's reasons seem to be Cartesian, mine are Kantian.[3] This is a contrast between a substantialist self in the world and a structural origin of experience that is not in the world. See Section IX below. For this reason, and because of the fact that it is not clear from data (C.D.) what exactly he takes an I or self to be, I wish very much that Chisholm had engaged in a proto-philosophical examination of his data.

Doubtless, Chisholm has in mind data of the following sort. Some sentences seem to change the truth value of what they formulate, even become senseless, when one replaces a person's first-person pronoun with descriptions of the person's body. For instance, 'I have (feel) a toothache' may express a truth, but 'this body has (feels) a toothache' is false. Is this enough to establish that I am not identical with my body? We know of many sentences in which two co-referring expressions cannot replace each other while truth or meaning is being preserved. Everybody knows about intensional contexts, negations of existence, quotation contexts, idioms, etc. Psychological sentences are the paradigm cases of intensional contexts. Sentences about selves, whether first-person or second-person sentences, are psychological sentences. It seems natural to regard them as intensional contexts. If so, one does *not* have a clear reason, from Chisholm's data (C.D.), to assume that a person's I (self) and that person's body are not the same. Here one must stress the methodological point made above: the sameness of the self and a body at a certain level of analysis of the data is compatible with their not being strictly identical in terms of the theory of the self one develops. This is comforting, but it cannot assuage the need for careful analysis of the data.

It seems, then, that Chisholm's problem (Q3) (which is supposed to be strictly identical with (Q2) and (Q1) above) is not the naive question one might have expected from the words of (Q1). It is already so high up on the theoretical pedestal that one cannot expect to answer it by asking for the sense of 'directly' and then simply proceeding to look at the facts. Compare for contrast the case of a man who claims that certain human children were born indirectly. Once he tells us that by 'being born indirectly' he means being born with midwifery assistance, everything is clear: We simply go and examine the birth of the children in question. Or take a conceptually harder case: Is Sweden a democracy? There are dozens of uses of the word 'democracy'. To decide the question we must first find out which one is intended and then look at the political facts in Sweden.

Chisholm's question is clearly of a different sort. To understand the question we must *construct a theory* of the self. To understand the question we need more than Chisholm's exposition of the senses of the key expressions 'be aware directly' and 'I' or 'subject of experience'. Palpably, the proposition he wants to defend, namely, that we are directly aware of the subjects of our experiences, must be defended as a necessary or philosophical truth. He will *give* meanings to the key expressions in such a way that he can derive his thesis. But his definitions must somehow illuminate the data and allow the illumination of further related data.

Chisholm's question is just one prong of a network of questions, others appearing in later chapters of his book, about the role of the self in experience. The general problem is what we may call *the first person structures of experience:* the formulation of both the principles that constitute those structures, and the principles connecting those structures to the other structures in each first-person proposition we believe or simply entertain, whether about ourselves or not. We glimpse at a segment of the design of those structures, and the principles connecting those structures to the other structures of experience and the world. But the whole structure has to be conjectured from a multitude of examples. That is why Chisholm's data (C.D.) constitute a magnificent rich collection of relevant data. A careful examination of the data can suggest points for hypothesizing parts of that design. Philosophical theorization is, like scientific theorization, hypothetico-deductive. The *deductive part* comes either at the beginning in the scrutiny of the data (e.g., when paradoxes are derived so as to single out negative points for the hypothezation of the grand design), or at the end, within the theory. We can make deductions from Chisholm's theory in order to test it, but we must *not* ask him to prove his theory.[4]

Chisholm's theoretical moves like (2) and (3) are crucial elements in his development of the theory of direct awareness of the self he is interested in. At bottom his plan is simply this: he finds a multitude of first-person truths; he also finds that those truths cannot be challenged in the referential part, even if they can be challenged in the attribution part; he finds that any claim to know anything about anything in the world involves some experience of the knower, so that he is related to the objects he knows. This is the role of the self Chisholm wants to call direct awareness. Hence his problem is simply to provide an account of it. The program seems to me perfectly satisfactory.

Now, Chisholm presents himself as being in drastic opposition to "two of the great traditions of contemporary Western philosophy—'phenomenology' and 'logical analysis' . . . with Sartre, with Russell and with Carnap. For at this particular point, if I am not mistaken, both groups have lost their way" (p. 23). Way to what? Chisholm is disagreeing with Russell on the non-discoverability of the self or subject and with Carnap on the subjectlessness of the given. But do Russell and Carnap mean to reject Chisholm's data (C.D.)? I doubt it. I doubt very much that those philosophers denied that we make in daily life first-person statements, or that at least some of the ones we make are true. I wonder, in fact, and will consider it later on, whether Carnap and Russell would have accepted Chisholm's account of direct awareness of the self.

In any case, it seems to me that the issue is not merely the factual one of getting straight on what Chisholm means by 'direct awareness' and then simply looking at the facts. Given the central role of first-person reference in our acquiring knowledge of the world, as I suggested above, it is obvious that in one sense we *have* direct awareness of ourselves. And I submit that Russell and Carnap would have agreed that in that sense we have direct awareness of ourselves. The issue then is about what sort of entity the self, or subject, is, how it relates to the other entities of the world, or of experience. Thus, I submit, Chisholm differs from Sartre, Russell, and Carnap on what they take the self to be: *on their theories.* I wish very much that Chisholm had made a detailed exegesis of what they were denying when they seemed to Chisholm to be denying that we have a direct awareness of the self. But enough of preliminaries.

IV. Chisholm's Informal Account of Direct Self-Awareness

Chisholm starts his informal account with these definitions:

(4) A proposition is known directly if it is self-presenting or presents itself.
(5) A proposition 'presents itself' to a man, if, first of all, it is true, and if, secondly, it is necessarily such that, if it is true, then the man knows it is true. (P. 24)

Thus, what Chisholm calls, in Meinong's terminology, self-presentation, is very much what others have called incorrigibility.[5] Chisholm is also in that tradition. The typically incorrigible propositions may be called *cogito-propositions,* namely, those that Descartes had in mind in his *cogito, ergo sum, viz.:*

(A) *Cogito propositions:* first-person present-tense propositions about states of consciousness: they are of the form "I am now E'ing such-and-such," where 'E'ing' is a variable standing for any occurrent state of consciousness.

These propositions, I gather, comprise Chisholm's data (1) of his first type. Now, *cogito-propositions* must be distinguished from (B) and (C):

(B) *Incorrigible cogitatum-propositions,* which are about incorrigible items, like pains, itchings, tinglings, sensory presentations (of the sort some philosophers call sense-data or sensa), etc. Propositions of this type are, whether formulated in language or not, of the form "There is a such and such here (over there)," where the such-and-such is not a physical object.
(C) *Physical present-cogitatum propositions:* These are nonegocentered propositions just about the physical contents of current perceptions. These are also of the form "There is a such-and-such over there" or "That (or this) such-and-such is so and so."

We shall speak of *cogitatum* propositions *simpliciter* to refer to both (B) and (C) types. Obviously, *cogitatum* propositions are part and parcel of the data one must consider in developing a theory of the self, of the mind, or of experience. Consider a time when one is experiencing pain and having the experience of there being a garden with a nearby maple tree and a somewhat more distant Chinese blue-green Wong tree, and a female bird flying back and forth from one to the other. It is certain that a pain is located where one is feeling it and that there is a visual presentation as described. Whatever Cartesian doubts one may have about the existence, i.e., physical existence of one's body, the trees, and the bird, those doubts leave unscratched not only that one is aware of them, but that the contents of consciousness are as described.

Patently, one question one must raise in the proto-philosophical examination of data (A)–(C) is: How do data of the three types relate to one another? This question leads some philosophers to think of reducing one type of proposition to the other. But reduction is a *theoretical* issue, and one has to deal with it later, much later, after one has scrutinized the datum-connections between the two types of proposition. At the proto-philosophical level, one question *of fact*, like all data, is this:

(Q4) Can one, or another creature less developed than we, be capable of experiencing, i.e., apprehending, considering, or entertaining, and coming to believe propositions of types (B) or (C) without entertaining or considering, much less believing, propositions of type (A)?

Clearly, the converse of what (Q4) asks is immediately ruled out for the case of considering or entertaining. It may be asked whether one can believe that one is feeling a pain even though there is no pain to be felt. But this presupposes that being a pain is not a quality that appears to feeling as it is. Now, it seems to some of us that the answer to question (Q4) is "Yes." I, for instance, many a time have been so absorbed in what I am conscious of that I have not been conscious of being conscious of anything. Apparently this is not an abnormality of mine. What phenomenologists call *'unreflective consciousness'* seems to me precisely of that sort.[6] It is a consciousness purely of a first order, and it does not appear to have a self or I to which it belongs. I submit, further, that such egoless consciousness is typical of the perceptions and bodily feelings of many animals, at least those that are not sufficiently advanced, like birds and crabs. Perhaps housedogs and domestic pigs have ego-owned consciousness. However, we do not have to decide on these facts. It suffices that we, in spite of our highly developed selves, are capable of moments of egoless episodes of consciousness, to be sure that there are facts that establish the affirmative answer to question (Q4). Hence, such facts of unreflective consciousness must be *added* to our collection of crucial data. Once we are safe on these factual data, we can appreciate the additional fact that it is not even crucial that there be such facts. It is sufficient that there *can* be such facts. We can consider, whether illustrated by any brute on Earth or not, a being that is capable just of unreflective consciousness. Such beings I have called *Externi.*[7]

Whether each animal around us is an Externus or not is an important question, and it is relevant to the inquiry that Chisholm is engaged in in the essay under examination. For one thing, the primacy of the self in the existence of experiences is diminished if there are actual Externi. But, more importantly, the phenomenon of human consciousness must *not* be treated in isolation. To use a word dear to Quine and others, we must *naturalize the study of man and mind.* I am using the word 'naturalize' only to make the point that *a theory of the self must be capable of being embedded in a larger theory of consciousness, whether ego-owned or egoless.* I certainly have nothing to do with reductionistic programs attempting to eliminate the mind altogether, or reduce it to the physico-chemical activity of a brain or a whole body.

Now, consider the question:

(Q5) Is an Externus directly aware of the subject of its experiences?

The answer would seem to be "No" in the obvious sense that an Externus does not possess the concept of the first-person, so that it is not capable of having thoughts that have as their contents the *cogito* propositions corresponding to its *cogitatum* propositions. Yet the answer to (Q5) *may* be "Yes," if we adopt an important stipulation laid down by Chisholm:

(6)   I suggest that whenever a person thus knows something directly then he may be said to have *direct knowledge* of himself; in Russell's terms, the man may be said to be *directly acquainted* with himself. (p. 24; Chisholm's own italics)

I said that with the help of (6) the answer to (Q5) *may* be "Yes," because Chisholm's stipulation (6) is unmistakably framed for persons and men. On the other hand, (Q5) refers to Externi. The difference is important. In the case of ordinary persons, even when we are engaged in an unreflective episode of consciousness, we are still in possession of our sophisticated concepts required for reflective consciousness: the move to reflectiveness is easily made: the spell of egolessness does not last very long. That is, although Chisholm's (6) is a stipulation, and we would like to know the rationale for it, we can accept it more easily in the case of persons and refrain from extending it to Externi.

In short, Externi are special cases. They are *not* within the data Chisholm included in (C.D.) Hence, they are not clear-cut counterexamples to the advisability of his stipulating (6). Yet they should be part of the data. My complaint again is that he did not do an adequate proto-philosophical exercise.

Chisholm justifies his stipulation (6) as follows:

(7)   For all the self-presenting *states we have referred to* are states of the knower himself. (p. 24; my italics)

As far as Chisholm's discussion has proceeded (pp. 1–24), there is no reason to object to (7), except to his connective 'For'. He has in fact referred to nothing but states of the knower as self-presenting, that is, he has referred just to *cogito* propositions. Yet he has so far said nothing that rules out incorrigible *cogitatum*-propositions as self-presenting. If we take them into consideration,

(7) cannot provide a good reason for accepting stipulation (6). Chisholm does, however, offer an argumentative gesture in support of (7), namely:

(8) To see that *these states* that are self-presenting *are* states of the knower himself, we have only to ask ourselves: What state which is *not* a state of the man himself is one which is *necessarily* such that, if it were to obtain, then the man *knows directly* that it obtains? That there are many people in the room, as we have said, could obtain without my knowing about it; that there *seem to me* to be many people in the room couldn't possibly obtain without my knowing about it. Thus Brentano has held that the only individual thing which can be an object of such direct factual knowledge is the knower himself. (p. 24ff.; Chisholm's own italics, except for those in 'these states')

I have quoted the argument in full because it is worthy of careful pondering.

Chisholm claims that "we have only to ask ourselves" the question he poses to see that only the states of the self can be self-presenting (or incorrigible, in another terminology). Is that so? I have asked myself the question many times in the last twenty years, and I have not been able to see the truth of Chisholm's thesis. Is it because of my obstreperous density? Perhaps. Is Chisholm perverse in his peremptory challenge? Much less likely. Well?

Undoubtedly, Chisholm is right in *his* own view in claiming that the simple asking of the question allows the answer to present itself. Chisholm has brought a train of assumptions with him that *his* asking the question suffices for him to see the answer. But I do not come to the question with the same assumptions. Perhaps the most crucial one at this juncture is Chisholm's assumption that *cogitatum* propositions have no bearing on the issue. He has not even considered them or the unreflective consciousness to which they properly belong as their contents. Why? This is a serious matter. Surely, *if* (so as not to prejudge the substantive issue and focus on the methodological one) there are individuals whose being or *esse* is *percipi*, i.e., 'perceived by a certain person', and those entities are *cogitata* rather than *cogitationes*, then propositions predicating phenomenal properties of such entities satisfy Chisholm's characterization (5) of self-presenting propositions. Obviously, Chisholm is assuming in his (7) that there are no such entities. But is this assumption justified? At first glance there seem to be such entities: bodily sensations, after-images, pains, sounds as heard, illusory particulars, etc., in short, all the entities that are said to be subjective (whose *esse* is *percipi*) and are not themselves states of consciousness but their contents. It would seem that Chisholm should at least consider some reasons for the eliminative *philosophical* theory that there are no such entities.

Chisholm does indeed offer some arguments later on (pp. 47ff.) where he attacks the sense-datum theory, but he does not connect them with the present issue. We examine them in Section XI below.

Chisholm has, thus, a theory of direct knowledge of self, and that theory is incompatible with the sense-datum theory. This conflict of theories is fine. It must be understood for what it is. Among other things, that conflict reveals that Chisholm's theory of direct knowledge of the self has to be *tested* against the data on which sense datum theorists base their theories. This is, of course, not an adverse criticism of Chisholm's theorization. Indeed, there is here an implicit praise for his theorization: Chisholm is proposing a theory that caters to a larger collection of data than those gathered in his (C.D.). Naturally, the more comprehensive the data for a theory, the graver the risks the theory runs of failing to illuminate its data. But the more enterprising a theory is, the more interesting and respectable it is.

The theoretical side of Chisholm's work in his informal presentation of his theory is clear. What perplexes me is the methodological side of that work. Chisholm should have faced squarely the fact that his theory requires not merely that sense-datum theories be false, but that there be no sense-datum or *entity* whatever whose being is *percipi*. Hence, Chisholm cannot mount his theory on data (C.D.), without the proto-philosophical exercise required for the taming of all the pervasive data consisting of experiences that seem to present us with entities whose being is *percipi*. Such data include the experiences of unreflective consciousness, which, quite properly, so much impressed Sartre, and Merleau-Ponty. (See Section XI below.)

Now, I demur at Chisholm's argument (8), and for several reasons. *First,* Chisholm's argument (8) has a step wanting elucidation, namely:

(9) that there *seem to me* to be many people in the room couldn't possibly obtain without my knowing about it.

It is an impressive step. It is meant as a paradigmatic example. Thus, Chisholm considers experiences in which I judge that there appears to be physical objects. Clearly, he is not considering that the contents of the experience (or judgment) be beings whose *esse* is *percipi*. This is in line with the general tone of his assumption as noted above. Let us, however, put that issue aside. The step has another important feature: it is a first-person present-tense example. Doubtless, if I *judge* that it seems to me to be the case that *p*, I am expressing a *cogito* proposition. Chisholm is right in claiming that such a proposition is incorrigible or self-presenting. That much is clear. However, the argument was supposed to show that in fact *all* self-presenting propositions are *cogito* propositions. The step would have been effective if it had taken up paradigms of what seem to be self-presenting *non-cogito* propositions, and then shown that they are after all *cogito-propositions*. Thus, step (9) and, hence, argument (8) need complementation.

Second, Chisholm's argument (8) is helped by the fact that (9) hides a subtle ambiguity. This ambiguity can be seen better in the past or future tense. Suppose that I had at time *t* an illusory experience consisting of a pink rat running on a certain wall. Thus I judged at *t*: "There is a pink rat over there!" We can describe the experience by saying "At *t* it seemed (or appeared) to

Castañeda (me) that there was a pink rat on that wall." Yet this description need *not* attribute to me anything more than an unreflective experience: that is, an experience that included no *cogito* judgment, but only a *cogitatum* judgment. And we must distinguish two kinds of cogitated content: the physical content, which is false, making my experience illusory, and the phenomenological content, which is incorrigible — or so it seems, until a really crushing argument against this is provided. Thus, the locution 'there seems to me that *p*' can be understood as expressing my judgment "It appears to me that *p*," or as expressing the fact that an appearance that *p* happens to me, even though I am aware of being appeared to. See Section XI for further discussion of this.

Third, Chisholm's argument (8) speaks of states of the person, rather than of the *cogitata* of those states. We shall discuss this in detail in Section XI below. Here we merely ask: why cannot a person, or an Externus, apprehend a state of his without realizing that it is a state or that it is his?

We have now a general idea of Chisholm's account of direct awareness of self. His desideratum is to articulate that idea in a system of definitions. Let us see the official version of his account.

V. Chisholm's Self-Presentation: Substrates and Predication

Chisholm's main official accomplishment in the essay under consideration is a series of eleven definitions. That series is his official theory of the direct awareness of the subject of experience. They are all carefully formulated and make clear the sense Chisholm gives his technical terms. I am somewhat quizzical about a theory that consists just of definitions. Fortunately, Chisholm always intersperses his definitions with a running commentary. This commentary does the real philosophical work. In this section we shall limit ourselves to the official theory. This eleven-definition theory is supposed to make precise Chisholm's "philosophical thesis" that we are, in Russell's terms used in (8) directly acquainted with ourselves. Note that no arguments for that thesis are to be expected: the theory merely defines the thesis. The arguments are presumably in the background informal discussion or may come in on the side in the commentary on the official definitions. Let us see what the definitions do.

Chisholm's account of acquaintance is developed in his first several definitions. The first two are as follows:

D. I.1   *h* is such that it is self-presenting to S at *t* =Df *h* occurs at *t* and is necesssarily such that, whenever it occurs then it is certain for S. (p. 5)

D. I.2   *h* is certain for S at *t* =Df (i) Accepting *h* is more reasonable for S at *t* than withholding *h* (i.e., not accepting *h* and not accepting not-*h*) and (ii) there is no *i* such that accepting *i* is more reasonable for S than accepting *h*. (p. 27)

Chisholm says (p. 26) that the certainty of a proposition (or state of affairs) is a normative matter, not a factual one, about what a person has a right to believe. Chisholm explains (in Appendix D) that it all has to do with epistemic preferability. And this has to do with our aiming at believing what is true. Thus, it would seem that a true proposition P that is compatible with the total set of propositions one already believes should be reasonable to believe, especially if P introduces some unity or illumination into a segment of one's beliefs. Presumably, then, such a proposition P is certainly more reasonable for one to believe than not-P, regardless of whether one comes to believe P or not. It is also more reasonable to accept than to withhold P (i.e., as Chisholm explains, to accept neither P nor not-P). All of this obtains whether one thinks of P or not. On p. 179 Chisholm says that "we could obtain a somewhat more restrictive, and possibly more useful, definition of self-presentation by further restricting the definiens. Thus we might say: '*h* occurs, S considers *h*, and . . . '." But Chisholm does not in Chapter I feel the need for any such restriction.

Yet such restriction as the one Chisholm contemplates on p. 179 seems to be required in order to avoid some strange-sounding results from his definitions. I am tentative here because I am not confident I have mastered Chisholm's system of definitions throughout his book. His difficult primitive concept *is necessarily such that* perplexes me immensely.

Apparently definitions D. I.1–D. I.2 allow that self-presenting propositions be not only *cogito* propositions but also *cogitatum* propositions and even propositions about physical objects. By way of experiment consider a true proposition P, namely:

P: the F exists and is G,

which is an instance of a generalization member of the consistent set H of propositions believed by a certain person, and that she alone believes the set H. Thus, it seems that P is certain for the H-believer. Obviously, it is a contingent matter that the H-believer exists; but it is not a contingent matter that P has the logical and objective relationship noted. P is necessarily such that whenever it occurs (i.e., is true), then it is certain for the H-believer. Hence, P is self-presenting to the H-believer, even if the H-believer does not believe P and cannot physically think of P, but can understand P.

I said that the preceding result is "apparently" allowed by definitions D. I.1–D. I.2. The reason is that a very plausible reply that overthrows that result is this: "In the expressions in definitions D. I.1–D. I.7 [see below] the variable 'S', which ranges over persons, cannot be replaced with definite descriptions: thus, 'the H-believer' is not a correct substituent for 'S'." Chisholm does not say this. He says so little about the logical structure of the formulas in his definitions. This is a serious matter because, as Quine has taught us, we *cannot* simply assume that the rules of quantificational logic can be combined with rules of modal propositional logic in a coherent way. Chisholm should have given a warning as to the proper substituends of his individual variables.

The issue is much more serious than merely giving precision to definitions D. I.1–D. I.7. Profound metaphysical issues about the *nature of individuation* and the *structure and types of predication* underlie the stipulations about the substituends for and the values of the variables in those definitions. For instance, the joint stipulation that (a) the substituends for those variables are not definite descriptions and (b) definite descriptions are to be analyzed in the Russellian way, has very significant metaphysical consequences. For one thing, since by the Russellian analysis all the predicative content true of an individual is separated from it, the decision not to allow definite descriptions as substituends of the quantifiable variables of those definitions amounts to making bare substrates the values of those variables. For another, the Russellian analysis amounts to the *anti-Meinongian* ruling that the values of the variables of quantification are existents and never merely possible individuals—let alone impossible ones.[8]

Chisholm does not raise the fundamental metaphysical issues of individuation and of predication in his metaphysical study. Some statements he makes seem to put him in the substrate camp. First he seems (p. 200) to adopt, as is customary, Russell's analysis of definite descriptions. Second, his definition D. I.5 (p. 29) distinguishes sharply between individual essences and the individuals that have them. Third, he comments on Sartre as follows: "but he adds, unfortunately, that 'consciousness' has nothing of the substantial; *L' être et le néant,* pp. 13, 23" (pp. 203f.). It is not clear, however, what Chisholm may mean by the substantiality of consciousness rather than of the self.

Fourth, he briefly attacks Hume's bundle-theory of individuation as follows:

(10) One is temped to say instead [of what Hume says] that our idea of a peach is an idea of *something that has* a particular taste, color, . . . But even this is not quite right. Our idea of a peach is not an idea of something that *has* the particular qualities, . . . but the *concrete thing* that *is* sweet and round and fuzzy. We also make clear, what is essential to our idea of peach, that the thing that is round is the *same* thing as the thing that is wet and also the *same* as the thing that is fuzzy. (p. 38; Chisholm's italics, except for those in 'concrete thing')

I am not sure I grasp fully what Chisholm is saying here. He says on the next page that his point "is a simple-minded one." Perhaps it is. My problem is that I do not see that it is inconsistent with Hume's view of individuals, except in the *non-trivial* and *far* from simple-minded sense that the concretion of things consists of a substrate, or substance, which is itself not a property or attribute, but the subject of attribution. Chisholm is not clearly committing himself to this. He seems to be limiting himself to reminding Hume that individuals are *subjects of predication*. But is this reminder a refutation of Hume? Shouldn't we distinguish the problem of what an individual is from the problem of the roles of individuals in states of affairs and facts and propositions? Given Hume's bundle-theory of individuals, the problem of predication and the problem of the structure of states of affairs are very pressing ones for him. But here is only a pair of problems yet: we can refute him only *after* showing that what he offers as solutions to those problems cannot illuminate the relevant data.[9]

In brief, Chisholm's attack on Hume's bundle-theory is in my opinion too cursory. The cursoriness of the rebuttals is, nonetheless, itself not important. What is important is that Chisholm, writing a metaphysical study, did not deepen the fundamental issues of ontological individuation and of predication. These issues are at the very foundations of his problems.[10] I hasten to clarify that, as I see it, a non-substrate view of individuation with a satisfactory account of predication and the structure of states of affairs can be developed.[11] On the other hand, although I am a bundle-bundle theorist of sorts, I hold that the substrate view is irrefutable: that is, a carefully developed substrate theory is as irrefutable as a carefully developed bundle theory.[12] Here I am envisioning an ultimate impasse, even more profound than Kant's antinomies in that it cannot be solved in one supersystem in the way that Kant proposed for his antinomies. I envision two irreconcilable systems of the structure of the world. The choice is in the end a matter of personality—or perhaps the physico-chemistry of one's body.[13] The crucial task is to face up to the problems within each view squarely and deal with them fully.

VI. Chisholm's Definition of Acquaintance

On the way to his analysis of acquaintance, Chisholm offers intrinsically interesting definitions. One of them is:

D. I.3   *p* entails the property of being F = Df *p* is necessarily such that (i) if it obtains then something has the property of being F and (ii) whoever accepts p believes that something is F.

This is an intriguing definition. Chisholm's concern is at bottom more epistemological than metaphysical, and his definition D. I.3 seems to me a precious epistemological gem. Propositions or states of affairs are objective, yet they are units of belief. But there is a problem: propositions or states of affairs have implications; however, nobody can believe all the implications of what he believes. Where can we draw the line? It is not easy. Chisholm's clause (ii) in D. I.3 is a very ingenious way of drawing one important segment of that line. Part of the force of clause (ii) is to make the property F a constituent of a proposition p that entails it—thus using the word 'entail' in its etymological meaning.

We shall see in Section VIII below that clause (ii) of D. I.3 is, on the other hand, a Waterloo of Chisholm's claims about acquaintance of the self, epistemological individuation (i.e., identification or pinning down an entity in the world), and individual essence.

There is a perplexing element in D. I.3, which appears also in Chisholm's later definitions, as we shall see. He has in clause (i) of D. I.3 the clause 'something has the property of being F', *not* the simpler clause 'something is F'. Yet this simpler clause is precisely the one that occurs in clause (ii). Is some important and subtle difference being insisted upon? Chisholm does not say. A casual reading of D. I.3 suggests that perhaps these are two stylistic variations of the same proposition, or state of affairs. (On p. 22 Chisholm does explain that "the letter 'F' may be replaced by any English predicate expression—e.g., 'red' or 'such that Socrates is mortal'.") But then why two styles, suggesting a non-existing difference? However, the passage quoted above (p. 18) labeled (10) suggests that perhaps Chisholm is on p. 38 drawing a distinction between having particular qualities and being such and such. Isn't this distinction applicable to the contrasts between 'is' and 'has' in Chisholm's formal definitions? I don't know.

I will, hoping that this exegetical hypothesis is valid, assume that 'a has the property of being F' expresses something equivalent to 'a is F'—equivalent, but not identical. (See pp. 4ff. above on equivalence, identity, and sameness.)

Chisholm's suggestion on p. 38 that the proposition *a has the property of being F* (or perhaps *a has F-ness*) is not identical with the proposition *a is F* is very important. I believe it to be true. But it must be embedded in a general theory of predication. Thus, once again, we see how Chisholm's definitions and arguments are, not only not so precise as they seem at first sight, but cry out for a metaphysical foundation on the nature of individuation and of predication.

Let us move on. Chisholm's next definitions are:

D. I.4   C is an individual concept =Df C is a property such that (i) it is possible that something has C and (ii) it is not possible that more than one thing has C at a time.

D. I.5   G is an *individual essence* (or *haecceity*) = Df G is a property which is such that, for every x, x has G if and only if *x is necessarily such that it has G, and it is impossible that there is a y other than x such that y has G.*

D. I.4 is straightforward: necessary uniqueness of instantiation makes a property an individual concept.

D. I.5 is, on the other hand, *not* an innocent definition—assuming, of course, that it is not an empty definition. Recall our discussion about substrates and variables of quantification in Section V. If the variable '*x*' in D. I.5 is to have substrates as values, how can one such value ever be necessarily G, for any property G that must be instantiated uniquely, or not instantiated at all? If the values of '*x*' and '*y*' are not bare substrates, how can we require that their substituends not be definite descriptions? How can we exclude substituends that represent as values entities that are not bare but have certain contents? If we allow as values of those individual variables not just bare substrates but substrates with their essences, these being properties, what role do the substrates play? What sort of data is illuminated by having substrates at all, rather than the bundles of properties that are essences? If we still insist on the substrate, how can the connection between the substrate, the pure individual, and its essence be necessary?

The preceding are only some of the profound questions that are just under the epidermis of Chisholm's definition D. I.5. It seems to me that the full understanding of what D. I.5 is to do metaphysically demands a full ventilation of those profound issues. At least this reader is perplexed by the contrast between individuals and individual essences assumed by D. I.5 and underscored in the commentary Chisholm appends to it, which begins with the following illustration:

> Thus the individual essence or haecceity of Socrates, if there is such a thing, has the following characteristics. It is a property which is such that, if anything has it, then that thing has it necessarily; hence *Socrates had it necessarily.* (But it was not necessary that Socrates had it, for *it was not necessary that there be a Socrates.*) (p. 29; my italics)

That it was not necessary that there be a Socrates is clear. One can say in fashionable metaphor: there is a possible world in which Socrates does not exist. But what is it for Socrates to *have necessarily* Socrateity (to give an ancient name to Socrates' haecceity)?[14] If Socrates were just the bundle of properties which Socrateity is, it would be clear. In some sense (which requires yet deeper metaphysical reflection to unravel) properties have a status that transcends possible worlds, or they hold (are, exist, belong) in all possible worlds. But Chisholm distinguishes Socrates from Socrateity. Does Socrates necessarily have Socrateity because somehow they go together, to continue the metaphor, in all possible worlds? (Let me emphasize that the use of the expression 'possible world' in the construction of set-theoretical models for formal "languages" is *not* metaphorical: it is a technical mathematical term in the way 'ring', 'field', 'group', 'pencil', and others are technical mathematical terms. What I call metaphorical is the commonly illustrated metaphysical or ontological use of the expression 'possible world'. Yet it need not be, and I think that it is a technical term in the writings of some philosophers, perhaps David Lewis and Alvin Plantinga, among others.) But what is there to Socrates besides Socrateity? A substrate especially fabricated for Socrateity, a matter specially suitable for its form, as an Aristotelian would say? Is the necessity of having a certain individual essence by an individual, which is itself not necessary, the suitability of the substrate to its essence? If there is no substrate in Socrates, what is there to Socrates besides Socrateity?

Other questions fight within me for expression. But I will not yield to their pressure. I have said enough to convey the depth of my quandary about the above quotation. The preceding questions make it palpable that the issues of metaphysical individuation and of predication are fundamental and unavoidable.

Chisholm's next definition is:

D. I.6 p implies x to have the property of being F = Df There is a property G such that (i) G is an individual concept, (ii) p entails the conjunction of G and the property of being F, and (iii) x has G.

This definition inherits my queries about the values of and the substituends for the variable 'x'. I surmise that it is supposed to work as follows. Consider a proposition of the form *The G is F.* The property being the G is an individual concept: *The G is F* is necessarily such that if it obtains then something has the conjunctive property being the G and being F: the proposition is also necessarily such that whoever accepts it believes that (something is F). These parentheses are meant to indicate scope, namely, that in a terminology I find distortive of the data, the sentence 'something is F' occurs *de dicto.* Hence, if the proposition is true, then it implies the G to have the property of being F. This sounds trivial, but it is not. The point is that if the H is the same (in the ordinary sense of 'same', which need not be strict identity) as the G, then *the G is F* also implies the H to have the property of being F. Definition D. I.6 allows us to partition the class of singular propositions into equivalent classes modulo sameness, whether necessary or contingent. D. I.6 does more, since non-singular propositions, like conjunctions of singular propositions, can be equally partitioned. If the above is correct, D. I.6 is a very nice definition.

Now we come to the first climax of Chisholm's definitions:

D. I.7   S is acquainted with x at t = Df There is a p such that (i) p is self-presenting for S at t and (ii) there is a property that p implies x to have.

It may be easier to understand Chisholm's notion of acquaintance if we unpack it all the way down to D. I.1, thus:

D. I.7A   S is acquainted with x at t = Df
          There is state of affairs p such that:
          (i.1) p is occurs at t, and
          (i.2) p is necessarily such that: whenever it occurs, then:
          (i.i) accepting p is more reasonable for S at t than withholding p, and
          (i.ii) there is no state of affairs q such that accepting q is more reasonable for S at t than accepting p; and

(ii) there is a property F and a property G such that:

(ii.i) G is an individual concept,

(ii.i′) if p obtains, something has the conjunction of G and the property being F,

(ii.ii′) whoever accepts p believes that something is F and G*, and

(ii.iii) x has G.

I have put 'G*' to produce the adjective corresponding to 'G' in the way 'F' corresponds to 'being F'. Does this matter?

The cumulative effect of my discussions of Chisholm's definition D. I.1–D. I.6 is simply this: it is hard for me to be sure as to what precisely D. I.7, or D. I.7A, amounts to. For instance, on that alternative interpretation that allows any proposition to be certain for rocks, a rock would be acquainted with every object. Similarly, on that interpretation that allows a proposition of the form "John is F and accepting this is more reasonable than withholding it for x at time t", the person x would be acquainted with John, whoever he might be, and regardless of any beliefs x has about John. In short, the imprecisions about the values of the variables and about the sense of 'reasonable to accept', etc., at the beginning tends to increase the imprecisions in the later definitions.

Notwithstanding the preceding overall difficulty, I find D. I.7 interesting, especially if it is modified so as to include a clause, like the one Chisholm himself suggests on p. 179, to the effect that the person S has considered or is considering the state of affairs p. Yet considering is definitely not sufficient. Something stronger like perceiving or being aware of the proposition in person, so to speak, must be added. Perhaps Chisholm means to build this into the notion of 'more reasonable to accept than to withhold'. I am not sure; on p. 135 he takes 'perceives (state of affairs) p' as primitive.

Perhaps clause (i.2) is too strong for the ordinary sense of 'acquaintance'. Suppose that there are two identical twins, a and b, and that Jones has no reason at all to suspect that a has a twin. One day the twins, for fun, decide to get together and exchange their worldly roles. Jones has had a two-hour visit with b, and has found nothing different from the a he has known in b's appearance and behavior. It would seem that in that case Jones has become acquainted with b, even though given his total system of beliefs, every proposition P that implies a proposition about b having some property F is less reasonable for Jones to accept than the corresponding proposition about a having F. Again, I am not sure that this is a counter-example for I am not sure of what 'more reasonable' means.

The queries raised above about Chisholm's formal definitions are quenched by the running commentary, which is discussed below. There is no full bridge between the two in the text. Nevertheless Chisholm holds in the running commentary the bold thesis, formulated in his informal presentation of his view of direct acquaintance with the self, that:

The second clause (ii) in D. I.7 and D. I.7A may well be redundant; for, it would seem, every state of affairs that is self-presenting for a given person is one that implies him to have a certain property. (p. 30; the qualifications on the claim seem to be merely expository)

Thus, it seems that acquaintance as intended in D. I.7 is to hold only for oneself, and not for objects or twin persons. This would, patently, be a very strong regimentation on the meaning of 'acquainted'. Clearly, for such a strongly stipulative definition, there is no point in looking for counter-examples in the ordinary use of the expression 'acquainted'. One has a *technical term,* and that's that.

VII. The Force of Chisholm's Acquaintance with the Self: Methodology

Let us try definition D. I.7A (and, hence, D. I.7) on first-person propositions. Let us consider one of the form *I am F now,* and let it be true, so that clause (i.1) is met. If being F is an experiential property, like being with a pain on the neck, being tired, being thinking that $2 + 3 = 5$, then conditions (i.2) *seem* to be met. Chisholm takes as the requisite individual concept the property of being identical with me. Clearly, *I am F now* logically implies that something is identical with me and is F now. Further, it would *seem* that whoever accepts that I am now F believes that something is identical with me and is F now. I am, of course, identical with me. Hence, it *seems* that clause (ii) is met. Therefore, as Chisholm wants it, it *seems* that I am acquainted with myself. We shall challenge this below. But for the moment assume that it is all right.

On that assumption, what has Chisholm really done? He has proven that given certain obvious facts and his technical definition of 'acquainted', each one of us is acquainted with him/herself. Now, is this proof what Chisholm led us to expect as a refutation of Russell's claim that the self is not empirically discoverable, or Carnap's that the given is subjectless? I do not believe so. I do not mean to bring back the previous observations about the imprecisions of Chisholm's definitions or the twin counter-example. I am for the purpose of this new issue assuming that Chisholm's definitions D. I.1–D. I.7 are perfectly clear, precise, rigorous, and that they unambiguously allow us to prove for instance, from the fact that I am in pain now, that I am acquainted with myself (me, my self). The point I want to make is that neither Russell nor Carnap nor Sartre denies, I believe, that there are facts that we describe by saying "I am in pain now." I feel very confident that none of those gentlemen denied that one *can define* a sense of 'acquainted with' so that it would be correct to infer from those facts that one is acquainted with oneself, or even acquainted with oneself and nothing else. Chisholm's definitions are especially devised so as to allow us to say that we are acquainted with ourselves. The insights those definitions provide do *not* pertain to the nature of the self as a particular in the world: they pertain to the way in which states of affairs involve properties.

To clarify the point consider the case of our ordinary experience of the apparent motion of the sun around the earth. We say that the sun rises in the east, fades into the west, that its movement around the earth takes about twenty-four hours, etc. We say those things and see that movement. Astronomical research has revealed to us that the sun does not really (physically) move around the earth. Evidently, an Aristotelian-Ptolemaean philosopher can construct a string of very precise definitions of what it is really to move at time t from place p to place p' with the aid of which from the ordinary observations about the positions of objects in the perceived sky we can conclude that the sun *really* moves around the earth. What is a Copernican to respond?

I do *not* claim that Chisholm's definitions are or are not Aristotelian-Ptolemaean in the above sense. I merely pose the methodological question: How can we establish that they are not? It is of the greatest moment that they *not* be Aristotelian-Ptolemaean.

One thing is evident to me. Russell's, Carnap's, and Sartre's remarks about the self are not meant to repudiate our ordinary ways of talking, nor were they meant to claim that the statements we take to be true in ordinary life, like 'I am in pain', etc. are not true. I feel strongly convinced that they were making *theoretical* claims, which were, besides, meant to be compatible with the ordinary truths. To see exactly where Chisholm collides with them, a careful exegesis of their remarks is required. There is no room, unfortunately, for such an exercise here. A few preliminary comments may suffice to indicate that the issues are complex.

The sort of thing Russell says lies naturally in a network of interesting assumptions. One of them is that, as Chisholm has also assumed (see pp. 98–99 above), the sense of 'I' used to refer to the subject of experience cannot be captured by expressions referring to one's body or to any other physical object. Another assumption is that ordinary individuals are in some sense substantial, they seem to involve substrates, and there seems to be no substrate in the pure subject of experience. Another assumption is that there seems to be nothing that may be called the internal structure of the self that can be the seat of mental powers. This is actually a part of the preceding assumption. A further development is that there seem to be correlations among the powers of the body and the mental powers, thus making the subject of experience ethereal. The lack of powers goes with the lack of nature and substance in those assumptions. (If mental dispositions (powers, abilities) correlate with dispositions of the body, and states of consciousness correlate with states of the brain (and the body and the circumstances), it would seem that the subject of experience correlates with the body. That leaves the self idling.) It is the substantiality of the self that is at issue. Thus, once again, we come to the need for facing the deep metaphysical issues about (ontological, not epistemological) individuation and about predication. See Section IX below on the non–worldliness of the self.

Carnap's remark about the subjectlessness of the given is important. He is seizing firmly to the data constituted by what we called above *cogitatum-propositions*. He is undoubtedly assuming a good deal of what Russell assumes. And because of an anti-substantiality program he views selves as systems of experiences. But the ordinary data are left as data, indeed they *are* enthroned as criteria of adequacy for those theoretical constructions. The self is to be constructed precisely because there *are* true ordinary statements in the first-person. These statements, on the principle that the appropriate theoretical constructions are filled in with empirical content, are expected to turn out to be true.

Let me underscore that I am not defending Russell's or Carnap's views. I am merely making the general methodological point that:

(M*) Theories about what there is are neither refuted nor established by definitions.

Theories must be refuted by being shown to be false, or inconsistent; by being shown to be unable to illuminate the data for which they were proposed; by being shown to be incapable of being extended to accommodate other data; or by being shown to be more complex in some interesting way than alternative theories that cater to precisely the *selfsame* data. Perhaps another methodological principle may be noted at this juncture:

(M**) A theory, especially one about what there is or exists, cannot be simply a string of definitions.

Because of (M**) Chisholm's commentary alongside his definitions turns out to contain his main philosophical contribution.

VIII. The First-Person Difficulty with Chisholm's Acquaintance of Self

At the beginning of Section VII I said that Chisholm's definition of 'acquainted with' *"seems"* to allow that I am acquainted with myself given that I now, incorrigibly, let us say, am in pain. But is this really so? Let us go through the computation slowly.

The crucial step I am interested in is the one involving definition D. I.3, the one implicit in clause (ii) of D. I.7, and appearing in D. I.7A as step (ii.ii′), namely:

(11) whoever accepts p believes that something is F and G*, (where G* is an adjective corresponding to the noun G, standing for an individual concept).

This clause, part of D. I.3, has been carefully formulated by Chisholm. Note the contrast between 'accepts' and 'believes'. Accepting is a relation between a person and a thing, which is a state of affairs, a species of which are propositions. The term 'believes' Chisholm analyzes as an "abbreviation" of a special construction involving 'accepts', as follows:

D. C.1   S believes that p = Df S accepts the proposition that p. (p. 161)

We have here, Chisholm says, "the paradigmatic expression of belief *de dicto*" (p. 161). Let us consider Chisholm's own example, but transferred to me, which he discusses on pp. 30f. Thus, I am applying definition D. I.7 (or D. I.7A) to *me*, in order to determine whether I am acquainted with myself. I use the following materials:

    p: *I am feeling* (feel) *depressed now* (p. 30);
    G: *being I,* or *being identical with me* (p. 31);
    F: *(being) feeling depressed now.*

Feeding these into (11) we find:

(12) Whoever accepts that *I feel depressed now* believes that *something is feeling depressed now and is I* (or, *is identical with me*).

But is (12) really an instantiation of (11)? No. To see this we need some obvious data about the first-person pronoun.[15] The minimal points are these:

(I*)   First- and second-person personal pronouns and demonstrative locutions have *always* the largest scope in the sentences where they occur. In the terminology Chisholm uses (but I do not like): they occur *de re*. I prefer to say that logically they are always external to the modalities and contexts containing them.

(I*.1) First- and second-person personal pronouns and demonstrative locutions always express references by the speaker.

(I*.2) First- and second-person personal pronouns and demonstrative locutions are *not* mechanisms for attributing demonstrative reference.

(Q*)   Demonstrative reference is attributed by means of quasi-indicators.

Let me explain (I*)–(I*.2) first, then return to (11)–(12), and then discuss the significance of (Q*) in Section X. Consider, in order to use another example of Chisholm's on p. 30, the *de dicto* construction:

(13) Jones believes that the editor of *Nous* is happy.

Clearly, part of the point in calling (13) *de dicto* is that the subordinate clause is *all* within the scope of 'Jones believes', to put the point syntactically. Semantically, the point is that if Jones were to express what he believes he would proffer assertively either the same subordinate clause, or a sentence that expresses the *selfsame* proposition (state of affairs, truth, choose your term) that 'the editor of *Nous* is happy' expresses. Ontologically, then, the prefix 'Jones believes that' expresses a modality of *the proposition* (whatever the words used to formulate it in any language):

(13.s) The editor of *Nous* is happy.

In terminology I have employed since 1968,[16] the subordinate clause in the *de dicto* belief construction (13) is *propositionally transparent* in (13): the whole of (13), by being *de dicto*, reveals the proposition that is the content of Jones' belief. In consequence, the speaker of (13) attributes to the Jones in question possible references to someone as the editor of *Nous* in order to attribute to him being happy.

Compare now (13) with its first-person counterpart:

(14) Jones believes that I am happy.

Evidently, *(i)* the speaker of (14) is not even suggesting that Jones can refer to the person to whom he attributes being happy in the first-person way; *(ii)* the truth of (14) does not require that Jones express what he believes by saying "I am happy" or some other sentence that includes a first-person pronoun; *(iii)* the reference expressed by I in (14) is made by the speaker to himself, and is not attributed to Jones; *(iv)* the logical form of (14) is

(14.a) I am the same as α and Jones believes that α is happy.

The point of (14.a) is primarily to indicate that since the first-person reference is not attributed to Jones, it logically belongs outside the scope of the prefix 'Jones believes that'. Naturally, (14.a) is only the formulation of a datum. Theories will have to start from there, and there are initially several alternative theories:

(a) 'α' is only a schematic letter representing substituends determined by context;

(b) 'α' can be taken as a variable of quantification, and the whole of (14.a), without Quine's corners, can be existentially quantified; etc.

Of course, theories of type (b) will have to spell out the substituends and the values of those quantifiers. I have my views[17] on the matter, but this is not the place to discuss them. In my terminology since 1968, (14) is *propositionally opaque*. The pronoun I in (14) merely occupies, as registered in (14.a), the place of an expression, coreferring with the use of I in (14), but a third-person expression available (*modulo* translation into other idiom or language) to Jones. Hence, there is a gap or opaque element in the information provided by (14) about the content of Jones' belief. Although (14) tells us what the property predicated in the proposition Jones believes is, it does not tell us what the subject is. There is a certain converse relationship between Quine's referential opacity and my propositional transparence. But things are more complicated.[18]

Let us return to (12). Taking our cue from (14.a), we can reveal the ontological content of (12) as follows:

(12.a) I am α and now is time β and: whoever accepts that α feels depressed at β believes that something is feeling depressed at β and is α (is identical with α).

Whichever theory ((*a*) or (*b*)) we adopt about 'α' and 'β', the fact is that the individual concept *being I* cannot literally pass the test demanded by D. I.7 (and D. I.3), namely: the test of being part of a proposition in the epistemologically interesting sense conceived by Chisholm: *first-person individual concepts seem to be private to each person, and cannot be thought by others in the way Chisholm envisioned in D. I.3 and D. I.7.*

The preceding difficulty is momentous. Chisholm's claim of direct acquaintance with the self is grounded on *precisely* those features of first-person reference that break definitions D. I.3 and D. I.7. The predicament comes forth very forcefully in the following passage:

> In other words, 'being identical with me', when I use it, has as its intention my haecceity; when another uses it, it has as its intention that person's haecceity. There is no contradiction or absurdity in affirming this and also affirming that 'being identical with *him*' does not intend anyone's haecceity. This latter view will, in fact, be suggested below. (p. 198, note 14)

In short, third-person references do not express or intend anybody's haecceities, only first-person references do. This is the idea of the primacy of the self and what intimates the view that one's states are alone self-presented to one, and that one is acquainted (in Chisholm's technical sense) with oneself only. Put informally this involves a truth of great importance. This is the truth, in my 1967 formulation, that:

> [N]o first-person proposition is identical with any third-person proposition, if both are in *oratio recta*. [The restriction belongs to quasi-indexical reference. That is,] Propositions about a given I can be the full objects of belief (knowledge, assumption, assertion, etc.), only if the belief (knowledge, etc.) in question belongs to that same I. (Castañeda 1968b, 263)

This important truth is the one that Chisholm's definition D. I.3 runs up against: its clause (ii) requires that *all* concepts, whether individual essences or not, be necessarily intersubjective: that the very selfsame individual concept be necessarily part of the proposition *everybody* accepts to be part of an identifying proposition! But by the very nature of first-person concepts they cannot pass that intersubjective test. Chisholm's definitions D. I.6–D. I.11 inherit the first-person malady from D. I.3.

The difficulty is actually much more serious than what I have indicated. It is not only the first-person reference, built into the individual concept G, which creates trouble. This is the α-problem of (12) and (12.a). The third-person indexical reference made with 'now', which is part of the property being F, also creates havoc. This is the β-problem of (12) and (12.*a*). Obviously, there are similar problems with demonstrative references to place (expressed with 'here'), demonstrative references to objects and persons (made with 'this', 'that', and compounds containing them), and second-person reference (made with 'you'). The reader can rehearse the moves by him/herself.

In brief, definitions D. I.3 and D. I.7 make it impossible to establish that one is acquainted with oneself, when this self-acquaintance is constituted by first-person reference—or whenever some demonstrative reference to oneself, to others, or to places or times is involved. They founder on the ineliminable *de re* character of indexical reference.

Can one use D. I.7 to establish, *not* that one, but that others are acquainted with their own selves? Which proposition are we to use as the proposition *p* of the definition? It is not clear, which one I can use. Given Chisholm's views about acquaintance with the self, those propositions should be first-person propositions for the others—but *we* are going through the reckoning demanded by D. I.7, and for us such propositions must be third-person propositions. As Chisholm nicely says in the preceding quotation from p. 198 of his book, the phrase 'being identical with *him*' (and any third-person phrase of the form 'being identical with X') "does not intend anyone's haecceity." Hence, we cannot use D. I.7 (or D. I.7A) to establish that other persons are acquainted with themselves.

In sum, definition D. I.7 does not allow us to establish that anybody is acquainted with him/herself, if acquaintance is connected with first-person reference.

It is of the utmost importance to understand the nature of the special first-person difficulty and the general indexical difficulty. They do not, in the customary dialectics of philosophical definition, provide counterexamples to Chisholm's definitions D. I.3 and D. I.7 (and the others built on D. I.3). Counterexamples can be serious; but they might in principle be surmountable in the standard way: revise the definition with a restrictive clause, so as to paralyze the proposed counterexample. The indexical difficulty hits at the root of Chisholm's program. Since there are no *de dicto* indexical constructions simply *there are no states of affairs or propositions that can even be subjected to the test encapsulated in Chisholm's definitions!*

Chisholm can, doubtless, pursue another, related program. He may, for instance, engage in the project of arguing that all indicators *hide* propositions of the sort he has been concerned with. I suppose that such an argument would involve a deep theory of predication and of individuation. But such an argument will have to find its data. Since it rejects the ordinary rich data provided by the extant mechanisms of reference, new mechanisms of reference will have to be invented. And the rationale for this invention must not involve circularities.

I want to conclude this section with some methodological remarks. Before that a topical preface: the problems of the self, i.e., of self-reference, are both partly the general problems of indexical reference and partly some specific problems. For this one must place the problems of the self within the larger context of demonstrative or indexical reference. Here is a case in which one must complicate the data in order to see the patterns of their structure. Otherwise, one runs the risk of reading into first-person reference more peculiarities than it actually has.

IX. The Non-Worldliness of the Self and the Demonstrative Particulars

Chisholm is definitely correct in speaking of "the primacy of the self" (p. 36). That primacy is chiefly epistemological, not metaphysical. Chisholm is also correct in adhering to the tradition that views the self, i.e., each I, as not strictly identical with a body, any body. This can be established by the arguments that show that no first-person proposition is identical with a third-person proposition. But those arguments do *not* establish that each self is not the same as a body. Recall in this connection our remarks about identity and sameness in Section II.[19] I will not rehearse these matters.[20] What I want to discuss briefly is the interesting fact, which gives concretion to several points made in the preceding sections, that the self is strictly speaking a non-worldly entity; furthermore, this is a categorial structure that the self (i.e., the subject of experience) shares with all demonstrative particulars. This follows from the indexical laws (I*)–(I*.2) formulated in Section VIII above.

Consider any sentence of English, however long and complex it may be, containing a demonstrative expression, or a personal pronoun of the first- or second-person D, say:

(15) $(- - -D \ldots)$

By law (I*) governing indicators, (15) is either logically of the form (15.a) or logically equivalent to a proposition of the form:

(15.a) D is the same as α: $(- - - \alpha \ldots)$.

Now, in the case in which D lies only in the scope of propositional or other extensional connectives there is not much point in moving from (15) to (15.*a*). We can easily regard both (15) and (15.a) as expressing different, but logically equivalent propositions (i.e., logically in the sense of ordinary logic and the "logic" of demonstratives). On the other hand, when D appears in the scope of intensional connectives, which create referential opacity, then things are wholly different. As we noted above in the case of (14), "Jones believes that I am happy," demonstratives occur *de re* always. They are referentially transparent in referentially opaque contexts. They are, therefore, propositionally opaque in such contexts. Consequently, *there are no propositions expressed with de dicto indicators:* there are no such sentences. Hence, the presence of intensional connectives, operators, modalities, or what have you, in whose scope apparently D lies, makes it clear that the proposition (truth-or-falsehood, state of affairs, situation) expressed by (15) is exactly the selfsame proposition that (15.a) expresses. I am prepared to say that the same happens in the case in which, grammatically, apparently, D lies in (15) just in the scope of extensional operators. Here, as often, the more complex cases alone reveal the nature of the elements.

Taking all the evidence into account, sentences of the form (15) are *mere* abbreviations of sentences of form (15.a). In general, then, the following principle holds:

(I**.1)   A sentence $S(i_1, \ldots, i_n)$ containing indicators $i_1, \ldots, i_n$, whether demonstrative terms, or first-person, or second-person terms, is a mere abbreviation of, or logically equivalent to (only if no i_j is in a referentially opaque position), a corresponding sentence of the form $S(i_1//\alpha_1, \ldots, i_n//\alpha_n)$, where i_h is (congruent with, or) the same as α_h, for $h = 1, 2, \ldots, n$.

Notes:

1. The singular terms $\alpha_h (h = 1, 2, \ldots, n)$ are not indexical.
2. Expressions of the form $i_h//\alpha_h$ signify that *all* occurrences of i_h are replaced with free occurrence of α_h.
3. The n sameness conditions are not conjoined to $S(i_1//\alpha_1, \ldots, i_n//\alpha_n)$ in order to stress the crucial fact that the indicators are logically (or ontologically, if you wish) never in the scope of any connective. This is not absolutely crucial: we can allow indicators to be in the scope of conjunction, negation, and existential quantification, but certainly not in the scope of non-extensional connectives or modalities.
4. The expression 'is the same' cannot be strict identity, since the sameness in question is contingent, not necessary.
5. What sense of 'sameness' is here involved, i.e., what laws govern this sameness relation, is a matter to be elucidated by a theory of indexical reference.

The important syntactical law (I**.1) goes hand in hand with the following semantical law:

(I**.2)   An indexical or demonstrative truth expressible with a sentence of the form $S(i_1, \ldots, i_n)$ is the truth of a nonindexical truth expressible with the corresponding sentence of the form $S(i_1//\alpha_1, \ldots, i_n//\alpha_n)$ and the indexical truth of each and all of the propositions of the form i_h is (congruent with, or) the same as α_h for $h = 1, 2, \ldots, n$.

Laws (I**.1) and (I**.2) are of the greatest importance. They show the way in which all the truths of the world are either non-indexical or indexical. They further reveal how the indexical truths are merely the congruences between indexical particulars and non-indexical ones. Furthermore, those laws show how the whole content of the world (broadly speaking) can be divided into the *content proper* and such congruences. The content proper may be called the *strict world*, or the *world (simpliciter)*. Clearly, the indexical particulars are the items we find in experience. Hence, laws (I**.1)–(I**.2) show how the world (broadly speaking) divides neatly into *the world and experience*.

Patently, experience is a personal matter: the uses of indicators are private to each person. This, naturally, leads to the view of private perceptual fields. But I have no spacetime to pursue these magnificent issues here. (See note 20.)

Laws (I**.1)–(I**.2) reveal an evident and important sense in which neither the self nor any indexical particular is part of the world. The non-worldliness of the self is, thus, only a special case of the non-worldliness of the contents of experience. The I, the Here, and the Now are the experiential guises of that *physical reality* that the certainty of the Cartesian *cogito* reveals. Elsewhere I have articulated this physicalistic anti-Cartesian character of the *cogito*.[21] The I is the point of Origin within each experience. That Origin is certainly revealed. In that sense we are certainly acquainted with the self. But the Origin is revealed as the way experience is organized, hence it is in a sense not empirically discoverable, as Russell said. Kant's description of the self as the unity of experience is correct, but incomplete: the organizational aspect is left out.

I do not have spacetime for an exposition of the theory of the self either. The discussion in this section has been in part meant to be methodological: how an examination of the data reveals important laws about the pervasive structure of the world (broadly speaking), and how this divides in such a way that the self is not within the strict world.

Perhaps it may not be amiss to point out some small points. Laws (I**.1)–(I**.2) apply universally. They do not describe peculiar features of English. Here we have a truly *linguistic universal*.

Given this generality, (I**.1)–(I**.2) apply *a fortiori* to alethic modalities. Thus consider:

(16) It is necessary that I be F;
(17) It is impossible that I be F;
(18) It is possible that I be F.

By those laws, these are, respectively, abbreviations of some sentences of the following forms:

(16.a) I am the same as α: it is necessary that α be F;
(17.a) I am the same as α: it is impossible that α be F;
(18.a) I am the same as α: it is possible that α be F.

Any proposition of the form [I am the same as α] has to be a contingent proposition: recall that α is a (third-person) non-indexical term. Then it is also contingent and empirical whether there is such an entity as α denotes. Thus, the second part of each (16.*a*) and (17.*a*) is false. If the modal logic in question is of S4- or S5-type, then those propositions are necessarily false, and so are (16.*a*) and (17.*a*). This shows not only the contingency of the self, but shows that that contingency is really vicarious, parasitic on the contingency of whatever in the strict world happens to be the same (in the relevant sense) to the self. *The self is really beyond the modalities:* neither necessity nor contingency applies to it: it is truly beyond the world. The proper realm of contingencies is the strict world. The self and all the demonstrative particulars *simply* are, and are congruent with the true contingencies.

The preceding has a bearing on Chisholm's definition D. I.5 of individual essence or haecceity. Applying it to what Chisholm takes to be one's haecceity, each one of us should have:

D. I.5.i Being I is an individual essence or haecceity =Df Being I is a property which is such that, for every x, x has being I if and only if x is necessarily such that it has being I, and it is impossible that there is a y other than x such that y has being I. (From p. 29; by instantiation.)

Some philosophers would be put off by the construction 'x has being I' or 'x has being identical with me'. We are, however, interested in the roles of the first-person pronoun. By laws (I**.1)–(I**.2), the definiens of D. I.5.i has nothing but *de re* occurrences of 'I' (or 'me' in the variant instantiation using 'being identical with me'). Hence, it is merely an abbreviation of something of the form:

(19) I am the same as α: being α is a property which is such that, for every x, x has being α if and only if x is necessarily such that it has being α, and it is impossible that there is a y other than x such that y has being α.

Clearly, in case (19) is true, it may perhaps establish that [being α] denotes an individual essence. I do not want to question this. We have already in Section VI queried whether Socrateity, or being Socrates, is necessarily had by Socrates. The point here is that 'being I' and 'being identical with me' do not denote an individual essence in the sense of Chisholm's definition D. I.5.

In sum, because of the laws governing indexical reference, no indexical expression, whatever its grammatical person, can express or denote an individual essence as Chisholm defines this locution in D. I.5.

X. Attribution of Indexical References and Individual Essences

First-person reference is the form of genuine self-attribution. But self-attribution, as emphasized above, is a special case of indexical reference. This is emphemeral and personal. As noted above, others cannot make our indexical references. But they can be captured and they can be made non-ephemeral and inter-personal. The conceptual (and linguistic) means for thinking and even expressing others' indexical references I have called *quasi-indicators*. The possession of a quasi-indexical mechanism of reference *and* attribution is a necessary condition for thinking of and communicating with others about third others.

Consider the old example:

(20) The editor of *Soul* believed in this house yesterday that he (himself) was a millionaire there then.

Evidently, (*i*), 'he (himself)' is in (20) a relative pronoun having as antecedent 'the editor of *Soul*'; (*ii*) 'he (himself)' represents in the context of (20) an occurrence of the first-person pronoun in the editor of *Soul's* language: had he expressed in English what according to (20) he believed, he would have said: "I am a millionaire here now". Further, (*iii*) 'he (himself)' is not an indicator—indicators have no antecedents; (*iv*) 'he (himself)' is both grammatically and logically in the scope of the prefix 'the editor of *Soul* believes that'; (*v*) the antecedent of 'he (himself)' i.e., 'the editor of *Soul*' is not in the scope of 'believes that'. Hence, the psychological verb 'believes' separates the quasi-indicator 'he (himself)' from its antecedent. Moreover, (*vi*) the quasi-indicator 'he (himself)' *cannot* be replaced with its antecedent (or any expression co-referring with its antecedent) *salva propositione*—let alone *salva veritate*. To see this crucial point compare (20) with

(21) The editor of *Soul* believed in this house yesterday that the editor of *Soul* was a millionaire there then.

Clearly, (20) can be true and (21) false: for instance, in case that the editor believed that he was a millionaire but had yesterday no idea at all about his being appointed to the editorship of *Soul,* and thought that the editor was still poor old Richard Penniless. Moreover, (21) can be true while it is the case that (20) is false: for example, the man who was yesterday attending the probation of a will bequeathing two million dollars to the editor of *Soul* was just before that, unbeknown to him, appointed the editor of *Soul.* Hence, neither (20) implies (21), nor (21) implies (20). Obviously, the same holds for any term replacing 'the editor of *Soul*'.

Evidently, the word 'then' in (20) is also a quasi-indicator, having 'yesterday' as its antecedent: the six conditions (*i*)–(*vi*) hold for 'then' and 'yesterday' *mutatis mutandis*. Likewise, the word 'there' and the phrase 'in this house' satisfy conditions (*i*)–(*vi*) *mutatis mutandis*. Thus, 'there' is in (20) a quasi-indicator.

Obviously, not all uses of the words 'he (himself)', 'there', and 'then' conform to (*i*)–(*vi*). Sometimes they are indicators; sometimes they have other roles. For convenience, I have introduced the semi-technical terms 'he*', 'there*', 'then*' to represent the quasi-indicators above described.

Now, on page 37 of *Person and Object*, Chisholm considers a segment of the preceding data that pertains to the first-person pronoun. He tries to bring it under his program of explaining self-awareness in terms of individual essences. The segment of the data he caters to is this:

> Castañeda has shown that the statement of self-attribution, such as 'Jones believes that he himself is wise' (S), is not implied by the corresponding quantified statement, 'There is an x such that x is identical with Jones and x believes that x is wise' (Q). (p. 37)

Chisholm sees the problem of the quasi-indicator 'he*' as follows:

(Q6) What, then, does (S) tell us that (Q) doesn't? (p. 37)

This question is undoubtedly the proper one to ask in the light of the datum singled out for treatment. Yet I must enter a methodological *caveat:*

(M***) One must theorize taking into account *all* the relevant data available at the time of theorization.

I hurry to clarify that (M***) is a most difficult principle to follow in philosophy. The data are so widely scattered, and they are so hard to muster and process, that one is bound to leave relevant data out of consideration. One can only try to theorize on comprehensive data. Clearly, we must avoid the not uncommon *coffee-pot approach*. Imagine a scientist claiming to be interested in nothing but the data pertaining to the transfer of heat from the electric wire, to the iron burner, to the coffee pot, and to his coffee water: he is not, he says, interested in the claims about heat obtained from fancy laboratory experiments; hence, for him the old caloric theory is good enough.

Chisholm has my admiration for having gathered the rich collection of data (C. D.) described in Section II; and, as we have seen, he has added more data along the way. My complaint is that there are more data about quasi-indicators (and indicators) than the datum he is trying to do justice to.

In any case, Chisholm embodies his solution to (Q6) in his last formal definition in chapter 1 *of Person and Object*, namely:

D. I.11   S believes himself to be F =Df There is an individual essence C such that (a) a proposition implying S to have C is self-presenting for S and (b) S accepts a proposition which entails the conjunction of C and the property of being F. (p. 37)

Chisholm comments that:

(Ch)   If I am right in suggesting above that no one knows any proposition expressing the individual essence or haecceity of anyone other than himself, then we may simplify D. I.11 by dropping clause (a) altogether. (p. 37)

Thus, D. I.11 and (Ch) constitute an account of our attribution of self-reference to others: an account, then, of the quasi-indicator 'he*' illustrated in (20) above. Let us reflect on this account.

One preliminary: the form 'S believes himself to be F' is ambiguous in ordinary language. It is sometimes used to express that a person X believes a certain person Y to be F and that X happens to be Y, whether known to X or not. It can also be used to say that a person X has self-belief: the proposition X believes is a first-person proposition. I prefer, in order to avoid ambiguity, and for greater generality as we shall see, to use the form 'S believes that he* is F' or 'S believes that he (himself) is F'. These forms clearly place the quasi-indicator in the scope of 'believes'. Chisholm's definiendum in D. I.11 is too narrow: the English infinitive does not have the richness of the indicative mood—let alone the combined richness of the indicative and the subjunctive and the optative moods. We must turn to the 'that'-construction, anyway, as in, e.g., 'S believed that he* would be happy a month later' and 'S believes now that he will be happy'. Hence, I will read D. I.11 charitably as having in its definiendum a general 'believe-that' construction.

The exciting thing about D. I.11 is, of course, its definiens. The first remark is that, as discussed above, there seem to be no individual essences in the sense Chisholm defines in D. I.5, especially if individual essences are to involve first-person reference. This is the first-person difficulty we explained above in detail. Clause (b) of D. I.11 sends us back to definition D. I.3, which is the one that requires an impossible intersubjective test. Yet (b) is, as Chisholm emphasizes in (Ch), the one indispensable clause in D. I.11 because of that required first-person reference. The internal tension in D. I.11 is as intense as it is palpable. Recall further that the first-person difficulty is only one prong of the multiple-prong indexical difficulty.

D. I.11 has another problem of its own, viz. *the quasi-indexical difficulty.* Consider this example:

(22) The editor of *Soul* believes that he* is a millionaire.

Let us try D. I.11 out on (22). It yields:

(23) There is an individual essence C such that (a) a proposition P implying the editor of *Soul* to have C is self-presenting for him, and (b) the editor accepts a proposition Q which entails the conjunction of C and the property of being a millionaire.

So far so good. Which property is C? Which propositions are P and Q? We should be able to tell. One would expect with all the information available to be able to develop (23) into:

(24) There is an individual essence C, *namely: – – –* such that a proposition P, *namely: – – – . . .* a proposition Q, *namely: – – –. . . .*

But we can't. The individual essence C cannot be *being identical with the editor of* Soul. This involves no self-reference: recall property *(vi)* of the quasi-indicator 'he*'. The individual essence C cannot be *being identical with me.* This would be the individual essence of the person who utters sentence (22): recall properties (I*)–(I*.2) of indicators. The individual essence C cannot be *being identical with him* (or X), where 'X' is a third-person non-quasi-indexical term: recall that Chisholm has said that this expression denotes no individual essence: besides, it lacks self-reference, so that it cannot capture the force of 'he*': recall property *(ii)* of 'he*'. The individual essence cannot be *being identical with himself*:* recall properties (i), *(iii)*, and *(iv)* of quasi-indicators: they are relative pronouns and are internal to a clause in *oratio obliqua*, i.e., lie logically and grammatically in the scope of a psychological verb (they are *de dicto* in customary terminology): the 'himself*' there would be dangling.

The preceding shows not merely that we cannot tell which individual essence C is in the sense that we lack knowledge of it. We do have the relevant knowledge. What is missing is the essence itself. The difficulty is ontological, not epistemological. Epistemologically the definiendum of D. I.11 is perfectly clear—aside, to be sure, from the ambiguity discussed above. In fact, the definiendum 'S believes that he* is F' is ontologically very clear. It is *propositionally transparent*, in the terminology explained above: it tells us quite openly that the person S has a state of believing whose content is a first-person proposition. And we already know that first-person propositions are about the non-worldly origin of S's experiences. Since believing is a dispositional state, the experiences in question are exercises of thinking that count as manifestations of that disposition. Because of this and many other reasons deployed in my papers I have claimed that the quasi-indexical mechanism for the attribution of self-reference is *irreducible* to other mechanisms of reference. I have urged this thesis as one prong of the more general thesis that each of the different quasi-indexical mechanisms is irreducible. I insist, however, that I have not proven this thesis. But any disproof has, in accordance with (M***), to consider *all* the data so far gathered. Fortunately, a large amount of data has been packaged together.

XI. Cogitatum Propositions and Consciousness

We are now ready to reflect on Chisholm's final section of Chapter I (part (v) of Section I above): his informal discussion of our awareness of the self. That section deals with the crucial assumption left pending in Chisholm's argument (8) examined in Section IV above. Recall how heavily, although Chisholm does not remark on it, his account of direct awareness of self rests on his ignoring *cogitatum* propositions. As noted, if there are entities whose *esse* is *percipi*, such entities and their perceptual properties compose states of affairs that will necessarily lie in the consciousness of the perceiver in relation to whom they exist. Yet even if the perceiver in question is capable of thinking such states of affairs, he (or it) may yet not be able to think of himself in the first person way. That perceiver would be an Externus. I have already pointed out that Chisholm's view of awareness of self does not seem to allow of a development to a general theory of awareness, which also accounts for the different degrees of the awareness of animals. Chisholm, of course, need not be moved by this naturalistic argument. In vintage Cartesian tradition he may simply insist that animal consciousness is just a *toto coelo* different thing from human consciousness, which requires awareness of self in the first-person.

In Section IV we discussed ordinary human unreflective consciousness. This still seems to me to be a serious problem for Chisholm (wholly independent of the indexical and quasi-indexical difficulties discussed above). There are two degrees of the problem:

(a) *cogitatum* propositions about physical objects;
(b) *cogitatum* propositions about entities the *esse* of which is *percipi*.

Let us take case (a) first. Suppose that:

(25) Jones is lying on the grass watching the maneuvers of a team of ants. He is totally absorbed in what he is seeing: he is having an unreflective train of experiences. Among other things he is thinking something of the form (whether he uses words or not, although it may simplify things to suppose that he is thinking aloud): *(a) This ant* is now turning back; *(b) That ant* is lazier than the others.†

We have now the powerful understanding of indexical data gained in the preceding sections. We know, for instance, that, because of properties *(i)*–*(vi)* of quasi-indicators, discussed in Section X, the indexical references in *(a)* and *(b)* are personal to Jones, and are ephemeral, besides. But we also know that by means of quasi-indicators, everybody, including Jones himself, can freeze, so to speak, those references thus making them omnitemporal and interpersonal.

Let us focus on (25)*(a)*. The indexical reference formulated by '*This ant*' in it is Jones' own reference. It has the role of placing a certain ant in Jones' experience. Hence, that indexical reference involves *a relation to Jones*—indeed it involves a *multiple relation* to Jones. Yet the multiple relation involved in Jones' unreflective reference in *(a)* and *(b)* is *not* an internal part of the concept formulated by '*this ant*': the multiple relation to Jones merely *under-lies* Jones' *making* of it. Jones thinks of what the experience presents, but he does not think of those contents as presented, much less as presented to him.

The preceding paragraph formulates succinctly the crucial considerations that clarify Chisholm's cursory discussion of the relative and the non-relative uses of the expression 'that thing' on page 35. Chisholm leaves the matter in a very inconclusive situation, as follows:

> Which interpretation of 'that thing' is the correct one, and how are we to decide? The only way to decide, so far as I can see, is first to decide whether or not

† This example is labeled '(26)' in the text, but because there is no '(25)' and '(26)' labels a different example below, we have used '(25)'. —Eds.

to accept the thesis that I can pick out *per se* certain entities other than myself. The thesis, then, seems to remain problematic. (p. 35)

The expression 'individuates *per se*' is defined by Chisholm in D. I.10. But I will bypass this definition. I propose to look at the issue and the facts; the technical definition may turn out to be an Aristotelian-Ptolemaean gambit, of the sort discussed in Section VII above.

The fact of unreflective consciousness must be reckoned with. It prevails throughout the lower animals, because they lack the concept of the first person; and it is widespread throughout human experience, because of its *survival or economical value*. If every episode of awareness of the external world were to be accompanied by an encompassing awareness that the episode in question belongs to oneself, then one would have a deficient focusing mechanism built in in one's power of consciousness. Hence, I submit the following evolutionary hypothesis about human natural consciousness:

(HNC*) Unreflective consciousness is, on the one hand, the first stage in the natural development of conceptual consciousness; but in human consciousness it is, on the other hand, more than a stubborn vestige: it is a necessary condition for the development of most efficient mechanisms of focusing attention.

It seems to me, thus, that a look at the whole realm of conscious beings reveals that there are non-relative demonstrative references.

Now, does that show that we "can pick out *per se* certain entities [like ants, in (25)] other than ourselves"? Yes, of course, if 'picking out *per se*' means referring to entities as individuals and referring to them *without thinking* of them as being related to us, the thinkers. That kind of reference is precisely the one that takes place in unreflective consciousness. Yet, even in the unreflective consciousness of absorbing perceptions, objects are referred to, picked out, by virtue of their relations to the experiences of the perceiver. Hence, there is a sense in which every object one picks out in unreflective consciousness is identified in relation to oneself. After all, as Kant said, all experiences must belong to one self, and must be *able* to be accompanied by an "I think." Therefore, we must distinguish between (i) a person S identifying an object O by thinking of it as being related to himself in some way or other, and (ii) S identifying O demonstratively, which involves S's finding O in experience, i.e., S's finding O as a consequence or result of S being related to O by an experiential relation. Obviously, in either of the cases there are always underlying causal relations that make it feasible for S to think of O, whether as related to him, or as not related to him. As one should have expected, this distinction is exactly the same one we discussed in Section IV concerning the ambiguity of the locution 'it seems to me'.

We can agree with a weaker thesis that Chisholm does not formulate: *We can identify objects only* in relation *to ourselves.* This gives us a clear sense of the primacy of the self he wants. But unreflective consciousness, whether of Externus type or not, establishes that a person does identify objects *without reference* to himself. The fact is that reference just is more variegated than Chisholm allows; in the light of hypothesis (HNC*), this fact is of great significance regarding the connection between consciousness and the world.

Let us proceed to case *(b)*. Here again we must insist on the distinction between identifying an entity in relation to oneself and identifying it with reference to oneself. We are now dealing with entities whose *esse* is *percipi*, e.g., afterimages, optical illusions, itchings, and pains. In unreflective consciousness I can be aware of an afterimage. Thus, I may be identifying the after-image without referring to me. But since the afterimage is causally mine, its very existence is relative to me, and my identification of it is relative to me. Similarly for the other examples.

One can, it seems, apprehend *cogitatum* propositions without apprehending *cogito* propositions. This, as we have seen, collides with Chisholm's claims. And he, correctly, takes up the issue of sense-data in the concluding section of his essay. Unfortunately, *sense-datum theories are not really at issue.* Those theories include highly specialized tenets that are irrelevant to the problem confronting us and Chisholm now. Thus, some of Chisholm's arguments are only of marginal interest for our present purpose, although some of them are very important. Furthermore, our issue here pertains to the *data* involved in unreflective consciousness, and it should be dealt with in their own terms, without bringing in conflicts among theories. Fortunately, however, in addressing himself to the sense-datum theories Chisholm does produce some relevant data. His theory disavows the act/content distinction in consciousness, and it is relevant to nonphysical-*cogitatum* propositions.

On pages 46ff. Chisholm makes some shrewd observations about the self. Then he asks on page 47:

(Q7) Could it be that a person might be aware of himself as experiencing *without* thereby being aware of himself?

He tackles this question by considering sense-data or appearances. I am puzzled by this turn of events. The issue that was left pending in Chisholm's informal exposition of his view (pp. 24ff.) is whether his tenet (6) above is correct, namely: whether whenever a person knows something directly he knows himself directly. This is the issue involved in unreflective consciousness and entities the *esse* of which is *percipi*. Question (Q7) is *not* what we want. We can immediately agree that the answer to (Q7) is "No." We still want to know whether one can know directly some entities without at the same time knowing oneself. This is the issue whether or not Chisholm's tenet (6) above is true.

To set aside irrelevant matters, let us agree that phenomenalism is mistaken: physical objects are not systems, collections, bundles of sense-data:

when we perceive a physical object, we are perceiving the object, not a sense-datum from which we infer or are otherwise led to believe that the object is before us. We grant that Prichard was right in chastising the sense-datum fallacy. Hence, there are no sense-data in the sense required by the phenomenalists or other foundationalists.

Our problem concerning Chisholm's tenet (6) still remains. The issue is whether there are entities the being of which is *percipi*. Such entities need not be the constituents of physical objects, or the epistemological foundation of our knowledge (or beliefs) about physical objects. Such entities can be known immediately *without* the knower knowing himself in the sense that his knowledge of himself involves first-person reference.

I submit, once again, that afterimages, illusory presentations in the visual field, itchings, pains, etc., in unreflective consciousness fill the bill perfectly. One can know them to exist without knowing that one has them, or is "perceiving" them. At this juncture Chisholm's arguments against sense-data become relevant. Let us look at them in order.

Chisholm's first argument is his endorsement of Prichard's sense-datum fallacy (pp. 47ff). We conceded, for the sake of enlightenment, that there is such a fallacy. Thus, we accept here that it is fallacious to infer as Chisholm describes thus:

> It was assumed . . . that whenever we have a true statement of the form 'Such-and-such a physical thing appears, or looks, or seems so-and-so to Mr. Jones', we can derive a true statement of the form 'Mr. Jones is aware of an appearance which is in fact so-and-so'. (p. 48)

What does 'fallacy' mean? This: The arguments of a certain form under consideration are not all valid: it does *not* mean that arguments of the given form are all invalid. The crucial point is this: *Statements of fallacies* (let alone labels) *are not principles of refutation.*[22] Thus, Chisholm can prove the existence of the sense-datum fallacy with an example. The example he actually gives is not satisfactory because it involves an ambiguity on the word 'appearance'. Sense-datum theorists use the word to refer to particulars; in Chisholm's example it refers to a complex of properties. In any case, assuming the example to be effective, we have no proof that examples of the form of inference in question cannot be valid. (I happen to believe that properly understood, after ambiguities are clarified, that type of inference *is* valid. But this is not crucial for our present issue.)

The sense-datum fallacy covers only one family of cases: those in which we perceive physical objects. There are cases, however, in which no perception of a relevant physical object is involved. Thus, even if the solid-called sense-datum fallacy were, *per impossibile*, a principle of refutation, it would still leave open those experiences that involve no perception of physical objects, e.g., awareness of pain, hallucinatory experiences, etc.

At this point Chisholm offers a general and really different *perspective,* namely, that states of consciousness have no objects, but have adverbial qualifications. He presents this perspective through a discussion of examples, and then generalizes reinforcing his claim with some creative grammar.

Let us be crystal clear about what is going on. We are not offered definite arguments, but a *theory*. This is fine. But theories must be based on data, and the data Chisholm offers are actually rather scanty. A good deal of weight is given to the grammatical innovations. Yet these innovations *cannot* be considered as evidence. At most those grammatical innovations show how we could express perspicuously, although with difficulty, what the theory claims. This is a precarious situation; yet I understand that it would have been hard for Chisholm to develop a detailed and full discussion of comprehensive data that would make the theory really plausible. Nevertheless, the full support of that theory of consciousness *is* an indispensable ground of his view about the direct awareness of self. We must determine how firm that ground is.

Chisholm's first datum is this:

(26) I feel depressed.

He argues persuasively (pp. 48ff.) that 'depressed' is in (26) like an adverb, saying how the speaker feels. There is no object that is felt, which has the property of being depressed. This seems persuasive.

There is, of course, a lot more to be said about feeling depressed. Feeling depressed is not a simple perceptual matter like feeling the chair for small bumps, or even feeling pain. The depression one feels has an overall character: *the whole of one is depressed*. The shift from 'feels' to 'is' is important. When one is depressed, one may not know that one is: one just reacts in the ways that count as exhibiting one's depression. When one *feels* depressed one knows something: one knows truths about oneself. Thus, it appears that (26) is not unrelated to

(27) I feel that Chisholm is coming today; I feel that *p*.

Many speakers use 'feel that' in the same way they use 'think that'. Yet in 'feel that' there is the suggestion that the thought is not fully articulated. Since the sentence following 'thinking that' does articulate the proposition that is thought of, 'feels that' tends to convey uncertainty or unclarity about the reasons for what is thought, and some overall vaguesness or imprecision. That seems to me proper. Even if 'feel that' converges with 'think that', the two verbs have different overall areas of application. 'Think' is the general verb to indicate the relationship between a person and a proposition, or parts of propositions. Thus, 'think' has an *atomistic* or *individuating* character: it singles out propositions in their unity, and signals some structure of the propositions thought of. 'Feel' in its sense related to 'think', and not in the sense relating it to touch in the way 'see' relates to vision, is *massive*: it tends to denote the relationship of thinking with less articulation, globally taking a mass of propositions as what is thought of.[23] Thus 'feel' in that propositional sense takes as companions more appropriately nouns and adjectives, which globally pinpoint a topic, which is severally dealt with by an unspecified class of propositions the person in question thinks of massively, without articulating them, and without differentiating them from each other.

In brief, I submit that (26) does tell us that the speaker is related by believing to an undifferentiated, unindividuated, and unarticulated mass of propositions about his mental state. *That mass of propositions is the object* of the feeling in question, a form of thinking, not of sensory awareness.

The propositional character of feeling (in the sense in question) is clear from a quick examination of examples. Just consider 'to feel how the axis moved', 'she felt along the wall for the lock', 'to feel insulted by his smile', 'to feel strongly about the environmental decay', etc.

Three points emerge from this extremely brief discussion of Chisholm's datum. *First,* the datum is initially more persuasive than it turns out to be after the required proto-philosophical examination. *Second,* it is wholly open whether the example, were it really satisfactory, can be the basis for a generalization to other types of consciousness.

In particular, in order to gain a sense of direction, it is not clear how much analogy there is between awareness of overall states of oneself and perceptions of particular matters, where we seem to be presented with individuals that possess definite properties. *Third,* we must engage in more careful proto-philosophy, in accordance with methodological principles (M*) and (M**) above, before we can be sure about Chisholm's ontological proposal for (26).

Armed with his adverbial role for the adjective 'depressed' in (26), Chisholm moves swiftly to perceptual consciousness. He considers examples like:

(28) I am aware of a red appearance.

He proposes to interpret (28) "in the way in which we interpreted 'I have a depressed feeling' . . . The adjective 'red' . . . is used adverbially to qualify this undergoing," i.e., the state of consciousness (p. 49). Here is *no* evidence, just a proposal. Chisholm notes that he is distorting things: the adjective 'red' is *not* an adverb. This fact about the data should be subjected to careful scrutiny. Besides, there is the rest of the grammar. Yet Chisholm tells us rather casually:

> Despite their grammatical or syntactical structure, neither sentence tells us that there are *two* entities which are related in a certain way. (p. 49)

When such a pervasive feature of the data appears, one must have a detailed exposition as to why it must be set aside. The feature is indeed very pervasive; it is not an idiosyncrasy of English syntax. Chisholm does give a reason later on. For the time being we must ask:

(Q8) What sort of evidence can there be for the claim that (28) does not say that a person (or self) and an appearance are related by awareness? What sort of evidence *can* there be for that?

This question, the absolutely unavoidable question at this stage, has no easy answer.

Chisholm proceeds immediately to *propose* that instead of (28) "we might say" (p. 49):

(29) I am appeared to redly.

This, patently, *cannot* count as evidence for the claim that the truth of (28) does not consist of a relation between two entities. Several remarks are apposite here. *(a) First*, why is the ostensive appearance of (29), which seems to be about just one entity, more reliable than the two-entity appearance of (28)? Obviously the answer has to be non-circular, which implies that we must produce the evidence for the claim about the alleged deception of (28). *(b) Second*, this becomes clearer when we remind ourselves that we are told that what (28) says about the world is what (29) says about the world. If so, why cannot one argue thus: since (28) is about two entities in the relation of awareness, so is (29), which, not being the natural way of describing the fact in question, has an imported artificial deception? *(c) Third*, obviously, an innovation in grammar cannot either create new entities or destroy existing ones. Hence, we *must* have access to those reasons that prove that (28) deceptively predicates a relation to two entities, when there is just one.

Remarks *(b)* and *(c)* can be strengthened. Consider

(30) John is taller than Mary.

Obviously, (30) is equivalent to:

(30.1) John has the property of being taller than Mary.

Have we got rid of Mary by noting the equivalence between (30) and (30.1)? Obviously not. Here we argue in accordance with *(b)*, and we claim that since (30) predicates a relation of two entities, then the state of affairs (30.1) does not show that Mary has vanished.

Clearly, the fact that both (30) and (30.1) are correct sentences of ordinary English *cannot* be counted against them. And matters will not improve were we to introduce the following new grammatical construction:

(30.2) John exists being-taller-than-Mary-ly

creating a new fancy adverb, so that we can claim that Mary has finally vanished as is perspicuously revealed by the adverbial form of (30.2). We have no relations, but just adverbial modifications of existence. Why is this unpersuasive? This is also, really, a difficult question.

Points *(a)*–*(c)* are there to save Mary from the annihilation that the adverbial account of tallerness suggests. But they are not powerful by themselves to save Mary. What really saves Mary is the fact that we are treating John and Mary differently. To be sure, tallerness is an asymmetric relation; but the roles of the relata stand in an *ontological symmetry*. We cannot annihilate Mary and preserve John. The converse relational fact, that Mary is shorter than John, will lead to the annihilation of John and the preservation of Mary. This is the internal tension that in the end vanquishes the preceding ontological analysis of (30).[24]

Now we must ask:

(Q9) Do selves or persons and the physical objects they perceive and think, on the one hand, and do selves or persons and their appearances, bodily sensations, illusions, etc., on the other hand, stand in the same symmetric ontological relation in which John and Mary stand?

This question must be answered in the negative for the adverbial analysis of the contents of consciousness to be plausible. The only way to find a justified answer to questions (Q8) and (Q9) is to turn our backs on theories and look into the data. *Innovative grammar does not help in the proto-philosophical task.* The data *alone* can help us.

An affirmative answer to question (Q9) will be supported by the contents of consciousness having certain individuality, and certain independence of our awareness of them. Furthermore, if a satisfactory description of our experiences reveals certain common elements or features from state to state, we have to provide an account of those elements or features: they must be conceived as segregated from each state and considered as individual points that account for the unity of states. But we had better look at the data.

Note, to begin with, that when one asks whether a certain entity exists or not, and the entity is an experienceable one, the proper advice is: search for the entity, and if it appears in experience it exists. Now, this obvious and pedestrian advice runs against the ontological claim underlying the grammatical innovation illustrated by (29). I have found in my experience appearances, afterimages, pains, etc.

Consider an afterimage once again. It is there, with its colors and its design. It moves with me, but it also moves by itself, depending on the conditions surrounding me. My afterimages go quickly to white walls, and if the walls recede they recede with the walls. Some move high up into the sky. Suppose the afterimage is red. Then I am appeared to redly. But this is only part of the story. I am appeared to redly, all right, but I am appeared to so *because there is a red afterimage that I am seeing.* The afterimage has a short existence, and its *esse* is *percipi;* its *esse* depends on me, on causal facts about my optical mechanism. But all *this creates* the afterimage: creation is not destruction. Afterimages are very interesting. In spite of their existential dependence on their perceivers, they have certain independence, for instance, as noted above, in their motions, in their sizes, in their duration, etc. Their colors depend primarily on the colors of the objects the seeing of which causes their existence, but they have the complementary colors.

The same considerations apply to pains and so-called bodily sensations. Pains occupy space and have volume, even disembodied space, as in the case of so-called phantom pains. They do not occur at the places where injury occurs as in the case of reflected pains. They move, as, e.g., when a big bite goes down your esophagus. Here again we must note that the movement of the swallowed stuff causes, creates, *not* destroys, the movement of the pain or discomfort. I doubt that with their objectivity, although not intersubjectivity, my afterimages and pains can be annihilated by mere grammatical innovations.

The same appears to be true from the studies by psychologists. They report that their experimental subjects' afterimages behave very much like mine. To be sure, afterimages are not material objects. They are not even physical objects in the sense in which shadows are. They do not obey the laws of physics: e.g., they collide easily with other objects without physical changes. They are not intersubjective. But so what? My world, just as Chisholm's, contains other entities besides physical individuals and their properties. The crucial thing is that a series of experiences have a unity that can be accounted for very nicely by recognizing afterimages for the particulars they seem to be. I find it puzzling that some anti-phenomenalists, in order to defend the view that we see physical objects and that these are not systems of sense-data, take it to be necessary to hold that we do not see particulars the *esse* of which is *percipi* (like afterimages and appearances). The reductionist bias seems to me as misplaced in the one case as in the other. Whole realism is wholesome realism.

Chisholm, as said before, offers reasons for thinking that his grammatical innovations eliminate perceptual particulars whose *esse* is *percipi*:

> What is the reasoning behind the present way of interpreting appearances? For one thing, [(A)] it seems to me, *we multiply entities beyond necessity* if we suppose that, in addition to the person who is in a state of undergoing or sensing, there is a certain *further* entity, a sense-datum or an appearance, which is the object of that undergoing or sensing. And for another thing, [(B)] *when we do multiply entities beyond necessity, we tangle ourselves in philosophical puzzles* we might otherwise have avoided. ('Does the red sense-datum or appearance have a back side as well as a front side? Where is it located? Does it have any weight? What is it made of?') (p. 51; my italics, except those in 'further')

Patently, Chisholm's second reason (B) depends on the first reason. If there *are* such entities as the objects of acts of consciousness the being of which is *percipi*, then questions about their relations to the rest of the world *must* be asked. To ask such questions is, perhaps, to become entangled in philosophical questions, and we might perhaps have avoided them, but to ask them and to answer them is, then, required, if we want to increase our understanding of the world and our experience of it. We can, therefore, set Chisholm's second reason for preferring his adverbial view aside with total equanimity. We must concentrate on reason (A).

Chisholm is certainly right in asserting that multiplying entities beyond necessity is a bad theoretical policy. To believe that there are entities that are not is an error; and when the belief belongs to a whole category of entities, then the error is egregious. So much for the principle.

We must, however, have a *minor premise*, namely, that to believe that there are entities like afterimages, pains, etc., which are themselves not states of consciousness but are the objects or contents of states of consciousness, is to multiply entities beyond necessity. Now, how can one show this? One effective way is this: show that there are no such entities. Obviously, to believe that entities that do not exist exist is indeed to multiply entities beyond necessity. This has not, however, been done by Chisholm. The evidence examined above is all the evidence he offers in the essay under consideration. Not only is it very slim, but as noted, it rather seems that experience reveals to us that there are afterimages, pains, itchings, appearances, etc.—individuals the *esse* of which is *percipi*.[25]

Yet, when all the above is said and stressed, we must recognize that perhaps there is no argument that can conclusively show that there are no particulars that are not physical objects and yet are the accusatives of acts of *some* episodes of consciousness. Perhaps all we can have is a very comprehensive dialectical argument that shows that the denial of such particulars is a better theory than their acceptance. I am prepared to settle the matter on these terms. And how can this be achieved? Not simply, I fear. What we need is to set out the two types of view, gather a large collection of data, and then see how the two views fare in their explicatory power with respect to the selfsame data, as described at the end of Section VII above. This Chisholm has not attempted to do in the essay under study, although other writings of his bear on the issue. Thus, I conclude only that Chisholm's fundamental premise concerning *cogitatum* propositions has not received any reliable support in *Person and Object*. Hence, from this side, too, his theory of direct awareness of the self has not been established; but, the problems on this side are of an entirely different sort from the ones created by the indexical and quasi-indexical difficulties. Here the issues are much broader and cannot perhaps be settled conclusively. All the theories we can construct are fragmentary in that they can always be, and must be because of the progressive dialectics of philosophy and in science, embedded in more comprehensive theories. Thus, the dia-philosophical exercise of examining truly competing theories may be not only exceedingly difficult, but also inconclusive: further extensions of a theory presumed defunct may resuscitate it. (See note 13.)

XII. Conclusion

I have now come to the end of my present reflections on Chisholm's essay "The Direct Awareness of the Self." I have *not* exhausted this essay: it is a very rich mine, to which I hope to return, in order to learn more about the topics it deals with. I have tried to delve into Chisholm's views in order to glean its truths, and in order to isolate what may be dead alleys. The spacetime allocated to this study has not permitted me to do a more penetrating analysis that Chisholm's work deserves. This is part of the method that finitude imposes: each wave of exegesis must be incorporated in a deeper wave, and so on.

I have made a special effort at making methodological commentaries. This is part of a deeply ingrained belief of mine. We are fortunate in having seen a great theoretical growth in philosophy in the last decades. This has created some confusions in methods and in goals. This was inevitable after the dominance of the classical analytic philosophy concerned with the analysis of concepts or uses of words—often done piecemeal, with the disclaimer of theorization. There is, in my opinion, an urgent need for serious methodological studies that can put some order into the exciting, brilliant, and diverse philosophical activities of the present generation. My interspersed commentaries are meant to be notes for a future discourse on philosophical method, which somebody should write.

The greatest philosophical illumination comes forth from the striking of competing theories against each other. For that reason I have pointed out at different junctures where alternative theories may appear. However, that was subsidiary to the task of squeezing rich and crucial data from our examination of Chisholm's essay. I believe that the data here collected can be ignored by theorists on the nature of the self and of consciousness only at their peril.[26]

Notes

1. Putnam 1975a, 132.
2. Chisholm 1976.
3. See, e.g., Castañeda 1968b, 1967a, 1977a.
4. The role of proofs in philosophical works is not seldom deeply misunderstood. Some philosophers expect philosophers to give proofs for their theories. Many are the essays written with the purpose of refuting the proofs philosophers have allegedly offered for their views. The fact is that philosophical arguments are deductive, but they do *not* belong at the connection between data and theory. Careful deductions (like Bertrand Russell's argument about the classes that are not members of themselves) must be formulated in the proto-philosophical examination of the data. Naturally, there are deductions linking the fundamental theses of a theory with the derived theses of the same theory. Thus, I am somewhat suspicious of Chisholm's examinations of the arguments he attributes to Hume and Kant in the very essay under scrutiny. Just as I do not expect Chisholm to offer deductive proofs of their respective views. This is *not* to imply, however, that philosophical views can or should be propounded without reasons. Just the opposite: I insist that there be evidence for each theory: moreover, I insist that the data should be rich, complex, and comprehensive.
5. It is not essential for our purpose here that *cogito* propositions be incorrigible in the sense that each one of them implies that the person in question, the one whose *cogitationes* are being considered, knows it. The relation between X's *cogito* or *cogitatum* propositions need not imply that X knows them. It is sufficient that in some important sense of

evidence, they have the strongest evidence for X, even if X can be in principle, or sometimes is in fact, mistaken about some of those propositions. They may be called, in Firth's expression, self-warranted. For convenience I will continue to use the term 'incorrigible'.

6. I am not here endorsing Sartre's or Merleau-Ponty's views on consciousness. All I am endorsing is the fact of unreflective consciousness. They and their coreligionists deserve credit for having stressed it. See Sartre 1943. Of course, other philosophers have insisted on that in spite of widely divergent points of view, e.g., Grossmann 1965, especially pp. 14–23, and Strawson 1959, especially 202–210, where he discusses *feature-placing statements,* which can certainly constitute the contents of an Externus-type of consciousness. See Geach 1956, and Castañeda 1967d.

7. See Castañeda 1970.

8. See Castañeda 1977a, 314–318, for an examination of the ontological commitments of Russell's analysis of definite descriptions.

9. Naturally, the illumination in question need not be a straightforward deduction of the data from the theory. Some auxiliary hypotheses about the use of language or about some empirical properties of experience or of a certain type of phenomena may be required. See note 4 above.

10. For a setting of the problem of individuation, see Castañeda 1975c. This paper accomplishes three main tasks: (i) separates the problem of individuation from the problem of differentation, with which it has often been confused in the history of philosophy; (ii) provides a metatheory of the problem, giving seven criteria for its adequate solution; (iii) offers a solution within the ontological theory of the papers mentioned in note 3 above. The issues are pursued further in Loux 1976, and Castañeda 1976.

11. See, e.g., Castañeda 1974 and Castañeda 1977a, mentioned in note 3 above. The nature of the system developed in those essays is further detailed in the exchange between Clark 1978 and Castañeda 1978a.

12. For a comprehensive substrate view see Rapaport 1978. For a recent classical formulation see Bergmann 1964.

13. In Castañeda 1978a I suggested that the highest philosophical discipline, still in the future, consists of the partial isomorphisms of very comprehensive philosophical views. That discipline I call *diaphilosophy.* Those partial isomorphisms of truly competing and incompatible views would be the ultimate structure of reality. I believe that the substrate view and a bundle-bundle view of individuation are great divides between types of theory for the diaphilosophical mill.

14. For a powerful study of necessary predication and kindred topics see Plantinga 1974. My view of proper names is different from Platinga's in this book. My view appears in Castañeda 1974 and 1977b. See also Castañeda 1979b.

15. The data about first-person reference deployed here is a very *small* fragment of the data deployed in the papers mentioned in notes 3, 7, and 14. These papers contain not only direct data about first-person reference, i.e., data pertaining to the use of the first-person pronoun, but also indirect data pertaining to the use of quasi-indicators through which one attributes first-person reference to others. Direct data of variegated sorts is found in practically all old and new discussions of the self. The literature of this sort is too huge to even start culling it. A nice representative collection is Perry 1975. Interesting data appear in Johnstone 1970, Shoemaker 1963, Jaeger 1977, and Sellars 1972. Of course, Hume, Kant, Fichte, and Hegel, Husserl, and Sartre are still very useful.

16. See the papers mentioned in note 14.

17. See the papers mentioned in notes 3 and 11, which deploy the Guise Consubstantiation-Consociation-Conflation theory.

18. See Castañeda 1974 and 1977b.

19. For a systematic effort at treating in unison seven apparently different types of puzzles where a distinction between identity and sameness appears to be required, see Castañeda 1975b. Those cases are synchronic; thus, the diachronic identity or sameness through change is not treated in the same unitary way. It is suggested that it may be of a radically different sort. This is the sameness that has interested many other philosophers. It is dealt with in detail and from many different perspectives in Perry 1975 and Rorty 1976.

20. See the papers mentioned in note 3 above. Concerning private demonstratives see Castañeda 1967e.

21. See Castañeda 1977a, II.4

22. It is so tempting to use the so-called fallacies as principles of refutation that even John L. Austin fell victim to it in his celebrated "'If's and 'Can's" (Austin 1956). He argued that Moore's analysis of 'I can' as a causal conditional 'I will if I choose' was incorrect because 'I can if I choose' implies 'I can'. The fact is this implication is a *necessary* condition of adequacy of that analysis. In general, let A be the conditional '*If* P, then Q' in some appropriate sense of '*if*'. Consider the conditional '*If* P, then A', in that sense of '*if*'. Clearly, this new conditional is '*If* P, then '*If* P, then Q'. And for the conditionals Austin mentioned, logical, material, and causal, the last conditional is equivalent (or at least implies) '*If* P, then Q', which is A. Hence, A is implied by '*If* P, then A'. The fact is that Austin's observation that 'I can' is implied by 'I can, if I choose' rather than refute Moore's tentative analysis is evidence for it. Austin discovered, unwittingly, a very interesting case which proves (again) that the so-called fallacy of detaching the consequent of a conditional is *not* a principle of refutation.

23. The massiveness of the content of feeling depressed should be understood in the light of what in Castañeda 1977a is called the *zero-guise* of a proposition (or state of affairs). The doctrine of propositional guises is introduced in that paper in order to account for the increase in the contents of attentive perception. The doctrine provides also a solution to Moore's paradox of analysis. Chisholm's example of feeling depressed suggests further uses for that doctrine, in connection with states of mind that take classes or masses of propositions, without differentiation, as contents. This would in part alter the distinction between perceptual and non-perceptual consciousness as drawn in Castañeda 1977a.

24. Perhaps we should point out that some philosophers would regard the vanquishing of all individuals as the proper result in their way to consider all truth as predicating something or other of the Absolute. In this connection see King-Farlow 1978, Parts III and IV.

25. For recent discussions of the adverbial view of perception see Cornman 1975; the review of this book in Grossmann 1976; Jackson 1975; Tye 1975; Sellars 1975; and Rapaport 1979b.

26. I am grateful for corrections of grammar and style to Karen Hanson, and for valuable philosophical queries and comments to Myles Brand, Earl Conee, Karen Hanson, William Hasker, Robert Jaeger, John King-Farlow, Mark Pastin, Irving Thaiberg, and James Tomberlin. To Tomberlin I owe the suggestion of a revision in law (I**.1).

5

Self-Consciousness, Demonstrative Reference, and the Self-Ascription View of Believing

This is an admiring understanding-seeking phenomenological and linguistic investigation of David Lewis's and Roderick Chisholm's view that all cognitive states and all thinking episodes involve the self-ascription of properties.

Introduction

1. The Accusatives of the Propositional and Practical Attitudes

There have been several criss-crossing disputes concerning what a speaker refers to when she makes first-person references, e.g., by asserting "I love to read philosophers' autobiographies," and concerning what exactly it is that believing relates a believer to. Lately the two have converged, and new ways at looking at the contents of thinking episodes and acts of stating have evolved. A fascinating development, due to David Lewis[1] and Roderick M. Chisholm,[2] is the Attribute/Self-Ascription View of believing (and intending), according to which the fundamental doxastic state is a very special state of directly self-ascribing an attribute of property. This Attribute View has been offered as a better alternative to the Classical Proposition View for which the fundamental state of believing consists of a relation relating a thinker to a proposition. The Attribute View is claimed to be better because of the way it handles first-person reference: it dissolves first-person reference by making it ubiquitous throughout mental propositional attitudes and acts—thus, paralyzing the questions about the referents of first-person references—and, ultimately, treating first-person reference as just cross-reference in psychological states.

Proposition Views have always been attacked by nominalist defenders of versions of the Sentence View, which conceives of believing as a relation between a believer and a special sentence or a class of sentences. Doubtlessly,

This essay appeared in *Philosophical Perspectives 1, Metaphysics* (1987): 405–454. Reprinted by permission of the editor.

there will be nominalist counterparts of the Attribute View according to which the primary doxastic state is a relation involving a believer and a predicate or a set of equivalent predicates. There are reasons for suspecting that there may not be enough classes of sentences or attributes to support nominalistic reductions.[3] They heighten Lewis's and Chisholm's pristine version.

Before proceeding any further, let us introduce an aseptic piece of terminology. It is customary to speak of the objects or contents of belief, or of thinking. Yet both expressions have been suspected by some philosophers as prejudicial. To cut through some verbal disputes, aiming at a problem-posing neutrality, I will continue to use the word 'accusative', or the locution 'internal accusative', which have fewer connotations. Since the fundamental dispositional contemplative mental state about the world is believing that something is the case, we will for convenience simply speak for the most part of *(internal) doxastic accusatives*, or accusatives of belief, or of thinking.

The talk of "accusatives of the mental attitudes" leaves it open for some sophisticated views to distinguish between the accusatives of belief and those of merely thinking or those of knowing. In this investigation we assume that the accusatives of thinking episodes, which include rehearsings of states of believing, are the same as doxastic accusatives. On the other hand, because what is known is true, the accusatives of knowing are better taken to be a subset of, or (to beg no questions) a domain in one-one correspondence with a subset of, doxastic accusatives. Furthermore, it is widely accepted that the accusatives of believing are the same as those of intending. I have, on the contrary, opposed this tradition for over 30 years. I distinguish between *propositional attitudes*, the central case of which is believing, and *practical (practitional) attitudes*, the central case of which is intending (oneself) and wanting (intending?) someone to do something. Thus, intending and believing differ in their internal accusatives as well as *qua* psychological reality, i.e., in the causal structures that constitute them, and, furthermore, the latter difference depends on the former. This is my old *proposition/practition* distinction. It is grounded on an enormous collection of data. Thus, I just cannot see how the current monolithic Attribute View is satisfactory. But I conceive of an exciting two-tier Propositional/Practitional Attribute/Self-Ascription View. Here, however, we cannot enter into this topic.[4]

2. Chief Objectives and Major Plan

Here my major objective is to investigate what and how much illumination the Attribute/Self-Ascription View bestows upon our experience in general, and in particular our experiences that explicitly involve self-reference. Since self-reference is a special case of indexical reference I expect to learn a good deal about indexical reference. Since for the most part we live our experiences through using a natural language, I hope to improve my understanding of the functions of the indexical mechanisms of reference in experience. Since thinking episodes are individuated by their accusatives, I anticipate learning about how in thinking we handle those accusatives.

Our plan is to place the tenets of the View in the middle of certain experiences to ascertain the structures of those experiences. This attempt at incisive delving into both experience and the View may sometimes distill some *problems* for the Attribute View. I mean exactly that: questions for the View to develop and become more illuminating. I do not wish to refute any philosophical approach. I believe that *all* plausible views on a given philosophical topic ought to be developed—really developed to the hilt. Thus, there is no point in attempting to refute other views in order to defend one's favorite view. Deep philosophical illumination is bound to ensue from the comparison of alternative theories, provided they are comprehensive and provided they cater to exactly the same rich collection of data. For one thing, dia-philosophical comparison may reveal that theories that look very different are under different terminology the same, or at least mappable into one another. But the theories may be really different. Then we gain philosophical insight by seeing the world, or a domain of phenomena, in different ways. Here Wittgenstein's reflections on the duck-rabbit design are relevant.[5] We should endeavor to see all, the rabbit, the duck, the gazelle, the tiger, and so on embedded in the master design of reality or of our experience.[6]

In any case dia-philosophical comparisons can be enlightening. They can help us appreciate better the elucidating power of a theory for a given area of phenomena. We will thus occasionally cast our glance on to other theories. In fact, let us start off with an overall comparison between the Classical Proposition View and the Attribute/Self-Ascription View. An appreciation of the former should deepen our admiration for the latter.

I. The Classical Proposition View as a Foil: Some Indexical Problems

1. The Main Tenets of the Classical Proposition View

The old-fashioned Classical Proposition View described below may be a theoretical reconstruction that perhaps no philosopher ever held in its entirety. But many seem to have written presupposing something like that. At any rate it is an excellent foil against which to see the new Attribute View shine. The view assigns to propositions a manifold of functions. Propositions are at once:

(i) *Psychological units*, as the accusatives *of all* dispositional states of mind, e.g., believing and intending, and of *all* acts that manifest or rehearse such dispositions;

*(ii) *Ontological units*, by being the possessors of truth-values in the primary sense of 'truth';

(iii) *Ontologically objective and intersubjective complexes;*

(iv) *Metaphysical units*, by having truth-values objectively and tenselessly
—'tenselessly' does *not* mean: at all times;

*(v) *Logical units*, by being the primary possessors of implication relations;

(vi) *Linguistico-semantic units*, by being the complete meanings of declara-
tive sentences, and being the core meaning of other types of sentence;

(vii) *Linguistico-communicational units*, by being the full unitary contents of
speech acts of stating: statements are stated or statable propositions,
and are the units of message suitable for the communication of information.

It is not clear whether propositions were by definition all of (i)–(vii), or
whether propositions are definitionally *(ii) and *(v), perhaps (i), and the
other theses some sort of *a priori* truths about them. In any case characteristic
*(ii) seems to be most commonly accepted as the identifying mark of propo-
sitions. The other properties may belong to propositions but not exclusively.
This seems to be the unifying pattern of the debates.[7]

The view composed of tenets (i)–(vii) is fascinating for its simplicity. All
those *unit convergencies* are powerful tools with which to build a most elegant
and unitary account of mental activity, of the connection between language,
thinking, and reality, and of the informational communication between
minds. Historical accuracy aside, that seems to be essentially the view propounded by Gottlob Frege[8] and George Edward Moore[9], although they both
condoned the violation of tenet (iii) by allowing propositions with private
components. Other philosophers, e.g., Bolzano, also deserve credit for having
contributed to its development.[10]

2. Elegance and Synchronic Virtue of the Classical Proposition View

The main virtue and power of the Classical Proposition View lies in the fact
that all those units the view equates with each other must somehow converge.
If language is to be an efficient means of thinking, then meaning and thought
content must coincide or be closely connected; if language is to be both a
means of thinking and a means of communication, then thought content and
communicated content must at least sometimes coincide, or have a high degree of intimate correspondence; if one's beliefs are to succeed in seizing
upon a real world, some of them will have to be true; if it is the same world
we cognize as we act upon, then shouldn't belief and desire coincide? Shouldn't
the accusatives of intending and will be thinkable content suited to enter the
world? Shouldn't there be a pre-established harmony between belief accusatives and intention accusatives? Frege expressed this intuition (hunch, or Idea

of reason in Kant's sense[11]) by holding that what can be believed is what can be desired, commanded, required, asked about, and so on.

Yet there are problems with the Classical Proposition View. The major problem, to phrase it as a general Kantian Idea of reason, is simply this: The View seems to be successful synchronically, but lacks dynamism. Freeze at a moment, or take an instantaneous philosophical snapshot of, a public candid and efficient communicational flow of thinking and speech. Those convergencies seem to jump into sight. There seems to be an identity between the dispositional state of believing and its manifestation in the captured thinking episode; what is thought is there, it seems, in the spoken words, a message ready to be carried to hearers by the movement of those words. The snapshot represents an ideal in which everything is open: thinking occurs out loud, language is steady and reliable, communication is frank and sincere. The discrepancies among the several units involved crop up when the frozen situation is seen as a slice within a diachronic flow, as it occurs within contexts pervaded by different and conflictive purposes, and as something that has to be prepared by undergoing shifting experiences about a steadily changing world.

In particular, we must have direct contact with the world both to place ourselves in it and to locate objects that demarcate our place in the world. This is experience. Its backbone is a succession of *performative* references to particulars, performative in that they *place* such particulars as the (our) contact points with the world. This is precisely the executive-experiential role of indexical reference: reference to items *as experienced*, or *as posited in experience* as of this or that type, in some way or another (as is executed through reference expressible by demonstrative pronouns ['this', 'that'], demonstrative adverbs ['now', 'then', 'here', 'there']), or *as experiencers* (as they are posited through reference expressed by personal pronouns 'I', 'he-she', 'you').

No wonder, then, that the Classical Proposition View comes into trouble when it confronts experience, i.e., indexical reference.

3. Some Indexical Data[12]

Consider the particular statements reported by the sentences (1)–(3) below as translations of corresponding French sentences (F1)–(F3) proffered out loud by Armand Duval, on a particular occasion on which he was reflecting on his passion for Marguerite Gautier:

(1) I love Marguerite Gautier too deeply.
(2) Gaston believes that I love Marguerite Gautier too deeply.
(3) I know that I love Marguerite Gautier too deeply!

Consider also the related statements reported by sentences (4)–(5), which are translations of the appropriate French sentences (F4)–(F5) uttered by Armand's father upon, unobtrusively, overhearing Armand's soliloquy:

(4) Armand knows that he (himself) loves Marguerite Gautier too deeply.
(5) Armand knows that Armand loves Marguerite Gautier too deeply.

For convenience we shall, when need arises, use locutions of the form 'state-ment (n)' to abbreviate 'statement made by the use of sentence (n) or of a sentence translated as (n) on the speech occasion under consideration'.

Obviously the expression 'he (himself)' in (4) represents, is proxy for, Armand Duval's uses of the French first-person pronoun 'je' in making or remaking statement (1). Patently, statement (1) is *somehow* involved in state-ments (2)–(4).

4. First Problem for the Classical Proposition View

Here he must be disjunctively imprecise to avoid begging serious questions. Roughly, to think that p, whether p, why p, is somehow to produce a repre-sentational or symbolic token that is part of a representational system. Obvi-ously, although Armand reflected out loud for our philosophical benefit, he could have reflected without muttering any sounds. Hence, the crucial sym-bolic system is an internal one consisting of patterns of brain activity, which exercised in appropriate tokenings constitutes or embodies somehow Armand's thinking. Indeed, Armand's utterances correspond really to peaking crests of the internal flow of symbolic events. This is not disagreeable to the Proposi-tion View. The distinction between episodes of sentence production and epi-sodes of thinking is already within the View: that is why it postulates the convergence between sentence meaning and thought content. The Proposition View does not have to identify an episode of thinking that p with an event in the brain, or in the whole body, which consists in some kind of occurrent representation of that p. The mind-body problem is not at stake here.

Now, the above description of Armand's reflection is built upon an impor-tant distinction, widely nowadays accepted, even though its implications are often not fully appreciated. The required application of this distinction breaks the elegant array of Unit Coincidences of the Classical Proposition View. This is the distinction between a symbolic system and its application, the distinc-tion so much underscored by Ferdinand de Saussure between *langue* (a lan-guage system) and *parole* (speech).[13] This recognizes the dynamics of language, and it is itself not inimical to the Proposition View. Nevertheless, its applica-tion to the case at hand is destructive. The above straightforward description of Armand's meditation necessitates, and casually applies, the distinction be-tween *knowing* the meaning of sentence (1) above, 'I love Marguerite too deeply'—not an exact synonym of Armand's (F1), *J'aime à Marguerite de trop*—and *using* the sentence to make a statement, to say something true or false. Thus, patently, sentences and words have meanings as parts of a lan-guage system, whether a dialect or an idiolect, whereas reference and state-ments and truth belong to what is *actually* said or thought. Patently, e.g., most of us know tacitly, i.e., have built-in in our speech dispositions, the language-system meaning of the sentence "I have one ounce of potassium compounds in my liver", yet probably no one has ever produced a token of it to make an assertion, and clearly we do not know whether it expresses a truth or a falsehood. Therefore, sentence meaning and truth-value possession do *not* coincide at least for the case of sentences containing indicators. If we continue to call propositions the subjects of truth-values, then tenet (vi) must be shunted.

This obvious result deserves some pondering. We may say that meaning in the *semantic* sense is a *lectic* matter, whether dialectic or idiolectic, using here the word 'lectic' as the adjective corresponding to Saussure's *langue* (i.e., as a succinct translation of his *appartenant à une langue*). On the other hand, in a standard terminology (after Charles Morris), reference and statements are a semantico-pragmatic affair. And here is a consequence not often appreciated: to the extent that the syntactic form of a sentence captures reference and what is said or thought, full logical syntactic form is also a semantico-pragmatic affair. Thus, semantics and semantic syntax are *schemes* built into our speech habits and dispositions, and compose the enveloping framework within which communication and thinking occur. The thought contents and the communicated messages are both fillers and further specifications of those schemes.

We must *not*, therefore, go along with the Classical Proposition View and equate the meaning of a sentence containing indexical expressions, like (1), with the doxastic accusative reported by a speaker's utterance of the sentence. What, then, is such an accusative? E.g., what is the doxastic accusative of Armand's thinking episode embodied in his uttering (F1)?

5. The Peculiar Intangibility of What "I" Refers To

At first blush an adherent to the Proposition View may respond to the preceding question straightforwardly: The doxastic accusative of Armand's thinking episode embodied in his uttering (F1), *J'aime à Marguerite de trop*, is simply the proposition we can express in a slightly regimented English as *I [Armand Duval at time T (of his reflection)] love Marguerite too deeply*. Quickly, however, this answer acquires a bad taste.

What is the role of our bracketed expression '[Armand Duval at time T]'? Why isn't the doxastic accusative in question the proposition *Armand Duval at the time of reflection loves Marguerite too deeply*? Why not, indeed? After all, our bracketed expression merely reveals what Armand is somehow aiming at, and isn't his thinking surely successful because it reaches that target? Yet this does not seem right: we must account, not only for the role of the bracketed content, but also for the role of the *bracketing* itself. The bracketing is something *we* have done to interpret Armand's utterance; the bracketing is not Armand's, and what is bracketed is not part of *what* Armand thinks when he utters sentence (1F). For one thing, Armand was reflecting but was not aware that he was doing so. In fact, secondly, he was so immersed in his reflection that during it he forgot entirely that he was Armand, that he lived where he lived, that his father was to visit him, indeed he forgot that he had any parents at all. Hence, it may very well be that:

(3) I know that I love Marguerite Gautier too deeply

and

(4) Armand knows that he (himself) loves Marguerite Gautier too deeply

are both true, whereas

(5) Armand knows that Armand loves Marguerite Gautier too deeply

is false. And vice versa. It may be that (3)–(4) are false and (5) true. Having become amnesiac Armand may know a lot of things about the man Armand Duval, e.g., that he was abandoned by Marguerite Gautier, without knowing that they are true of himself. He may pity the poor Armand Duval for having such an indomitable passion for the courtesan Marguerite, yet having no *reason* to indulge in self-pity because he does not realize that he himself is Armand Duval.

In general, a simple reflection reveals that for each third-person way of referring to Armand Duval, say, *h*, such that Armand Duval is (the same as) *h*—e.g., Gaston Rieux's friend, the Receiver General's son, the man competing with the Count of Giray for Marguerite's affection—we have a statement (5*h*) that can be false while its counterparts (3*h*)–(4*h*) are true, and vice versa too. Each third-person way of identifying Armand may be utterly unknown to Armand.

In brief, then, whereas others must use third-person ways to think and gossip about him, not only does Armand *not* need such third-person ways to think about himself, but he MUST use the first-person way to really think about *himself*, to think of himself as *himself*.

REMARK I. The two italicized 'himself''s in the preceding sentences are, like the 'he (himself)' of sentence (4) above, mechanisms especially devised to depict first-person reference. They are special cases of *quasi-indicators*: mechanisms needed both to capture ephemeral and personal indexical references and to depict them both inter-personally and non-ephemerally. From now on, we may write 'he*' to indicate the quasi-indexical use of the pronoun 'he/she (him/herself)'.

REMARK II. This semantico-pragmatic contrast between indicators (e.g., the inflections of the first-person pronoun) and their corresponding quasi-indicators (e.g., the corresponding inflections of the pronoun 'he*') is both a fundamental part of our living language and crucial clue to the solution to the problems of reference and semantics. I take the difference to be a fundamental conceptual universal and expect *every* language to signal it in some way or another.

As words are normally used with their normal meanings, the doxastic accusative that (1) represents is a most peculiar one. We may still say that this accusative is *I [Armand Duval at time T] love Marguerite too deeply*, leaving it open what sort of entity it may be.

The Proposition View is, it seems, forced to recognize that what is thought by tokening a sentence containing a first-person pronoun, whether in a natural language or in the language of the brain, cannot be some *objective* feature or entity in the world available to everybody. Thus, first-person reference clashes with tenet (iii) of the Classical Proposition View. Worse, it clashes with the opposition to everything private so well entrenched in the current philosophical mainstream. Given the present passion for intersubjectivity, the mere hint of a need to posit privately accessible egos, or selves, or I's, not to mention sense contents or pains, as the referents of actual uses of singular-referring terms, is a serious predicament. It rings absurd, "crassly implausible to postulate a *surd in nature as* the referent of a use of the first-person pronoun," cry out Stephen Boër and William Lycan.[14]

Furthermore, the Classical Proposition View cannot, it seems, maintain that the units of thinking content are identical with the units of communicational content. And once these units diverge, one question pops up: Are the units of reality, or of measuring reality, true propositions, the same as the communicational units, or are they the same as the units of thought content, the doxastic accusatives, or must they, too, also go their own separate ways?

Let us turn to a novel view that cuts the Gordian Knot of first-person reference right at its root.

II. The Attribute/Self-Ascription View

1. Enter the Attribute/Self-Ascription View: Its Major Tenets

The Attribute/Self-Ascription View is a brilliant piece of radical theorization that clears up the stage. It sharply cuts the Gordian knot of the first-person reference and puts the whole medusa of the Theory of the Self to perish by starvation. The View includes the following tenets, labeled and formulated in my own words:

(AT.1) All propositional attitudes have a uniform type of accusative.
(AT.2) That accusative is an attribute.
(AT.3) The first-person pronoun refers to nothing: it functions like a free variable representing a thinker as the subject of a psychological state he/she self-ascribes.
(AT.4) Sentences containing tokens of the first-person pronoun are used performatively to express self-ascription.
(AT.5) The self-ascription consists of a thinker being related in a unique doxastic way to attributes.

(AT.6) Persons are doxastically related to propositions via the self-ascription of attributes of the form *such that p*, where *p* is a proposition and *such that* is a universal one-one function mapping propositions into attributes.

(AT.7) Propositions are composed of purely objective and intersubjective components.

(AT.8) English quasi-indexical sentences of the form:

(f) X believes that he* is F

are preliminarily analyzed either as:

(f.a1) X believes-himself to be F,

or as:

(f.a2) X believes-that-he* is F.

Again, the asterisk '*' signals quasi-indication.

(AT.9) Propositional attitudes are not only the contemplative ones (believing, supposing, etc.) but also the practical attitudes (intending, wanting, etc.). They are all analyzable in terms of, or include, self-ascriptions.

REMARK. My formulation of (AT.8) differs in a major way from what Chisholm has proposed as his analysis of the quasi-indicator 'he*'. He defines the formula (f.a) in terms of his quasi-indexical primitive predicate. This is why I am referring to (f.a1) and (f.a2) as preliminary analyses. I am assuming a deepening Chisholmian thesis (AT.8.d) that delves down to Chisholm's final analysis of (f). That deepening provokes interesting questions about his reductionistic program. The discussion of Intensional Requirement g) in the next section is relevant to this.

Tenets (AT.1)–(AT.9) constitute the Core Attribute/Self-Ascription View. They seem to be common ground to the two (main) versions of the view known to me: David Lewis's and Roderick M. Chisholm's. Before examining them we need an additional framework of requirements for *any* theory of doxastic content.

2. General Comparison between Attribute and Proposition Views: Intensionality Adequacy Requirements

The Attribute/Self-Ascription View possesses the great merit we have explained above. But it has other virtues, some of which it shares with the Proposition View. To see this is a rewarding dia-philosophical exercise. One central constraint on any theory of doxastic accusatives is the family of Intensionality Requirements. These have to do with the internality of propositional content. Perhaps the most general way of characterizing this requirement is by means of this fundamental principle of the mental:

(Int.R*) No type of mental state or act is closed under any form of implication (logical, causal, or whatever) pertaining to its internal accusatives. In general it is NOT the case that: if P implies Q, then if at

> time T thinker X thinks (believes, supposes, knows, ..., intends, wishes, ...) P, at T X thinks (believes, supposes, knows, ..., wishes, ...) Q.

This formulation of (Int.R*) attempts not to beg any question in favor of propositions.

(Int.R*) is connected with other requirements. Let us briefly discuss some of them because they will have to be referred to in our ensuing meditation.

a) *Propositional transparency and the diaphanousness of consciousness.* The intensionality of mental states and acts is involved in the nature of a mind capable of self-consciousness, not just able to make self-references to self as such, but also to apprehend immediately the contents or internal accusatives of current mental acts for what they are. To be self-conscious that one is thinking P is to know immediately what P is. On the assumption that such accusatives are propositions then self-consciousness involves the transparence of such accusatival propositions. Furthermore, being able to enjoy self-consciousness involves a direct knowledge of the type of consciousness one is living and of which one is conscious. Thus, merely to be able to see requires consciousness of what is seen, or presented to sight, but it does not require consciousness of self. But if one can be *self-conscious* when one is seeing an object O, one must be able to be aware that the experience one is undergoing is one of seeing.

b) *Universals and their predicational function.* The proper content of thinking—and this should be called here *Plato's Principle*—is that the most suitable content for mental acts is universals. They do not have to appear as abstract individuals, but only as predicative content. To illustrate, when one sees something red one sees in one piece the *whole* of the species of redness one sees: this is the one (uni-) in the versal (diverse): the one in the many. Properties or universals are so unitary and so fully exhausted in their unity that they explain the diaphonousness of consciousness and the transparency of mental content. They also explain how there is a unity of exemplification linking the perceived to the unperceived to the unperceptible instances of the same attribute. In these respects the Attribute View is most commendable. Yet it has no definite advantage over the Proposition View. As composed of attributes propositions have all the universality of attributes, whatever it or they may be.

c) *Abstract vs. concrete.* Thinking of universals seems less problematic: they provide us with the means of distinguishing individuals from one another. The problem is to explain how we can think of individuals. At this juncture the Proposition View forks into several versions, and so does the Attribute View.

In this respect the conservative Abstract Attribute/Self-Ascription View, which rejects concrete or particularized properties (like being Napoleon's fifth son and being in between Cicero and Caesar), and sticks to abstract properties (like being a son, being in between other objects), seems to be more satisfactory than the liberal Concrete & Abstract Attribute/Self-Ascription View. Again here is no definite advantage over a Proposition view that rejects particularized propositions. (See Section 13 below.)

d) *Finite vs. infinite.* Apparently we are bound to think, so to speak in person, primarily, or exclusively, of what is finite, and only vicariously of the infinite: infinities covered by one attribute or potential infinities partially constructible by applying a rule that allows positing *another* item in a sequence. The finitude of the mind underwrites (Int.R*). Here the Attribute and the Proposition Views need not differ.

e) *Extensions vs. intensions.* Attributes, sometimes called properties and relations in intension, are the fundamental content of thinking and are presupposed by thinking of classes of instances or extensions of attributes. Clearly, classes of objects cannot be presented in person to consciousness, unless they are demarcated in some finite way and are unified by a finite attribute. We can see a set of ten cows as such if the ten cows are within view, and of course the class is unified by the property cowhood, or by some other property, e.g., being taller than the dog in sight.

The important consequence of the preceding points is that thinking of an individual as a member of class presupposes the ability to think of that individual as being so-and-so, say being F, for some property Fness:

f) *Predication is at least psychologically more basic than class membership.* Thus, an Attribute/Self-Ascription View that takes attributes genuinely so, as properties in intension, rather than as properties in extension, as what a thinker self-ascribes conforms to the fundamental Intensionality Requirement of thinking and believing. Again, in this respect there need not be any gain for Attribute views over Proposition views.

g) *Predicational thinking of a property is more basic than thinking of the property as itself subject of predication.* This is a most important requirement that complements f). That is, the primary ability necessary to possess the concept of F is the ability to think thoughts of the form *x is F*, even if one cannot think yet thoughts of the form *Fness is G*.

3. David Lewis's Attributes/Self-Ascription View

David Lewis invented the term '*de se* belief'. He starts out with the tenet that propositions have nothing non-intersubjective in them. Hence, the subjectivity of first-person reference becomes problematic. He offers an argument for his Attribute/Self-Ascription View. The argument reveals the other tenets listed above, as well as some special tenets of his own. The argument is, like all philosophical arguments, persuasive to those who accept the premises, whereas those who reject some premise can find assistance in the argument by supporting an attack on that premise by *modus tollens*. Here is the argument nearly in its entirety:

We can imagine a more difficult predicament. Consider the case of two gods. They inhabit a certain possible world, and they know exactly which world it is. THEREFORE they know EVERY PROPOSITION that is true at their world. Insofar as knowledge is a propositional attitude, they are omniscient. Still I can imagine them to suffer ignorance: neither one knows which of the two he is. They are not exactly alike. One lives on top of the tallest mountain and throws down manna; the other lives on top of the coldest mountain and throws down thunderbolts. Neither one knows whether he lives on the tallest mountain or on the coldest mountain; nor whether he throws manna or thunderbolts.

. . . But IF it is possible to lack knowledge and not lack any propositional knowledge, then the lacked knowledge must not be propositional. IF the gods came to know which was which, they would know more than they do. But they wouldn't know more propositions. There are NO more to know. Rather, they would self-ascribe more of the properties they possess. One of them, for instance, would correctly self-ascribe the property of living on the tallest mountain. He has this property and his worldmate doesn't, SO self-ascribing this property is not a matter of knowing which is his world.

I think these examples SUFFICE TO ESTABLISH my second thesis: SOMETIMES PROPERTY OBJECTS WILL DO BUT PROPOSITIONAL OBJECTS WON'T. SOME BELIEF AND SOME KNOWLEDGE CANNOT BE UNDERSTOOD AS PROPOSITIONAL, BUT CAN BE UNDERSTOOD AS SELF-ASCRIPTION OF PROPERTIES. (Lewis 1979, 520ff. the capital emphasis is mine)

This argument hinges on the relevant senses attached to the words 'property' and 'proposition'. Lewis of course explains his intended senses:

Not everyone means the same thing by the word "proposition." I mean a set of possible worlds, a region of logical space. My target in this paper is the view, until recently my own, that objects of attitudes are propositions in the sense of sets of worlds. I need not quarrel with the view that they are propositions in some other sense.

The word "property" also is used in many senses. I mean a set: the set of exactly those possible beings, actual or not, that have the property in question. That means that I shall confine myself to properties that things have or lack *simpliciter*. I shall speak of properties that SEGMENTS of the road or the person simply have or lack. (Lewis 1979, 515; the capital emphasis is mine)

There are many important things in these quotations, but we must limit ourselves to a few pertinent observations.

REMARK 1. It seems to me that possible worlds are not suitable for the role of internal accusatives of thinking. They are too large, too infinite to satisfy requirement d) of finitude and requirement a) of transparency. If mathematical set-theoretical truths belong to all worlds, then their magnitude is staggering. See Note 3. I am delighted to see Lewis demote possible worlds from the role of doxastic accusatives he had bestowed upon them.

REMARK 2. Possible worlds do not seem to me to be proper subjects of truth-values. Again I want to understand this intensionally: truth-values are intensional properties that propositions (by definition) have. Thus, since Lewis has no quarrel with propositions understood differently from classes of possible worlds, on this score there is nothing to disagree about.

REMARK 3. Because of the primacy of predication over set membership we have a concept of proposition that is small enough to be a finite content of thinking episodes. Thus, it seems more pleasurable to think of possible worlds as classes of propositions. Since they are infinitely large, the problem is to identify them in terms of either some individuals or in terms of some propositions. But perhaps we cannot individuate such classes. (See Grim 1988.)

REMARK 4. Lewis asserts that his properties are sets. If this is so, then his Attribute View does not satisfy the above intensionality requirements b), c), and f). Some of the sets he is interested in may be too large to satisfy the requirement of finitude. Yet sets of individuals are in general more manageable for thinking than are possible worlds.

REMARK 5. Except for the demand that propositions have nothing private or subjective, it is not clear why possible worlds cannot include indexical propositions. There seems to be no logical or set-theoretical or semantic reason why models cannot have unique entities that play a formal role of representing selves. A possible world can be conceived as a composite of a basic core that contains public, physical individuals, and extensions around that core containing all the I's, other indexical individuals, and all private individuals proprietary of an entity in the core. The uniqueness of Lewis's notion of counterparts is more suitable for sub-domains of private objects. Overlapping structure would be a total world, and each extension would be my *world* for each person in the world. Thus, Lewis's premise that the two gods are omniscient and they know all the true propositions there are before knowing that they are at this or that place is not evident, even if we equate propositions with sets of possible worlds. It is noteworthy that in his long argument the premise is initially a wholly uncontroversial conditional: see the capitalized 'IF's.

REMARK 6. Similarly, the claim that perceptual knowledge is non-propositional is not obvious. To the extent that perceptual beliefs involve demonstrative reference, the issue is whether possible worlds can have ephemeral and privately demonstrated particulars.

REMARK 7. The idea that *I's*, *now's*, *this's*, and *that's* are privately knowable has a point. Yet that they must remain wholly inexpressible by others is not quite right. As observed above it is precisely the function of quasi-indicators to capture other persons' indexical references by means of interpersonal and non-ephemeral quasi-indexical references.

To conclude. Our discussion of Lewis's view has dealt exclusively with the extensionalist theses peculiar to his own version of the Attribute/Self-Ascription View. Therefore, our ensuing examination of Chisholm's version of the Attribute View, which will consider the common core of the approach, is relevant to the study of Lewis's view.

4. Chisholm's Self-Ascription View: General Assessment

Let us continue our reflecting saga on Armand Duval's reflection. Recall his statement:

(1) I love Marguerite Gautier too deeply.

Recall also Duval Sr.'s statement:

(4) Armand knows that he* loves Marguerite Gautier too deeply.

According to the Core Attribute View Armand's uttering sentence (1) is simply his act of self-attributing the attribute *loving Marguerite Gautier too deeply*, and the pronoun 'I' is not really a referring expression. Likewise, in sentence (4) the quasi-indicator 'he*' is not a referring term. But there is an interesting initial asymmetry between (1) and (4). 'I' represents a *logical* gap that makes a sentence (1) a mere predicate. On the Core View 'I' is a dummy grammatical subject that functions as a logical free variable and has a performative role; it contrasts with the dummy subject 'it' in 'it is raining' and 'it is hailing' pragmatically and semantico-syntactically: in these sentences 'it' neither has a similar performative role nor is a free variable. On the other hand, for the Core View in sentence (4) 'he*', in spite of its depicting Armand's uses of 'I', neither possesses the performative role of 'I' nor represents a logical gap, or functions as a free variable. This is captured by *the* hyphenation in the preliminary analyses recorded in tenet (AT.8) above in Section 2:

(4.A1) Armand knows-himself to love Marguerite too deeply;
(4.A2) Armand knows-that-he* loves Marguerite too deeply.

The hyphenation shows that here is no dummy subject, or singular term, to account for: the word 'himself' and the locution 'that he*' function merely as syllables of the main verb, or as signals of the relevant sense of 'knows', just as indices attached as suffixes to words to disambiguate them—as we have illustrated with the appended '*' as a signal that an expression functions as a quasi-indicator.

Normally one tends to explain the senses and roles of expressions in clauses in indirect speech in terms of, and against the background of, the sentences in direct speech represented by those clauses. The Core View seems to produce an important semantico-pragmatic reversal: the special reflexivity straightforwardly meant by the quasi-indicator 'he*/she*' is precisely what is brought into existence by acts of first-person reference: the performative uses of the indicator 'I' are better understood in terms of the quasi-indexical morpheme 'he*/she*'.

Given that direct speech is basic to, and presupposed by, indirect speech, this reversed asymmetry has engendered a general suspicion about the Core View, to wit:

Contention. I suspect that the Core Attributes/Self-Ascription View is:

(A) more suitable for the semantics-*cum*-pragmatics of sentences containing quasi-indicators, like (4), than for the semantics of sentences containing the first-person pronoun, like (1);

(B) an excellent account of the involvement of the self in non-reflective consciousness, but needs complementation to account for the role of first-person reference in reflective consciousness;

(C) in need of development to account for the relations between oneself and others, as well as between oneself and the world;

(D) in need of development to account for the other types of indexical reference, which connect us directly with the world;

(E) more illuminating of the semantics and pragmatics of sentences containing quasi-indicators of degree one, like 'he*' in sentence (4), than of the semantics and pragmatics of sentences containing quasi-indicators of higher degrees.

DEFINITION. An occurrence Q of a quasi-indicator is of degree N if and only if Q's immediate antecedent, explicit or implicit, appears in a psychological embedding sentence that subordinates N-1 nested psychological sentences and the (N-1)th embedded clause contains Q.

We have seen above that a crucial ontological issue from which the Attribute View sprung forth is the perplexing peculiarities of the thought-of referents of tokens of the first-person pronoun. Among those peculiarities lies the apparent subjectivity or privacy of referents of indexical reference. Yet there is an important issue that underlies the question of subjectivity, namely: whether all properties and relations are abstract—e.g., self-identity, triangularity or being a triangle—or whether some are *individualized* or concrete—e.g., being identical with Richard M. Nixon, being taller than Ronald Reagan. Each of the different answers to this question seems to be compatible with the Core Attribute/Self-Ascription View. Chisholm, for his part, has opted for the following tenet:

(C.AT.1) All properties or attributes (including relations) are abstract. There are no individualized relations.

Obviously, (C.AT.1) raises a most serious question: If we think attributes only, how can we think of individuals? Chisholm's major task is precisely to answer this question. His task is narrowed down, and made more challenging and exciting, by his commitment to a program of ontological reductionism to stay within the most parsimonious ontological inventory.

5. Chisholm's Self-Ascription View: Intensionality

Chisholm's view is deliberately intensional. His ontology includes properties, genuine properties in intension, as fundamental entities. Concerning thinking he is adamant on there being two ways of thinking of objects as having properties, which ways may be said to determine two senses, or uses, of predicates: a comparative and a noncomparative way. Further, he insists that the fundamental concept is the non-comparative one, namely, the one used in thinking that an object is F, given a monadic property Fness, *without* any reference whatsoever to other objects as F. Here my philosophical prejudices are with Chisholm. To think comparatively that *a* is red like *b*, presupposes the ability to think *simpliciter* that *a* is red *period*, and that *b* is red *period*.[15] Of course, *in* neither case are we thinking, or *do* we need to think, of class membership.

Concerning classes Chisholm, always parsimonious, wants to reduce them to properties (pp. 8ff.). This is, however, another story. The Intensionality Requirements we have registered above do not include this reduction, nor is it evident that the Attribute/Self-Ascription View is better served by such a reduction. The View arose from the puzzles of self-reference, and its acquiescence of classes *as* irreducible could very well allow it to deal more adequately with thoughts about sets and class membership. Here we shall ignore this part of Chisholm's ontology, leaving it open whether class membership is also another primitive aspect of reality or of thought content.

In sum, Chisholm's Attribute View seems to satisfy all the Intensionality requirements deployed above in Section 2.

6. Two Types of Self-Ascription: Unreflective Consciousness and Self-Consciousness

For the powerful reasons we know, the Core Attribute/Self-Ascription View, on the one hand, eliminates the self, and I, as the object to which we attribute properties in a first-person statement, and, on the other hand, makes all thinking episodes, and all states of believing, instances of self-ascription. Thus one's thinking episodes are one's own in two ways. To think of X or that *p* is to relate oneself to X or that *p*, but at one level this is trivial, just as one relates oneself to a chair that one kicks or sits on. Here is a *self* component all right, but there is no self-reference. In thinking, besides creating a relation, one *attributes* to oneself a property, and this oneself is not an I, or ego, but simply the very same massive infinitely propertied entity that others see as making noises or kicking chairs. It is a nice picture. The View is nicely Fichtean in a moderate sense: all consciousness is diffusely self-consciousness, and all reference is tacit self-reference.[16]

The View is very adept at handling experiences of the type Sartre called unreflective or egoless consciousness.[17] Just ponder this example:

Marybel and the ant colony. A young woman, Marybel, is watching an ant colony. She is attending to the ants' antics with no self-awareness. Her train of thoughts (whatever her language may be, and we may suppose that she is thinking out loud in English for our philosophical convenience) includes this fragment:

> (MC) That ant is moving faster than this one; the ant over there! Coming out of the big hive. It is running toward that one; it is stealing the load from it . . .

Marybel seems to be doing precisely what Chisholm and Lewis say: she is relating to herself everything she is contemplating. And she is doing it through demonstrative references to what is in her visual field.

This *de facto* self-attribution seems to pervade all of our thoughts, whether perceptual or not. Armand thinks: "Gaston loves no one" and he is thinking of a person somehow cognitively related to *him*, *his* Gaston, or one of his Gastons. The Core Self-Ascription View accounts for this very well.

The View can be used to place human thinking in a scale encompassing beings that have, besides sensitive consciousness, only perceptual thoughts, lacking altogether the concept of self or of the first-person. We may say that they have only an Externus type of thinking.[18]

There is also a type of egoless experience that intrudes into oneself, and for this too the subdued self-consciousness of the Self-Ascription View seems correct. To illustrate: Marybel is so involved in her experience that even the parts of her body in view, say arms and legs, appear to her as mere parts of the scene. We may suppose that she is so fully stuck to what she is experiencing that for a short while even her bodily sensations appear to her as being there in the world, as another realm of reality, not as unified as *hers*. She may think:

> There on that leg is a little pain expanding down toward that foot, under and along the movement of that ant. The itch of this knee is growing in intensity. Now it is squashed by this finger . . . [19]

Children seem to think egolessly about all sorts of things in their environment before they think first-person statements. But in their second year something extraordinary takes place in their development, and they are never the same again. They start making first-person utterances in which they attribute to themselves something new. They now seem to be self-attributing I-properties of the form *being such that I am F*—just as on the Attribute View they had been, and will continue to be, self-ascribing cat- or Motherproperties of the *form being such that the cat [Mother] is F*.

Once we acquire the power of self-reference we are mature thinkers, but maturity here is cumulative. As we all know, sometimes we become so immersed in thought that we forget ourselves. Then something goes wrong: we discover a mistake, a sudden noise tears our ears, a little itching grows, an unexpected thought or image of something hated, or loved, crosses our minds, and then we become aware of ourselves.

In general, a little phenomenological reflection reveals this:

(H.C*) *Hierarchy of consciousness*: There are three suffusive tiers of consciousness, each one encompassing and remaining present in the following tier:

    (I) sensitive consciousness;
    (II) cognitive unreflective consciousness;
    (III) cognitive reflective consciousness, or self-consciousness.

We must distinguish between the unreflective self-*ascription* of levels (I) and (II) and the reflective *self*-attribution of level (III). This difference in self-attribution is of the utmost importance for human life, even the uncivilized one. It plays a role in building our *auto*-biographies. Because of this, we leave open at this juncture that tier (III) may itself be composed of several suffused tiers.

Urgent Clarification. In the preceding discussion we are not making a linguistic claim to which Chisholm would object, namely, that the use of the first-person pronoun explains self-consciousness or self-reference. The use of the first-person pronoun is evidence for others that self-references are being made. Whatever the connection may be between learning to master some syntax or vocabulary and acquiring a concept or a particular thinking ability, the point here is that over and above the basic egoless experiences that children and we all have, there are experiences of another type, namely; they seem to be I-unified. We discuss more profound cases in Sections 11–13, where the above hierarchy (H.C*) reveals that reflective consciousness is not one single level but a manifold sub-hierarchy.

To sum up, in my opinion the Self-Ascription component of the Core Attributes/Self-Ascription View is most insightful. Something like the self-ascription this View postulates as primitive seems to be what is going on in cases of unreflective consciousness. Because of the suffused cumulativeness established by (H.C*), unreflective consciousness is also present as a base for reflective consciousness, hence, the self-ascription posited by the View seems to be present in all episodes of consciousness. Further, we may accept that what is self-ascribed in those cases is precisely an attribute. At the moment we leave it open whether attributes may be, or have to be, individualized. The problem here is the higher story of reflective consciousness. We seem to need at least one more type of self-ascription. (See Section 10 below.)

7. Self-Ascription and the Other Types of Indexical Reference

For over twenty years I have been claiming that the several types of indexical reference are mutually irreducible.[20] If this claim is sound, the Attribute View has to be extended. First-person or *de se* reference is only the first step. We should also acknowledge belief *de te* (you), *de nunc* (now), *de hic/ibi* (here/there), *de hoc/illo* (this-that). Chisholm rejects my claim. Impelled by his reductionistic proclivities, he has proposed to analyze the uses of all indicators in terms of first-person reference. His work on this project is, however, only program-matic. For instance, a bit too hurriedly he submits that the following "analysis does not presuppose that there is an 'indexical property' which constitutes the sense of the expression 'this thing'":

(C.AT.Th)   'This thing is F' is used in English to express the following property of its utterer: believing himself to be such that the thing he is calling attention to is F. (Chisholm 1981, 46)

Consider this actual example: A little while ago, looking at and thinking of my copy of *The First Person*:

(Th.1)   I asserted: "This book is profound and brilliant!"

According to (C.AT.Th) then what happened was this:

(Th.C1)   I expressed my property: believing myself to be such that the book I am calling attention to is profound and brilliant.

Calling attention? Whose attention? I am here alone facing my computer and my own thoughts struggling with Chisholm's definitions. I uttered (Th.1) to vent my feelings—some of my feelings—about the book. Even if I had not uttered (Th.1) I would have *thought* indexically of that book. It is the thought content that we are anxious to understand. Doubtless, somebody will insert that Chisholm is in (C.AT.Th) furnishing only the analysis of the communi-cational uses of "This thing is F". This restriction of the analysis may be fair. But it acknowledges that we do not have a fundamental systematic treatment of the thinking uses of 'This thing is F'. This is a serious lacuna in a book devoted to building an account of reference on the intentionality (and inten-sionality) of thinking.

Be things as they may, let us examine Chisholm's analysis (C.AT.Th) re-stricted to the communicational uses of 'This thing is F'. Suppose, then, that my utterance (Th.1) was communicationally made to Tomis Kapitan, to whom I communicated my self-ascription:

(Th.1r)   I am such that the book I am calling attention to is profound and brilliant.

This does not seem right. Let us meditate on (Th.1r).

First, a most important element of demonstrative reference is missing in (Th.1r), to wit: the *performative* role of indexical reference. To refer to some-thing as a "this" (a "now," a "here," a "you") is to place the referent in ex-perience in focus in its proper niche. Sentence (Th.1r) is too bland: describ-ing my action as one of calling attention to something does not have the punch of actually calling attention to the thing in question. You might say: "But recall that the uses of 'I' have a performative function, and this role is bequeathed to all of Chisholm's analysands in terms of 'I'." This is not enough. The uses of 'I' are performative in a very special sense: they *self*-attribute or rehearse a *self*-ascription of a property, and as we shall see in Section 8 below they possess a holistic character. Now, however, we are confronting a different type of performative function: the placing of the item in experience, or even the calling attention to it. This performative role of 'this' present in (Th.1) is missing in (Th.1r).

Second, to pursue the preceding point consider a use of the following 'This thing is F' sentence by Professor Moriarty, who, in front of a map of London displayed on the wall, is talking to his current gang of criminals:

(Th.2) *This is* what we are going to do: You [patting John on his back with his left hand] bring *this gun* [giving it to him] and station yourself here [pointing to a spot on the map with the pointer in his right hand]; you, Paul, put *this gun* [gives it to him] in your briefcase and wait for Art *here* [another pointing at the map]; you [pointing to Mike] carry *this gun* [puts it on a table] attached to your leg; . . .

(NOTE: The italics represent my meta-linguistic emphasis; Dr. Watson recorded that Moriarty did not himself underscore any words at all.) By analysis (C.AT.Th) all the uses of the expression 'This gun' in (Th.2) will simply convey and self-attribute the property being such that the thing the speaker x IS [new emphasis] calling attention to is a gun. Each use of 'this' is a performance of singling out a gun, not, as we shall see, of a self-ascription. Each of these performances of singling out a gun must be carefully distinguished from one another; self-ascription would at best be a common underwriting performance.

Third, a follower of Chisholm might reply that the analysans in (C.AT.Th) has a present tense, the one in the *above capitalized 'IS'*, and that it captures the time and executive function of each use of 'this'. That reply may not satisfy Chisholm, for it introduces an ineliminable demonstrative *now* reference to the present time through the present tense.

Fourth, one important result is this: Each use of the indicator 'this' represents an autonomous, individual episode of reference. Nevertheless demonstrative references of the *this* type can be nested. This is illustrated by the very first 'this' in (Th.2).

Fifth, sentence (Th.2) as a whole falls out of Chisholm's analysis (C.AT.Th). This deals with predicational 'This is F' sentences, whereas the first 'This' of (Th.2) is a term in a statement of identity: (Th.2) is not of the form 'This is (the same as) A'. Statements of identity are troublesome, and indexical identities are particularly puzzling.

Sixth, now, to self-attribute a property is, as (Th.1r) illustrates, to take the property internally, predicationally, *de dicto*. Chisholm's analysis (C.AT.Th) seems to be excessively conceptual. One can do something without knowing that one is doing it. One may call one's hearers' attention to something without realizing that one is so doing. You might rejoin that this distinction does not apply when we are dealing with cognitive activity. But it does. Recall the hierarchy (H.C*) of the suffusive layers of consciousness (Section 6 above). Perhaps the mental operation of thinking something as a *this* cannot escape consciousness at all. That is, it must be present to sensitive consciousness, and perhaps even to unreflective consciousness. But it often escapes reflective consciousness. Recall that the lower degrees of consciousness are present in their higher degrees.

Here we seem to face the converse situation of that for the self: The Self-Ascription View was excellent for unreflective consciousness, whereas now for the case of demonstrative reference the proposed account, by reducing it to self-consciousness, is less apt for the basic phenomenon of unreflective demonstrative reference.

Seventh, this takes us back to Marybel and her absorption in contemplation of an ant colony. Recall her indexical statements (MC) in Section 6 above. She referred demonstratively to items in her visual field without having any awareness of herself. Her indexical references were unreflective. The same obtains for an Externus's experiences, and for Marybel's egoless references to her bodily sensations. Here we have the difference between the performative function of first-person reference and that of demonstrative reference sculpted in high relief.

Eighth, the concept of calling attention to something is very complex. Possessing it *presupposes* having the ability to make indexical references. Suppose that all demonstrative references were instances of calling attention to what is demonstratively referred to. Then to think that a case of demonstrative reference is a case of calling attention to is to classify it. Now, there are very good reasons, pertaining to vicious regresses, for supposing that one must be able to perform basic mental operations without classifying them. This is an operational counterpart of the primacy of unreflective consciousness. This point is of the utmost importance. It appears everywhere. One intriguing case is this. To believe that p (at least on the Classical Proposition View) is to take the proposition that p as true. This taking as true is itself a nonjudgmental mental operation, it involves no classification of the believed proposition as being true, much less thinking of it as, further, being related to the property truth. Thus, to come to believe that p is to perform a non-classificatory attempt at placing that p on the truth bin; on the other hand, to believe that that-p is true is, among other things, to classify that p as true.

Ninth, taking a clue from what Chisholm says about the so-called paradox of analysis, namely, that analysans and analysandum are not identical, someone might suggest that there must be a gap between (Th.1) and (Th.1r). Since (Th.1r) is the analysans of (Th.1), that someone might continue, they do not have the same self-identical content, hence, all the previous comments establishing such a gap are not inimical to the analysis of 'This thing is F' propounded by (C.AT.Th). This is perplexing. Unfortunately, there is no time on this occasion to delve into Chisholm's view of analysis. (See Section 13.) Nevertheless, concerning the meaning and uses of 'this', the response misses one point: this gappy view of analysis should help to establish a gap between the information thought of by the speaker in the analysans and the information thought of by him in the analysandum. But this gap in information is not the gap in performance we have been discussing. We just need more theory.

To round out our examination of the use of 'This is F' sentences, we must proceed to studying Chisholm's account of the use of 'I am F' sentences. We excuse ourselves from examining Chisholm's analyses of the other indexical expressions. Since these analyses are couched in terms of calling attention to something, the above comments about his analysis of 'This thing is F' apply. Note in particular the two uses of 'here' in (Th.2) above. The cumulative result is that each of the different indexical references has its own performative role and its own type of role. This is one of my reasons for holding that they are not inter-definable.

8. Self-Ascription: Its Holistic Character

The kingpin on which Chisholm's analyses of indexical sentences pivots is his analysis of 'I am F', to wit:

(CA.I) The locution 'I am F' has as its primary use in English that of expressing the following property of its utterer: directly attributing the property of being F to itself. (Chisholm 1981, 42)

It is uncertain how to assess (CA.I). Chisholm declares that the primary use is that in terms of which the other uses are explained. But to make this order of dependencies clear requires a less hurried treatment of the topic. For instance, we have seen in (Th.2) above that for the case of 'this' and 'here' each used token of the indicator is autonomous. Is 'I' the same? What counts as a sentence of the form 'I am F' for the distribution of the performative function described in (CA.I)? We know (more or less) what counts syntactically as an English sentence of the form 'I am F', and we know that such sentences are governed by a closure rule: a combination of an 'I am F' sentence with other sentences is also an 'I am F' sentence. For the sake of concreteness, consider a statement by a famous philosopher:

(11) If [a] sometimes I am not tolerant or am disdainful, [b] it is because I am anxious not to waste my time.

Clearly, neither the antecedent [a] as a whole nor the consequent [b] as a whole nor each of the smaller clauses within them containing 'I' is used to express or perform the self-ascription of the attributes denoted by them. If there is any tenuous doubt of this in your mind just suppose that (11) functions as the major premise of that philosopher's deduction by *modus tollens* of the denial of [a].

Presumably the *whole* conditional is the sentence 'I am F' to which Chisholm's (CA.I) applies. Thus the whole of (11) expresses semantically the property directly self-attributed, namely: being such that if sometimes x is not tolerant or x is disdainful, it is because x is anxious not to waste x's time. Thus, the tokens of 'I' contrast with the tokens of 'this' and 'here' in not being autonomous but requiring a unified wholesale interpretation.

9. Myself and Others: Quantification and Counting

As we have seen, the Self-Ascription View is excellent as the centerpiece of an account of egoless experiences. However, many an experience includes at least an apparent reference to an I as the subject of the experience; besides, some such experiences include references to an I as one among other individuals. Consider, for instance, Armand Duval's reasoning:

> (R)   Marguerite eventually makes all those who love her unhappy; I love her inordinately, just as much as the Baron of Varville. Hence, some time she will make the *two* of us unhappy. And this one; and that old goat, too. Four unhappy lovers to be!

Here we do not care about Armand's logical acumen or the validity of his reasonings. Correctly, or incorrectly, Armand is instantiating a universal proposition into the particulars he calls "I", and "the baron of Varville," with no sense of an invidious logical asymmetry between them. On the Self-Ascription View he is not doing such a thing: there are no I's to serve as values of our universal quantifiers.

Furthermore, Armand is counting unhappy lovers: "The Baron of Varville and I make two." Whereas this, as Chisholm says, is on his view not literally true, Armand does speak *with truth* (Chisholm 1981, 44). Armand is ascribing to himself the property of being such as to make himself with the Baron of Varville two. This seems fine. The pronoun 'I' may be taken to function as a blank or an unbound variable in the phrase 'He and I make two', so that this phrase expresses, in the lambda notation, the property λx[he and x makes two], being an x such that he and x make two. We can add that the point of using 'I' instead of 'x' is to perform the self-ascription. This self-ascription is one *effect* of counting: *He, one; I, two.* The role of being *counted* is, however, submerged. In the counting process the function of 'I' is not so much to act as the free variable signaling that we are dealing with a property predication-ally, but to seize an item that is supposed to be individuated and differentiated from the other items being counted: it is at best a free variable satisfying at least two *semantico-pragmatic* conditions: (a) it is a sorted variable that captures the sort of entities being counted, and (b) it is a flagged variable that has a particular value.

Condition (b) deserves further comment. It might be adduced that the performative use of 'I' includes the assignment of a particular value to the free variable that 'I' is. This is not, however, the issue now. The semantico-pragmatic point (b) goes beyond that. Counting is an operation, a *performance*, not a mere Platonic one-one correspondence between the set of instances of a property and a subset of the natural numbers. A performance of self-ascription of a property is, as we have just seen, an operation on the whole property; a performance of counting operates on each counted item. We must distinguish between the *piecemeal* assignment made at the particular use of 'I' in the count; *he, one; I, two; two prospective unhappy lovers*, from the overall, *holistic* assignment involved in the self-ascription of the total property in question. Each counting use of 'I' takes an autonomous assignment made to the variable 'I' as made there; it is like each autonomous use of 'this', discussed above, singling out a counted item, as when Armand counts: "Varville, one; I, two; this, three; that old goat, four; four unhappy lovers to be."

10. The Manifold Semantics of Self-Consciousness and
the Syntactic Undimensionality of the Self-Ascription View

The problem is still the difference between unreflective and reflective consciousness. This is a semantico-pragmatic, thought-contentual distinction, and it collides with the uniform syntax of Chisholm's Self-Ascription View. As I see it, regimenting Chisholm's View within a second-order logic, what the View essentially does, very cleverly, is to offer a free variable of quantification as the self-referential mechanism, allowing the variables to range over ordinary physical objects and persons. The View allocates to free variables in sentences about propositional attitudes two roles: to pick out a thinker, and to represent the attribute predicatively self-ascribed: the prefix 'self' merely signals the fact that it is the same variable that both occurs at the subject position and is the mark of the predicative role of the self-ascribed attribute. (Chisholm may perhaps disapprove of this precisification.) Consider:

(12) Gaston believes that he himself is not in love with Marguerite.

Let us suppose that 'Marguerite' occurs in (12) *de dicto*, or internally as I prefer to say. Chisholm would analyze away the proper names in (12) in a Russellian-Quinean style. The result is a quantificational frame within which lies a core that can be summarily represented as follows:

(12.A) Gaston-x believes himself to be such that: not (x is R-Marguerite to just one y & x is in love with y).

There is a question as to whether the negation *not* is within, or without, the scope of the quantifier *just one*, which the analysis introduces. The decision is important. Scope differences matter, and there is a tension. On one side, the Russellian analysis preserves semantic unity if it is fixed systematically with the lowest scope; on another side, the referential use of the terms is better understood as having the largest scope; on the third side, the best choice for the *de dicto* content of belief may be maximal scope within a belief context.

In any case, as I estimate the elucidatory force of the View, the cross-reference depicted by the sheer repetition of the variable x is the self-reference the theory offers. To me this is an illuminating logical account of unreflective consciousness: the unity of the free variable expresses the *unattended* unity of consciousness. The question is whether this is all there is to self-consciousness and self-reference.

The semantics of thinking and consciousness, as recorded in (H.C*) above, is twofold. Besides unreflective, merely cross-referring self-reference to 'x', there is reflective, genuine self-reference, which not just refers back to x, but refers back to x qua the thinker x is. My answer is "Yes." Furthermore, I am prepared to find within reflective consciousness several layers of thinking. Consider:

Gaskon's Latest Adventure. Gaskon has recently moved into his fully mirrored mansion, with walls covered with different types of mirrors. Two evenings ago some of the most charming and creative philosophers surprised him with a most pleasurable entertainment. They talked about self-identity, self-recognition, and they took full advantage of the mirrors and arranged and re-arranged them to illustrate different types of epistemic situations. After seeing everybody out, or so Gaskon thought, he turned around and saw as if in a dream a man who looked like a cross between John Perry and David Kaplan, yet he felt as if he were looking at himself; Gaskon even thought quickly of some movie where a character talks to his inner self both played by James Stewart—or was it Cary Grant? They were staring at each other; then Gaskon heard himself in the mirror saying: "You and I are different types of persons; we have different tastes in metaphysics." He recognized his voice. The staring continued as painful as the enveloping silence. Then Gaskon blinked, and the truth dawned upon him. In fact, his friends had arranged a recording to sound out at a certain time. Nonetheless, Gaskon is now not sure that he heard the words, or just imagined the utterance. He understood. In Los Angeles one can become high with a spirited metaphysical conversation. As soon as he understood, Gaskon was elated. He mailed a circular letter to the people working on indexical reference, describing his exciting experience. In my copy I have marked this passage:

(13) It was unnerving. There I was ostensibly telling myself that I was different from myself. I realize now that for a moment I believe that I thought that I was not identical with me.

Some of his friends were proud of having caused, in their own words, that:

(14) Gaskon acknowledges that for a moment he* believed himself* to think that he* was not identical with himself*.

Chisholm's view as described above interprets Gaskon's uttering (13) as his expressing his self-ascription of the property being an x such that:

(13.A) x realizes (now) that x believed himself to be such that: x believed himself to be such that x was different from x.

Recall that all the occurrences of 'x' are to be interpreted at unison, holistically. For (14) we obtain:

(14.A) Gaskon-x acknowledges that x believed himself to be such that x thought himself to be such that x is not identical with x.

The story suggests that Gaskon was justified in believing *I am different from myself*, which does not contain the contradictory property of being not self-identical. Gaskon seems to have been dealing with a contingent sameness $x \equiv y$, where the different variables are to receive different values. How can we introduce a variable 'y' that picks out a different value than the one that 'x' picks out, for such values to be appropriately empirically the same? Recall that the values of the variables are full persons and physical objects, and that self-reference is nothing but back- or cross-reference.

It is of the utmost importance to appreciate that merely positing selves both as referents of first-person reference and as distinct from bodies or persons does not solve the problem of explaining the semantics of (13) and (14). Apparently we need at least two different selves connected to Gaskon: the self from which he speaks (presumably anchored directly to Gaskon's body) and the self of which he speaks (presumably anchored indirectly to his body through the mediation of his mirror image). Palpably, Gaskon's latest adventure is not very sophisticated. We can expect that at their next surprise party his friends will bring it about that:

(15) Gaskon will know that he*(1) believed that he*(2) believed that. . . . he*(n) believed that he*(i) is different from he(j).

In (15) n must ultimately be a measure of Gaskon's intellectual ability to figure out a chain of identities.

We seem, thus, to need a fine-grained ontological semantics. Frege's with his Sense/Referent distinction may be helpful, especially if it includes Frege's hierarchy of senses. We must reckon, however, with the mix-location of the senses of 'he*(i)' and 'he*(j)' that appear in the scope of $n + 1$ psychological verbs. Guise Theory has enough resources to distinguish all the individual guises, including I-guises, that may be required to account for the enormous richness of what humans can think. Individual guises are a good deal like Frege's senses, but differ in crucial respects, e.g., in their relations to Fregean referents, in their roles as contents of thinking and speech acts, in their not being part of a hierarchy.

The preceding discussion, again, does not refute the Attribute View. It just gathers questions that any development of the View should attend to.

11. Others' Thoughts about Me: Indicators in Indirect Speech

Chisholm's primitive concept is *the property of being F is such that x judges himself to have it*, where the substituends of 'F' are adjectival or predicative

expressions. He clarifies what that primitive involves by means of some definitions. Two crucial ones are:

D2 x believes himself to be F =Df The property of being F is such that
       x judges himself to have it.

NAI: x indirectly attributes to y the property of being F =Df There is a
       relation R and a property P such that: (a) x judges himself to have
       P; (b) x bears R only to y; and (c) P is necessarily such that: (i)
       whoever conceives P conceives the property of being F, (ii) whatever
       has P bears R to just one thing and to a thing that is F. (Chisholm,
       1986)

Consider, Armand's statement:

(16) Gaston believes Armand to love Marguerite.

Continuing to ignore 'Marguerite', (16) presumably is analyzable as:

(16.A) There is a relation S such that: Gaston is S just to Armand, and Gas-
        ton believes himself to be: S to just one person, and such a person
        loves Marguerite.

Assuming 'Gaston' analyzed in the Russellian way, (16.A) is a proposition
that predicates of Gaston the property, represented by the predicate obtained
from (16) by substituting the free variable 'x' for 'Gaston'. Now, Armand believes (16) and goes on to assert:

(17) Gaston believes that I love Marguerite.

Thus, for some relation R by which he is related only to Gaston, and a certain
property Gness, Armand believes himself to be G. Presumably (17) is an 'I
am F' sentence, and as luck would have it Armand proffered (17), in English.
Then what he asserted is that he is one object y such that:

(17.A) y bears R just to just one person x (namely Gaston), and there is a
        relation S such that: x is S just to y, and x believes himself to be: S to
        just one person, and a person who loves Marguerite.

    This seems to me a very illuminating analysis. To put my praise slightly
invidiously, aiming at a dia-philosophical exercise: it is very similar to the
analysis I offered in "Indicators and Quasi-indicators" (1967). I gave up that
analysis for reasons that seem more valid today. On the one hand, the analysis
makes very high conceptual demands: (a) it takes properties as subjects of
predication, instead of merely taking them in their predicative function (recall our discussion of predication in Section 3 above); (b) further, it makes use
of quantification over properties. On the other hand, these conceptual resources are beyond the ken of many persons who think of others as having
beliefs about them.
    The fundamental achievement of the View here is twofold: it conforms with

the intensionality thesis that the main contents of thinking are universals and it satisfies the epistemological requirement that singular reference hinge on identification of referents by properties they uniquely exemplify. These requirements MUST certainly be complied with by any theory of singular reference. Yet at least for the purpose of dia-philosophical illumination we should attempt to satisfy them while doing justice both to the fact that certain persons do not rise up to the level of quantifying over properties, and to the fact that thinking abilities develop, the ability to quantify over properties being a later acquisition. We need, hence, a theory of thought content and of semantico-pragmatic referents that neither demands nor proscribes that the attributions to others of thoughts about oneself involve properties as subjects of predication—let alone require quantification over properties. This was one major impetus for the development of Guise Theory.

I have said that Chisholm's view delivers an analysis of (17) "very similar to the analysis I proposed in 1967." There are two major differences.

First, Chisholm's view of self-ascription demands that every object in the world referred to singularly be singled out by a relation that has *explicitly* the thinker as one relatum. This is precisely the force of his self-ascription. That is his subdued Fichteanism. I have never required that. Nonetheless, I concur that singular reference to objects in the world is essentially to objects in *one's* world. This provokes the question as to how this all-encompassing involvement of self in one's acts of reference is to be conceived. There is no room here to broach this topic, except for some brief hints. On the alternative view I propose, the reference to oneself involved in the identification of objects in one's world is primarily the *implicit* self-reference of unreflective consciousness. This has to do, as it might have been expected, with the suffusiveness of the tiers of consciousness recorded in hierarchy (H.C*) above in Section 7, and with the greater thermodynamic cost and preciousness of self-consciousness. This hierarchical suffusiveness allows us to account for psychological development and to place human consciousness and mental activity within a larger natural scheme. From Fichte remains only the schema of self-reference as this is deployed in experience. Thus, the implicit references to the thinker are not brought out every time she identifies an object, but are *holistically* built into the contents of experience. Indexicality and contextuality are, albeit different, closely connected.

Doubtless, by putting all self-references out into the open, Chisholm's View is simpler than the view I have wrought out, which distinguishes not only tiers of self-consciousness, but also between indexical references and contextual referential frameworks. This difference in the views is immaterial for my eulogy of the Self-Ascription View in Section 6 above. The fact is that Chisholm's present view, though simpler, does deliver more *complex analysantia* than the Contextual View I prefer. Obviously, by simply requiring that everything be made explicit the view creates piecemeal complexity.

Second, the other major difference between my 1967 analysis of (17) and

Chisholm's consists of our different attitudes concerning Russell's analysis of definite descriptions. Even in 1967 I was not interested in analyzing the definite article 'the' à la Bertrand Russell. I was happy to regard it as a primitive. My reasons had to do with reference to non-existents, which lie at the heart of thinking and believing, and also because the Russellian reduction worked havoc in deontic contexts. (Later on this defensive attitude paid off in terms of an account of individuation, which grounded the development of Guise Theory.)[21] Chisholm on the other hand wants all possible reductions, and his analyses of 'I am F' sentences include a built-in Russellian analysis of identifying references. This of course leads to additional piecemeal complexity in the resulting analyses.

Patently, assertive utterances of 'I am F' sentences in which the substituends of 'F' contain no clauses in indirect speech need not raise the problems discussed above. The problems appear when 'F', as in the case of sentence (17), contain a clause in indirect speech. Since subordination of indirect speech is iterative, we should expect a *crescendo* effect of the above problems for sequential attributions to others of references to oneself. Just reflect on Armand's discovery:

(18) My father believes that Gaston knows that I suspect that Marguerite does not really love me.

12. Nested Attributions of Self-Reference: Quasi-Indicators of Higher Degrees

In Section 11 we considered some special cases of attribution of self-reference, mainly Gaskon's self-attribution. Let us dwell a bit longer on the third-person case and its quasi-indexical mechanisms. Recall the definition of degree of quasi-indication in Section 5 above. In Castañeda 1967a it is claimed that tokens of quasi-indicators of higher degree than one are reducible to quasi-indicators of degree one. The proposed analyses involve property quantification. Chisholm can adopt them as basis for his deeper analyses.

Chisholm for his part (Chisholm 1981, 120) treats a somewhat complex schematic example adopted from Castañeda 1967a, namely:

(19) J believes, with respect to K, that he, K, once thought that he, J, was F.

Here 'he, J' can be ambiguous. Presumably it is intended as a quasi-indicator of degree two; but 'he, K' is not a quasi-indicator. In Castañeda 1966 'he, K' was pedestrianly called an (F)-'he', because it illustrates the use of 'he' listed as (F). The difference is clear: 'he, K' is a mere variable having the preceding 'K' as antecedent, and does not tell us how J or K refers to K—being, thus, propositionally opaque.[22] On the other hand, 'he, J' is propositionally transparent, although it has a *de re* force, in that it clearly represents first-person references by J. Thus, (19) can be rephrased as:

(19*) J believes of K that he(K) once thought that he*(2) was F.

Chisholm analyzes (19) this way:

(19.A) There are relations R1 and R2 and properties H and G such that: (i) J directly attributes H to J;

    (ii) H is necessarily such that for every z, z has H, iff z bears R1 to just one thing and to a thing which, when it has G, bore R2 to z and only to z; and

    (iii) G is necessarily such that for every y, y has G iff y bears R2 to just one thing and to a thing that has F.

(Chisholm 1981, 120; on the first line I have replaced 'F' with 'H', since 'F' is not bound by any quantifier)

This analysans was wholly unexpected. Given that sentence (19) contains two verbs of propositional attitude, I expected its analysans (19.A) to mention explicitly two states of self-ascription, one belonging to J and the other to K. Given the non-reversible sequential order of the nesting of indirect-speech clauses, I expected this order not to yield the symmetric biconditionals of clauses (ii) and (iii). Further, there is a question about the interpretation of the linkage of 'when' to the rest of clause (iii): is it linked conjunctively, or conditionally? The conditional interpretation seems to be too weak. Yet the conjunctive interpretation does not look strong enough to make up for the aforementioned unexpected features of (19.A). I wonder whether the following properties H and G and relations R1 and R2 constitute a counterexample cleaving (19.A) from (19)?

H: having just one immediate neighbor on the South who has just one immediate neighbor on the North when he had just one immediate neighbor on the North, and this was F.

R1: having an immediate neighbor on the South;

R2: having an immediate neighbor on the North;

G: having just one immediate neighbor on the North, who is F.

Perhaps the contrast between (19.A) and the analysis of it in Castañeda 1967a may help firm up the previous remarks:

(19*.A) There is a property $h$ness such that: K = the h, and J believes that there is a property $g$ness such that: the g = he*(1) and the h once thought that the g was F.

In (19*.A) we see the allegedly irreducible quasi-indicator of degree one, and also the irreducible 'the' of definite descriptions.

13. Some Crucial Ontological Issues

My time is up. I have enjoyed meditating on the Attribute/Self-Ascription View of belief and the accusatives of thinking. The examination has been very educational. I wish there were time to scrutinize the major ontological tenets undergirding Lewis's and Chisholm's different version of the View. It will be rewarding to ponder Chisholm's thesis that there are no particularized properties. It deserves and needs a thorough evaluation. It lies at the heart of the problem of the nature of thinking content and connection between thinking and reality. If thought content is purely universal and abstract, how can we make thinking contact with the particular? Recall that Chisholm does not merely allow that singular terms be composed of expressions denoting pure universals only, he goes on further to analyze singular terms away altogether (as I understand him) either in terms of free variables with the performative role of expressing self-ascription, if they are indicators, or by means of the Quinean-Russellian technique. This raises the questions Peter Strawson raised about the gap between asserting that there are objects that uniquely exemplify this or that property and actually referring to them as singled out individuals.[23] (See the comment on scope about example (12.A) in Section 10.) But we cannot say more here.[24]

Let us suppose, then, that to secure the connection between thinking and particulars we allow particularized properties, or even as Kaplan and Kripke do, particularized propositions.[25] Then the problem is that, given the mainstream fashionable metaphysics, such propositions and properties contain as components the very massive particulars of the world, with infinitely many properties. It really does not matter whether those massive particulars are physical or mental, or whatever. The problem is that, because of the Intensionality Requirements, discussed above in Section 2, those objects are too large to be thinkable in person as the wholes they are.

Here is the chief dilemma of doxastic accusatives: pure universals seem too remote; particularized properties or propositions are too huge. At this juncture Guise Theory, as well as some recent Meinongian views, offer a way in the middle: particularized properties particularized to very thin finite individuals. But all we can do here is provide references.[26]

I understand that in response to Tomberlin and others Chisholm has adduced that the conjunction "y *believes himself to be F* and x is F is analyzable as x is G," does not imply y *believes himself to be* G. This is an illustrator of the paradox of analysis. In my opinion Chisholm is right in denying this implication. He admirably builds this denial into his analyses by systematically including a condition of conceivability. (See for instance NAI in Section 11.) That suggests that there is a *surplus* of thought content in the analysans being G that is not present in the analysandum being F. That surplus seems to escape the equations of analysis. Perhaps no ontological surplus escapes any analysis and the surplus is merely an internal contentual creation of thinking episodes and their underlying dispositional propositional attitudes. Yet we cannot be content until the View is complemented with the theory of the surplus content that explains how Chisholm may claim analysis without identity. Perhaps he can use Guise Theory, which centrally distinguishes between strict identity, governed by an absolutely unrestricted Leibniz Law, and a family of sameness relations. Guise Theory utilizes the sameness relation called *conflation* and the concept of property and propositional guises to handle the paradox of analysis.[27]

This is really all we can do here.

Appendix: Boër and Lycan's
Sellarsian-Davidsonian Account of
the Quasi-Indicator 'He Himself' of Degree One

In their *Knowing Who* (1986) Stephen Boër and William Lycan mollify somewhat their early attacks (Boër-Lycan 1980) on my thesis that both singular indexical first-person reference and its corresponding quasi-indexical reference are conceptually irreducible. They acknowledge a certain *linguistic* irreducibility of first-person reference. Their book is an excellent and most impressive treatise on the propositional attitudes. It is well grounded on data and it represents a powerful and illuminating theoretical accomplishment, carried out rigorously. Here I wish to vent briefly some queries pertaining to our present topics.

At bottom, aside from the symbolism, the Boër-Lycan analysis of:

(1) Armand believes that he himself is happy

amounts to this:

(1.A) [The triadic relation] BELIEVES relates Armand, an empty sequence of objects, and [the demonstrative] THAT → [which points to the type of sentence that in any language has the same general behavioral role as our sentence] '*I am happy*'.

In (1.A) the arrow '→' indicates the speaker's pointing; the expressions I have bracketed constitute the analysts' commentary on what the immediately following expressions are or do. The demonstrative 'THAT' captures Davidson's view of indirect speech: it points to a sentence that the speaker produces, which is merely juxtaposed, phonetically or graphically, to the psychological verb. The reference to the role of the pointed-to sentence is Sellars's, and, after him, they put dot quotes around 'I am happy'. The dot quotes around an expression signal the role that tokens of that type play in the behavioral economy of the speakers; hence, a dot-quoted 'red' names the same role as dot-quoted (French) 'rouge's, Spanish 'rojo's, and German 'rot's. This is insightful.

Yet many questions beset this nominalistic analysis of 'he himself', and of 'I'. First, there is the diagonal argument of Note 3. Besides, realists always wonder how objects and pieces of behavior can be identified and differentiated from one another without qualities or relations providing criteria of classification and role demarcation. However, let this pass. It seems to be mere wishful thinking to assume that the sentences of all languages nicely partition themselves in behavioral equivalent classes and that such partitions correspond in their uses across all the languages, past and future.

More likely there are areas of overlapping correspondence within the wide divergences among such vague partitions. Consider a trivial case: to the English 'I am coming' correspond in Spanish the indicatives 'vengo', 'yo vengo', and the subjunctives 'venga', 'yo venga' with diverse ranges of uses, which overlap with some of the uses of 'I come', and 'I will come', the areas of use of which in their turn overlap in varying patterns with the Spanish forms 'vendré' and 'yo vendré', not to mention the crucial fact that the English '(to) come' has a *second-person perspective* that contrasts with the requisite *first-person perspective* counterpart, in which cases the forms of '(to) come' correspond rather to forms of the Spanish 'ir' (often translated as '(to) go"). The discrepancies in areas of behavioral equivalence grow when we consider other constructions.

The point is that there are no easy syntactic correspondences, and then there are semantic divergences and pragmatic non-correspondences. Beyond that lie diverse ranges of vagueness and imprecision. Of course we can use Sellars's dot quotes to name one linguistic role of sentences: the propositions they express. Thus *I am happy* can be used to name first-person propositions. Similarly for predicates: dot-quoted they name attributes. Since we can tell some attributes from others we can now organize the areas of divergency and overlap of the expressions under consideration.

Thus interpreted the Boër–Lycan analysis is illuminating: propositions or attributes, names in dot-quoted expressions, are what Davidson's demonstrative of indirect speech points to. Now we must formulate questions pertaining to nested belief sentences and quasi-indicators of higher degrees.

Consider a simple case: Gaston's statement:

(2) Marguerite believes that Armand believes that she* does not love him*.

The first 'that' might be said to be Gaston's demonstrative; but the second 'that' has to have another function: it should be taken to represent, be proxy for, Marguerite's demonstration of some sentence, presumably a French one. But then the second 'that' is a quasi-indicator. It introduces structure, which needs accounting for.

Another query: What is the proposition, that is, the dot-quoted sentence Gaston has pointed to?

Another question: What is the dot-quoted sentence Marguerite has pointed to? Suppose that she believes what Gaston says she does, but has said nothing? If Gaston is lying, is there such a Davidsonian demonstrative used by Marguerite? Let her, however, believe what Gaston says she does: What dot-quoted sentence is Gaston attributing to her? Perhaps: *I(1) do not love I(2)*, where the indices indicate different users of the first-person. Yet this requires some structuring of the pointed-to sentence into the subordinating clause. Besides, there seems to be no such sentence. We could have *You don't love me, I don't love you, I don't love him, She doesn't love me*, and others. To reach these, however, we need to build some structure relating subordinate clauses to main clauses.

It seems, then, that a paratactic view of indirect speech has to work hard with quasi-indicators of higher degrees. (See above Section 11.10–12, and Castañeda 1966 and 1967a.)

Notes

1. See Lewis 1979. Lewis discusses mostly first-person references, and says very little about demonstrative reference and attributions of reference. His notion of property is not the standard one. I am using here the term 'attribute' to cover mainly properties and relations, but in the case of Lewis's view it covers also extensions. See Tomberlin 1989.

2. See Chisholm 1981, 1986. His first exposition of the Attribute View is, I believe, Chisholm 1979. The topic made it appropriate for an exposition of the monolithic Attribute View.

3. In Castañeda 1975a, 33ff, there is a "diagonal" argument against equating propositions with classes of sentences. The key premise is that propositions are truth-valued. Consider a language L, perhaps infinite, and let A be the class of its sentences. Let B be the class of equivalent sentences to L. To make sure, let C be the power set of B. Let $c(X)$ denote the cardinal of X. Then: $c(A) \geq c(B) \leq c(C)$. Consider now the class T of true propositions of the form: *member of B is a member of a member of C*. Then $c(T,) \geq c(B)$ and $c(C) \geq c(B)$. L, therefore, does not have enough resources to equate classes of sentences with the above propositions—barring ambiguity. I am still persuaded by these facts. More so in fact after having read Grim 1988, an illuminating discussion of a battery of issues pertaining to truth and the infinity of propositions. Blackburn 1975 rebuts attacks against the Classical View of Propositions. For nominalistic views of doxastic accusatives see Sellars, Quine, Davidson, and many others. Rosenberg 1974 develops a Sellarsian reduction of universals to linguistic roles. Boër-Lycan 1986a combines Sellarsian and Davidsonian aspects. Some questions are posed for it in the Appendix.

4. The monolithic Attribute View is defended in Lewis 1979, Chisholm 1979, and Brand 1983 and 1984. I have argued for the need to distinguish practical from contemplative (propositional) attributes in my "Reply to Brand" in Tomberlin 1983. Brand's rejoinder in 1984 leaves the issue as it was then. My argument hinges crucially on mixed conditionals, e.g., to close the window if I open the door, which is different from: to open the door if I open the window. Brand deliberately keeps conditional intentions out of his account in 1984, xi. See Tomberlin 1988a for additional discussion.

A large collection of data containing a plurality of experienced distinctions, all of which are subsumed under the unifying theoretical contrast between propositions and practitions, is displayed in Castañeda 1975a. The main thread is gathered in chapter 6, which refers to data in chapters 2–9; additional data appear in chapters 10–12. Further data are gathered in Replies to Bratman, Sellars, Tomberlin, and Aune in Tomberlin 1983.

5. See Wittgenstein 1952, 194–199, 205ff. But I do not want to attribute to Wittgenstein any views on philosophical theorization.

6. For a detailed defense of philosophical pluralism, an explanation of how competing views and systems are sym-philosophical contributions to philosophical understanding—

the whole profession being willy-nilly like a symphonic orchestra—, and the need of dia-philosophy, see Castañeda 1980a. For a defense of the dia-philosophical tenet that, although philosophical theses can be refuted, views or approaches cannot, see Castañeda 1980a, chapter 4, sections 4, 7–9.

7. The characterization of propositions as truth-valued need not involve the assumption that there are just two truth-values. Of course that characterization says by itself nothing against propositions having subjective or privately accessible components. These theses have to be established independently.

8. See Frege 1892 and 1918. Perry 1977 argues that Frege's Classical View of Propositions (Thoughts) could not accommodate his own observations about first-person references. See note 10.

9. See Moore 1922. Moore is generally credited with the paradox of analysis; it is only a special case of the paradoxes of identity, which Frege saw in a more general way. See Castañeda 1980a.

10. Being more traditionalist, I have proposed what may be called Refurbished Proposition/Practition View. It distinguishes propositions from practitions, recognizes private indexical properties and propositions, breaks down the classical conception of identity in a family of at least six types of sameness relations, and reveals propositions to be hierarchies of *propositional* guises related by the sameness called *conflation*. Propositional guises are truth-valued, have logical implications, and are internal doxastic accusatives. The earliest version, minus practitional guises, appears in Castañeda 1974; practitions and propositions are combined in Castañeda 1975a, chapters 2–3, 6, 12. My recent sources of immediate inspiration were Strawson and Cartwright. Propositional guises appeared with this name in Castañeda 1977a.

11. Kant 1781, A312–320 (B369–377). Perhaps this is an incorrect application of his Ideas. But their theory-guiding role has fascinated me.

12. What follows is merely a surface phenomenon of indexical reference. It and other phenomena are brilliantly discussed in Perry 1977 and 1979, which have become standard references. Perry acknowledges as sources Castañeda 1966, 1967a. These papers contain much data not yet tapped, especially concerning the roles and properties of quasi-indicators, e.g., the locution 'he (himself)' in sentence (4), and particularly quasi-indicators of higher degrees than one (see Sections 11.4, 11 and 12 below). For additional data, sometimes exegesized in detail, see also Adams 1983, Baker 1981a, Boër-Lycan 1980 and 1986a, Castañeda 1977a, 1982a, 1983b-h, 1987a, and 1989a, Grim 1985, Hintikka 1970a, Kaplan 1975 and 1977, Richards 1984, Saarinen 1982 and 1986, Smith 1982 and 1986, Tomberlin 1984, Zemach 1985.

13. See Saussure 1915. An important conceptual tool in Saussure's work was that concepts and linguistics mechanisms belong, not so much to words or morphemes, but to syntactico-semantic contrasts. E.g., the German plural is not a certain, or certain forms of words, but a family of pairs that include *Gast-Gäste*. This idea has been put to philosophical service in Castañeda 1980a, chapter 2. See Note 6.

14. From Boër-Lycan 1980. This excellent essay attacks the thesis of the irreducibility of first-person reference. Castañeda 1984c contains both a rebuttal of their formal critique and an account of their interesting Perry Mason example, which is indeed a valuable major datum. Boër-Lycan 1986a acknowledges a certain linguistic irreducibility of first-person reference. See Tomberlin 1987 and 1987a for discussion of these issues. See the Appendix to this study.

15. See, e.g., Chisholm 1957. For a criticism see Shirley 1987.

16. For Fichte 1794 all consciousness is self-consciousness.

17. See Sartre 1943. For a valuable discussion see Rosenberg 1981.

18. The notion of Externus was first introduced as such by Castañeda 1970. But it was assumed in Castañeda 1967a.

19. In Castañeda 1967a there is discussion of a solipsistic thinker, no longer an Externus, who thinks I-thoughts. But the I's it thinks are nothing but mechanisms for unifying experiences without involving a contrast between the thinker and others. Then he acquires the concept of other I's, as subjects of alien experiences, yet still wants our full concept of I: it lacks the concept of *you*. There are several sub-conceptual strands woven into our mature concept of the first person. Buber 1923 was right in contrasting two layers of our mature I concept as *I-It* and as *I-Thou*. He had a Saussurean idea that concepts (and word meanings) are constituted by their contrasts with others. Yet he missed an in-between strand: the *I-Other* sub-concept. Of course, I am not endorsing the conclusions he derives from those conceptual (linguistic) insights. For some recent discussions of I-constitution see Nozick 1981, Richards 1984, Mazoue 1986.

20. See in particular Castañeda 1967a, and Castañeda 1989a. Castañeda 1982a contains revisions of papers never published in English.

21. See Castañeda 1974 and 1977a. In the latter (Section 11.7) there is an explicit criticism of Russell's 1905 analysis of definite descriptions.

22. This notion was introduced first in Castañeda 1977b. It is a partial converse of Quine's referential opacity. What he calls "referential transparency" is actually exclusive speaker's reference. He is concerned with the *de re* aspects of communication, whereas I have been worrying about the *de dicto* aspects of thinking. In this paper there is also the view that proper names are really free variables of quantification.

23. Strawson 1952. For a celebrated discussion of the debate between Russell and Strawson see Donnellan 1966. Donnellan's famous distinction between referential and attributive uses of definite descriptions is a mixture of several crucial distinctions. See Castañeda 1977b, note 7.

24. Tomberlin 1985 discusses some of these issues, especially whether we can live our experiences without particularized properties.

25. Russell 1903, Kaplan 1977, Kripke 1972. Castañeda 1989c argues that Kaplan's Direct Reference is fine as an account of *external* targets of thinking and believing, but we need *internal* accusatives. The former can be massive Kaplan-Russell singular propositions; but the latter must be very thin, at most as Frege's and Moore's propositions. In fact thinner, like propositional guises, in order to account for the strong intensional nature of thinking contents, as this is manifested in the paradox of analysis.

26. See Castañeda 1974, 1977b, 1982a, 1986b; Clark 1978, 1983; Plantinga 1983; Rosenberg 1974, 1986a; Smith 1986; Sicha 1986; Tomberlin 1983, 1984, 1986; Lee 1984; Rapaport's studies; Parsons 1980; Fine 1984; Zalta 1983; Orilia 1987; Zemach 1985.

27. Compare the treatment of the paradox of analysis in Castañeda 1977a. Propositional guises and conflation allow a comprehensive solution of this paradox that also applies to the facts of growth of perceptual knowledge by attention.

6

The Self and the I-Guises, Empirical and Transcendental

Here is a mere prolegomenon to a general theory of self-consciousness—dedicated to Dieter Henrich with gratitude and with admiration for his illuminating contributions to our understanding of the nature of consciousness, selfhood, and self-consciousness.

Introduction

Hitherto persons have been human beings, that is, human bodies with experiences and with selves who own such experiences. Reflection shows that the fundamental, nuclear elements of selves are *I*'s, i.e., the strict denotata of purely indexical, singular uses of the first-person pronoun. Hence, we shall study first-person reference. Now, mysteries and perplexities arise easily when problems are treated in isolation. For that reason we shall start with an examination of singular reference in general and then apply the results to the special case of first-person reference. Thus we come to Guise Theory; within it we find the I-guises. Subsequently we shall focus on indexical reference. This is thoroughly experiential reference. Then we concentrate on the peculiar manifestations of some of the general features of indexical or experiential reference in first-person reference. With that background we become equipped for the apprehension of the nature of I-guises and of the selves they constitute. An I-guise is the subject of an experience intimately linked to the present and presented time and the presented space of the experience, i.e., to a Now-guise and a Here-guise. For these their *esse* is *to be involved in an experiencing*. This raises questions about the diachronic unity of I's and selves, about their roles in experience, about their places in the world, more specifically, about the structure of personal histories and autobiographies, about the connections of the Now-guises to physical time and of Here-guises to physical space. In that context we confront Descartes's *cogito* and Kant's tran-

This essay appeared in *Theorie der Subjecktivität*, edited by Konrad Cramer et al. (Frankfurt am Main: Suhrkamp, 1987), 105–140. Reprinted by permission of Suhrkamp Verlag.

scendental and transcendent selves. Of course, here we can do no more than glimpse at those questions and at the materials for a comprehensive theory of selves, I's, and self-consciousness.

1. Linguatic and Contextual Singular Terms

A singular term can be so constituted as to have an individual entity assigned to it by the very general rules of the language to which it belongs. For instance, the term 'the first atom ever to exist' either denotes an entity, or it does not, depending on the facts about the universe. The whole thing here consists of a matching between a language and reality, and no speech act involving the term is required. We may call such expressions *Leibnizian (linguatic) singular terms*. The adjective 'linguatic' is meant to connect with languages as systems of rules, with languages in the sense in which French and German are languages, i.e., with what Saussure referred to as *langues*, not with language in the ability sense in which cats lack (human) language.

Typically, however, a singular term gains a denotation through a more complex operation: the term has a general meaning fixed by rules in a language system, but these rules, not sufficient to assign to it a unique denotation, must be complemented with information provided by the context or circumstances of the use of language, whether in thinking inner speech or in communicational overt speech: the determination of a unique referent is thus a semantico-pragmatic affair: the general meaning of the term gains specificity by the context of speech and through this specificity the term acquires a referent. For instance, personal pronouns, demonstratives, and most descriptive terms we use in daily life, like 'the table' and 'my friend', are of this sort. As normally used, they involve, thus, three factors: the general rules of the language, the specifying role of speech contexts, and the individuating function of the matching reality. We shall call expressions of this type *contextual singular terms*.

Within the category of contextual singular terms we must highlight the subcategory of *indexical terms*. The difference has to do with the way in which the relevant elements of the speech context yield the uniqueness aspect of singular reference. *Merely* contextual singular terms gain their singularity in a given context of (possible) speech act by a mere matching of the circumstances of the context with the general semantic meanings of the terms in question. For example, a token of the term 'the table' has a unique referent in every context of use in which there is just one table. On the other hand, an indicator (e.g., a personal or demonstrative pronoun ['I', 'you', 'this', 'that']) or an indexical definite description (e.g., 'this table', 'that distinguished-looking young man') gains a referent in a context C of possible use, not by a mere pairing of its general meaning with the circumstances pertaining to C, but by the *execution* of an appropriate speech act by a language user. Briefly, a token T of an indexical singular term gains a referent by virtue of an actual *experience* lived through the tokening in context C of some sentence containing the token T. To illustrate, no object is really a *this* or a *that* or a *you* by merely lying in the neighborhood of a potential speaker. Something is a *this* only by being *selected* as the target of reference in an *encounter* with it. A *you* for a woman at a certain time *t* is only an entity the woman has *selected* as an addressee in a dialogal experience occurring at *t*. Similarly, an *I* is the subject of an experience conceived *qua* subject of the experience while the experience lasts. The distinctive feature of indexical reference is, thus, an *executive* (or performative) role of placing referents within experience. Indexical reference is executive and experiential.

2. Thinking Singular Reference as Semantico-Pragmatic Denotation

A distinction crucial for both semantics and the philosophy of mind is that between *the semantico-pragmatic referent* and *the doxastic co-denotata* of a singular term as this is used in a given sentence in a certain context of thought and speech. The semantic referent of a singular term is, roughly and initially, what the term strictly or exactly denotes given both the rules governing its meaning and the individuating role of the context of use. Given that thinking is symbolic or representational, a person thinks in person, *de dicto*, internally, of an individual, only if this individual is the precise denotation picked up by a term in a sentence, the tokening of which sentence by the person in question constitutes an episode of this person's thinking. Thinking reference must be strict semantico-pragmatic denotation.

The doxastic co-denotata of a term are the individuals, characteristically not thought of, believed by the speaker (for the most part tacitly) to be the *same* as the strict semantico-pragmatic referent of his terms. We will have to say a lot about sameness.

3. Total Experience and the Semantic Unity of Thinking

Now, thinking is the backbone of experience, whatever its type. And all the types of experience of a person are integrated in a *total experience*. The unity of the total experience of a person is at bottom the unity of all the trains of thinking that constitute the different experiences. The unity of thinking across the diversity of experiences must rest, therefore, on the semantic unity of the language the use of which embodies thinking. That is why the thinking of individuals is impervious to existence: thinking is intrinsically the same whatever the type of the experience the flow of thinking constitutes, whether it is a thinking of existents, or of fictions, or of hypotheticals, or of hypostases, whether the thinker realizes or judges what kind of thinking it is. This suggests that the individuals that are the targets of thinking reference, or strict semantico-pragmatic denotations, are rather thin individuals that can, by their very thinness, both move across different types of experience and secure the unity of the total experience of a person. But we must not get ahead of ourselves.[1]

4. The Paradox of Reference: a Reminder

As is well known, a fundamental philosophical problem is always a tension between an evident sameness and an obvious difference. This tension for the case of the semantics of our denoting terms and the referents of our thinking reference is forcefully brought forth by the widely pondered failure of substitutivity of co-referring terms in belief contexts. Thus, the interpretation of the terms in such contexts raises a serious problem at the intersection of general semantics, the contents of thinking, and the nature of the objects in the world. To ground this, let us reflect on a concrete example that will be of service later on.

History and standard principles of logic connive to distill a contradiction from the following seven statements, all of which seem to be true:

(1)   At the time of the pestilence Jocasta believed that both Oedipus' father was identical with Oedipus' father and the previous king of Thebes was not identical with Oedipus' father;

(2)   The previous King of Thebes was the same as Oedipus' father;

(3)   It was not the case that at the time of the pestilence Jocasta believed that both Oedipus' father was identical with Oedipus' father and Oedipus' father was not identical with Oedipus' father.

(T1) For any individuals x and y: if x is (genuinely or strictly) identical with y, then whatever is true of x is true of y, and vice versa.

(T2) The sentential matrix occurring in (1) and (3), namely: "at the time of the pestilence Jocasta believed that both Oedipus' father was identical with Oedipus' father and was not identical with Oedipus' father", expresses something true of (a property of) the individual denoted by the singular term that by filling the blank in the matrix produces a sentence expressing a truth.

(T3) The expression "was the same as" in (2) expresses genuine identity.

(T4) The singular terms 'Oedipus' father' and 'the previous King of Thebes' have the same denotation throughout premises (1)–(3), i.e., both in the direct speech and the indirect speech positions.

The contradiction arises from the tension between a sameness and a difference. In Jocasta's mind or doxastic system, there is the *difference* between Oedipus' father and the previous King of Thebes. This is the difference revealed by premises (1) and (3) taken together. On the other hand, there is the *sameness* between these two entities, formulated by premise (2); this sameness holds in reality, or at least in the mind of whoever believes premise (2).[2]

5. Frege's Two-Dimensional Semantic Solution
to the Paradox of Reference in the Category
of INDIVIDUAL

To resolve the Paradox of Reference, as is well-known, Frege introduced a
two-dimensional semantics, namely: the thesis of the double semantic connection between a singular term and the objects in the world. A term, e.g.,
'The previous king of Thebes', has always a (primary) sense and, sometimes,
a (primary) referent. Frege also introduced the thesis that a singular term in
oratio obliqua (indirect speech) refers to its (primary) sense. He apparently
postulated higher and higher senses and referents in order to account for iterated embedding of indirect-speech constructions in indirect-speech constructions. But we shall ignore this third thesis here.

Frege's solution consists of avoiding the collision between the sameness
and the difference in tension in premises (1)–(3) by assigning them to different entities: thus he removes the common ground where they could collide.
The sameness in reality (or in the doxastic system of whomever believes
premise (2)) Frege assigns to the *common primary referent* of the two terms
'Oedipus' father' and 'the previous King of Thebes'. On the other hand, the
difference in Jocasta's mind he assigns to the *different primary individual
senses* of these terms. Thus, Frege's solution belongs in the category of individuals, which he multiplies appropriately to his theoretical needs.

In sum, Frege rejects (T4), which to most of us seems *so* obvious and un-
questionable. By rejecting (T4) he claims that (T1) is inapplicable to (1) &
(2). Yet he maintains (T1), which thanks to him has been called Leibniz's law,
as a full characterization of genuine identity, but is inapplicable to psychological contexts. Nevertheless he maintains a version of (T2), thus allowing psychological properties, like the one postulated by (T2); these properties, however, turn out to be relations between thinkers and senses, rather than
between thinkers and primary referents. On the other hand, Frege accepts
(T3), thus not insisting on just one concept of identity or sameness. Moreover, Frege keeps a generally simple view of predication; nonetheless, it is not
clear how individual senses relate, on the one hand, to properties and, on the
other, to primary referents. It would seem that a different form of predication
should be needed to connect senses and properties, at least when these occur
within indirect speech.

6. Guise Theory: Its One-Dimensional Semantic
Solution to the Paradox of Reference within
the Nexus of Predication

An alternative to Frege's Sense/Referent solution to the paradox of reference
is Guise Theory. Like Frege's solution, it respects the three factual premises
(1)–(3) and endorses theses (T1) and (T2); it contrasts sharply with Frege's

View in both holding on to the commonsensical (T4) and adopting the apparently non-commonsensical denial of (T3). The guise-theoretical solution does not operate within the category of individuals; initially it looks to lie within the category of properties, but in the end it lies within the nexus of predication. Guise Theory eliminates the tension between the *sameness* in reality, or at least in the doxastic system of him who believes (1) & (2) & (3), which links the previous King of Thebes to Oedipus' father, and the *difference* separating them, in Jocasta's doxastic system, by taking this distinction between sameness and difference LITERALLY at face value. It explains that the tension arises because premise (T3) blurs the distinction by postulating just one sameness or identity. By jettisoning (T3) Guise Theory accepts that there are (at least) *two* distinct relations of the sameness family: genuine identity governed by Leibniz's law, i.e., (T1), and the contingent, factual, existential sameness postulated in premise (2), hereafter called *consubstantiation*. (Later on Guise Theory introduces other members of the sameness family.)

Genuine identity between Oedipus' father and the previous King of Thebes does not hold: they are distinct individuals. Their difference belongs both to reality and to Jocasta's mind; it underlies Jocasta's belief, recorded in premise (1), that they are, also, not contingently the same, i.e., not consubstantiated. The individuals, the previous King of Thebes and Oedipus' father, are different (i.e., non-identical); yet, in spite of Jocasta's belief, they are consubstantiated (i.e., contingently the same). They are, therefore, constitutive of a big unitary chunk in the world: they are thin slices of such a chunk, and we call them *individual guises*.

Obviously, the preceding linguistico-ontological analysis of the Jocasta argument is generalizable to all singular terms and to all speakers. Patently, any two singular terms that are normally said to be coreferring can be passed through a differentiating test like the one above involving Jocasta's beliefs and assumptions (T1)–(T4). A person's beliefs are, thus, sifting devices that discriminate between identity and consubstantiation, and between genuinely identical and distinct individual guises that are in some respect the same.

To place the guise-theoretical approach in a wider perspective, consider the parallel example:

(4) Karl believes that $3 = $ the square root of 9;
(5) $3 = \tan 71.565051$;
(6) Karl doesn't believe that $\tan 71.565051 = $ the square root of 9.

From (4)–(6) we can, with the help of (T1) and counterparts of (T2)–(T4), derive a contradiction. Again, the Fregean solution proposes to distinguish between the primary referent and the different primary senses of the singular terms '3' and 'tan 71.565051'. Here again Guise Theory shunts that common Fregean referent and proposes to fasten, like Frege, to the difference between the numerical guises *3* and *tan 71.565051*. Again, Guise Theory, still focusing on the counter-part of (T3), proclaims that the equal sign '=' in premise (5) [as well as in premises (4) and (6)] does not express strict or genuine identity; but in this case Guise Theory proposes to distinguish genuine identity, not from the empirical sameness of consubstantiation, but from an *a priori* sameness, which it calls *conflation*. Since we are here concerned with selves, which are empirical entities, we shall from here on limit our discussion to consubstantiation.

The preceding distinctions are fundamental laws determining a general characteristic of the mental. Both propositional attitudes (paradigmatically, believing) and practical attitudes (paradigmatically, intending and desiring), as well as propositional episodes of thinking something to be the case and practical episodes of thinking what to do, are *ontological prisms* that diffract massive objects of belief into thinkable guises. Since some of our beliefs about the world are true, the infinitely propertied objects of the world are composed at least in part of finite slices that are individually manageable by our thinking mechanisms; hence, such thin slices, our individual guises, are the strict denotata of our singular terms.

At this juncture two serious problems loom large:

First: What is the constitution of individual guises?

Second: How do individual guises enter into the composition of such massive chunks in the world?

Guise Theory would be an irresponsible artifact if it merely rejected (T3) and proceeded to derive the consequences above noted. It *must*, like any other theory, deal with the problems of predication, individuation, etc. This it does. It goes on to conceive of the two samenesses just mentioned as members of a larger sameness family, and then takes the members of this family as forms of predication. Thus, ordinary properties—as opposed to the sameness properties—are ultimately not predicative, but compositional of individuals.[3]

7. The I-Guises

A good deal of what we have said above applies to indexical terms. In particular, the application of doxastic sieves shows that the indexical uses of the first-person pronoun also refer to individual guises. Consider for concretion the following first-person statements that Jocasta *could*, but need not, formulate at a moment T during the Theban pestilence mentioned in the above premises (1)–(3):

(11) I believe both that I am Oedipus' wife and that I am not Oedipus' mother.

(12) I am the same as Oedipus' mother.

(13) It is not the case that I believe both that I am Oedipus' wife and that I am not I.†

---

† This numbering of the examples follows that of the published version, and is identical to the numbering found in an electronic text in Castañeda's files. Thus, no examples (7)–(10) were given. —Eds.

Here we have the same contradiction as in the preceding case. It is, however, easy to become confused with premise (12). The statements, that is, the *content* of the speech acts of stating that Jocasta would perform by assertively uttering sentences (11)–(13), are true, whether she states them or not. Were she jokingly to assert (12), in a masked ball at the palace, she would be saying something true. Jocasta's beliefs are sieves that discriminate between what at a given time she refers to as "I" and the infinitely many third-person individual guises she herself is contingently the same as.

The same point can be made by means of quasi-indicators. We can describe Jocasta's belief according to (11) by asserting:

(11.q) Oedipus' mother believes at time T that both she (herself) is Oedipus' wife and she is not (herself) Oedipus' mother.

Clearly, we cannot replace the embedded pronoun 'she (herself)' with its antecedent 'Oedipus' mother' *salva veritate*. On the other hand, we can replace the external occurrence of 'Oedipus' mother' with any coreferring term. Hence, no expression coreferring with 'Oedipus' mother' can replace 'she (herself)' with preservation of truth-value. The reason is that the relative pronoun 'she (herself)' is used in indirect speech to depict a first-person reference by the person that is the referent of its antecedent. That is why it is a quasi-indicator: it represents the *making* of an indexical reference being attributed to its antecedent.[4]

The indexical uses of the first-person pronoun have, therefore, no third-person content, whether this is demonstrative or not. As I explained almost twenty years ago, third-person demonstrative reference to oneself (or to an individual that happens to be the same [in the consubstantiational, contingent sense]) is not identical with first-person reference to oneself *qua* oneself. Of course, first-person references are also lacking in second-person content. Consequently, indexical uses of the first-person pronoun have as their proprietary referents very special guises. They are very special in that they refer to an individual guise that is essentially constituted by the making of a first-person to itself. *The essence and the substance of an I is just to conceive itself as a subject* qua *subject*.

This is so important, that we must come to it through other, convergent lines of development. Let us for contrast pursue now a historical route and enjoy the architecture along the sojourn.

8. Kant's Datum about the I THINK

Kant described the unity of consciousness by saying that an *I think* must be capable of accompanying all my representations. This is true for everybody, of course. The 'my' in question is a variable ranging over the proprietary makers of first-person references, whoever they may be. One way of interpreting this, giving it a linguistic twist (which slightly distorts, but perhaps does not drastically misinterpret Kant's intent), is to construe it as pointing to the principle that:

(I-OO) Every utterance expressing a thought (whether believed or not by the speaker) is in principle and at bottom subordinated to an implicit *I think that* (or, even, to an *I say that*).

A crucial consequence of (I-OO) is this:

(I-OR) Every statement lies implicitly, or explicitly, in *oratio obliqua* (indirect speech), and the only true or genuine *oratio recta* (direct speech) is the unspoken *I think*—this is Kant, but I wish to add—or, rather, *I think here now*.

9. The I in Descartes' COGITO

Principle (I-OR) was applied, but not conceived as such, by Descartes in his first *Meditation*. To be sure, he was very little concerned with linguistic analysis. His whole sceptical tactic is precisely an attempt to infect everything with doubt, that is, an attempt to subordinate, in principle, a complete exhaustive description of the world, let us call it THE BALLOON, and of the doubter's experience to the prefix *I doubt*, which is simply a special instance of the prefix *I think*. Then in the second *Meditation* Descartes reflects upon that subordination, and discovers that the doubting, thinking *I* is outside THE BALLOON, and so is the *doubting* itself—and so is the subordination. Although Descartes did not dwell upon it, not even the evil demon can cause me to subordinate every *I doubt* without thereby introducing a non-subordinated, but subordinating, *I doubt*. In any case, Descartes proceeds to extract items from the hypothesized all-encompassing exhaustive description of the whole world, from THE BALLOON. This was, as Kant well knew, a grave error. All we have a right to claim is that the transcendental structure *I-think-THE-BALLOON* has a *source* beyond THE BALLOON: this is Kant's negative concept of the noumenon. Hence, all we can do is to take THE BALLOON as the posited world, and each experience as a mere internal component of THE BALLOON that points to that noumenon beyond. All we can do is to study the internal nature of THE BALLOON: This is the Copernican revolution, which shunts transcendent metaphysics and adopts a phenomenological program.

Now, the structure *I-think-THE-BALLOON* underlies every experience: every experience is a piecemeal confrontation with the world, posited as encompassing the experience in question. In that sense the I of that structure is a mere form of the unity of the particular experience with the posited world at large. Furthermore, on the occasion of each experience one can raise the Cartesian hyperbolic doubt and uncover the underlying structure *I-think-THE-BALLOON*. But then the I of this structure is not in THE BALLOON, is non-worldly, and may be called *transcendental I*. On the other hand, that structure is the content of an experience, namely, the Cartesian experience of hyperbolic doubt. Hence, that transcendental I must be represented by a thinking subject within THE BALLOON itself. There must, consequently, be within THE BALLOON an empirical self, an I, that phenomenologically anchors the transcendental self—just as there must be a metaphysical source beyond THE BALLOON that grounds both the empirical I's and the transcendental I.

The metaphysical source of the transcendental I is forever beyond. We can peel off from it other slices of the transcendental I by iterating the transcendental reflection, and dwelling upon the content *I-think-that-[I-think-THE-BALLOON]*. This reflective iteration delivers both a new transcendent I and a transcended I, both outside THE BALLOON, but the latter inside an extended BALLOON. We have gained nothing about the transcendental thinking self. Evidently, the only direction in which the thinking I can gain substance or content is the phenomenological one: the transcendental I can have no more content than the sum of empirical identifications of the empirical selves equated with a given transcendental I with items in THE BALLOON. Not to see this is, as Kant diagnosed it, to commit a paralogism of pure reason.

10. The I of the Kantian I THINK

Kant seems to me to oscillate between taking the transcendental I to be the unspoken subject of the subordinating prefix *I think* (when this is unspoken and it implicitly unifies a network of experiences) and taking the transcendental I to be the I referred to in the explicit assertion of an all-encompassing *I think*. The two positions are compatible if the spoken encompassing *I think* is given a very special interpretation. Among the main features of that special interpretation are: (i) the pronoun 'I' does not denote an object —certainly not an object of experience, because all objects of experience lie within THE BALLOON; (ii) the verb 'think' does not express an action, event, or state —again actions, events, and states are all in THE BALLOON; (iii) the all-encompassing *I think* is tenseless; and of course (iv) it is spaceless; (v) the all-encompassing *I think* expresses the unity of the encompassed experience.

The force of (i)–(v) is to assimilate the spoken I of an explicitly encompassing *I think*, hereafter called *transcendental prefix*, to the unspoken subordinating I of the tacit *I think*. But the price is high. For one thing, it is a mystery why the words 'I' and 'think' are the appropriate ones to express the unity of experience. In what sense is there such an I facing the total balloon? Secondly, there are *I*'s and *think*'s within the subordinated balloon. How do they connect with those in the transcendental prefix? Thirdly, doesn't the thinking, let alone the saying, "I think" as the all-encompassing prefix of experience place the all-confronting I within experience, although not as an object? Fourthly, if the transcendental prefix is, not just *I think*, but *I think now*, or even *I think here now*, then to the extent that there is an I connected to experience by thinking, and both the I and the thinking are transcendental in that they represent somehow what lies beyond experience, then why isn't there in the transcendent beyond something corresponding to, although perhaps not necessarily analogous to, time and space?

There are other questions, but this must suffice to show how deep the tension within Kant's transcendental prefix is: on the one hand, it represents something that lies beyond experience, on the other hand it places something in experience. Because of principle (I-OO), the transcendental prefix depicts effectively the tension between the noumenon and the phenomenon in Kant's critical, transcendental philosophy. But let us move on along our historical route about the I.

11. The C-Kant-Frege Vanishment of Frege's Primary Referents

Combining the Kantian tenet (I-OO) with Frege's thesis—that in indirect speech a singular term denotes, not its Fregean primary referent, whatever this may be, but a Fregean sense—we obtain the C-Kant-Frege view. (The 'C' is meant to signal that perhaps here is a combination of curtailed, and perhaps contorted views of Frege and Kant.) A central tenet of this combined view is the above quoted principle (I-OR), according to which the only true genuine construction in direct speech is the transcendental prefix. An immediate consequence of the combination is that *the Fregean primary referents vanish*, except perhaps the referent of the singular term 'I' (perhaps also the referents of the terms 'here' and 'now') as this term (and 'here' and 'now') occur in the (extended) transcendental prefix *I think (here now)*. This has momentous consequences for the subjects of experience and the I's in the world.

An important ontological consequence of the C-Kant-Frege View (discarding Frege's third thesis of higher senses for the iterated embedding of indirect speech constructions) is that *all* singular terms, except perhaps 'I' (and 'here' and 'now'), refer to Frege's primary senses. To be sure, Frege's primary referents may still exist as autonomous, even somehow thinkable entities. But they break away from the semantics of singular terms.

The C-Kant-Frege view puts the semantics of singular reference in a new light by promoting, at least initially, Frege's primary senses to the status of being the *only* denotata of singular terms. Because of the disappearance of genuine direct-speech constructions, this combined view provides a unified semantics of reference by allowing, commonsensically, that a singular term denotes precisely the same self-identical referent both in indirect speech and in (apparent) direct speech. The view also presents a new ontology by eliminating Frege's primary referents from the semantics of singular reference.

Frege's primary referents may, as remarked, still be objects of belief and thought. How? Recall that the thinking singular references of a person P through a thinking episode embodied in an event of P's tokening a sentence S are precisely the semantico-pragmatic denotations of the tokens of the singular terms in the token of S. Therefore, the Fregean primary referents, if we are to posit them, cannot be the targets of thinking singular reference. If at all they will have to be referred to by means of *general* or quantificational reference, and must be identified through their connections with the Fregean senses, or alternative thin finite individuals, like the above individual guises, which are manageable units of finite thinking.

Therefore, Frege's primary referents must be connected to Fregean primary senses, or our individual guises, in a way that is both ontologically feasible and epistemologically accessible. Evidently, the simplest account that conforms to these desiderata is this: Fregean primary referents, which are exclusive targets of general reference, are especial structures or systems of Frege's primary senses or of our individual guises.

12. Guise Theory Again

We have seen above how Guise Theory is an alternative to Frege's Sense/Referent solution to the paradox of reference. Then we entered Guise Theory through two parallel distinctions: (a) between genuine identity and contingent, existential sameness, and (b) between genuine identity and a weaker necessary sameness. We now enter Guise Theory through the semantic destruction of Frege's primary referents. In the C-Kant-Frege View we have the promotion of Frege's primary senses to proprietary semantic referents of singular terms. But, obviously, once the contrast between primary referent and primary sense disappears, the remaining entities are the primary referents, indeed the *only* referents of singular reference, and they turn out to be governed by different laws. Certainly, the principles governing the vanished Fregean semantic contrast go by the board. Hence, it is somewhat of a misnomer to continue to call them senses. Let us call them *individual guises*.

Of course, the new name does not solve any problems. We must, as always, tackle the fundamental ontologic and semantic problems. We must still develop a comprehensive theory worthy of discussion, a theory that includes an account of individuation, identity, predication, etc. The C-Kant-Frege View must be developed. And developed it becomes: we merge it with Guise Theory by means of the theoretical leap that identifies the new individual guises, found through the historical Kant-Frege route, with the old individual guises subject to trivial, all-pervasive identity, which is truly and deeply self-identity, 'governed by the most unrestricted Leibniz's law', obedient to the laws of consubstantiation, conflation, and those of the other sameness-forms of predication. But we have no time to pursue this. Let us return to the self-guises.

13. Indexical Reference, Guise Theory, and Indexical Guises

In the preceding sections we have considered indexical first-person reference as a special case of singular reference. It has been rewarding to treat the nature of the self against the background of the individuals we find in experience, and it is delightful to find the convergence of different lines of analysis and development. Let us consider indexical first-person reference as a special case of indexical reference. Then we should have prepared the proper set-up for the discussion of the particular features that belong exclusively to first-person reference. Such features will then be more revealing of the peculiarities of the selves of the world and the manifold I's within THE BALLOON. Here is a fruitful example whose exegesis should prove beneficial:

(21) Mark McPherran believes that NOW I am working on Plato's views of relational facts in THIS DIALOGUE OF HIS MIDDLE AGE.†

The three fully capitalized expressions 'NOW', 'I', and 'THIS DIALOGUE OF HIS MIDDLE AGE' are indexical. I mean my (21) to have 'HIS' referring to Plato, not to McPherran. *Grammatically* the three terms occur in indirect speech, within the scope of the psychological prefix 'Mark McPherran believes that'. Yet *logically*, *semantically*, and *communicationally*, they lie outside the scope of this prefix. This is nowadays, at last, obvious and most philosophers would immediately say that the three indexical expressions occur *de re*, not *de dicto*, in sentence (21). I have a mild objection to this jargon.[5] One reason is that the expression '*de re*' tends to be used with its etymological force, as implying the existence of the entities (the *re*) referred to with terms that occur *de re*, and this existential import is not assumed to be part and parcel of other aspects that often, but not always, go together with *de re* expressions. Consider, e.g.:

(22) Christopher Columbus believed that Castro's island was China;
(23) Helmut believes that the hero of Cervantes's greatest novel was mistreated by Cervantes.

Palpably, in a normal use of (22) the term 'Castro's island' expresses speaker's reference only, and says nothing as to how Columbus referred to what the speaker calls "Castro's island." Similarly, Klaus, who in disagreement with Helmut claims that *Don Quijote* is Cervantes's best novel, may very well proffer (23) using the term 'the hero of Cervantes's greatest novel' with *external construal*, to express just his own reference to Don Quijote, without revealing how Helmut refers to this personage.

It is, obviously, of the utmost importance to fasten one's attention firmly to the differences between: (a) the distinction between the internal or external construal of a term in indirect speech; (b) the distinction between having or lacking existential import; (c) the distinction among expressing only speaker's reference or an attribution of reference to another or a mixture thereof. Otherwise we cannot do full justice to the richness of the experience that the richness of our language allows us to enjoy.

† Again, the numbering follows both the published and electronic text, and there are no examples (14)–(20). —Eds.

The indexical terms in (21)—'I', 'NOW', and 'THIS DIALOGUE OF HIS MIDDLE AGE'—play in (21) several chief roles, among which are:

I. *Pragmatic roles*:

  (i) They express nothing but speaker's reference;
 (ii) They express indexical reference made by the speaker and nobody else;
(iii) As such they have an executive or performative role of placing the items referred to indexically in the (speaker's) thinker's experience;
 (iv) Those indexical terms are *not* used to attribute indexical reference to Mark McPherran;

II. *Syntactico-semantic roles*:

  (v) They are syntactically absolute, and not relative pronouns, and connect, by virtue of their executive role, with their denotations immediately, not through cross-reference or back-reference to other terms;
 (vi) They have an external construal—like 'Castro's island' in (22);
(vii) They occupy in indirect speech positions that belong to expressions that would express how Mark McPherran refers to the items they denote; hence:
(viii) They represent positions of *propositional opacity* in (21) and more specifically in the subordinate clause of (21), namely: the positions where McPherran's own expressions would occur were he to express what according to (21) he believes through a sentence of the grammar illustrated by the indirect clause in (21).[6] Hence:

III. *Communicational roles*:

 (ix) There is no way of retrieving from (21) alone how McPherran has referred, or will refer, to the items the speaker calls "I," "now," and "this dialogue of his [Plato's] middle age."
  (x) Perhaps McPherran has referred, or would refer, to the *same* items by means of indicators, perhaps he may have used, or might use, the very same indexical expressions I have used in (21); in such a case, however, the tokens of these expressions produced by McPherran did, or would, express *his very own* acts of reference (different from mine) with his very own referential targets (different from mine), namely: the indexical I-, NOW-, and THIS-dialogue-of- HIS-middle-age- guises in MacPherran's own experience. (To belabor the point, clearly McPherran cannot use the first-person pronoun to refer to *me*; clearly the time of *his* reference is different from mine and his experience now is different from mine; likewise, his *this*'s are different from mine, and indeed some of them can very well be my *that*'s, and vice versa.)

Once again we face here a tension between a sameness and a difference. Once again, we can handle it by taking the sameness between McPherran's indexical experiential guises to be different from mine, but the same in the contingent-identity, i.e., consubstantiational sense.

The above ten points of information do not exhaust the semiotic content of the mere assertive profference of sentence (21). They establish that we need a logical notation that can formulate perspicuously the above exegesis of the type of message (21) conveys. The following is only a first step, which I call the *preliminary alpha analysis*:

(21.A) There is a person *alpha*, who is the same as I, and a book *beta*, which is the same as THIS DIALOGUE PLATO WROTE WHEN HE WAS MIDDLE AGE, and a time *gamma* which is the same as NOW, such that Mark McPherran believes that *alpha* is at time *gamma* working on Plato's view of relational facts in *beta*.

Patently, (21.A) accomplishes the task of exhibiting clearly all the features (i)–(x) distilled above.

Now, what happens when we embed (21) in another psychological prefix? Consider for instance:

(24) Jig-chuen Lee knows that Mark McPherran believes that I am NOW working on Plato's view of relational facts in THIS DIALOGUE OF HIS MIDDLE AGE.

Manifestly, the indexical references expressed by the fully capitalized terms are made by the speaker; nor are they made by or attributed to Jig-chuen Lee. Therefore, the preliminary alpha analysis applies to (24). More specifically, (24) should be equivalent to, indeed, should express the same content or proposition as the sentence resulting from embedding (21.A) in the prefix 'Jig-chuen Lee knows that'; let us call this embedding sentence (24.A). Clearly, the same rationale that leads from (21) to (21.A) through the preliminary alpha analysis leads from (24) to (24.A), namely:

(24.A) There is a person *alpha 1*, who is (the same as) I, a book *beta 1*, which is the same as THIS DIALOGUE PLATO WROTE IN HIS MIDDLE AGE, and a time *gamma 1*, which is the same as NOW, such that Jig-chuen Lee knows that there is a person *alpha*, who is (the same as) *alpha 1*, a book *beta* which is (the same as) *beta 1*, and a time *gamma*, which is (the same as) *gamma 1*, and Mark McPherran believes that *alpha* is at *gamma* working on Plato's view of relational facts in *beta*.

The general drift of analysis is apparent. (Genuine) indicators, by expressing uncontaminated speaker's reference, really belong in direct speech, and have behind them a chain of equations with unspecified, unrevealed ways of reference available to the persons mentioned in the chain of nested psychological prefixes. This is the way it seems. And this is true with some crucial exceptions. Succinctly, the exceptions are these.[7]:

(Ex.1) The tokens of the indicators 'I', 'here', and 'now' must *always* be brought out of all subordinate clauses in indirect speech by means of the alpha analysis —except when they are subordinated to tokens of themselves.

An example is this:

(25) I believe that now I am happy here.

The embedded sentence 'now I am happy here' expresses exactly what I believe, if (25) is true: there is no room for referential opacity: the indeterminateness that the alpha analysis introduces is out of order here. If the subordinating prefix of (25) were fully specified, it would become the extended prefix *I believe here now*.

(Ex.2) Tokens of the indicator 'you' behave similarly to the tokens of 'I', 'here', and 'now' in that they can be brought out of their subordinate position except when they are immediately subordinated to another coreferential token of 'you'; but the tokens of 'you' stay within an indirect speech clause subordinated to an encompassing *I think (here now)*.

(Ex.3) The tokens of the other indicators, i.e., third-person indicators with which we make demonstrative references to objects and persons, can always be brought out of their subordinate position in indirect speech, except when they are subordinated to an *I think (here now)*.

There are many important points and lines of exegesis lurking behind and awaiting a call to the stage. Nevertheless, we must leave them behind the curtains and limit ourselves to just a few remarks:

(I) The preliminary alpha analysis, which has been excellent in making perspicuous the features (i)-(x) of indicators in indirect speech, raises some fundamental questions of its own, in particular these two:

(A) What are the values of the quantificational variables *alpha, beta, gamma*?

(B) What exactly is the sameness relation postulated by the alpha analysis?

Naturally, different theories may issue as answers to these questions. One such theory is Guise Theory. It has the tremendous advantage of furnishing a ready made answer, which thus shows itself to be fruitful, not *ad hoc* in the pejorative sense of this expression. Guise Theory simply says: in response to question (A), let the variables *alpha, beta,* and *gamma,* have individual guises as values; in response to question (B), let the sameness at issue here be consubstantiation, but be prepared to replace it with some other sameness relation in other cases.

In brief, the exegesis of indexical reference in indirect speech, which led us to the preliminary alpha analysis, uncovers additional data, which in its own route takes us to Guise Theory.

(II) With respect to embedment and the alpha analysis, the fundamental co-ordinates of experience are the I-, the Here-, and the Now-dimensions.

All other indexical references are internal to the contents encompassed in THE BALLOON confronting the transcendental prefix. This includes all the *that*'s and *this*'s and *you*'s of experience. This is a signal of the impossibility of a logical refutation of solipsism.

(III) The fact that all indicators can be brought out of all indirect speech constructions except those in the scope of an extended transcendental prefix signals an important partition within the contents of experience. The ultimate canonical description of an experience, and ideally—in Kant's sense of ideas and ideals of reason—a total maximal description of the world, is thus of the form:

(B*) I think here now that: [THE WHOLE BALLOON, with prefatory equations asserting the consubstantiational sameness of strict indexical (experiential) guises with non-indexical guises, whether these are referred to singularly or generally, e.g.:] there is an *alpha 1*, an *alpha 2*, an *alpha 3*, . . . such that *alpha 1* is (the same as) THIS 1, *alpha 2* is (the same as) YOU 1, *alpha 3* is (the same as) the F, *alpha 4* is (the same as) NOW, . . .

The partition puts right under the transcendental prefix all the indexical references, and then in the rest of the subordinated BALLOON all the non-indexical facts of the world, psychological, physical, etc. The first layer, the indexical layer, is the layer of the purely experiential references. That is also the layer in which I expect to find all the purely phenomenal qualities and properties of experience. Hence, the alpha analysis (with its variables ranging over the appropriate values, e.g., guises, and its proper sameness relations) divides up nicely the contents of experience between *the purely experiential and private contents*, subordinated immediately to the transcendental prefix, and the rest, *the intersubjective, physical, psychological, and sociological contents of the world*. In this schematic division we have a signal of the grains of truth in empiricism and in phenomenalism.

(IV) The limitation of the application of the alpha-analysis to 'I', 'here', and 'now' is most significant. It suggests that the proprietary semantic referent of the embedded occurrences of 'I', 'here', and 'now' can be interpreted indexically and are not merely coreferring, but are tokens of exactly the same self-identical singular term. Here we have an indication that each I of Kant's transcendental prefix, peeled off from the transcedental reservoir that is the transcendental self, in the process of iterating the transcendental Cartesian hyperbolic experience, is a just another I-guise, whose content consists simply of being the subject of the higher-order experience of encompassing, bracketing, all the contents of a given network of experiences in a big BALLOON wherein skepticism runs rampant and indefeasible.

We have no room to outline a guise-theoretical account of perception, which should explain the role of indexical guises in perceptual consciousness.

Since indexical references are personal indexical guises are experiential. Since demonstrative reference is executive and locates indexical guises in perceptual experience, indexical guises are experience guises in perceptual fields. Here there are many profound issues, e.g., the structural differences between perceptual and non-perceptual experiences. Perhaps a discussion of these matters elsewhere may be helpful.[8]

14. The Transcendental Prefix, the Extended COGITO, and Experience

Let us now return to Kant's transcendental prefix *I think*. Recall the internal tension in the prefix. Again, it is a deep tension between a sameness and a difference: the sameness is that between the spoken I, referred to in the transcendental prefix, and the unspoken source of the experience to which the word 'I', or the concept *I*, points to in a pointing that transcends experience and full conceptualization; the difference is that between what that source may be in itself and what it appears to be. Again perhaps we should take this difference and the sameness involved at face value.

There is no transcendent I. There is a transcendent noumenon, beyond THE BALLOON, which underlies at once and *holistically* THE BALLOON, our experiences, and their subjects. Such an underlying entity is the *unspoken* and ineffable source from which arises within experience the actually encompassing I of an explicitly conceived (although perhaps not spoken) *I think*. If there is no encompassing, if there is no actually subordinating *I think*, there is no encompassing thinking and there is no encompassing I. This encompassing I, though only existing while encompassing, is transcendental in the sense that it quietly points to that source beyond the experience from which it issues. The whole conceptual foundation of the pointing to that source beyond is nothing else than the very fact of its encompassing THE whole BALLOON. All actual encompassings, expressed with the assertive utterance of "I think" and actually performed with the thinking "I think," take place in experience, regardless of how much this "I think" encompasses in the subordinated balloon. This encompassing I is, thus, a genuine I, an I-guise, having the higher-order experience of encompassing at a given time and at a given place. Hence, it lies wholly within, and is exhausted by, the encompassing experience. The place and the time in question are also internal to the experience of encompassing: they are a *here* and a *now*.

The true transcendental prefix is, it seems, the extended one: *I think here now*. By the same Cartesian considerations that led Descartes to the indubitability of the doubting I, we reach the indubitability of both the now and the here of the doubting. Those considerations are simply that all doubts, regardless of how radical they may be, can always be imprisoned in THE BALLOON and in so doing a new transcendental prefix springs forth. Here we encounter the extended *cogito*, which manifests the indubitability of the *I-Here-Now*'s.

This extended *cogito* is Cartesian only in structure. Its contents are anti-Cartesian. For one thing it provides only an I that at all lights is in time and in space. For another, as Kant insisted, it only delivers a genuine *I*—and, we must add, a *here* and a *now*—from inside experience. They belong inextricably together in their ephemeral uniqueness as co-ordinates of one experience. Each I lasts as long as its corresponding NOW and HERE—no more. Descartes for a moment had a lucid glimpse of this at the beginning of the second *Meditation*:

> . . . que cette proposition *Je suis, j'existe*, est nécessairement vrai, toutes les fois que je la prononce, ou que je la concois en mon esprit.

In this passage Descartes uses the French *nécessairement* both as the expression of a modality and in its etymological sense of not-ceasing. In any case the metaphysics of the substantial permanence of every I, not only lacks foundation, but has in the very nature of experiential, indexical reference a positive discouragement.

Of course, the main point of the *cogito* is to establish a metaphysical certainty. As Kant insisted, that is the certainty that *some* entity, the source of the experience, lies beyond the doubting I. This is fine, and it applies equally well to the HERE and the NOW of the doubting experience. Thus, something like space and something like time seem to lie beyond experience, and are in themselves exempt of the ephemeral experiential features of the HERE and the NOW. At any rate, the underlying source of the I is bound up with the underlying source of both time, to which each NOW points, and space, to which each HERE aims. Rather than foment, the extended Cartesian *cogito* strongly discourages the Cartesian metaphysics of disembodiment.

15. Identity of Empirical Selves across Time

We have seen how the I, the Here, and the Now of an encompassing higher-order experience are just guises within the experience. We have also seen how ephemeral and experiential indexical reference is. The I-guises, the Here-guises, and the other indexical guises, are all ephemeral. This raises a problem: How is it that we have first-person statements about the past? Don't such statements convey the information that a present self is the same as a past self? Don't they present changes as having been undergone by one and the same self, the same I, if you wish?

This is a serious and central task. Yet we must be nimble.

An I-guise is, in the light of the preceding discussion, a rather thin individual which is the proprietary subject of a given experience, and vanishes when the experience vanishes. Yet there is an appearance of lastingness beyond each experience. Consider, for instance, a truth I can testify:

(26) I was in Chantilly, France on November 15, 1976, celebrating Leibniz's termination of his sojourn in France on November 15, 1676.

At first blush statement (26) seems to be proclaiming that one individual, the one I am referring to as "I", existed in November 1976 and exists now. Assuming that individuals are not discontinued, then there is an individual that lasted from November 1976 through today. (I don't know today's date, in October 1985.) Which individual is that? Not the subject of the present experience, nor the subject of whatever experiences occurred to me then. But what does this "me" mean here? The same thing that 'I' does in (25). Thus, it would be circular and innocuous to leave the matter this way.

Guise Theory has useful resources to solve the problem. What we have is a present I, who, like every I always, is present to itself and proclaims in (26) that it is *contingently and existentially the same as* a good number of third-person individuals that were in Chantilly on November 15, 1976. Undoubtedly, that manifold of individuals was consubstantiated at each time with an I that was the proprietor of some experiences. But even when I (now here) remember some of those experiences from inside, that past I is a posit. For all I know those memories can be erroneous, the product of my present fantasy. Of course, I naturally make that posit, and I make it in the light of certain experiences and beliefs in accordance with certain inferential and abductive proclivities I (here now) possess.

The main point is that in this case we are not dealing with synchronic existential sameness, but with diachronic existential sameness, which we may call *transubstantiation*. The main differences between these two samenesses are these: in the case of consubstantiation we have the principles of a sameness that relate individual guises pairwise, whereas in the case of transubstantiation we have principles of sameness that tackle systems of guises; consubstantiation is less conventional than transubstantiation; consubstantiation deals with experiences at times and provides the basis for the principles of transubstantiation to apply. In short, the fluidity and richness of the sameness relations is what is needed here. By means of the preliminary alpha analysis expounded above, (26) can be put slightly more perspicuously thus:

(26.A) There is at least one person *alpha* such that I am (the same as, transubstantiationally the same as) *alpha* and *alpha* was in Chantilly, France on November 15, 1976 . . .

Persons are complexes of bodies that behave in certain ways, have certain types of experiences, and are, therefore, connected to particular families of I-guises along their histories. These histories include experiences of identification of given I's with other individuals, and these identifications cover a spectrum of cases that range from a theoretical leap involving an I-guise and a family of third-person guises to cases in which, through memory, an I is equated with persons, so to speak, from inside. Most commonly personal identifications involve combinations of these two models. Here we need the distinction between primary and secondary co-denotata of singular terms in contexts of speech or thought. For once a person has produced the external identification of an I of hers at a given time with some person, the use of the first-person pronoun will be available for the identification of future I's. Furthermore, external identifications produce a re-arrangement of memories and powers to remember, and it may even be possible that lost memories can be regained. For instance, in the case of a split personality, where each of the personalities has its own unshared repository of memories, it may be possible that a third-person identification of an I with the other personality may awaken the I in the identifying personality of the other's memories.

It is crucial, however, to hold on to the fact that remembering having done some action A, or having had an experience E, is not to remember a self or an I, in itself, so to speak, nakedly, doing A or experiencing E. Past selves—as Hume claimed for present selves—are nowhere to be found. What one remembers is a situation from a certain perspective, even if it is the merely intellectual perspective of a hierarchically organized set of beliefs, but often such beliefs include a scaffolding network of perceptual beliefs—and if the person in question has the powers of imagination, these perceptual memories can be recalled as if these were present and were perceived from one or more relevant perceptual perspectives. Thus, remembering *having done or experienced something* from the inside, as *having oneself* done or experienced something, as contrasted with remembering that something occurred, involves a mental time (and space) travel and the *re-living* of a network of indexical references, which constitutes the backbone of the remembered experience.

16. The Self and the I's

Each I or I-guise is the ephemeral proprietary subject of an experience, be this perceptual or purely intellectual, be it reflective or actional, and it is demarcated by the here and the now of the experience. Of course, each I is existentially the same as, or consubstantiated with, other individual guises; some of these are physical, some are psychological, and some are agents constituted by social roles, by duties and interdictions. There is a complex causal and rule-constituted framework of facts (brute, moral, social, etc.) within which an experience occurs. That framework does *not* determine the inner nature of an I: it only determines both the existence of the I in question and the realization of a network of *external* empirical samenesses, in particular a pattern of consubstantiations in the midst of which that I exists. Here we have the domain of first-person synchronic truths involving the I of a particular experience. The network of consubstantiations of a given I, especially the sub-network composed by consubstantiations of that I to psychological individual guises, may be said to constitute a *self* underlying the I in question.

Crucial consubstantiations are those relating the I's of experiences to the

I's of sub-experiences. Because experiences are built on specious presents, we have in these consubstantiations an ineluctable factual basis for the contingent identity of I's across time, i.e., their transubstantiation. Patently, there are as many selves underlying a given I as there are different ways in which the boundaries of the relevant network of consubstantiations can be drawn. Many of such boundaries are conventionally stipulated by institutional rules, and the boundaries are drawn differently in different institutions and even on different occasions.

A self is an enduring entity. This means that we use the word 'self' to refer, not only to networks of consubstantiations anchored to an I or to a sequence of I's overlapping through a sequence of shared specious presents, but also to networks of transubstantiations conventionally constructed. Again, there are many different selves, depending on the diverse institutional conventions we abide by in daily life. Each concept of self gives rise to a corresponding concept of person, and we know how conventional and risky the notion of personal identity is. The discussion of this topic will gain in explanatory power if it is carried out within some version of Guise Theory, which, by dividing the massive objects we believe to be infinitely propertied into individual guises or strands, can account for many more lines of identification than the usual discussions have at their disposal. But this is a problem for another time.

17. Conclusion: I's, Selves, Persons, and Substrates

An I-guise is the I of an experience. An I, a Here, and a Now, constitute the inner framework of an experience. They are mutually irreducible and irreducible to the contents of experience. They are all exhausted by the experience they demarcate: they are most ephemeral and subjective. Because I-guises overlap through overlapping specious presents, which underwrite the unity of the consciousness of each episode of consciousness of succession, there is a concept of a synchronic experiential I or self as a manifold of overlapping I-guises. Beyond the internal aspects of experience, there are concepts of self erected upon manifolds of experiential I's by layers of consubstantiations.

We also have operative concepts of the self as an enduring entity. These selves are simply networks of consubstantiations and transubstantiations built around overlapping I's as well as successive I's, embellished with physical, psychological, and sociological guises as is allowed by the context of surrounding environment and institutions we belong to. That context imbues such networks with special patterns of consubstantiations and transubstantiations. Such patterns are characteristic of the personalities constituted by given synchronic selves.

In any case, a fundamental truth is that there is no special substrate underlying the history of a self, nor is there any substrate underlying the possession of properties by an ephemeral I—indeed there are no substrates underlying the unity of mind and body, nor the histories of physical objects. Simply there are no substrates; there are only guises, and of many varied types and sorts, and their concatenations by means of the different samenesses. In particular, *I am a physical object* is, not, of course, a statement of genuine or strict identity, but one of contingent existential identity just as *The morning star appears in the evening* is a contingent identity, namely: consubstantiation—perhaps with a twinge of transubstantiation. This sameness is, of course, not a noumenal, but a phenomenal, hence, contingent sameness. With this Spinozistic note we may, perhaps, conclude these reflections.

Notes

1. For a somewhat detailed examination of the semantics of the unified language for total experience see Castañeda 1985/1986. For the initial formulation of Guise Theory as a comprehensive account of such a semantics see Castañeda 1974, included in Castañeda 1982a, and for criticism and further development see Plantinga 1983, Clark 1983, and Castañeda's replies to these, all in Tomberlin 1983, as well as Rosenberg 1986a, Smith 1986, Sicha 1986, and Castañeda's replies in Tomberlin 1986.

2. A methodological point may not be entirely amiss here. Since a contradiction can be solved only by substraction, the above argument about Jocasta gives rise initially to seven different types of solution, depending on whether one starts by rejecting (1)-(3) or (T_1)-(T_4)—if we assume, of course, that we do not want to tamper with the logic of the deduction. As premises (1)-(3) are singular propositions, rejecting one of them requires the rejection of some crucial principle in the background evidence for them. This is somewhat vague and one should at least intitially keep them fixed and theorize on the general premises like (T_1)-(T_4). Thus, these provide initially the four interesting approaches or types of theory for the solution of the paradox of reference; nevertheless, one should be prepared to build theories on the rejection of one of the singular premises (1)-(3). Given the present philosophical climate in the English-speaking world, it is fashionable for an "analytic" philosopher to reject (T_2) and hold on to (T_1) and (T_3). Here I want to experiment with the approach that starts off by holding on to (T_1), (T_2), and (T_4) but rejects (T_3). In this regard both the Fregean and the guise-theoretical solutions are not in the main stream of current fashion.

Being fashionable is not, however, our goal, not in any case our primary goal. And several points are worth keeping in mind. *First*, the problems of reference are only a major set of data in the pursuit of understanding of the general structure of the world and of our experience. Hence, we need theorizing that can deliver comprehensive theories of such structures. *Second*, the data cannot underwrite just one theory. *Third*, fortunately, the greatest illumination and understanding of the general structure of the world and of experience can be attained by living our experiences through different comprehensive alternative theories. Hence, *fourth*, we need as many different but comprehensive alternative theories as we can construct; then we will be able to bask in the illumination of dia-philosophical comparison. *Fifth*, given the powerful stimulation and band-wagon effect of the fashions, therefore, if one is to achieve the enormous benefit of a comparison of fashionable with non-fashionable views, some of us have to work on the erection of non-fashionable theories. *Sixth*, the emphasis lies on the comprehensiveness of the theories catering to rich and complex data—indeed, catering to *ALL* the data available at the time of theorization. Clearly, there is not much gain in the critical comparison of narrow-focused or local theories. For a more patient defense of philosophical pluralism and dia-philosophy, see Castañeda 1980a, and also Castañeda 1984c.

3. Guise Theory includes a non-substratist, bundle view of individuation. Individual guises are bundles of properties, and ordinary objects we believe to exist in the world are bundles of guises. This bundle-bundle character of GT allows it to escape the standard objections addressed to bundle theories. See the studies mentioned in Note 1 above.

4. The most comprehensive collection of data pertaining to indexical and quasi-indexical reference appears in Castañeda 1967a. See also Castañeda 1984a, Pilot 1984, and Pape 1984.

5. A run-down of the major distinctions blended together under the *de dicto*/*de re* distinction appears in Castañeda 1980b.

6. The notion of referential opacity† was introduced first in Castañeda 1977b. This essay also translated by Helmut Pape appears in Castañeda 1982a.

7. These exceptions are discussed in Pilot 1984.

8. A theory of perception is added to Guise Theory in Castañeda 1977a. This theory accounts for vexing problems pertaining to the perception of spatial relations through indexical individual guises. In order to provide a unifed account of both the increased information gleaned by mere perceptual attention and the paradox of analysis, the theory of propositional guises, already adumbrated in Castañeda 1967a in the discussion of perspectival properties, and even before, is developed. This leads to the thesis that the primary given in perceptual consciousness is a perceptual field composed of zero-propositional guises. Zero-consciousness is sensitive consciousness, and zero-propositional guises provide a solution to the serious ancient problem of the gap between the non-judgmental nature of the sensory given and the judgmental character of consciousness. This paper, very much revised, translated by Helmut Pape, constitutes Part iv of Castañeda 1982a.

---

† Presumably, Castañeda meant *propositional* opacity at this point, and not *referential* opacity as is written. —Eds.

7

First-Person Statements
about the Past

The Self and the I-Guises
1. The Kant-Fregean argument:
   Elimination of Fregean referents
   The I guises, and the transcendental I
2. Meaning and reference *de re* and *de dicto*
   The rule: "A use of an 'I' refers to the user."
   The rule: "Whoever uses 'I' refers to himself *qua* himself."
3. The I and its co-present co-consubstantiated guises
4. The I and its past co-consubstantiated guises
5. The I and its future co-consubstantiated guises

I. The Kantian-Fregean argument

The Fregean-Kantian argument establishes that the first-person terms denote individual guises.† But it also leaves unreduced the *true*, genuine direct speech terms: 'I', 'now', and 'here'. Consider expressions about the past:

This unfinished and previously unpublished essay is a compilation of two electronic files under this title found in Castañeda's computer disks. It is prefaced by a brief outline entitled "The Self and the I-Guises," though it appears to deal only with the first item on the outline. Its concern with self-identity over time and its mention of a "Kantian-Fregean argument" suggest that it may have been intended as a sequel to "The Self and the I-Guises." If so, it was likely written during the period 1985–1987. Printed here by permission of the Estate of Hector-Neri Castañeda. —Eds.

† It is not entirely clear what argument Castañeda is referring to here, and we have been unable to locate any place in his writings where he refers to an argument with this title. However, in Section 11 of "The Self and the I-Guises" he refers to the "C-Kant-Frege View" combining "Frege's thesis" that singular terms in indirect speech denote senses—or, as Castañeda subsequently argued, individual guises—with the "Kantian tenet" that every utterance is subordinated to an implicit *I think that*. The result is that all singular terms denote individual guises. —Eds.

(1) I am the one who suffered the worst ignominies.
(2) I believe that I suffered the worst ignominies.

QUESTIONS:

(A) Do I identify, i.e., posit an identity between I (an individual that exists now here) with a third-person individual in the past?
(B) Do I identify a past I and posit its identity *qua* I with me?

II. Dr. Shekill and Mr. Fabian

Dr. Shekill is a psychiatrist whom the Department of Police consults when they are investigating a difficult criminal case and want him to help establish a psychological pattern of the criminal.

Unbeknownst to him and to everybody else, Dr. Shekill has been undergoing drastic metabolic changes. Certain chemicals in the salad dressing he likes so much have been affecting him. He has reached the stage that when he has had his salad with his favorite dressing and then takes his regular nightcap, he becomes unconscious and then he wakes up with a new, nasty personality. His facial features also change. Lately he has been going out into the city and has committed crimes. As in the usual stories, he has been attacking prostitutes and nightclub performers. The effect of the drugs has been lasting longer, and now sometimes it lasts several days at a time. Thus he has rented an apartment in a rundown neighborhood and even gotten a job in a bar as peace keeper, throwing out drunkards and those who disrupt the standard disorder and noise level.

The last stage of the effects of the drug put our hero in a state of somnambulism. Sometimes in a form of sleep-walking he reaches his luxurious home and sleeps for several hours. Then he awakes with a renewed professional spirit and works intensely. Occasionally he fails to reach home and falls asleep in a nearby park. When he wakes up in the early morning, he finds himself being Dr. Shekill taking his morning constitutional stroll. In any case, he accounts for his long gaps as a deep-seated need for rest after the long hours of intense work. He thinks, however, these gaps are somewhat freakish both in his unusual, uncanny ability to concentrate on intellectual pursuits and in his immensely recuperative capacity through uninterrupted sleep.

He has advised the Police about the new crimes. The criminal has been heard by some witnesses to refer to himself as Fabian. And the Police have developed, with the assistance of Dr. Shekill, an excellent profile of Fabian.

One night Dr. Shekill leaves a hidden camera at the corner of 10th Street and 10th Avenue. That is a central location in the City's Red Light District. Dr. Shekill was, thus, able to photograph Fabian. He has himself developed the film and has several copies of the photographs on his desk. He has also written a brief note for the DP saying:

(A) This is a recent photograph of Fabian. He will attack within the next two weeks the Blue Azalia. Stake out this nightclub every night from now on. I suspect that he believes that I will predict the location of his next crime. You must be very careful.

Fabian has read in the newspapers about Dr. Shekill and how he has often predicted correctly where he will attack. He decides to have a talk with Dr. Shekill, for whom he has some admiration. Thus, he looks up Shekill's address in the telephone directory and takes a taxi to it.

When Fabian reaches Shekill's house, Shekill isn't there. He observes that the Doctor has his office nearby and walks toward it. He sees a light inside and decides to enter. He sees his own photograph on the desk, and reads the letter to the Police. He exclaims:

(B) Very good, Doctor! Yet you've got it wrong this time. I will not attack the Blue Azalia. I will attack the Red Locust!

These are all the data we need for the time being. The following bits of data, statements made by Fabian, are true, and we want to exegesize them:

(1) Dr. Shekill believes that I will attack the Blue Azalia.
(2) I will not attack the Blue Azalia within two weeks.
(3) Within two weeks I will attack the Red Locust.

As we have discussed many a time before, (1) does not attribute to Dr. Shekill first-person reference to Fabian. The first-person pronoun occurs in (1) somewhat misleadingly placed. In short, (1) is to be analyzed as:

(1.a) There is an individual a who is identical with me and Dr. Shekill believes that a will attack the Blue Azalia.

Similarly, Dr. Shekill's statement

(4) Fabian believes that I will predict the location of his next crime

is to be analyzed as:

(4.a) There is an individual b identical with me such that Fabian believes that b will predict the location of his next crime.

Now I want to examine two different situations:

S1. The situation in which Fabian, knowing that Dr. Shekill has certain beliefs about himself (Fabian), (suddenly) thinks that he is Dr. Shekill;
S2. The situation in which Dr. Shekill, knowing that Fabian has certain beliefs about himself (Shekill), (suddenly) realizes that he is Fabian.

I propose to investigate the effects of the believed identification on each person's beliefs. The readjustment that must take place has, perhaps, a minimal structure, which is to be found whenever such phenomena of recognition take place. If there is such a structure, then elucidating it should give us some insight into personal identity.

III. Situation S1

During the time Fabian is examining the documents in Shekill's office the effects of the drugs diminish slightly, but not enough for him to attain the sonambulic stage. He manages to see his own transformation and see himself gaining some similarity to Shekill's appearance. With the help of a full-size wall mirror, he compares himself with several photographs of Shekill that are spread about the office, and with those collected in a massive album of photos taken at professional meetings and ceremonies. Fabian's first reaction is one of bewilderment. A fleeting thought passes through his mind that the good doctor's office must be bewitched and that explains why he's acquiring the appearance of the dreaded enemy. Then he examines the doctor's photos with great patience, and he observes that in some pictures taken at some professional dinners Shekill has some characteristic features of his own, except for the degree of distortion and the number of simultaneous distortions. There is in some photos the slight protuberance of the cheeks, in others the distortions of the nostrils, in others the contortion of the lips. He suddenly considers that he may be related to Shekill. He becomes profoundly interested in Shekill's biography and searches for documents, encyclopedia entries, and other references where he can learn about Shekill. He goes avidly through everything he can get hold of. Then the idea enters his mind that perhaps he is not related to Shekill, but that he himself is Shekill! He exclaims:

(5) I am Dr. Shekill, and (as such) I have predicted the location of my next crime.

(6) I have predicted it wrong, but I have informed the Police.

Let us pause to interpret Fabian's statement (6). The situation is as follows:

i)   The first-person pronoun 'I' is used by Fabian to refer to his present self, the one that has the experiences he is in part describing.

ii) The original predictor is a past Dr. Shekill.

iii) Fabian expresses his identification of himself with the past predictor.

iv) This identification is derivative. It derives from the primary identification that Fabian makes of himself with Dr. Shekill.

v)   Both the primary and the derivative identifications are identifications of a present self with a past person conceived entirely in the THIRD-PERSON way.

vi) For Fabian to identify himself with the past predictor in the FIRST-PERSON way is for him to remember having (*himself*) made the prediction.

But what is it for Fabian to remember having himself made the prediction?
  Consider that Fabian can truly say:

(7) I do not remember having predicted the location of my next crime.

He may be *positing* that he made the prediction, but he cannot recall having made it. To remember having made the prediction Fabian has to identify himself with the past predictor from, so to speak, inside his experience of the prediction. He lacks by hypothesis any experience of the prediction. He cannot remember circumstances in which he made the prediction. Yet this is not necessary. In principle he could remember having made the prediction even if he doesn't remember the circumstances. It is necessary that he believes firmly that he made the prediction. But now that he thinks that he is Dr. Shekill he believes that he made the prediction. Yet it does not seem sufficient that he believes that he made it personally.

There seems to be a spectrum of cases, clear at the extremes but not so clear in the middle. The more isolated his belief that he made the prediction, the less clearly is the case one of remembering. If a person simply claims to remember having made a prediction but remembers nothing else about the prediction, his claim is indistinguishable from the claim of a person who has acquired the firm belief that he made the prediction, perhaps based on nothing at all. A clear-cut case of remembering having done something involves remembering something else, namely, some of the circumstances in which the action was performed. Apparently, we must adopt some structural principle like this:

(M.C*) Memories come in clusters: each supporting the others by structural relationships, e.g., perceptual relationships, causal connections, underlying intentions, and temporal and spatial locations.

Furthermore, besides the fact that beliefs come in networks, we must consider the role of the agent. Since the remembered action is seen from the inside of the doing of the action, the perceptions (if any) involved cannot include a perception of the agent, unless it is a perception of certain parts of his/her body or an image of the whole body as reflected, e.g., in a mirror. This is important also because the perceived objects should be remembered as from the perspective of the agent's location. The networks of perceptual memories that assign a clear-cut spatial position to the agent are excellent support for the agent's claim of remembering his having done the action in question. The clearer the position of the agent in a perspective origin, the more personal the memories look and the more firmly they can anchor an agent's having done something.

The problem with purely intellectual actions like predicting an event is that they need not involve perceptual perspectives or definite locations in space. Yet a network of perceptions locating the external circumstances of the agent at the time of predicting, or the motivations for making the prediction, or the circumstances of the communication of the prediction, do anchor the action in the world.

In brief, memories come in networks that place the experience in a context.

Images, feelings have a role to play in placing the remembered item in context, but they are not required. Whatever images or feelings occur must be interpreted and it is this interpretation that counts. For instance, an image representing a perceptual perspective from the place at which the agent did something or underwent an experience is helpful. Naturally, there can be conflicts in the network of alleged memories.

IV. Situation S2

In his office Dr. Shekill is studying Fabian's photographs. He becomes hungry and goes to the kitchen to fetch something to eat. He makes a sandwich and to improve its flavor he adds some drops of his favorite salad dressing. He returns to his desk. Then he goes to the bathroom with two photos of Fabian's that have attracted his interest. There he feels sick and watches himself in the mirror, and sees some slight changes that he is undergoing. He realizes that he is becoming like the man in the photographs. He recalls his sudden periods of sleep or actual disappearance from daily life. After some reflections, he comes to believe that he* is Fabian. He exclaims:

(8) I am Fabian, and I have predicted the location of my next crime.

Sentence (8) is just a token of the type of which (5) is another token. But the propositions they express are different. The subjects are different. These are distinct I's. Each of these I's is determined by a different experience, and this occurs as the apex of a chain of events. Furthermore, the two propositions are in tension. If one is true, the other is not. In detail, what the two sentences represent is of the form:

(5a) I [a subject presently experiencing and existing, determined by the history, especially the inner history, of Fabian] am Dr. Shekill, and . . .
(8a) I [a subject presently experiencing and existing, determined by the history, especially the inner history, of Dr. Shekill] am Fabian, and . . .

We have here the suggestion that each I is determined by physical guises as parameters.

V. The Problem:
First-Person Past-Tense Statements†

In the Shekill-Fabian story we have first-person statements of identification. We have two personalities (persons) each one with its own history and its own center of consciousness. What happens is that one person identifies itself with the other, but the identification starts from a first-/third-person affair. It is

† Here begin the contents of a second file. The title of this section is Castañeda's, though we have supplied the section number. The abrupt breakoff suggests that the section is incomplete. —Eds.

only an empirical matter that the other person gains (if he/she ever does gain) access to the other's memories, thus making genuine first-/third-person extensions of the reservoir of beliefs that accrue to the new enriched person.

Obviously, the first-/third-person identification of Shekill with Fabian, or vice versa, is just an extremely rich and special case. But the richness is not necessary. The phenomenon is structurally the same whether we have two richly distinct persons that by having a common bodily basis can identify with each other, or whether we have one person who identifies him/herself as the such and such who did some action A or had a certain experience E he does not remember. Patently, there is the person who did A or the person who experienced E; there is the center of consciousness of that person at the time of the action or of the experience. The fact that that person does not re-appear as in the case of Fabian is immaterial.

To construct a bridge between the two cases just consider the situation in which Dr. Shekill vanishes completely and Fabian identities himself with the missing Dr. Shekill. The only difference between this case and the isolated lost memory is that between the thinness of the latter and the richness of the former.

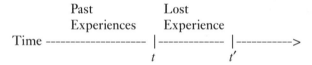

The isolated lost experience has a self referring to itself in the first-person way and one that has all the previous memories of the common self up to time t. The use of 'I' at t' could be said to refer to the subject of the experience at t', but could also refer to the self that has that experience and had the previous, past experiences. What I want to argue is that this past self being referred to at t' is only the present self of t' identified with past selves. Thus, the first-person pronoun used indexically refers to a self co-terminous with a here and a now, the dimensions of the specious present of an experience. How?

The view I want to defend is that each I goes with the now and the here of an experience, so that there is no permanent I that underlies the history of a person, but only a succession of I's, some of which are interlocking, overlapping because specious presents are overlapping. There is a continuous consciousness from time t to time t' and there could be an encompassing I that endures from t to t', yet there *need* not be such an I. Within that encompassing I there could be a succession of smaller overlapping I's.

What about the representation in memory of one's own experiences and intentional actions? Memory cannot establish that there was an I that has lasted from the past to the present. Yet memory can provide an internal representation of past actions. Consider my memory that I did something, say, e.g., wrote "Thinking and the Structure of the World." I remember having written it. That is, I have memory images of how pieces of paper with paragraphs on that paper looked to me as if I were writing them, some by handwriting and some by typing them. I also have abilities to say things that are connected with the contents of that essay and with other papers of mine and other experiences, etc. In short, the memory in question is in part a network of representations of perceptual experiences from a certain perspective, namely of a writer with my writing habits looking at his writing while doing it.

This does not establish that there is one self underlying the whole sequence of changes I have undergone.

(1) The changes I have undergone.

What does this mean? Perhaps the following?

(1.a) There are persons p_i at previous times i such that $C^*(I, p_i)$ and there is a change Ch of p_i at i.†

WHAT'S THE DIFFERENCE BETWEEN remembering that one did an action A or had an experience E AND believing that one did A or experienced E? Let's consider actions.

One remembers having done an action A. This construction is very suggestive. It has no surface agent. Of course, we know that there is an implicit quasi-indicator 'one', and that one expresses what one remembers in the first-person way: "I did A." Yet the lack of the subject pronoun is representative of an important feature of memory, namely, that *there is no I in the memory*.

To remember having done something is in part to be able to produce first-person past-tense statements and to assent to them. It is in part to be able to produce mental images as representatives of the contents of the experience of doing the action in question. To the extent that 'remember' is used with a success condition, then part of remembering is that the appropriate truths obtain.

The statements and the mental images one can produce when one remembers that one did A constitute the description of a perceptual situation in which one could use indicators—if one performs the appropriate mental space-time travel that underlies the use of the so-called historical present. It is THE PATTERN OF INDEXICAL REFERENCES THAT CONSTITUTE THE BACKBONE OF AN EXPERIENCE, AND, HENCE, THE BACKBONE OF A MEMORY.

1. mental space-time travel
2. pattern of indexical references
   (i) personal and ephemeral;
   (ii) intersubjectively depictable through quasi-indicators;
   (iii) subjectively capturable in imagination;
   (iv)

---

† It is difficult to make sense of this unless (1) is reformulated as a sentence. Perhaps Castañeda intended (1) to be something like "I have undergone changes." The operator 'C*' is Castañeda's symbol for the relation of consubstantiaton; see Castañeda 1974. Here follows a distinct break in the text. —Eds.

8

Metaphysical Internalism, Selves, and the Indivisible Noumenon (A Fregeo-Kantian Reflection on Descartes's *Cogito*)

1. Modest Transcendental Realism: The *Cogito*, the Balloon, and the True

The most radical forms of skepticism force us into Metaphysical Internalism. This is, very roughly, the view that all thought and talk about the world and the reality underlying it are internal to experience, whatever reality may be in itself beyond experience, indeed, even if there is no reality beyond experience.

The world we encounter might certainly be all illusory, exhausted in its own appearance. Our lives could be coherent hallucinations created by an Evil Demon. Each of us could be a brain in a cask, perversely, or happily, manipulated by a clever experimenting scientist. I might have always been just an immobile, computerlike artifact at the center of a huge spaceship the likes of which will not yet be dreamed of on earth for centuries, and my experiences and beliefs, piecemeal hallucinatory, could be caused by the interaction of cosmic rays and waves impinging on my electronic parts made of some unfathomable materials.

These are, of course, mere philosophical fantasies. Nevertheless, they are philosophically salutary—if we do not, depressed, stay with them. They can be neither proved nor disproved. Obviously, any argument offered, whether pro or con, if its premises are not inconsistent, can always be rejected by an opponent. The rejection recipe is simple: Choose one premise, claim that *at it* the argument begs the question, and demand a proof of that premise; repeat the procedure for the new argument, and for each of its successors; if, at some

This essay appeared in *Midwest Studies in Philosophy, XII* (University of Notre Dame Press, 1987), 129–144, edited by P. French, T. E. Uehling Jr., and H. K. Wettstein. Reprinted by permission of the publisher.

round of argumentation, you are tempted by the premises, complement the argument with a modus tollens, and take it as a proof that the least attractive premise is false.[1]

My purpose here is neither argumentative nor dialectical. I am not concerned with building an argument that finally, and conclusively, establishes radical skepticism. I immediately surrender to Descartes's nondemonstrative hyperbolic techniques of doubt. Thus, obversely, I desire NOT to engage in a refutation of radical skepticism to secure the metaphysical basis for our daily living. Radical skepticism is cathartic: It *can* be treated optimistically: In the final analysis, it must be swallowed whole in one gulp and then allowed to do its job in oblivion. (But I understand the manifold passions for professional skepticism.) My aim here is hermeneutical and constructive, namely, to subject the phenomenon of radical skepticism to exegesis in order to distill the deep reality-content of the world in which we find ourselves.

Most of us do not believe the skeptical arguments. But are we justified in supposing that there is a reality beyond, and underlying, experience?

The mere affirmative answer to this question is *Minimal Transcendental Realism*. It is compatible with Metaphysical Internalism. As I interpret Kant, his Copernican Revolution is his adoption of Metaphysical Internalism. Some philosophers would say "antirealism"; this expression is, however, not adequately descriptive. Kantian terminology, albeit archaic and tainted with the suggestions and images of Kant's own views, is more apt: Radical skepticisms strangle our complacency with transcendent metaphysics and thrust us into transcendental idealism. The outcome is that, with the exception of the account of what he calls the problematic noumenon, we are limited to do, as I have sometimes called it, phenomenological ontology.[2] His claim that, properly speaking, we have only a *negative* concept of the noumenon is his endorsement of Minimal Transcendental Realism.[3]

According to Metaphysical Internalism, I must not try to break my possibly nonexisting head attempting to beat the skeptical arguments: I must yield to the deepest skeptical doubts and concede that all my experiences could, in principle and in fact, be illusory. I must, then, turn to inside experience and follow Leibniz's internalist advice,[4] making my problem that of understanding the contents and the structure of the experienced world, however illusory these may be. I must understand them from *inside*, not from without, as God may see them; even the skepticism of the past, whether composed of events in the external world or of speech acts that have a semantic unit across time, should be granted, and acknowledge that the past is posited within the bounds of present experience.

Enter Minimal Realism. We fasten to a minimal transcendent-pointing framework—we may call it *transcendental*—within which we must vicariously and holistically connect our experiences to a reality beyond merely pointed to. Within the structures of that framework, we can posit a hierarchical quilted world with varying degrees of uncertainty. By fastening to those posits, we can live our autobiographies with variegated degrees of limited certainty. Happiness? It must lie somewhere in the interaction of those posits and the succession of our experiences.

Minimal Realism is indispensable if the whole of experience is not to become lost in a total circle of fiction. Clearly, a character in a fictional story may be said to engage in, say, skeptical doubts concerning the possibility of an Evil Demon who deceives him at every thought. But the character is *said* to do that, he does not *actually* do anything. This difference spans the difference between literature, or science fiction, and artificial intelligence. Thus, when I (whatever I may really be) engage in that reflection, I indeed *engage* in it. More generally, as Descartes pointed out (at the beginning of his second *Meditation*), regardless of how much the Evil Demon may deceive me, he cannot deceive me about two things: (i) that I think, and (ii) that I am having such and such thoughts. These are for real.

(D.2) But I am persuaded that there is nothing in the world. . . . But [I have supposed] there is and I don't know what that deceives, too powerful and too cunning, who uses all his skills to deceive me always. Then there is no doubt that I exist, if he deceives me, and that regardless of how much he deceives me to the full extent of his wish, he will never be able to make me nothing, as long as I *think* that I am something [whatsoever mistaken this thought may be]. This way then, after thinking attentively, having examined all these matters carefully, it is necessary to end [conclude], and to record as a constant [i.e., as an unchangeable truth] this proposition *I am, I exist*, which is necessarily true whenever I assert it, or I conceive it in my mind.

This is the end of Descartes's methodological, nondemonstrative doubt. He was making several connected points.

First, in (D.2) Descartes is remarking that we can conceive all alleged truths about the external world to form an exhaustive set or whole, which I will hereafter call *The Balloon*, and, further, that the arguments for radical skepticism put the doubter in a position of transgressing all particular experiences in which she deals with parts of the world, in order to transact with the world as a whole, thinking The Balloon, so that the situation can be depicted thus:

(1) I think that (The Balloon).

In other words, Descartes was making a wholesale application—of the sort Kant would have called "transcendental"—of Kant's general *I-think* principle: "It must be possible for the 'I think' to accompany all my representations" (Kant 1781, B131).

Second, Descartes in (D.2) observes that the Evil Demon can make me doubt The Balloon in its entirety, the whole of it, and, distributively, each part of it. But the prefix *I think that*, hereafter called (in Kantian style) the *tran-*

scendental prefix, is beyond doubt. Therefore, its components, which we shall henceforth call the transcendental *Thinking I* and the transcendental *Think*, reach metaphysical rock bottom. Of course, it is part of that rock bottom that the *Think* has The Balloon as its total tail, whether this is wholly illusory or not, and that on particular occasions of customary thinking certain parts of The Balloon will function as partial tails of my thinking. The Balloon may be a fiction, but that I exist thinking The Balloon or parts thereof is NOT a fiction. Hence,

(mTR*) There is a minimal transcendent dimension of experience underlying what is thought through the transcendental Thinking I.

Third, a crucial point Descartes makes in (D.2) is that the certainty of *cogito* (I think-I exist) is NOT the certainty of a deduction. As he well knew and insisted all along, his search for a fundamental certainty cannot be derived from anything else. The certainty of the *cogito* is fundamental because it is the terminal certainty of his quest. He makes deductions: His skeptical arguments are deductions and generalizations; but the proceedings culminate with reflections on the role of the Evil Demon's deception or the wholesale illusion of experience for whatever causes. These reflections are doings and they conclude, that is, end up, with the doubter's *metaphysical-phenomenological grasping* of an ultimate reality—this is the metaphysical aspect of the grasping—that appears—this is the phenomenological aspect—as a thinking I confronting a whole but perhaps wholly empty world, including the I's own embodiments in that world.

Fourth, the transcendental I of the methodological doubt exists with certainty only *during* the skeptical experience. Descartes says "with necessity," but it is not clear that by 'necessary' he means, etymologically, nonceasing, that is, constant, which is another word he uses. The doubter's existence as well as his or her thinking are constant parameters during the whole skeptical proceedings. In any case, Descartes leaves it, in (D.2), quite open that the transcendental I of a particular skeptical experience may vanish when the experience ends, that if the experience is repeated, the transcendental I's involved may be entirely different.

This brings us to a *fifth* crucial point that pervades (D.2) throughout, which Descartes did not appreciate fully—at least he did not dwell upon it as fully as he should have done. The point is that the I on which the hyperbolic doubt concludes is not internal to The Balloon. That is why Kant called it *transcendental*, transcending The Balloon without being transcendent in the sense of being beyond experience, that is, the experience of the methodological hyperbolic doubt. That I is beyond the world in The Balloon, and it is all of reality as this can be grasped in that encompassing doubt. Hence, the empirical I's within The Balloon may be different from the transcendental I thinking of them as the same as itself inside The Balloon.

Descartes did not savor fully the nonworldliness of the transcendental I of his *cogito*. Having realized that the *cogito* ended with an existent, but with no content, aside from facing a whole world of experience, he hastened to ask *what am I*? But this question involved a tremendously important, though apparently insignificant, shift of sense and referent in his new use of the little word 'I' (or 'je' and 'ego'). This question is NOT the question about the transcendental I that thinks The Balloon. This latter question would ask about the structures connecting the transcendental I without and The Balloon within or as the accusative of the transcendental Think. Descartes's question, on the other hand, is about *an I within The Balloon*.

We must ask the unasked question and then try to fill in an account of the connection between the nonworldly transcendental I and the many I's within The Balloon.[5]

Now, the *cogito* possesses a second dimension of transcendental realism. It has to do with the transcendental *thinking* of The Balloon. The thinking of The Balloon is also externally real, as real can be, indeed *thinking* as such is the internal, experienced manifestation of whatever it may be in the reality beyond, which underlies experience. Thinking is itself a real representing— whatever this may ultimately really be—of a perhaps empty representation of a hallucinatory world.

Moreover, in the reality beyond experience lies the source, the *transcendent source*, of the thinking of what is thought in The Balloon. The nature of that source is, of course, at the level of the radical skepticism of the Evil Demon, as unknowable as the transcendent self underlying the transcendental I. For instance, according to the Evil Demon "hypothesis," the transcendent source is the Demon's network of deceptive operations; according to the Clever Scientist "hypothesis," the Scientist's manipulations; in the case of the self-propelled isolated computer or brain, it is the electric or physicochemical activity inside the computer or brain. To be sure, wilder hypotheses come forth with their own unknown transcendent sources. In particular, the self-propelled computer shows that the transcendent self may be at the core of the transcendent source. We include both dimensions of transcendence under the heading of Minimal Transcendental Realism. Of course, none of these so-called hypotheses is a genuine hypothesis. They are nothing but suggestive analogies of how noumenal reality could be conceptualized within our experiential resources; there is absolutely nothing to elicit a preference for one over the others. This total parity concerning their validity shows (as Kant well knew) that once we recognize the force of radical skepticism, we must simply acquiesce in the ineffability of the underlying reality.

Two additional aspects of transcendence must yet be latched on to Minimal Transcendental Realism.

To begin with, The Balloon is precisely what may be wholly illusory. Yet it also has a two-directional dimension of transcendence. On one direction, it has a transcendent source. At worst, exactly the same transcendent source of my *thinking* The Balloon is also the very same source of my thinking *the con-*

tents of The Balloon. On the other direction, there is an internal pointing to transcendent reality within the experiences inside, composing The Balloon. The fundamental *attitude* we must take toward the world is that of transcendent realism. We must live our ordinary experiences as if normally what we experience is real beyond them. Any questioning stops the natural flow of one's autobiographical living; it may, of course, start a stream of philosophizing. After all, the metaphysical possibility of error does not affect the order of experiences. We simply take—and must take—it for granted in our basic daily experiences that we are not the toys of an Evil Demon or the thinking gadgets of a clever scientist, or the accidental connivance of we do not know what that causes us to have wholly illusory experiences.

Second, experience is hierarchical. We ascertain within it different layers of *irreality*. We have within our experiences of The Balloon what we call simple illusions, misperceptions, delusions; we distinguish within experience tiers of fiction: original fiction, and fiction created within fiction, and so on, and variegated mixtures of so-called reality and fiction. These hierarchies of internal nonreality presuppose a *ground floor* of The Balloon on which we set them up.

The metaphysical doubt is, in effect, the overall doubt about the ground floor we need. This is the realm of physical objects orderly interacting in spacetime. It is this ground floor of The Balloon that we take in our naive attitude to be real in the strongest metaphysical sense. Thus, our transcendental pointings of our naive attitude are pointings to the reality beyond experience of the ground floor. The metaphysical doubt is, in effect and essence, a sweeping doubt about the physical ground floor of The Balloon. It succeeds, its polemical tone aside, in establishing that the customarily unquestioned ground floor taken for granted in daily living is not logically or mathematically secure.

Notwithstanding, still, within the morals of what Descartes taught us, each of us can affirm a transcendental experience of radical skepticism:

(Di*) Regardless of how much Evil Demon, the Mad Scientist, or the Reality Beyond may deceive me, it cannot make me doubt that I need a ground floor of believed content of experience at the basis of, and inside, The Balloon, through which I point in every act of thinking the contents of that ground floor to the transcendent reality underlying experience holistically.

Doubtless, here we still lack metaphysical certainty about transcendent reality. We merely acquire an *ontologico-epistemological* dimension of realism: Experience rests on a fundamentally transcendental taking for granted both that it has a ground floor and that, so to speak, each placing of a tile on that ground floor, through the rehearsal of a belief about physical reality, is a pointing to the reality beyond experience.

The transcendental *Thinking I* and the transcendental *Think* deliver pointings to transcendent reality. They deliver transcendent reality as target, so to speak, as blindly and merely hooked at the ends of their long harpoons. The Balloon delivers a network of pointings. For instance, each perception we take to be veridical, each belief we come to adopt considering it to be true, is a pointing in the direction of transcendent reality. The pointing is, continuing to use Kant's jargon, transcendental: It reveals that something lies beyond, but it does not reveal *what* it intrinsically is.

What the transcendental *Thinking I* harpoons and what the transcendental *Think* harpoons may, for all we can ever *really* know, BE one and the very *same* thing. That same thing is precisely what, in constructing The Balloon, we may be pointing to. Indeed, we can say very little more than this about transcendent reality. It is of the utmost importance to appreciate that as far as we can consider it, it is an INDIVISIBLE WHOLE. As Kant remarked about his negative problematic concept of the noumenon, it is so far beyond our experience that even calling *it* "it" is already too presumptuous, if we do not dissociate from this use of 'it' semantic contrasts that give it its meaning—for example, its being a singular pronoun; of course, the plural 'they' is by far much more misleading.

Frege appreciated well Kant's insight into the noumenon. He understood deeply both the holistic role of the noumenon in the total unified experience of the world at large and its iterative role in the piecemeal transcendental pointings to it in each of our believings. In each claim of truth we make we point holistically to the problematic noumenon, and for us then the only-blindly pointable transcendent reality is what underlies and undergirds the undifferentiated *The True*, which Frege postulated as the ultimate indivisible convergent referent of all true propositions. Propositions, or Thoughts, are internally to experience what they really are, and when we take them to be true, we represent to ourselves a GUISE of a small part of The True. But there is no reason to suppose that that part is a transcendent part of The True. *Frege's The True is inside experience the fundamental internal guise of the Kantian noumenon.*[6]

We have discussed three several-pronged, transcendental dimensions of the transcendental prefix. Together we shall call these *Modest Transcendental Realism*. Patently:

(MI.Mr*) Modest Transcendental Realism is compatible with Metaphysical Internalism and anchors it to transcendent reality (The True, the Whole Indivisible Problematic Noumenon).

NOUMENON [THE TRUE: indivisible
whole: existence certain]

	self	world
[certain] I Think that:		(The Balloon) [uncertain]

2. The Ontological Semantic Dimension of
Ordinary Words

The three aspects of the noumenon, subsumed under Modest Transcendental Realism, are about all we can say concerning transcendent reality. From there on, everything we can say will have to be *internal* to the complex:

(1) I Think (The Balloon).

In particular, the vocabulary for making reality claims—for example, first-order mechanisms like existentially meant verbal inflections and words like 'exists' and 'really', as well as second-order mechanisms like 'true'—have full-fledged metaphysical applications only as allowed by Modest Transcendental Realism. That is, these words serve their speakers to *perform* metaphysical pointings to The True, but their meaning consists of their essentially internalistic, or phenomenological use.

In the most common, internalistic, use of the word, reality is the ground floor of The Balloon, in particular, the physical world. The Balloon, of course, includes much more. As we observed, it has a hierarchical structure: reality or brute facts at the bottom, our experiences thereof, and the diverse tiers of nonfacts or nonreality above—illusions, hallucinations, dreams, conjectures, unverified hypotheses, intentions, unrealized plans, obligations, unfulfilled duties, fiction, and so on.

The ordinary vocabulary of natural languages for claims about reality has an *ontological semantic dimension*. Ordinary reality claims are about the ground floor of the world we confront in experience. Each making of a reality claim includes a pointing in the direction of transcendent reality as well as a positing of a part of the ground floor, and carries with it the suggestion that what is so posited may, in fact, be itself in, or have a counterpart in, The True beyond. To illustrate, while being deceived by the Mad Scientist, I distinguish between my veridical perceptions and my dreams, and from both my imagined situations and my creation of pieces of fiction. By claiming that my perceptions are veridical, I am claiming, *internalistically*, that the acquired perceptual content belongs to the ground floor of the totality of my experienced contents, to the (internalistically) real world, namely, the ground floor of The Balloon. Underlying this internalistic claim of reality is the deeply seated *taking it for granted* that there is *beyond* a noumenon, which is somehow responsible both for my having the perceptions in question and for these possessing the content they have.

3. The Fivefold Ontological Dimensions
of Certainty

Reflection on the Evil Demon challenge, or on its alternatives, has unveiled two dimensions of *cogito* certainty:

(a) The *metaphysical* certainty of the three aspects of Modest Transcendental Realism: This is a wholly existential and contentually unspecific knowledge that there is simply a reality, to which we can point as a whole in every experience, which underwrites the metaphysical fact that there is experience of a (perhaps wholly illusory) world, and which is directly but blindly harpooned by the Thinking I (whatever and however this may in itself be).

(b) The *ontological* or *semi-internalistic* certainty that the transcendental Thinking I of the radical doubt exists confronting, even surrounding, the world, indeed The whole Balloon, with its Thinking.

A quick reminiscence suffices to remind us that The Balloon may very well contain, so to say, its local I's. There are inside The Balloon many first-person propositions (possible states of affairs, thought contents) like the following:

(B1) I am shorter than Robert Sleigh, Jr.
(B2) I feel a pain on my neck.
(B3) I read Sellars's *Science and Metaphysics* many years ago.

The Evil Demon may definitely sweep away (B1)–(B3) with its tornado of doubt. My height and my eyes, Sleigh and Sellars, my neck and Sellars's book, all might be mere figments of my imaginings forced by the Evil Demon. Can He make me believe that I have a pain that does not exist? Here I want to set this question aside. Here is something of much greater importance. This is I. Can the Evil Demon mislead me about me, that is, I as I appear in (B1)–(B3), *inside* The Balloon? We have grasped the indubitability of the I without The Balloon, which doubts (B1)–(B3) and the rest of The Balloon. But here we have local, internal (empirical) I's. *If* these I's are the SAME in some strong sense of 'sameness' as the Thinking I of the transcendental prefix of (1), then the certainty of the Thinking I spills over into The Balloon over the local I's. Hence, if so, two further dimensions of certainty surface:

(c) The *metaphysico-ontological* or *trans-internalistic* certainty that the local I's in The Balloon are also anchored to transcendent reality.

(d) The *phenomenological* or *internalistic* certainty that within the domain of the appearances constitutive of The Balloon, the local I's in The Balloon are on the ontological ground floor of The Balloon: The ultimacy of the reality of the transcendental I supports The Balloon, and this support also spills over the local I's and disperses throughout them. The force of this internalistic certainty is epitomized in the following implication (signaled by the double-stemmed arrow):

(C*.Ex) *Internal Cogito Axiom:*
$$S(I) \Rightarrow I \text{ exist}$$
where 'S(I)' is any sentence in direct speech, containing uses of the indexical first-person pronoun signaled by 'I'.[7]

This ground floor, dispersed existential certainty of the transcendental I, requires the certainty of the embodiment of those local I's, that is:

(e) The *phenomenological* or *internalistic* certainty that every local I in The Balloon must be tied down to, that is, must be the *same* as, a ground floor resident of the world, that is, a resident so chained by the structure of the world that it cannot leave The Balloon. Such a native resident of the world is, of course, a natural victim of the radical skepticism of the Evil Demon. Thus, here again, we find the certainty of the phenomenological necessity of *there being* something in the ground floor, but not the certainty or necessity of anything in the ground floor that realizes or embodies any local I.

4. Selves, I-Guises, and the Multifarious Semiotics of First-Person Reference

According to (c) the I's in The Balloon have a full-fledged transcendent existence, (but, to be sure, unspecifiable in transcendent content)—provided that, and to the extent that, they are the *same* as the Thinking I of the transcendental prefix. This proviso needs attentive examination. Undoubtedly, from the mere linguistic fact that we have the same mark 'I' in (B1)–(B3), it follows neither that the three occurrences of 'I' are used to think the very same entity, nor that what they denote is exactly the same as what the word 'I' denotes in the transcendental prefix of (1). The issue is *not* that different persons may be uttering (B1)–(B3). We are assuming that there is a personal unity of reflection, experience, and world throughout this meditation. In a general sense all the uses of 'I' that we are considering are uses of the first-person pronoun by the same ordinary person. In that sense, we assume that they all are used by that speaker to refer to the same entity. But obviously, there is more to the thinking reference of the speaker than that general sameness. The meditation occurs in the first person, for the first person, and all the samenesses that the thinker-speaker does not know are unavailable to her. Yet her thoughts have a definite content. Thus, by using the first-person pronoun, the speaker is somehow referring to an entity—which in *some* sense, loudly crying out for analysis, is, of course, the *same* as the speaker. Besides all that, which may be inaccessible to her, she is thinking of an entity *as* a thinker of such thoughts in such and such circumstances. And this makes an enormous difference. For instance, the thinker engaged in the transcendental meditation responds to the brain-in-the-cask "hypothesis" without any assumption of her being embodied; the thinker that thinks (B1) to be probably true must perforce be embodied; the thinker thinking (B3) must think of himself as having a history. This raises a serious question about the sense of diachronic identity between I's.

Let us say that an entity conceived *as* in some way or other is a *gross individual guise*. We may say that a gross individual guise is an ordered pair (x, G), where x is conceived as, *qua*, the G. Applying this idea to the I's we have been considering, let us introduce some terminological order. We call each I-thought in a given unitary propositional text pertaining to the ground floor of The Balloon an *empirical gross I-guise*. Temporarily, let us conceive the unitary manifolds of such gross I-guises as somehow constituting entities to be called *empirical selves*.

The metaphysical certainty of one's own existence is the assurance that there *exists* something problematic, unspecifiable, beyond experience, which underlies one's own uses of the first-person pronoun. These uses are semiotically complex. The uses of 'I' in the transcendental prefix I *Think* in (1) have at least the five crucial roles we pass on to discuss.

First, 'I' in (1) represents a successful gesture of *pointing to* the transcendent self.

Second, 'I' depicts in the context of sentence (1) the semi-internalistic role of the Thinking I vis-à-vis The Balloon. To think proposition (1) is to think of oneself as without The Balloon; yet this *without is* not a transcendent 'without'. The I-Thinking-that in (1) is apprehended in (1) as at the boundary of The Balloon, and it is *internalizable* by its being thought of within a larger Balloon:

(2) I Think that {I think that (The Balloon)}.

In proposition (2), we have the Extended Balloon: {*I think that (The Balloon)*}. This process is iterative with no end. This iterativity makes it clear that the Thinking I is already in (1) a Thought-of I. In a sense, then, the true Thinking I is the *unthought of* I, which thinks (1), or (2), or any other more encompassing proposition of this sort. The iterative embedding of (1) or its successors in a more encompassing Extended Balloon merely introduces *another* thought-of I, thus, revealing by adumbration a semi-internalistic, inexhaustible reservoir of Thinking I's from which Thinking-Thought-of I's can be extracted. Let us call that inexhaustible reservoir the *transcendental I*.

This brings in a *third* role of the first-person pronoun 'I' in (1) and (2): Also semi-internalistically, each use of 'I' points to the internalizability of the transcendental I, or rather, to its sliceability in Thinking-Thought-of slices (hereafter called *transcendental gross I-guises*) that can be internalized in Extended Balloons.

A *fourth* role of depiction by the first-person pronoun in (1) is this: The internal inexhaustibility of the transcendent I is an internal representation within (extended) experience of the inaccessibility of the transcendent self.

Fifth, as already noted, the 'I' in the transcendental prefix of (1) anchors the uses of 'I' to denote an empirical self within The Balloon.

The structure of the internalistic certainty of the empirical I's includes the substructures of indexical reference in general. Referring to oneself *qua* oneself as in the midst of the world is to refer as such to a thinker as *presently* involved in the very experience of making the referring in question.

The nonworldliness of the transcendental I infects the empirical I's. But we cannot go into this here. Furthermore, first-person reference is just one case of demonstrative or indexical reference to items that are presented or present in an experience, which is lived through the very structure of the references in question. Therefore, to understand fully the structure of the internalistic certainty of one's existence, it is necessary to place the psycholinguistic phenomenon of first-person reference within the context of its general type of *indexical reference*. Additional aspects of the semantics of the first-person pronoun become crucial. And the nonworldliness of the I's turn out to be hand in hand with the nonworldliness of the strict denotata of all other indexical references.[8]

5. The I-Manifold: Strict Semantic Denotation Versus Doxastic Denotation

We have encountered a somewhat bewildering multiplicity of entities at the end of the semantics of the first-person pronoun. We have also felt pressure for some sort of identification among them. Here we cannot tackle the problem in full. If we yield to the pressure for identification, we find a long, impressive array of equations. We deliberately formulate them by means of the problematic word 'same', intending to pose a problem at it. To begin with, we have, where for convenience the adjective 'gross' is left tacit:

Ontological Unity of the World of a Given Subject:
(TI.TI*)   Each transcendental I-guise, that is, each Thinking-Thought-of I, is *the same as* its corresponding transcendental I.
(TI.TI*.1) I [Thinking an Extended Balloon] am *the same as* my (semi-internalistically) underlying transcendental I.
Metaphysical Anchoring of Experience:
(MA*)   The transcendental I is *the same as* its transcendent self [which underlies from beyond experience its thinking a Balloon].

By equation (TI.TI*) all the members of the iterative infinite sequence of Extended Balloons have the unity of one and the same underlying unthought-of transcendental self. Since each Extended Balloon thought of is explicitly encompassed by a transcendental I-guise, (TI.TI*) derivatively unifies both the Balloons and the possible experiences of a given subject. Equation (MA*) is, by contrast, a *metaphysical*, trans-semi-internalistic principle tying the knowable world of experience to the (problematic, indivisible) noumenon.

Moving into The Balloon we find the *empirical I-guises*. Here, again, positing a unity of reference is the simplest and most straightforward justification of the use of the first-person pronoun. We postulate:

Internalistically, within The Balloon:
(Ei.ES*)   Each empirical I-guise is *the same as* the empirical self.
Semi-internalistically, a Bridge between the Prefix and The Balloon:
(Ti.Ei*)   Each transcendental I-guise [of the prefix], is *the same as* each of the empirical I-guises [in its corresponding Balloon].
(TI.ES*)   Each transcendental I *is the same as* the empirical self it encompasses.

Some of these equations can be derived from others by the transitivity of sameness, but this is part of the problem. Also by transitivity, (Ei.ES*) identifies all the empirical I-guises. This requires investigation concerning the unity and identity of empirical selves across time. Equations (Ei.ES*) and (TI.ES*) raise, and are contributions to, the fundamental problem of the synchronic unity of an I.

By the above equations, all the uses of the first-person pronoun captured in (1), (2), and (B1)–(B3), from the perspective of one person, denote the same everywhere. This cries out for elucidation.

As we have pointed out, we are considering entities as they are thought of and referred to by a thinker putting her world together after the skeptical devastation brought about by the Mad Scientist, or the Evil Demon. Thus, we found the thinker thinkingly referring to individual guises. If that thinker's thinking is deployed or embodied in language, then there is a *fundamental semantic dimension* in which the *strict semantico-pragmatic denotations* of the thinker's terms are precisely what the thinker refers to, namely, individual guises. Otherwise, the terms are not capable of carrying the thinker's thoughts. If the terms in question gain their denotation in the pragmatic context of use, then these, as they exist in the thinker's psycholinguistic speech habits, do not have a denotation. Their general meaning is, then, a schema to be filled in by the pragmatics of the context of use. (In more fashionable jargon: The general meaning of a term is only a function that assigns a function of the context that assigns a denotation to the term.)

We must, therefore, distinguish different ways in which a proffered singular term, or the corresponding mental content it overtly represents, can be said to refer to, or aim at, its denotata. Here we are concerned with the referential uses of the first-person pronoun. Clearly, then, each token of 'I' *strictly (semantico-pragmatically) denotes* an I-guise being thought of; it *mediately denotes doxastically* the transcendental I, by virtue of being part of an expression of thought that *occurs* within a network of beliefs, which includes the assumption of a unity of the thinker's experience; and *it points* to, or *most mediately denotes doxastically*, the transcendent self—which in the naive attitude of daily living is not even conceived, but underwrites the naive realism of daily attitude.

6. The Variegated Sameness in the I-Network

The above principles establish, but only programmatically, subject to an acoming theory,† the unity across the I-manifold. That theory has to deal with the problems mentioned, as well as with others. For instance, by the transitivity of sameness, the preceding equations also imply:

† This clause is incoherent in the original text. Perhaps 'acoming' was meant to be 'an encompassing.' —Eds.

(TS.Ei) The transcendent self [BEYOND the inexhaustive transcendental prefix] is *the same as* any empirical I-guise [IN The Balloon].

This contains an important grain of truth, namely, the one that underlies the dimension of certainty (c) described earlier. But (TS.Ti) must not be understood as transferring the properties of an empirical I-guise to the transcendent self—the noumenon. This is precisely Descartes's error in his *Second Meditation* when he derives from the certainty of the *cogito* that he is a transcendent mental substance. Pointing out this error is the main task of Kant's "Paralogisms."

We must, consequently, interpret (TS.Ei) in such a way that the sameness it proclaims is *not* strict identity. Since (TS.Ei) is a consequence of the previous equations, there is at least one sameness in the latter that is not strict identity.

Having differentiated sameness from strict identity, we need a general account of identity, sameness, predication, and guises. *One* such account, built on the distinctions drawn between strict semantico-pragmatic reference and doxastic reference and pointings-to, can be found in Guise Theory.[9] Since we are now dealing with the structures inside The Balloon, we may stop this round of investigation. Perhaps one small appendix may not be amiss to round out our discussion.

7. The Transcendental Prefix and Experience

Our reaction to the Evil Demon hypothesis followed Descartes in considering the whole world and experience, The Balloon, encompassed by Kant's transcendental prefix I *think*. This is, however, a serious error, for as Descartes himself had casually shown, the Kantian prefix is only a fragment of the relevant prefix, to wit: *I think now*. This is, to be sure, at the heart of Descartes's claim that thinking and extension are two distinct attributes characteristic, respectively, of the mental and material substances. A comprehensive study of indexical reference suggests that the true transcendental prefix is, therefore, the extended one: *I think here now*. By the same Cartesian considerations that led Descartes to the indubitability of the doubting I, we reach the indubitability of both the *now* and the *here* of the doubting. Those considerations are simply that all doubts, regardless of how radical they may be, can always be imprisoned in the subordinated Balloon, and in so doing, a new transcendental prefix *I think here now* springs forth at every turn:

I think here now that (I think here now that [. . . The Balloon] . . .).

We may speak here of the extended *cogito* and of the indubitability of the transcendental *I-Here-Now's*.

This extended *cogito is* Cartesian only in structure. Its contents are anti-Cartesian. For one thing, it provides only an I that exists in time and in space.

For another, there is the problem of transferring the transcendental *I-Here-Now's* into The Balloon and determining the sense, scope, and laws of the different sameness relations connecting the transcendental times and places with their empirical counterparts, and those between the empirical counterparts themselves. Patently, we need the Guise Theory of times and places to go hand in hand with that of the I-guises and selves, and of physical objects.

Kant would have insisted against Descartes that the extended transcendental prefix delivers only an I, and that we must add a *here* and a *now* from inside experience. The question arises in relation to Kant: Does the fact that a transcendent reality underwrites the transcendental I-Now guises also extend, first, to there being in the noumenon something like time (duration, or becoming, as Bergson suggested)? If so, is there in the noumenon something like space that underlies the Here-component of the extended transcendental I-Here-Now guises? Of course, Kant might have, on the one hand, resisted recognition of the extended transcendental I-Here-Now guises. On the other hand, he would have insisted that, although his official theory about the limits of knowledge precluded knowledge claims about the noumenon beyond its negative concept, his official epistemology and philosophy of mind made ample room for *metaphysical faith*—just as they did for theologico-religious faith. Thus, *unofficially*, one can believe—without knowledge—that the noumenon is this or that, indeed, that it is exactly as science and intersubjective experience tell us the phenomenal world is.

Notes

1. For details see Castañeda 1984c.

2. In the context of developing a material and experiential semantics for ordinary language, I contrasted transcendent metaphysics with phenomenological ontology in Castañeda 1974. The proposed phenomenological ontology-semantics was later on called Guise Theory.

3. See Kant 1781, 1787, Preface to the Second Edition, A286ff, B287ff.

4. Leibniz 1690. He formulated his Internalism as follows: "Indeed, even if this whole life were said to be only a dream, and the visible world only a phantasm, I should call this dream or this phantasm real enough if we were never [internally] deceived by it when we make good use of reason." (In Loemker 1976, 364.)

5. Descartes should have moved the rest of *Meditation* II beginning with its fourth paragraph to *Meditation* IIbis.† What follows above in the main body of the essay is one (anachronistic) way of furnishing the "missing" part of what "should" have been *Meditation* II.

6. See Frege 1892.

7. Descartes is not denying (C*.Ex) when he replies to Gassendi:

† This is a misprint in the original. We assume that Castañeda intended to write Meditation III. —Eds.

> For when you say that I could have indifferently concluded the same thing
> [that I exist] from each one of my other actions, you seriously misinterpret
> me, for there is nothing in them of which I can be entirely certain, that is the
> metaphysical certainty which is the only one at issue here, except thinking.
> For, for example, THIS INFERENCE WOULD NOT BE SOUND: *I
> walk, therefore, I exist*, if only the interior knowledge that I have is of a think-
> ing episode, from which alone the conclusion follows. (At the end of section
> I of the third response to the Fifth Objections to the *Meditations*, capitals are
> mine.)

Descartes is merely pointing out that at the transcendental level of the methodological hyperbolic doubt, the premise of the quoted inference is false, hence, an
unsound transcendental argument. The inference is, of course, valid, and internalistically sound if the premise is true.

8. For a preliminary treatment of these matters see Castañeda 1981. For a sustained
discussion of the self see Castañeda 1987b, and for a most comprehensive account of indexical reference see Castañeda 1982a, 1989a. See also the studies by Robert M. Adams,
John Perry, and the replies to them in Tomberlin 1983, and the studies by Esa Saarinen
and by David W. Smith in Tomberlin 1986.

9. For an account of Guise Theory, criticisms of it, and responses, see the essays by
Alvin Plantinga, Romane Clark, and replies to them in Tomberlin 1983; the studies by Jay
Rosenberg, David W. Smith, Jeffrey Sicha, and replies to them in Tomberlin 1986; see also
Tomberlin 1984 and subsequent reply.

9

Persons, Egos, and I's

Their Sameness Relations

"There are also dreams in which MY EGO appears together
with other persons, who when the identification is resolved,
again, reveal themselves to be my ego . . . I may also give my ego
multiple representations in my dream, either directly or by
means of identification with other people . . . That ONE's EGO
should appear in the same dream several times or in different
forms is fundamentally no more surprising than that IT should
appear, in conscious thoughts, many times and in different
places or in different relations: as, for example, in the sentence:
'When I think what a healthy child I was'."
—Freud, *The Interpretation of Dreams* (1900/1938, p. 349)

1. Introduction

This is an inquiry into the nature of what we, whether in dreams or in waking
experience, think as "I". What does one refer to internally, *de dicto*, when one
uses assertively a sentence containing an inflection of the first-person pronoun? What sort of entity is that referent? How does such a referent relate to
the person calling himself or herself "I"? Consider for example Freud's wishful self-assuring statement:

(1) Sometimes I think what a healthy child I was!

We shall say that a token of a form of the first-person pronoun used to
make a thinking singular reference strictly or internally denotes an *I* [*ein
Ich*]. This is a neutral piece of terminology. It leaves open that an *I* be nothing
at all even in the most liberal conception of referent. We are, thus, inquiring
into the constitution of *I*'s, if there be such, the roles they play in experience,
and the ontological structures enveloping them. These ontological structures
may, again, be such as to determine the annihilation of all *I*'s. This topic is
of the greatest intrinsic importance. It is, of course, of special value in attempting to understand Freud's, as well as other philosophers' and psychiatrists', views of the ego or the self. Indeed the above passage from Freud constitutes an excellent initial datum.

This essay appeared in *Psychopathology and Philosophy*, edited by M. Spitzer, F. A. Uehlin, and
G. Oepen (Berlin: Springer-Verlag, 1988), 210–234. Reprinted by permission from Springer-Verlag.

2. I and My Ego: Some Questions

2.1 My Ego Is Myself

Undoubtedly, Freud thought that what he called a person's ego [*das Ich*] is in some sense identical to the person's *I* or *I*'s. Let's reflect on the last sentence of the above passage (the capitals are added to express my emphasis):

(2) That ONE'S EGO [*das eigene Ich*] should appear in the same dream several times or in different forms is fundamentally no more surprising than that IT should appear, in conscious thinking, many times and in different places or in different relations, as, for example, in statement (1).

The capitalized pronoun 'IT' refers back to 'one's ego'. The ego that appears as such in the dream is oneself—referred to in the first-person way. It is Freud's EGO that the pronoun 'I' of example (1) denotes. Hence, as Freud reveals in (2):

(FI.1) One is (the same as) one's ego.
          I am (the same as) my ego.

(FI.1) is a sort of semantic axiom characterizing what Freud meant by the ego *(das Ich)*. But what does 'my' denote in the locution 'my ego'? What sort of sameness is that?

On a conceptually economic interpretation Freud is being verbose in (2): 'my ego' is simply short for I, and 'one's ego' for 'one'. On this interpretation, (2) is a verbose version of:

(2.A) That ONE should appear in the same dream several times or in different forms is fundamentally no more surprising than that ONE should appear, in conscious thinking, many times and in different places or in different relations, as, for example, in statement (1).

There seems to be something right here. A patient must express in the first-person the identifications, brought forth by psychotherapy, that she has executed in her dreams. For instance, Tayra's:

(3) I dreamt that George [my undersexed husband] was anxiously, very tenderly, trying to feed *me*. I kicked him hard at the groin. He groaned, but stopped offering *me* the food. Immediately the food became a liquid column that fell very slowly to the ground, and then vanished. . . .
I see now that in my dream I was George, and George was ME. In kicking him I was refusing him. Also blaming me for his real refusals.

The first-person pronoun in (3) is crucial. It threads the unity of the person who lives the dream, has the underlying psychological states, and undergoes the ensuing interpretive waking experiences. This first-person overall unity is what Freud emphatically signals in (2).

2.2 I Cannot Be My Ego

Yet the sameness between one's ego and oneself postulated by Freud's (2) is not the strict identity proclaimed by the verbose interpretation. To begin with, let's ponder his tantalizing statement in the above text:

(4) I may also give my ego multiple representations in my dream, directly, or by means of identification with other persons.

This separates my ego from me. I am like a playwright, my ego a sort of historical personage about whom I write a kind of fable narrated in the first-person way. The personage is carved into different characters in the dream fable. The direct representation of my ego is the first-person character that narrates the story; the indirect representations are the third-person characters. These need not be real persons. Indeed, why should they be ordinary persons, at all, and not, as in genuine fables, animals, or non-existing animated, even inanimate, objects? In any case, there is the internal ego or I of the dream story, the external ego that appears piecemeal multiply manifested in the story, and I that create the story. In some sense, I am my ego. Hence, there is this meta-external ego that composes the dream. There is also the I that interprets the story. Presumably they are all the same. These levels of sameness cry out for elucidation. It is clear, however, that all these samenesses operate within a background of fundamental differences. None of these samenesses is the strict identity of the verbose interpretation.

For Freud the phrase 'my ego' was really not just a verbose version of 'I'. He meant by 'ego' (*das Ich*) a special part of a person's mind centering about his/her powers to undergo episodes of consciousness. Each of us has an ego, but one also has other psychic parts. Later on he posited an Id and a super-ego as in some sense parts of oneself, but not of one's ego. Patently:

(5) I am (the whole of) the person H-N. C.

is true, whereas:

(6) My ego is (the whole of) the person H-N. C.

is false.

Freud is better construed as claiming in passage (2) and its surrounding text that:

(FI.2) One's ego is in some sense (at least) the same as one's thinking part—the part of oneself that enjoys episodes of consciousness.

Perhaps one's ego is more than one's thinking part. Nevertheless, there are many things one is that one's ego is not. In particular:

(FI.2Ph) For every physical property Fness, one may be F but one's ego is not F.

For instance, I weigh 160 pounds, but my ego apparently has no weight. One can be at places where something else in some appropriate relation to oneself is at, e.g., in a law court when one's proxy or one's lawyer is performing his representation function. But one's ego is not the one so related to a lawyer, or what is vicariously present at the law court.

In passage (1) Freud declares—truly, we suppose—that *he (himself)* was a healthy child. This 'he himself' is a quasi-indicator depicting the first-person of his statement (1).[1] Perhaps there existed an *I* of Freud's (the whole person) that was a healthy child; yet Freud's ego was neither a healthy child nor an unhealthy one. (Toward the end of this essay we return to this topic.)

There is an important tension between (FI.1) and (FI.2). I do *not* claim that Freud in (2) is contradicting himself by holding that a finite whole is the same as one of its proper parts. I want, rather, to pursue the semantic eluci- dation of the first-person pronoun to ascertain what an I is. This elucidation should help us understand Freud's consistent, and profound, tenets about the ego.

The sense of 'part' in (FI.2) is very special. To be sure, one is also one's id as well as one's super-ego in the sense in which they are one's own psychic components. However, the identification between oneself and one's ego is spe- cial. (FI.2) alone can mislead. The ego is not merely the thinking part of oneself, but is that part of oneself that one thinks of as operating in the first- person way. This is precisely what (FI.1) brings forth. The hermeneutic task is to specify in detail the complementarity between (FI.1) and (FI.2).

Patently, (FI.1) and (FI.2) are semantic axioms characterizing what Freud meant by the ego *(das Ich)*. They are, though obscure, analytic or logical truths in the logic of the ego. (FI.1) is an abridging principle connecting a person's ego [*Ich*] with his/her *I*'s [*Ichs*]. (FI.2) connects the ego to the op- erational powers of thinking, rather than to the psychological context within which those powers function.

2.3 I's and Persons

In the background of Freud's identifications lie, of course, many identificat- ions which one acknowledges in daily life. For instance, I am (the same as) Hector-Neri Castañeda, the Editor of *Noûs*, the Mahlon Powell Professor of Philosophy of Indiana University, the father of Frieda Xmucane Wiebeck. We summarize all these identifications with the master equation:

(*I.3X) There are (infinitely) many unique personal characterizations Xness such that:
  One is (the same as) the person X.
  E.g., I am (the same as) the person X.

Postulate (*I.3X) is a logical truth in the logic of the embodiment of the I's. It is a pervasive truth prior to psycho-analysis. Freud assumes and uses it in reporting his cases. On the other hand, each particular truth (*I.3j) that instantiates (*I.3X) is contingent and empirical.

Postulate (*I.3X) is a Pandora's box. To the extent that one thinks oneself the (*I.3X) equations, things look (though just look) clear and calm. Those equations also identify what a speaker refers to as I with what others refer to as *the person X*. Yet strict identity must fail here. What one thinks, *de dicto,* i.e., the internal content that one thinks, when one thinks in the first-person way, is entirely different from what others think in the third-person way. Yet a necessary and sufficient condition of being a person, or being fully a person, is to be able to think of oneself as *oneself,* in the first-person way. Others must perforce think of one in the third-person way. This contrast is enormous and enormously important.

Consider a totally amnesiac person. She cannot forget to refer to herself as I. However, for any third-personal characterization Xness whatever, she may fail to know that *she herself* is (the same as) the X one. (Here again, 'she herself' is a quasi-indicator depicting the amnesiac's use of 'I'.) Let's focus on the moment at which, having been transported in a state of coma to a strange place, she first awakes with total amnesia. To be sure when she asks: "Where am I? WHO am I?" she is groping for some true equations of the (*I.3X) type. Patently she is not inquiring whether logical reflexivity holds for her: "Am I I, the same as myself?" For practically every property Fness, she may believe (and think) that some person X—who happens to be the same as she— is F without believing that she herself is F.

To underscore this fact observe that one can refer to oneself demonstratively without making a first-person reference. One can see oneself in a mirror and, without realizing that it is oneself one is seeing, think demonstratively "THAT person looks pitifully tired!" The surprise one experiences at seeing such a pitifully looking person may show on one's face, and seeing it reflected into the mirror one may proceed to think:

(7) That man must be thinking that I am horrified by his thinking that I am pleased by thinking that I am so different from him that I could never look like him.

Then the mirror disappears, and one may never realize that once one thought that one was not oneself. One may of course learn later on that it was oneself:

(8) Once I, without realizing what was happening, saw myself in a mirror with a horrified expression at looking at myself in the mirror, and thought then that I in the mirror, looking intently at me, must be thinking that I was so horrified by my mirror image thinking that I was pleased by thinking that I was so different from what I saw myself looking like that I could never look like that.

Undoubtedly, what one thinks in the original mis-identification experience involves no contradiction. It hinges on a lack of I-integration. What one thinks in the later, recognitional experience need not involve a contradiction. It must for consistency provide an I-identification that corrects, yet respects the earlier lack of I-integration. This is all within normal experience. It merely hints at psychiatric possibilities.

What I strictly think as *I* is not the same as what others think when they refer to me. What the others think is more or less clear: they think of a person (whatever this may be) that has for them certain uniquely differentiating properties. But what do I think as this *I* that I am and that in principle I can think as having no property other than being currently involved in some experiences? In brief:

(*1.4)   Where being F is not simply being myself, all propositions of the form *I am F* are synthetic *aposteriori* in Kant's sense, i.e., not tautological.

The predicate F of any such proposition contains something not contained in the subject. The attributions of experience are additive to what 'I' means. They are empirical, requiring the existence of the experience in question to be true. Let's go over this in some detail.

To attribute some property to an object X, that is, to think something of the form *X is F*, presupposes that the attributer has differentiated and segregated (individuated) that subject of predication from all other individuals. Thus when one thinks something of the form *I am F* one must individuate oneself as an *I*, as the subject of Fness. How does one accomplish this feat?

Compare the case of a physical object. We can differentiate and individuate it as a subject by means of some identifying properties. Suppose that we individuate an object as *the tallest man in Heidelberg in 1986*. Then we can attribute to it all sorts of properties, e.g., we can think "The tallest man in Heidelberg in 1986 was a Swede, was an engineer, was a grandfather, . . . " And we can think tautologically, analytically in Kant's sense: "The tallest man in Heidelberg in 1986 was a man, was a very tall person, was in Heidelberg, lived in 1986, . . . " This tautological thinking we cannot do with one's *I* or *I*'s, with *oneself.* By (*I.4) no property Fness, physical or psychological, can serve to individuate an *I*. The utilization of any such property presupposes that one has already, so to speak, in one's hands a constituted subject of predication—an *I*.

Yet what I think as *I* must be the same as what others think when they refer to me. How is that feasible? What sort of sameness is that? What exactly is an I?

2.4 Main Problems

The task of determining the way in which (FL.1) and (FL.2) complement each other must be carried out in the context determined by the truths conforming to (*I.3X) and (*I.4). We must investigate the experience of first-person reference. There we can study the living semantics and the pragmatics of first-person language. There we can establish what exactly the I's [*Ichs*] are. (We cannot examine now Freud's texts to ascertain what he calls a person's ego (*das Ich*).) We focus on the fundamental *sameness* relations. We attempt to elucidate the general principles (*I.3X) and (*I.4), and the interpretive sameness, illustrated by (3), examples of which psycho-analytic practice aims at finding. We cannot tackle here the corresponding problems of the *individuation* of the I's [*Ichs*], the persons X each one of us is, and Freud's egos [Ichs].[2] Thus, we cannot deal with normal lack of I-integration, not even with the trivial case like those illustrated by examples (6) and (7), let alone the exciting psychiatric cases of synchronic *Ichstörung*.

3. Indexical Reference as the Structural Core of Experience

3.1 Subsumption of the Problem of the I's under Indexical Reference

The problem of the I's is a central piece in the problem of the self. Here we will not consider the self in general. We must, however, generalize our problem in a different direction. Evidently first-person reference is a special case of indexical reference. Personal pronouns and demonstratives form a unified semantic category. Most discussions of the self or of the I, nevertheless, adopt a type of referential atomism. They deal with the I's in isolation, neglecting the place of THE I's within the general phenomenon of indexicality. I propose to examine this general phenomenon first in order to build an appropriate background, and distill some guidance, for the study of the I's.

3.2 Confrontational Reference to Objects

To live one must deal with objects and persons in one's environment as the individuals they are. One must locate them by confronting them *in propria persona* in some experience, or by connecting them to confronted objects. In confronting an object one places it in present experience thereby constituting it both as present and as a presented referent. Confrontational perceptual experience is fundamental. Its core is indexical reference, whose sole function is to pinpoint items in experience. In the normal, doxastically default case of perception, we believe that what we are appeared to is physically real. That is, we equate items internal to the experience with items in the external world. Furthermore, in the veridical sub-case our indexical experiential equations are true. Let's consider a visual experience as a model:

The Austin-Künne Datum. Krista is driving us to her summer house perched on a high hill in the Black Forest. The road twists and turns in a long

chain of loops; we don't complain, for we are enjoying the beautiful kaleido-
scopic landscape. Suddenly Krista makes a very sharp turn left, and, keeping
her hands firmly glued to the steering wheel, says:

(21) That tiny white dot on the very right is my house, where I live in July.

As Künne has pointed out,[3] Krista's (21) does not imply:

(22) I [Krista] live in a tiny white dot.

This lack of implication of (22) by (21) I have called the Austin-Künne
Datum.[4] As I interpret this datum, it establishes that the property being a
tiny white dot is not predicated in (21) of a physical object. We must, however,
go on to ask: What has that property? Patently, it must be something internal to Krista's perceptual content. If Krista succeeds in communicating her
thoughts to her guests that property will also appear instantiated in her
guests' perceptual experiences. Still, what is the subject having that property?
A new look at (21) furnishes the answer. Statement (21) presents the property
of being a tiny white dot as exemplified by what Krista calls "That." Krista's
sentence (21) expresses compactly the selfsame statement as is expressed,
with its structure more visibly, by the sentence:

(21*) That, which IS a tiny white dot, is my house, where I live in July.

Krista's *that*, as an internal item in her perceptual field, has really the
properties it appears to have. In the logic of perception, Krista's statement
(21) is equivalent to, but not identical to, Krista's statement:

(23) *That*, which *looks like* a tiny white dot, is my house, where I live in July.

This raises a profoundly important question: What is the meaning of the first,
capitalized 'IS' in (21*)? Clearly, it is an equational 'is'. It is short for 'is the
same as'. What sort of sameness is this?

3.3 Identity, Consubstantiation, and Consociation

According to the story, Krista's perceptual experience is veridical. Hence her
visual judgment (21), identical with (21*), is true. This helps in determining
its truth conditions and the sense of 'IS' in (21*). To be sure (21) may be
false. Krista may have confused her house with another, or she may have been
joking. No matter. If (21) is true, there exists in the physical word a house
where Krista lives, which she sees, and, furthermore, it is really (the same as)
what she calls *that*. Thus, (21), or (21*), is a mixed equation of the form:

(21.A) That   *is the same as*   my house,
        which is [looks like] a tiny white dot   where I live.

This sameness relation is very exciting. Krista's *that* is just an internal part
of her perceptual presentational content. Her house is an external object in

physical space. They are not strictly identical. By strict identity I mean Leibnizian identity: total unrestricted indiscernibility. The Austin-Künne Datum is a masterful stroke. It differentiates at once between Krista's subjective perceptual *that* and her house, and between strict identity and the subjective-objective sameness of (21).

The Austin-Künne Datum shows further that the sameness proclaimed in (21) is *non-communitarian*. By this I mean that each of the items said correctly to be the same have properties that do not transfer to the other items across the sameness relation. We have already seen how the properties of being a tiny white dot, being a dot, being white, being tiny, possessed by Krista's *that* do not transfer to Krista's house. In fact, later on we learned in confirmation that Krista's July residence is a huge blue three-story house. None of these properties transfers to Krista's visual *that*.

With the sameness posited by Krista in her statement (21) we must compare a homogeneously objective sameness, say, the one in:

(24) Krista's huge blue three-story house is (the same as) the *villa Il Ritiro* built by Braunschweiger in 1775 where Baron Karl von Falkenberg and Baron Franz von Frankenburg fought a mortal duel for the affections of the Attendant to the Marchesa Francesca di Soavia.

This sameness is communitarian. All the properties of Krista's house mentioned in (24) transfer to the *villa Il Ritiro*, and vice versa. For example, (24) implies each of the following:

(25.1) Krista's blue house was built by Braunschweiger;
(25.2) Krista's huge house is where Von Falkenberg and Von Frankenburg fought for Francesca's Attendant;
(26.1) The *villa Il Ritiro* is a blue house;
(26.2) The *villa Il Ritiro* is a huge building, where Krista lives in July.

We must, consequently, distinguish the sameness of (21) from the sameness of (24), and both from strict identity. Both samenesses are contingent. Both are epistemologically empirical: they must be known on the basis of experience. The thoroughly objective, existential sameness of (24) we call *consubstantiation*. The paired items that are the same in this sense all belong to the real world in one unitary entity: they constitute one physical substance. The reality of this existential sameness needs in general no experience to obtain. On the other hand, the hybrid sameness of (21) is inherently, ontologically empirical: it is *experiential*. To have an experience is to confront such subjective indexical items through which the external world reveals itself. Thus, Krista's very visual experience creates her visual *that* is wrapped up in its apparent *sameness* to a physical object. This subjective-objective sameness includes a component association established by an operation of a finite mind. This is the kind of association a novelist creates who lays it down that the murderer of XXX is XXX's lover. It is the association of John F. Kennedy and the Attorney General of the United States in 1962 in the mind of a person who confuses the Kennedy brothers. This mind-made *sameness* we call *consociation*.

A full account of the structure of experience and of the world we confront in experience requires other sameness relations. These are copulational relations, that is, forms of predication. Here we cannot go into these matters. We speak of existential or consubstantiational predication to refer to the having of properties by existents *qua* existents. We call consociational the possession of properties by objects through stipulation, or through mental activity, whether in confused thinking about the world or in literary creation. It does not matter whether the consociated items do not exist. Strict identity, or self-identity, is the most pervasive, absolutely reflexive, wholly trivial, and utterly necessary form of sameness valid for everything, whether existing or not.[5]

3.4 Perceptual Judgments: This's and That's

To sum up our discussion of demonstrative reference in perception let's outline an analysis of perceptual judgments. Recall Krista's visual judgment:

(21)   That tiny white dot is my house, where I live.

The first step in its analysis is:

(21.A) That (which is [looks like] a tiny white dot) *is the same as* my house (where I live).

This reveals the following components of (21):

(a)   The central hybrid sameness proposition: THAT *IS THE SAME* AS MY HOUSE;
(b1) The is-predication of the subjective element: THAT IS A TINY WHITE DOT;
(b2) The *looks-like-predication* of the subjective element: THAT LOOKS LIKE A TINY WHITE DOT
(c)   The objective predication of the objective element: MY HOUSE IS WHERE I LIVE.

Undoubtedly, there are several illuminating theories that can be erected to account for these data. I propose, tentatively, to interpret the copulational relations present in (a)–(c) as follows:

A.   The sameness predication in (a) is consubstantiation;
B.   The predication in (b1) is consociational;
C.   The predication in (b2) is consubstantiational;
D.   The predication in (c) is consubstantiational.

By **A** we secure in veridical perception an access to the external world. In veridical perception every subjective *that* [*this*] forms the same substance with the perceived physical individual. Physical objects, when perceived, grow demonstrative tails by means of which the perceivers apprehend them. By **B** we secure a general non-transferability of the properties of the subjective item to the physical objects with which it forms the same substance. The actual manifestations of things in perceptual consciousness are subjective. They may be causally matched in other persons' perceptions of the same things. Nevertheless, each one has his/her own experiences with his/her own perceptual contents. Thus, consubstantiation is transitive, but consociation is not. It is the combination of **A** and **B** that makes the sameness of (21) non-communitarian. Thus, the ostensive sameness of (21) is, as observed, a compacting of **A** and **B** and **C**. **C** secures the transferability of the *looks-like* properties of the subjective elements to the perceived physical objects. Clearly, *what* things look like is personal; but *that* they look like such and such is an intersubjective matter. **D** secures a wholly objective sameness in the physical world.

3.5 Confrontational Reference to Time and Space: Now's and Here's

Perceptual confrontation with objects is the placing of objects in the world. To place objects in the world is to place them in the causal structure of the world. This involves placing them in the spatiotemporal structure that underlies the causal order. Therefore, to experience a confrontation of objects in the world is to experience a confrontation of the space and the time of the world.

As we have seen, confrontations of objects pivot on demonstrative reference of the *this [that]* type. The demonstrative individuals are the subjective protrusions of the perceived physical objects. Clearly, we must have the undergirding subjective protrusions of space and time. These are the internal contents strictly referred to indexically as *here [there]* or as *now*. Hence, the same considerations about identity, consubstantiation, and consociation we deployed above about *this*'s and *that*'s apply to *here*'s and *now*'s.

3.6 Confrontational Reference to the Experiencer: The I's

Elsewhere I have argued, siding with Sartre, against the Fichtean thesis that all consciousness is self-consciousness.[6] The fundamental type of consciousness is non-reflexive, egoless. Furthermore, reflexive consciousness is mounted on a base of unreflective consciousness of objects. This in its turn is mounted on diffuse, inarticulated sensory consciousness. This cumulative hierarchical structure of consciousness is crucial. Of course, unreflective consciousness of objects is, as discussed above, built on third-person indexical reference.

Here we are interested in reflexive, *I*-anchored consciousness. An episode of self-consciousness has as its top echelon a sub-experience of confrontation with the experiencer in *propria persona*. Again, the backbone of this confrontation is indexical reference: reference to oneself in the first-person way. This exhibits the same pattern of indexicality found above in the analysis of Krista's visual demonstrative reference to her house.

An *I* is, thus, strictly speaking, a subjective, experienced item. It presents itself as existing, and as being, like Krista's visual *that*, consubstantiated with a physical individual. Consider this example:

(27) I, who feel at the moment exhilarated, am the author of TSM, an unknown treatise, where he discusses an agent's occasional moral duty to change his moral code.

Its basic logical form is the general pattern of indexicality:

(27.A) I (who feels [seems to feel] . . .) *am the same as* the author of TSM (who discusses . . .)

Again, we have here the following components of (27):

(a) The central hybrid sameness proposition: I *AM THE SAME AS* THE AUTHOR OF TSM;
(b1) The is-predication of the subjective element: I FEEL AT THE MOMENT EXHILARATED;
(b2) The *looks-like-predication* of the subjective element: I SEEM TO FEEL EXHILARATED;
(c) The objective predication of the objective element: THE AUTHOR OF TSM DISCUSSES AN AGENT'S MORAL DUTY . . .

Again, the copulational relations present in (a)–(c) are as follows:

A. The sameness predication in (a) is consubstantiation;
B. The predication in (b1) is consociational;
C. The predication in (b2) is consubstantiational;
D. The predication in (c) is consubstantiational.

Of course there are most important differences between third-person and first-person reference. These have two sources. On the one hand, the role of subject of experience is a fundamental structural element of experience. On the other hand, the role of subject has certain unique and peculiar epistemic features. Let's discuss these features briefly.

3.7 Dimensions of Certainty in Indexical Reference

The epistemological accessibility of reality to a thinker requires that there be in principle a *manifestation* of reality *in* experience. This requires a structure within which the manifestation can occur. That is precisely the experienced space-time structure. This is a network of *now- and here* [*there's*]-*positions* for experienced *this's* and *that's*, and for experienced *I's*. That network is fundamental for experience. It not only constitutes the framework for indexical items representing objects. It must be accessible in itself. There cannot be uncertainty about these experiential coordinates. This is the first dimension of certainty, *subjective certainty*, of indexical reference.

If we are to gain any access to reality, the experienced spatio-temporal framework must *somehow* correspond, must be fastened, to the structure of reality. There must be a certified hook-up between experienced space and time and physical spacetime. This hook-up must make itself present in every experience. Hence, each experienced *now* is underlain by an interval of real physical time, and every experienced *here* or *there* is underwritten by a volume of real physical space. However, this implies logically nothing about the actual geometrical, or causal, nature of physical space or physical time. Nor does it imply that experienced spaces and times have all the same geometry, let alone the geometry of physical space.[7] Physical geometry and specific causal principles are needed to give a precise sense to the above underlined crucial 'somehow'. In any case, here is the second dimension of certainty, *structural objective certainty*, characteristic of indexical reference to time and space. This certainty secures no specific feature of physical time, other than its being the time of the experience in question and being part of a special network of ordering relations.

The subjective and the structural objective dimensions of certainty undergird non-reflexive consciousness. Recall the cumulative-hierarchical character of reflective consciousness. Because of it the indexicality of unreflective consciousness, together with its subjective and objective certainties, is an integral part of reflective consciousness.

The onsetting of reflective consciousness requires access to current episodes of thinking. In principle there can be awareness of one's current mental acts without awareness of oneself *qua* oneself. Thus there may be consciousness of unowned episodes of thinking and feeling.[8]

The highest degree of reflexive consciousness requires, besides, access to the agent, not merely as an experienced item, but as a subject, that is, as an experienced experiencer. Thus, there must be an *objective certainty* that a real entity appears as a thinking I. The general validity of this certainty yields an equivalence (a consubstantiation of sorts) between objective *certainty* and *structural intersubjective certainty*. There is, however, no certainty of any particular consubstantiation between an I and a physical embodiment of it. This is precisely the force of postulate (*I.4) above in Section 2.3.

On the other hand, experienced *this*'s and *that*'s, which in veridical perception are the subjective tails of physical objects, lack objective certainty. They may fail to be in fact such subjective tails. They have only a general causal certainty that something causes the episodes of thinking in which they exist as such subjective tails—perhaps bereft of physical objects.

The arguments for radical skepticism about the reality of an external world bring forth a profound dimension of certainty of indexical reference. Those arguments undermine not only the local objectivity that may lie behind a given *this* or *that*, but also the general causal objectivity mentioned above. Yet, as Descartes argued in his celebrated *Cogito: Sum*, I can conceive of the world as wholly failing to exist, yet in so conceiving I secure my own existence. Kant saw perfectly well the purely structural nature of this certainty and enshrined it in his distinction between noumenon and phenomenon. In his honor we call this the noumenal certainty of first-person reference. Apparently in agreement with Descartes I also attribute *noumenal certainty* to our references to experienced *now*'s; but, in disagreement with him, I further attribute certainty to experienced *here*'s. As against Kant, I hold that both *now*- and *here*-references also possess noumenal certainty. I substitute a noumenon formally structured by space-like and time-like networks for Kant's wholly indivisible and holistic noumenon.[9]

4. Fleeting Experiential Particulars and Evanescent I's

4.1 First-Person Reference and Experiential I-Equations

The many-dimensional certainty of first-person reference is part of the logic of the I's. That is, some implications are valid for first-person reference, which have no counterparts in demonstrative reference to objects. To illustrate let's return to (27). Its surface analysis is:

(27.A) I (who feels [seems to feel] . . .) *am the same as* the author of TSM (who discusses . . .)

By virtue of general indexicality the experiential properties are equivalently predicated of the I of the experience in the consociational form (*feels*) and in the consubstantiational form *(seems to feel)*. Yet both forms of predication allow transferability of properties to the physical individual thought to be consubstantiated with that *I*. The patterns of sameness involving an *I* are communitarian. This is grounded on the objective certainty of *I*-reference. There is always a real individual that can receive whatever properties the *I* has in experience.

There are also further structural features of the *I*'s. Demonstrative reference to objects is particularized because of the plurality of objects that we may encounter at a given time. A perceptual experience presents a field which in principle can, and typically has, many *this*'s and *that*'s. Each sub-experience has a fundamental unity of consciousness, and its own I. The unity of each experience and the necessary objectivity (that is, embodiment) of the *I*'s yield together a fundamental principle in the logic of first-person reference. Let P(I) be any proposition expressed by a sentence containing any number of forms i of the first-person pronoun, let $P(I/x)$ be the proposition schema or property that is predicated of what i denotes, and let '$\rightarrow$' express logical implication in the logic of the I's. Then:

(I.1*) $P(I) \rightarrow$ There exists an individual x such that: I am consubstantiated with x and $P(I/x)$.

The unitary role of each I is signaled here by unifying all the I's that may figure in $P(I)$ into one single I. The objectivity of the I is represented by the implied consubstantiation of the I with an existent individual, i.e., an individual that has a place in the causal order. Principle (I.1*) is the necessary truth underlying the equations between oneself and the persons X, discussed as (*I.3X) above in Section 2.3.

4.2 The Fleetingness of Indexical Referents

A little reflection shows that indexical reference is perforce *personal*: one refers indexically to what one confronts in one's experiences. Indexical reference is essentially *ephemeral*: the subjective indexical items one finds in experience are different from experience to experience. Palpably, the thisnesses and thatnesses of the objects one perceives are exasperatingly fleeting. A *this* quickly turns into a *that*, and soon enough it is lost to experience and is not even a remote *that*. Nothing is intrinsically a *this*, or a *that*. One bestows this status on several very different things in succession: "This [pointing to a man] is older than this [pointing to a woman] and shorter than this . . . " A *you* goes away and is replaced by another, and then there is just oneself alone fretting about something or other. Nothing is really an enduring *you*. Likewise, no moment can claim to be a *now* beyond itself—except perhaps the whole of time as confronted by God. No place has a proprietary right to be a *here* or a *there*—except perhaps the whole of the world space as confronted by God.

Is there at least an I that abides through the vicissitudes of its experiences? If so, which I? Mine? Well, this is the only I I can refer to singularly at this moment by using these tokens of the first-person pronoun I. But how enduring is it? How long can I exist? I believe, of course, that I *have* lived for over sixty years. Yet doesn't this believing amount to *I-now* believing to have lived, i.e., to *I-now* believing that something, or, perhaps, a sequence of something has existed for over sixty years?

Subjective indexical particulars exist only during the experience in which they play their evanescent roles. The I's are no exception.

The personal character of indexical reference raises an important problem. Having experiences is the fundamental property of a mind or person. The power to make indexical references is a basic category of a person. Hence, to think of something as a person one must be able to represent to oneself that something's indexical references. We need others to cooperate with them and to share with them the world that we all both cognize and act upon. For valuable cooperation sometimes we need to communicate transparently others' thoughts.

How can we represent to ourselves others' indexical references? The answer to this lies in the mechanism of *quasi-indexical reference*, of which we have taken some glimpses above. Quasi-indicators are pivotal mechanisms of reference in the language of other minds or persons. They capture our indexical references, ephemeral and personal though these are, into propositionally transparent, enduring, and interpersonal depictions. This of course requires a harmonious match of world, thinking, and language. It requires a comprehensive ontology that can be semantically anchored to the syntax of our language. We cannot discuss this here.[10]

4.3 The Enduring World and the Evanescent I's

The ephemeral nature of indexical reference creates a serious problem. How can we refer to the same things again and again? To carry out plans we engage in we find ourselves confronting some of the same objects and persons again and again. Our plans require a diachronic unity of both the world and the agents. Such a unity must be established in experience. How do we do it, if the core of each experience is a manifold of evanescent particulars?

This is a profound question. It falls beyond the scope of these meditations. The answer has to lie partly in the nature of the world. But partly however the answer involves our conceptions of transubstantiation: the patterns of changes that determine the diachronic unity of substances. These conceptions are mobilized in the particular experiences of a person who posits a past reality. And this has to be done, or so it seems, by a fleeting *I* confronting a domain of evanescent particulars. Again, how? Perhaps some brief comments may not be amiss.

The world of experience is, first of all, not a Heraclitean chaos. It has some abiding hierarchical logical and causal structure. (The noumenon underlying the world and our experience is, of course, another topic.) In the second place, each *I* is the *I* of an experience. Like all indexical particulars, it is evanescent and exists only for the duration of the experience in question. An *I* exists only in the present. Third, the thread of the answer is this: An *I* is nothing but a subject and its contents are literally the contents of the experiences of which it is its subject. This opens the door to the *I* of the experience identifying itself by consubstantiation with anything in those thought-of contents.[11] Fourth, the unity and order of the world is registered in the memories of the thinker. These memories are in the doxastic pedestal that support the thinking episodes constitutive of the experience. The mobilized beliefs, assumptions, and takens-for-granted make the world with its posited past a common framework for all judgments. This mobilization yields beliefs and thinking episodes about continuant physical entities in stretches of the history of the world. These are all consubstantiations and posited instances of diachronic sameness *(transubstantiation)*. The *I* of the experience appears consubstantiated with some contemporaries that have undergone those transubstantiations. Yet there is literally no enduring *I*, except for its duration in a specious present. Except perhaps God.

An *I* is intrinsically nothing but a subject of experience. It corresponds to the maximal unity of the experiences that are, at a given time, internally unified as one total experience by virtue of their being co-consciousness of a manifold of contents. An *I* is in itself the hypostatic construct of the unity of the experience of which it is its subject. Of course, as we have insisted above, behind each *I* lies a physically real, even a noumenal existent. Let's consider an example:

Friedrich's Bee Watching. At a park Friedrich is watching some bees descend on some flowers, pick up some pollen, and then fly away. He is fully aware of himself. His whole experience hinges on a succession of overlapping *I*'s existing alongside a succession of overlapping specious presents. Friedrich is enjoying several sub-experiences. He is attending to one big yellow jacket. He sees it move from a red flower to a yellow one. This seeing occupies a specious present: "From here to here." There is thus the subject of that seeing. During that interval he hears several drones from different bees. Each hearing has its own subject, an *I* that lasts less than the seeing *I*. Similarly, during the same interval he throws off several ants crawling up his legs. Each one of these seeing and throwing episodes has its own subject, again very short-lived. Also about the middle of Friedrich's seeing his favorite yellow jacket he feels an itching on his head; he scratches. An itching I, a scratching I, and an itching-and-scratching I come into existence and quickly vanish.

The itching-and-scratching *I* overlaps the other two *I*'s. During the first moment of just itching the itching *I* coincides with the itching-and-scratching *I*. Then this *I* is the subject of the integrated experiences of itching and scratching. Likewise, Friedrich's whole experience of seeing the yellow jacket fly from one flower to another pivots on one *I*. This ensues from the integration of the different sub-experiences into one comprehensive reflexive consciousness. That *I* is a unit built up from the subjects of the sub-experiences. The real *I* at a given time *T* is the reflexive subject of the maximal co-conscious integration of experiences at *T*. The specious present determined by a succession of overlapping of co-consciousness determines in the normal human cases the short-lived *I* of the interval.

Nothing so far precludes that there be one *I* unifying experiences across different persons or bodies. On the other side, the sub-experiences of a person at a given time may fail to unify into one subject of experience. In principle, for instance, Friedrich may have been mentally disorganized. Some of the experiences mentioned above may have failed to integrate at all, or may have integrated only partially. These are empirical matters that may appear in many different degrees. Psychiatric practice may have (and undoubtedly has) established many types and families of such failures of *I*-integration.

4.4 The Hierarchy within Self-Consciousness and Psychiatric Possibilities

The reflexivity of self-consciousness, as remarked, has an internal, contentual cumulative hierarchical structure:

(1) conceptually inarticulated sensory consciousness
(2) egoless better: I-less, articulated consciousness of objects
(3) unowned consciousness of occurring mental episodes
(4) I-consciousness

At the second level a primitive relation of CO-CONSCIOUSNESS links the contents of a simple experience (or sub-experience) as the contents of *one* (sub-experience). Each experience (or sub-experience) has its own *now-here[there]* spatio-temporal framework. More or less simultaneous experiences normally combine into more comprehensive experiences. This requires an intimate organization of the different synchronous experiential spaces and times. Let's call CO-INTEGRATION the network of structural relations through which a unified total experience is built. Thus, the unity of a person's normal, fully organized total experience at a given time *T* is wrought out by a system of low-level instantiations of CO-CONSCIOUSNESS, and by a thorough system of instances of CO-INTEGRATION. Let's call META-INTEGRATION the relations that structure unowned reflexive experiences. Let's call SUBJECTIONS those structural relations that subordinate an experience to a subject, that is, through which an *I* is posited, or hypostatized.

In the normal case every mechanism runs perfectly and all run in marvellous unison. In the normal case of self-consciousness all the contents of the experience are unified into sub-experiences, and these into a fully unified experience, each sub-experience is experienced as a strand of consciousness that forms part of a unified experience and is owned by an *I*. In such cases the *I* referred to is the maximally integrated and unified *I*—the *I* subsuming all the *I*'s of the unified sub-experiences. Likewise, the *now* of the total experience is the hierarchical cumulation of the *nows* of the sub-experiences.

In an abnormal case a single mechanism by itself or a combination of such mechanisms fails to work properly. Abnormal cases are data about the distinctness of strands in reality that normally go together. The closer the togetherness in question the more informative is the abnormality that breaks it. For instance, a person whose mechanisms eliciting the CO-CONSCIOUSNESS, CO-INTEGRATION, and META-INTEGRATION relations work well may yet suffer from disruption of a SUBJECTION mechanism. He may experience a sub-experience as if it were not his.

The preceding list of mechanisms engaged in the production of self-consciousness is of course nothing but a very crude armchair-philosophical schematic typology. This is precisely one juncture where psychiatry can, and should, guide the philosophy of mind.

4.5 Past Attributions to Oneself: "What a healthy child I was!"

First-person attributions always posit a present *I*. Yet consider Freud's example (1) above:

(1) Sometimes I think what a healthy child I was!

Evidently Freud thinks sometimes a proposition he expresses by means of a first-person past-tense sentence:

(0.I) I was such a healthy child!

On the surface the situation is of the same type as those in which we ourselves use a third-person past-tense sentence to capture (part of) what (0.I) asserts, for example:

(0.SF) Sigmund Freud was a very healthy child.

   Both propositions agree on one point: that a certain individual had a certain property *in the past*. They differ dramatically concerning the utterance present, i.e., the time of utterance. Proposition (0.SF) is neutral concerning the present existence of that individual: he may very well not exist at the time of utterance. In fact, as far as (0.SF) reaches into the world, the Sigmund Freud under consideration may have died as a child, or later but before our utterance. On the other hand, Freud's proposition (0.I) decidedly asserts the present existence of the subject of predication. Both propositions agree only partially concerning the diachronic identity of the subject of predication. Neither posits that the past subject is literally identical with a later subject. (0.SF) leaves it open whether the past subject, the child, was not then a Sigmund Freud. Likewise, (0.I) leaves it open whether the child had any experience, hence, any I at all.
   Let the child last long enough to exist at the time of utterance. According to (0.SF) in such a case a continuous biological entity exists through the whole period. Yet (0.I) does not posit a continuous entity lasting through the mentioned past through the utterance present; furthermore, it rejects any continuity of that entity as an I, and leaves it undetermined whether there is a continuous biological or physical object lasting throughout that time.
   Statement (0.I) is of the logical form:

(0.I.A) There is [in a tenseless sense] an individual X such that: X *was* (consubstantiated with) such a healthy child, and X and I are [transubstantiationally] diachronically the same.

Apparently Freud was not committing himself to the lastingness of an I from his childhood to the present of his statement. In the exegeticized text (2) above he cautiously says: " . . . it [=my ego=I] should appear, in conscious thoughts, many times [*mehrmals*] and in different places or in different relations, as in statement (1)." He is not saying: "it appears in different times (*Zeitungen*)." Nevertheless, he does claim that one's ego lasts through many experiences, through illness and the therapeutic treatment and thereafter.

4.6 Future I's

First-person future-tense statements also speak of utterance-present I's. Just as statements about one's past incorporate memories, statements about one's future incorporate expectations. Here is, however, a serious question. One can trust the past to remain constant; but the future is not so reliable. Here lie interesting issues, which we cannot go into. Perhaps we should record only that predictions about oneself depend for their truth, *not* on the preservation of an I, but on criteria of personal identity. This is another large topic.

5. Conclusion

5.1 The Evanescent I's, the Persons, the Ego, and the Soul

No permanent I underlies the history of a person. There exist successions of ephemeral I's, some of which are interlocking, overlapping because specious presents are overlapping. As long as there is a continuous consciousness from time t to time t' there could be an encompassing I that endures from t to t'. Yet there need be no such an I. It all depends on the degree of organization of the experience of each moment during the interval (t, t'), and on how much overlapping and integration by co-consciousness and meta-integration the successive experiences have.

The crucial ontological point is that the I's, exactly like all other indexical individuals, are ephemeral and subjective. They exist in the present. They link the person who has the experiences with the objective world. They, together with all other indexical items, provide the experience of reality, namely, the reality of the present. All of them are intrinsically simple items, and function as subjective epistemic handles of the experienced existing persons and objects.

An I is the creation of a process of a thinking episode that includes co-consciousness of the unity of the thinking and its contents. As we have remarked it has several dimensions of certainty. It certifies its own existence and its own role in experience. It points to the person whose thinking it is. It reveals that the person has thinking powers. But as such it reveals nothing else. The person underlying an I may be anything whatever. Even the underlying entity postulated as enduring in past- or future-tense statements need not be an enduring physical person, or a metaphysically transcendent substance. As Kant observed a duration of consciousness is compatible with a succession of underlying substances.[12] Each *I* indeed points to a noumenon underlying all of experience. Thus there is a strong temptation—a dialectic illusion deeply seated in the nature of the process of thinking—to equate the experienced ephemeral referent with the pointed-to experiencer in the world and with the pointed-to noumenal reality. Even Kant was not free of this temptation.

The temptation must be resisted at all levels. Nonetheless, it is of the utmost importance to fasten to three facts: (i) the evanescence of the *I*'s presupposes some underlying constant phenomenal as well as noumenal reality; (ii) that evanescence neither requires nor runs against the view that the constant element in phenomenal reality is a pattern of diachronic connections among physical individuals; (iii) likewise, neither is the lastingness of the *I*'s required for, nor does its fleetingness oppose, the thesis of a noumenal soul.

Freud's ego is not identical with an *I*. It is an enduring set of powers to think in the first person. The sense in which an ego is the same as an *I* is at best that of consubstantiation. Hence, a person's ego is at best transubstantiated with a broken sequence of *I*'s.

Summary: This is an inquiry into the nature of what we think as "I". What does one refer to internally, *de dicto*, when one uses assertively a sentence containing an inflection of the first-person pronoun? What sort of entity is that referent? How does such a referent relate to the person calling himself or herself "I"? We shall say that a token of a form of the first-person pronoun used to make a thinking singular reference strictly or internally denotes an *I*.†

In the normal case these mechanisms run perfectly and all run in marvellous unison. In the normal case of self-consciousness all the contents of the experience are unified into sub-experiences, and these into a fully unified experience, each sub-experience is experienced as a strand of consciousness that forms part of a unified experience and is owned by an *I*. In an abnormal case a single mechanism by itself or a combination of such mechanisms fails to work properly. For instance, a person whose mechanisms eliciting the CO-CONSCIOUSNESS (integration by simultaneous occurrence within consciousness), CO-INTEGRATION (integration of different contents into one unified experience), and META-INTEGRATION (structuring reflexive experience, thought) relations may work well yet suffer from disruption of a SUBJECTION mechanism (subordinating experience to a subject, thus producing the character of mine-ness of experience). He may experience a sub-experience as if it were not his. Thus psychiatry can, and should, guide the

† The first paragraph of the conclusion is repeated at this point in the text. It is deleted here. —Eds.

philosophy of mind in trying to delineate the different types of integrating and unifying relations as structures at work in every experiencing person.†

Notes

1. On quasi-indicators, see Castañeda 1967a and Tomberlin 1983.

2. The general ontological and semantical theory from which I am approaching the problems in this paper is Guise Theory. It contains a full account of the different sameness relations discussed here as well as of others. This theory was first formulated in Castañeda 1974. This is reprinted in Castañeda 1982a and 1989a. Guise Theory is discussed in Plantinga 1983 and in Clark 1983, and in Castañeda's Replies to these authors in Tomberlin 1983. Further discussions appear in articles of Rosenberg 1986a, Smith 1986, Sicha 1986, and in Castañeda's Replies (Tomberlin 1986). More recent discussions can be found in Küng 1990, Heckmann 1990, Kapitan 1990a, Rapp 1990, Burkhardt and Dufour 1990, Jacobi 1990, and Castañeda's replies to these authors, all in Jacobi and Pape 1990. Guise Theory has been discussed and developed into an alternative ontology by William Rapaport in several papers (1978, 1985/1986). Francesco Orilia (1986, 1988) has also developed an alternative.

3. See Wolfgang Künne 1990. He refers to Austin 1962, 98, 136.

4. See my reply to Wolfgang Künne in Jacobi and Pape 1990. For additional delving into perceptual indexicality see Pilot 1990, Prauss 1990, and my replies to these papers in Jacobi and Pape 1990.

5. On identity and the other sameness relations, see the materials mentioned in Note 2.

6. See Fichte 1794 and Sartre 1943. My latest discussion of an Externus-type of consciousness appears in Castañeda 1987c.

7. These are the fundamental premises behind Kant's view that space and time are forms of perception. He also saw the structural objective certainty of references to perceived time and space. This led him to what I call *Kant's Unifying Hypothesis about Time and Space.* This is the thesis that physical space [time] and all perceptual spaces are one and the same. See the *Transcendental Aesthetic* of Kant's *Critique of Pure Reason.* This hypothesis has been shown to be false. There is an enormous literature on perceptual spaces. For my ontological discussion see Castañeda 1977a. This is an abridgement of the last two chapters of Castañeda 1982a.

8. In Castañeda 1967a a level in between unowned consciousness and full self-consciousness is recognized. It is a level that has the contrast between what is internal and what is external. Vacuous I's are posited to collect the internal. Full self-consciousness involves, besides, the contrast between oneself and other persons. Later on I realized that my two levels of self-hood correspond to some extent to Martin Buber's distinction between two strands of *I-ness.* One is the contrast *I-Other,* and the other is the contrast *I-Thou.* See Buber 1923. In fact we have three strands in the concept of I: *I-That [it]*, *I-That [He/She]*, and *I-Thou.* Since the days of *Indicators and Quasi-indicators* I believe that the most complex and exciting English indicator is *you.*

† The last three paragraphs of this summary are duplicates of three paragraphs in the conclusion and have been deleted here. Also, we have deleted the German translation of this summary which appears at the end of the essay. —Eds.

9. See Descartes's *Meditations*, Kant's first *Critique* (Paralogisms), and Castañeda 1987d. This study complements Castañeda 1987b.

10. See materials mentioned in Notes 1 and 2.

11. Here is a fundamental indexical premise for Kant's refutation of idealism in his first *Critique*. See also the paper by Harald Pilot mentioned in Note 4.

12. See Kant's refutation of Mendelsohn in the first *Critique*.

10

I-Structures and the Reflexivity of Self-Consciousness

> Phenomeno-logic is the study of the logic of phenomena. Phenomena are what appears in experience. That is, the phenomeno-logic of X is the logic of the consciousness of X. . . . The phenomeno-logic of self-consciousness studies the structure of the consciousness of the appearance of self. To carry out such a study is to be conscious of the form of self-consciousness as this is experienced. . . . One major tool of phenomeno-logic is phenomeno-logical linguistics. It investigates how the contents of a type of experience become encoded in the language used to live that experience.
>
> —Tor Daschein, *The Reflexivity of Self-Consciousness*

1. Introduction

Here I continue "Persons, Egos, and I's: Their Sameness Relations," presented at the 1988 Freiburg conference on Psychopathology and Philosophy. That paper tackles basic ontological and semantic questions: What does one strictly refer to, that is, think, by means of the first-person pronoun? What sort of entity is a thinking referent? How does what a person calls "I" relate to that person? To gain a better understanding of these questions we subsumed the problem of first-person reference under the general case of indexical reference. We found that the *I*'s—like the *now*'s, the *here*'s, the *this*'s, and *that*'s—are irreducible fleeting subjective individuals, existing only as contents of experiences. They constitute the framework of the experience they belong to. Their ontology is exhaustively epistemological. They exist merely to make present to the experiencing person objective referents with which they are the same in an appropriate representational sense. That this sameness is not literal self-identity is of the utmost importance: the ontology of the

As indicated in the Preface to this volume, the present essay combines Castañeda 1989b and 1990a, published respectively in *Philosophical Topics* XVII, No. 1 (1989), 27–58, and in *Philosophy and Psychopathology*, edited by Manfred Spitzer and Brendan A. Maher (Springer Verlag, 1990), 118–145. The latter essay, reprinted by permission of Springer Verlag, is used as the base text. Passages from the former, reprinted by permission from the Editor of *Philosophical Topics*, are inserted when appropriate and indicated with brackets. The title reflects the amalgamation we have attempted here.

fleeting I's can ground neither an empirical theory of a particular embodiment of consciousness nor a metaphysical doctrine about an immortal soul.

The initial focus of the present paper is the reflexivity of self-consciousness. This is a twofold reflexivity: an external, pedestrian one, and an internal, exciting reflexivity, which rests on the former. The internal reflexivity hinges on I's. We develop complementary evidence for the evanescent and subjective nature of the I's. This nature explains their essential ontologico-epistemological role as points of integration and unification of experiential contents. These are organized in the framework constituted by the I-strands. Experiences need not be owned by I's, and when they are the I-integration presupposes the unity of the owned experience. Thus we reject the Fichtean thesis—still widely held even among philosophers and friends of Artificial Intelligence—that all consciousness involves self-consciousness. (Thus we take issue with Kant's view on the role of apperception.) The Fichtean thesis demands a downwards unity of the contents of consciousness from the experienced-experiencing self to the non-self contents. This runs against the facts of experience, and prevents a unitary account of animal consciousness. Indeed, even the postulation of an experienced-experiencing self arises from an unjustified conflation of the external with the internal reflexivity. Hence, whereas there is a momentous problem about the I's, there is no problem of a self-referring self.

Even though no theory of a person's body can be derived from the intrinsic nature of the I's, the phenomenological facts of I-experiences reveal certain structures of bodily mechanisms that make those experiences feasible. Thus we may distill a "physiological" schema underlying self-consciousness, that is, the minimal form of a network of bodily mechanisms upon which not only consciousness, but self-consciousness emerges. Its guiding assumption is clear: Discriminations in the contents of what is thought or experienced signal differences in the bodily abilities underlying the making of such discriminations. This assumption must be accepted both by Cartesian dualists and by reductionist physicalists. The Cartesian sees those signals as contingently required by the intimate connection between an embodied mind and its body. The reductionist sees them as analytically necessary, given his reductionist program; he might concede that those necessary truths can, even must, be discovered empirically. We can set aside the modal issue in order to attain the shareable truths. However, here we do not pursue the formulation of the schema of the self-conscious body.

No I is a naked or isolated individual. On the contrary, every I is a focus of connections to different types of entities in the world, even out of the world, and to the world itself. Since I's exist only as, and only while being, thought of, those connections are constitutive while thinkable. They are instantiations of the possible I-structures. These determine the nature of the I-contents. Patently, the I-structures signal general features of a body upon which self-consciousness accrues.

2. Self-Consciousness and Self-Reference

2.0 Problem, Assumptions, and Major Theses

[Consciousness (in the primary sense of this word) is an *occurrent* condition. It is a general condition, as when, for example, we re-gain consciousness by coming out of surgical sedation or a coma. Crucially, this condition permeates, and exists in, particular episodes of being conscious of this or that. There is, however, a dispositional sense of 'consciousness'. For instance, Marxists speak of the plutocrats' class consciousness and of the social consciousness of the labor class. This consciousness is not (occurrent) consciousness, but a complicated network of attitudes and propensities to act in special ways, tolerate certain types of actions, promote certain species of behavior, experience feelings of certain kinds, have beliefs of certain types, and argue in appropriate ways. These attitudes and propensities exist even though they are not manifested, but when manifested they will naturally deploy themselves in episodes of consciousness of the pertinent contents.

Here we consider occurrent consciousness only. More precisely, we focus on episodes of *self*-consciousness. These are episodes in which ONE is conscious of ONEself *qua oneself*. Our topic is the reflexivity of self-consciousness. The reflexivity in ONE referring to ONEself as *oneself* is twofold. There is the external reflexivity of ONE referring to ONEself, and the internal reflexivity of ONE referring to something, whatever it may be, as *oneself*. We must take both reflexivities into account. The internal reflexivity is the peculiar core of *self*-consciousness.

Self-consciousness is executed in episodes of thinking about oneself *qua* oneself. The contents thought in such episodes are expressed in utterances of sentences containing (at least apparently) singular-referring uses of the first-person pronoun. For this reason we may more accurately speak of *I*-consciousness. A thinking episode is of course not an event of uttering. It is embodied in—indeed, in some *appropriate* sense of 'sameness', a thinking episode is the same as—an event or process in the thinker's brain, or whatever the thinking box of the thinker may be. Here we neither endorse nor oppose the reductionist physicalistic thesis that mental events are just second-order causal properties of physical events. We must, however, insist that mental events and mental dispositions are in the world and are part of the causal order. We must accept causal equations of the mental and the physical, and raise the fundamental issue of the nature of the sameness involved in such equations. Here, however, we do not enter into this issue.[1] One thing is clear to me: the sameness in question cannot be conceptual or analytic equivalence, much less literal (self)-identity: hence, such equations cannot provide a reduction of the mental, more specifically, of consciousness, to the physical. Yet they may secure the causal dependence entrenched in the hierarchical emergence of mental states and particulars on and off physical states. In fact, consciousness seems to be an irreducible emergent. This is, however, not the occasion to tackle this topic.[2] In any case, reductionist functionalists are, or should be, firmly concerned with the reflexivity of self-consciousness. The better we understand what it appears to be, the more detailed and secure our reductionist programs can be. Likewise, Artificial Intelligence, whether practiced with a reductionist bent of mind or not, has a vested interest in the reflexivity of self-consciousness. Clearly, the production of facsimiles of human behavior or of mental states and activities needs only the causal dependence of the mental on the physical. Self-consciousness is the apex of mentality.

Here we are not concerned with development, but with the structures of self-consciousness. Our subjects are mature, fully competent thinkers who enjoy or suffer full episodes of *self*-consciousness. Such subjects have acquired the requisite abilities to think thoughts of the form *I am such and such*. We assume that they have mastered a natural language by means of which they relate to others, with whom they engage in social activities and practices. In brief, our mature thinker has a natural language that she uses both as a means of communication and as a means of thinking. Thus, there is as good a match as is feasible between our thinker's brain events embodying her thinking episodes and some linguistic utterances available to her that express the contents of such episodes. That is, her sentence tokens in her varying contexts of thought and speech can formulate the internal contents constitutive of those thinking episodes. We further assume for convenience that our mature thinker is, at least in the cases we discuss, *candid*: her sentence tokens reflect, within the normal limits, and subject to applicable standard contextual constraints, what she is thinking at the time of utterance.[3] The assumption of speaker's candidness is subordinate to the chief assumption that language is spoken. To be heard, or overhead, language must be spoken. Thus, though we are interested in the hearer's perspective, we are deeply concerned with the speaker's point of view. This involves a needed departure from the standard philosophizing carried out in English. Surely to investigate *self*-consciousness is to attempt to get into the thinker's most intimate standpoint. Nonetheless, assuming a hearer, we initially pose the problem as the exegesis of attributions of self-consciousness. This is the problem of ascertaining what a speaker thinks and what a thinker thinks when the former attributes self-consciousness to the latter.

Armed with the preceding methodological assumptions we can discuss the thought contents of episodes of *self*-consciousness as they manifest themselves in the pragmatico-semantic content of tokens of first-person sentences. We need not worry about the neurophysiology or the engineering of the thinker's processes embodying such episodes. For our task here it does not matter whether the sequential order constitutive of such processes is compositionally syntactic or connectionist, or whatever.[4]

At the risk of provoking hostile opposition, as well as greater expectations than can be fulfilled here, I want to deploy the general view of *self*-consciousness urged by the examination of central data. It is constituted, among others, by the following theses. *First*, contrary to a widely held Fichtean tradition, not all consciousness is *self*-consciousness. *Second*, the different degrees of consciousness are essentially cumulative and hierarchical: more advanced degrees not only presuppose but include suffusively the lower degrees. (This does not show that brain events embody thinking or consciousness compositionally. It does show, however, that the surface operations of the brain, those that ultimately deliver consciousness, have a general compositional syntactic structure.) Thus, *self*-consciousness is built up on layers of self-less consciousness which remain as an internal basis for reference to oneself as *I*. *Third*, consequently, the unity of an episode of consciousness is not explicable by virtue of that consciousness belonging to a self, or, better, an *I*.[5] On the contrary, it has to be accounted for in its own terms. Besides, if an episode of consciousness is internally owned by an *I*, then the unity of that owned consciousness is, rather, an element in the constitution of that ownership, and an internal presupposition of that *I*. *Fourth*, the hierarchy of content of full *self*-consciousness is twofold. On the one hand, it includes a structural hierarchy of formal contrasts—a structure of *conceptual negativities*. On the other hand, those contrasts have to be realized in specific contents—a network of *empirical positivities*. These are identifications of what one is, and raise a question about the sense of the requisite identity or sameness.

Fifth, the vital role of an episode of *self*-consciousness is exhausted in current experience: it is organizing and monitorial. Here lies one part of the solution to the biographical paradox of *self*-consciousness. Consciousness is an expensive commodity worth sparing. To live is fully to immerse oneself in action, that is, in full obliviousness of oneself, developing techniques of habitual and immediate, but adequate response to problems. Obversely, as Plato remarked,[6] the best life is an examin*ed*, a fully consciously examined life; yet an examin*ing* life is not the best form of living—if living it is. *Sixth*, the experiential function of first-person reference is of one piece with the experiential role of all other indexical reference. *Seventh*, THE MECHANISMS OF INDEXICAL REFERENCE CONSTITUTE THE STRUCTURE OF SUBJECTIVITY. The strict referents of acts of indexical referring are fleeting subjective particulars that serve to harpoon the external referents being experienced. In the case of perception, we aim at harpooning, and we typically harpoon, (perceived) physical entities; in the case of first-person reference we harpoon thinking persons with their bodies. *Eighth*, hence, indexical particulars, which are ephemeral and subjective, have a twofold epistemological primacy. On one side, indexical particulars enjoy a basic intrinsic incorrigibility: they exist as and inasmuch as they are experienced. On the other side, since their role of harpooning external reality is their *raison d'être*, their subjective incorrigibility typically and normally transfers to the physical realities they harpoon as the latter's immediacy of presentation in experience. The ontology of indexical particulars is wholly exhausted in their epistemological roles. *Ninth*, first-person reference is true to its indexical character. The *I*'s, strictly referred to in episodes of *self*-consciousness, are evanescent particulars whose function is to harpoon, through reflexive thinking, persons as subjects of experience, whatever they may otherwise be. *Tenth*, one peculiar feature of the *I*'s is their effective transfer of their incorrigibility to the reality they harpoon for the experiencer. (This is the Cartesian truth of the fundamental certainty of the *cogito*.) *Eleventh*, there are no lasting *I*'s. This raises an interesting problem about first-person past- and future-thoughts and statements. Of course, underlying each evanescent *I* there *may*, logically, be an enduring physical entity, or a sequence of such entities, or even an eternal soul. However, the ontology of the *I* grounds by itself neither an empirical theory of a particular embodiment of consciousness nor a metaphysical theory of the soul.]†

2.1. The Reflexivity of Self-Consciousness

Ultimately we want to understand the manifold of powers whose joint activation ensues in episodes of *self*-consciousness. In such episodes ONE is conscious of ONEself *qua oneSELF*. They are doubly reflexive, and reflexive in two ways. There is the external reflexivity of ONE referring to ONEself, as when shaving ONE accidentally cuts ONEself, rather than another. Externally referring to oneself is, like cutting oneself, a matter of *doing* something, rather than of thinking a certain content. Like the reflexivity involved in cutting oneself, the external reflexivity of reference to oneself can be unintentionally and unwittingly executed. Thus a forgetful painter may think that the painter of a certain picture is a very good painter without realizing that he himself painted the picture. There is, on the other hand, the internal reflexivity of ONE referring to something, whatever it may be, as *oneSELF*. The internal reflexivity is the peculiar core of *self*-consciousness. It is the reflexivity of a content of thought, namely: what one expresses by thinkingly using sentences containing tokens of the first-person pronoun '*I*'.

Both forms of reflexivity are necessary for self-consciousness. Indeed, self-consciousness rests so firmly on its external reflexivity that the expression 'x refers to x as himself' sounds out of order if 'refers' is meant in its strict sense. Merely to refer to something is simply to pick it up in thought as a subject of properties and as an object of a propositional attitude, e.g., believing, doubting, supposing. The use of 'x refers to y as herself' suggests that it would be a special instantiation of 'x refers to y as z' for the case in which x *happens* to be the same as y, and 'as herself' instantiates z. The fact is that one cannot just refer to another person as oneself. One can, to be sure, refer to another person and think that she is (the same as) oneself. But then one is

† The foregoing is taken from Castañeda 1989b, 27–31. —Eds.

referring to oneself as oneSELF. In short, letting '⟶' express logical or analytic implication connecting the concepts in question, we have the following
principles or meaning postulates:

(SC.ER) x (merely) refers to y as herself ⟶ x is the same as y.
(SC.Ex) x refers to x as himself ⟶ x exists.

Clearly, the two occurrences of the suffix '—self' have a very different
meaning in the matrices' 'one refers to ONEself as *one*SELF' and 'x refers
to HIMself as *him*SELF'. Yet it is very easy to think that it has exactly the
same meaning and role in both occurrences. Undoubtedly, in some sense that
cries out for elucidation, the two occurrences of '—self' express a sameness
of referent. If one then—as is customary—mobilizes a monolithic concept of
identity or sameness, one sees the very same self-identical entity as outside of
and as inside the referring act. Of course, that entity is called *self*. Then one
has the difficult problem of explaining how a self can be at the same time both
the subject of and the object of one and the same experience. This is a *ficti-
tious* problem. There is no such a self. Here one must tread with care. That
problem of the self does not exist. This, however, in no way justifies a Humean
conclusion that there is no self in experience. In fact, Hume was also the
victim of his conflating the external ONEself with the internal *one*SELF.
There is no external self; but there is an internal SELF. The latter is an important philosophical problem. Since the internal SELF is what one refers to
by using the first-person pronoun 'I', we should perhaps say more perspicuously that whereas there is *no* problem of the self, there is a serious problem
about the *I*'s.

We can, then, concentrate on the internal reflexivity without loss.

Self-consciousness is executed in episodes of thinking about oneself *qua* oneself. The contents thought in such episodes are expressed in natural language
in utterances of sentences containing (at least apparently) singular-referring
uses of the first-person pronoun. The internal reflexivity of self-consciousness is the appearing of the thinker to HIMself as himSELF, that is, as an *I*.
Self-consciousness is *I*-consciousness. Not because we identify *I*-conscious-
ness with the use of the pronoun 'I'; but because the uses of 'I'-sentences
reveal the speaker's thinking *I*-contents, and, consequently, his having a brain
I-representation. A thinking episode is not an event of uttering. It is embodied in—indeed, in some *appropriate* sense of 'sameness', a thinking episode is
the same as—an event or process in the thinker's brain, or thinking box,
whatever this may be.

Here we do not endorse the reductionist physicalistic thesis that mental
events are just second-order causal properties of physical events. We must,
however, insist on an insight that underlies physicalism: mental events and
mental dispositions are in the world and are part of the causal order. We must
accept causal equations of the mental and the physical, and raise the fundamental issue of the nature of the sameness involved in such equations. Here,

however, we do not enter into this issue [see note 1]. One thing is clear to me: the sameness in question cannot be conceptual or analytic equivalence, much less literal (self)identity: hence, such equations cannot provide a reduction of the mental, more specifically, of consciousness, to the physical. Yet they may secure the causal dependence entrenched in the hierarchical emergence of mental states and particulars on and off physical states. In fact, consciousness seems to be an irreducible emergent. This is, however, not the occasion to tackle this topic [see note 2]. In any case, reductionist functionalists are, or should be, firmly concerned with the reflexivity of self-consciousness. The better we understand what it appears to be, the more detailed and secure our reductionist programs can be. Likewise, Artificial Intelligence, whether practiced with a reductionist bent of mind or not, has a vested interest in the reflexivity of self-consciousness. Clearly, the production of facsimiles of human behavior or of mental states and activities needs only the causal dependence of the mental on the physical. Self-consciousness is the apex of mentality.

2.2 Reference and Consciousness†

We are concerned with thinking reference, the reference a thinker makes to what he thinks, whether he is reflecting by himself or engaged in a dialogue. What does it consist of?

Let us examine the *as*-moment in the general formula:

(GR) *X refers to Y as Z.*

This is a requisite background for our study of the moment *as oneSELF* in self-consciousness.

An act of referring is a real event in the world. It is, therefore, a part of the causal order. It involves a relation which can have the selfsame entity in the positions of agent and accusative. Hence, there is a causal relation that includes an external dovetailing of reference on to its source. This dovetailing is, as we noted above, not only required for self-consciousness, but implied by the internal reflexivity of the moment *as oneSELF*.

An act of referring is a mental event. As such it has an internal content. This is what the sub-form 'as Z' of (GR) alludes to. Content Z is what the thinker thinks of, refers to thinkingly. What does this amount to?

The physical-physiological process of thinking something about Z, say, that (. . . Z . . .), is undoubtedly thoroughly computational. It may include a multitude of computations of brain states, terminating in a complex B of brain events that contains a *representation* of that (. . . Z . . .). That is, either there is an isomorphism between some systematic parsing of that (. . . Z . . .) and

† No section 2.2 appears in Castañeda 1990a; the paper goes from section 2.1 to 2.3. However, the outline of an earlier draft indicated that there should be a section 2.2 with this title. We think this is the place in the narrative where the section should begin. —Eds.

a parsing of B, or there is a mechanism for constructing such an isomorphism, or there is a general causal function that assigns (... Z ...) to B. However, for X to think that (... Z ...) the occurrence of that representational event is not enough. That representational event must deliver a *presentation to the thinker* of what he is thinking of. This is of the greatest importance. The representations of what the thinker refers (or purports to refer to) as Z when he thinks thought content (... Z ...) may be stored in different ways in his brain. This storage is not thinking. Those representations may move from storage to occurrence, yet this transition may not suffice. This is so even if the representation were a perfect replica or image of the object thought of, and the thinking occurrence of the image consisted in its being a faithful replication of the stored image in the thinking box, screen, or whatever, in the brain. Certainly, to embody an act of referring (or purporting to refer), the occurring representation of the referent must occur in the proper location required by the engineering of the brain. It must, further, occur in the proper presentational way: It must yield the molar state of the possessor of that brain being *presented* with Z through being *presented* with (... Z ...). The word 'presentation' is of course in the family of words meaning consciousness as its basic sense. The threat of circularity indicates that, although, of course, certain amounts of unconscious events, states, or objects do *cause* consciousness, no amount of unconscious states or objects can constitute an episode of consciousness.

The purely mental and crucial sense of '[refers to, thinks of] as (*qua*) Z' is governed by this fundamental principle of the embodiment of thinking:

(Th.PR) In the general sense of '(thinkingly) refers to' (and 'thinks of') what the referrer is presented with is the *selfsame* item as what he strictly refers to (thinks of).

2.3. The Chinese-Box Structure of Attributions of Reference

Let us continue our exegesis of the formula (GR): "X refers to Y as Z." In terminology I don't like, the locution 'as Z' expresses a *de dicto* attribution of content to a mental act. Here, as always, though often not attended to, *de dicto* attribution is attribution by *depiction* of the internal, presentational content of such an act. Suppose I declare: "John believes that Leibniz was a lawyer." Evidently, my subordinate clause discloses to the hearer, not John's words—let alone John's brain representations—, but my alleged replica or picture of John's belief content. The picture purports to reveal, first, an isomorphism between certain doxastic representations of his, concerning Leibniz, with a corresponding representation of mine; the picture purports also to reveal the psychological equivalence between the components of our isomorphic representations. Hence, expressions that occur internally, *de dicto*, in attributions of mental state have, on Peirce's term, an *iconic* function.

The formula (GR) *X refers to Y as Z* is of a mixed nature. The component *to Y* is, as we said, external. It is, in one sense of a companion terminology I also dislike, *de re*. The point often made with this expression is that what a substituend of 'Y' denotes exists. This is of course often true. However, it is just a special case of what people think. The underlying function of so-called *de re* expressions, like 'Y' in the formula (GR), is to express, not existence, but *speaker's (intended) reference*. It is the person proffering (GR) who expresses *his* thinking of what *he* calls Y. The whole formula expresses that the speaker, *not* the person X, identifies what he calls Y with what X calls Z —regardless of whether Y exists or not. Obviously, to express this identification of his the speaker himself also represents Z as Z. Clearly, then, expressions in *de dicto* positions are points of referential *cumulation*.

Accessing another's thought contents requires connecting those contents with the shared world. For this we must think ourselves those contents, whether we believe they are veridical or not. (This is referential cumulativeness.) Thus, the general sense of (GR) can be diagrammed as follows:

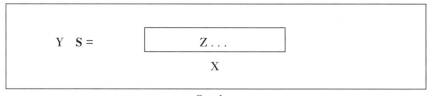

Speaker

where 'S=' denotes the speaker's identification of X's Z with his Y, and each box represents a fragment of the world as conceived by the person mentioned immediately under it.

Statements of the form (GR) are little windows which the speaker opens to her hearers to let them peep into her (conceived) world; these windows reveal internal open windows on the said referrer X's world. To speak (candidly) is thus to perform an act of revelation, of one's-world-window opening.

Internal, *de dicto* expressions are depictions of representations the speaker exhibits as SHARED by him and the person he speaks of. *De re* expressions just vent the speaker's references. *De dicto* indirect speech has a Chinese-box structure, each box revealing the presented representations constituting thinking content—regardless of the existence of what is thought of.

A statement of form 'X refers to Y as Z' discloses to the hearer that the speaker is presented with thinker X as thinker X, with item Y as Y, with item Z as Z. Further, it reveals that the speaker takes Z to be an intersubjective thinkable. This is simply the cumulative character of the *de dicto* occurrence of Z in 'X refers to Y as Z'. By equating Z with Y the speaker reveals, besides, that Z has an objective status in her world. This status need not be existence. Even if X in fact refers to the speaker's Y as Z, Y may be only an intersubjective thought of item. In short, the externality of the moment *to Y as Z* in

(GR) consists of its expressing the speaker's positing the *objective intersubjectivity* of Z as Y.† She locates X's referred to item Z in her world, or in the thinkable surroundings of her world. To be sure, the speaker may be in error in equating her Y with Z as thought of by X. It does not matter. The point is that she claims to have penetrated X's mind and have found Z there: Z is shared. Thus, the internality of the moment *as Z* of (GR) is the subjectivity of Z within X's experience, yet it manifests an accessible *intersubjective subjectivity* of Z. Again, this is the referentially cumulative function of *de dicto* expressions in the Chinese-Box structure.

2.4 The External (de re) Target of Reference and Existence

To understand fully the nature of the acts of referring we must understand (GR) in as general way as thinking reaches. Doubtless, an episode of thinking is typically and primarily oriented toward the physical environment. Typically we think of real objects as having certain properties, and we succeed: the objects we think of exist and have the properties we predicate of them. Occasionally we make mistakes. Sometimes the objects we think do not have the properties we think them to have; sometimes the very objects we assume to exist do not exist. A comprehensive account of experience, thinking, and how language functions, requires acknowledgment that we must sometimes refer (if you wish, purport to refer) to non-existents—as when we conceive failed plans to make certain things, or erroneously postulate certain entities to explain some events. An episode of thinking as a psychological reality is exactly the same whether what one thinks exists or not: the same brain events, the same representational structure. (Just imagine your thinking of a distant existent, which vanishes while you are thinking of it; yet its vanishing does not lame your thinking.) In sum, we must not equate externality of reference with existence.[7]

Thinking is impervious to existence. The sense of 'refers to' and 'thinks of' we need in (GR) lacks an existential commitment to what is thought of. We keep, on the other hand, an existential commitment to X, the referrer. Thus, we subsume the problem of the reflexivity of self-consciousness under a more general problem of thought content.

On the assumption that the speaker makes true statements, what his world windows show is part of the real world. Of course he may be in error; or he may be trying to deceive. The entity Y he locates in his world as being the same as Z as conceived by X may not be real. Clearly, what the speaker calls "Y," his Y, is—like Z in X's alleged act of referring—just a presentation typically (in the default case) pointing to the world. Thus, the item Y is no different in ontological status from the item Z. Both are aspects, faces, *guises* of thought of objects. In the typical episodes of thinking they are posited as real,

---

† It may be that Castañeda intended 'Y as Z' rather than 'Z as Y' as it here occurs. —Eds.

that is, as existing aspects, faces, guises that compose unitary objects in the real world. If they are real then they have infinitely many properties not thought of in the thinking that the statement reports.

On the assumption that the speaker is telling the truth, we the hearers take it for granted that the aspect, face, *guise* Y put forward by the speaker for consideration is real. That is, we take it for granted that Y has a place in the causal order, and doxastically posit a whole infinite system of existing faces or guises each *existing as being the same as* Y. Under this positing we can equate the speaker's Y with some item H in *our* world and say: "The speaker says of H, to which he refers as Y, that X referred to it [Y] as Z." Thus we become speakers, and assign to Y an intersubjective subjectivity: we and the (previous) speaker think of Y as such. This is the basis for our assigning to Y an objective intersubjectivity through our equating it with H. In its turn, Z gains a deeper intersubjective subjectivity: Z is then a shared item located in the innermost box of a three-membered Chinese Box we have created.

Our H may not be real. We take it to be real, and our (conceived) world is the one we have beliefs about and act on. Metaphysically the basic fact is that we have NO access to an external point of view. All reference is from *our, one's* point of view. (As is well known, here lies the kernel of Kant's Copernican Revolution.)

The speaker's posited sameness between Y and Z need not be recognizable by the person X. It is not the strict self-identity of Y=Y, Z=Z, X=X. As always, the elucidation of sameness is a serious matter (see note 1). Consequently, we must not prejudge the nature of the sameness involved in referring acts. We remain open to there being several different types of sameness required for the elucidation of storable mental representations, and for their occurrences yielding thinking presentations to a thinker.

[Let us abbreviate 'is the same as' by 'S='. We allow that 'S=' may turn out to be a *sameness* variable. We reserve the sign '=' for strict or genuine, necessary identity, self-identity, governed by a wholly unrestricted Leibnizian indiscernibility of identicals—including psychological and modal contexts. Hence, whereas some cases of sameness are bound to be contingent and empirical, strict identity is absolutely necessary. The symbols 'X', 'Y', and 'Z' have singular terms, not variables, as substituends. Clearly, "(Y=Z) does not imply (Y S= Z)"; but the converse is trivially valid. Let 'Y S= Z' express the appropriate sameness relation suitable for each type of entity Y and the nature of what the speaker takes X to be thinking. Let 'Z<X,*t*>' denote the item Z as it appears in X's world at time *t*, according of course to some speaker's view of X's world. Let '→' express analytic or logical implication, and '↛' its denial, these symbols having large scope. The basic logic of referring acts in general includes the following postulates, where *t* is a time:

(Id.S)   Y S= Z → (Y=Y & Z=Z)
(GR.1)   At *t* X refers to Y as Z & X S= X' & Y S= Y' → at *t* X' refers to
          Y' as Z

(GR.1.1) At t X refers to Y as Z & X=X' & Y=Y' $\longrightarrow$ at t X' refers to Y' as Z

(GR.2)   At t X refers to Y as Z & Z S= Z' $\nrightarrow$ at t X refers to Y as Z'

(GR.2.1) At t X refers to Y as Z & Z=Z' $\longrightarrow$ at t X refers to Y as Z'

(GR.3)   At t X refers to Y as Z $\nrightarrow$ Y S= Z

(GR.4)   At t X refers to Y as Z $\longrightarrow$ Y S= Z<Y,t>

(GR.5)   At t X refers to Y as Z $\longrightarrow$ at t X refers to Z as Z

(GR.5.1) At t X thinks that (. . . . Z . . .) $\longrightarrow$ at t X refers to Z as Z.

(GR.5.A) At t X refers to Z as Z $\longrightarrow$ at t X thinks something of the form (. . . Z . . .).†

Here we leave it open whether some converse of (GR.3) holds.‡ The contrast between (GR.1) and (GR.2)–(GR.5.A) is only one part of the contrast between the externality of the moment *referring to* and the internality of the moment *referring as*. The reflexivity of reference to oneself as Z, not necessarily as *oneself* (hence, not necessarily *self*-reference) is a special case of the externality of referring; it is, as already remarked, like the reflexivity of the self-eating tiger of the above example. (GR.4) connects internal thought content with external thought of referent; (GR.3) puts a limit to that connection. (GR.5) and (GR.5.A) are partial expressions of the presentational role of what is thought. They establish a necessary aspect of reflexivity in every act of reference, *a fortiori*, in the self-reference of self-consciousness.

Undoubtedly, there are three-position reflexive statements and facts of the form *X refers to X as X*. For instance:

(2) The wisest man of Freiburg referred to the wisest man of Freiburg, to HIMself, as the wisest man of Freiburg.

By (GR.5) and (GR.5.A), it suffices that the wisest man of Freiburg thinks, for example, this: The wisest man of Freiburg will exert great influence in the cultural changes in the Albert-Ludwigs-Universität. Palpably, in his mere thinking episode reported in (2) the wisest man of Freiburg does not refer to HIMself as *himself*. This is so even if he knows that he himself is the wisest man of Freiburg. This piece of knowledge may indeed be operative and un-

---

† Castañeda may have intended 'Z<X,t>' in place of 'Z<Y,t>' in (GR.4), since the '< >' notation indicates that one is talking about how X represents Z. Given this adjustment, the sameness in question would have to be something like consociation, the relation whereby thinkables are in fact together insofar as they are thought to be together (see Castañeda 1974); otherwise the principle would not hold. (GR.5.1) seems incorrect; given what Castañeda writes in the next paragraph he may have intended it as a non-implication principle. However, given that he later (1989b, 40) cites this principle to derive the following: "At t X thinks (. . . I . . .) $\longrightarrow$ There exists an entity u such that u S=I<X,t>" then it seems that the consequent of a corrected version of (GR.5.1) should be "there exists an entity u such that u S= <Z,t>". —Eds.

‡ This sentence is difficult to understand unless the sameness in question is something like consociation. In a draft of "The Reflexivity of Self-Consciousness" on electronic disk, Castañeda wrote that it is "left open whether some converse of (GR.5.1) holds", rather than a converse of (GR.3). —Eds.

derwrite his thinking what (2) reports in a context of impersonality. Obviously, then, three-position reflexivity of referring is *not* necessary for *self*-consciousness; it is actually inimical to *self*-consciousness.]†

2.5 The Internal [de dicto] Reflexivity of Self-Consciousness

Now we come to the third prong, 'as (*qua*) *oneSELF*,' of our initial formula of *self*-consciousness:

(I*) In an episode of *self*-consciousness ONE refers to (thinks of) ONEself *qua oneSELF*.

We turn to the meaning of the suffix '-self' in the italicized pronoun '*one-SELF*'. In (I*) this is a relative pronoun having 'ONE', *not* 'ONEself' as its antecedent, whose character it takes. In our schematic formula (I*) the antecedent 'ONE' is a variable; hence, '*oneSELF*' has a variable aspect: its substituends have as antecedents the corresponding substituends of 'ONE'. These substituends of 'oneSELF' are reflexive pronouns that depict first-person reference: '(he) himself', '(she) herself', 'themselves', 'yourself', 'myself'. Thus, '*oneSELF*' and its substituends are *quasi-indicators*.[8] For example:

(3) The author of "Self-reference and Self-awareness" is thinking [of HIMself] that *he himSELF* wrote *Self-Knowledge and Self-Identity*.

Here the pronoun '*he himSELF*' refers back to its antecedent 'The author of "Self-reference and Self-awareness" ' and depicts this author referring to HIMself as "I."

Doubtless, the external target of self-reference is ONEself. One always succeeds in harpooning ONEself if one thinks of ONEself as *oneSELF*. But what is the presentational representation with which one harpoons ONEself? Evidently, it is what a use of the first-person pronoun reveals that the speaker is presented with: an *I*. This is a unique, ephemeral, and irreducible representation. The uniqueness and privacy of *I*-reference is established by the fact that nobody can refer to another person in the first-person way. The peculiarity and subjectivity of each *I* is established by the fact that for any third-person individual *i* which is the same as a person X, X may fail to know that he himSELF is (the same as) *i*. The first-person pronoun has a general meaning that determines a framework within which, on each occasion of its use, a speaker confronts a unique and personal representation of the reality he or she is.

In sum, the indexical uses of the first-person pronoun have these central features: (i) they express an ineradicable privacy of the presentational *I*-representations; (ii) because each of these representations is a presentational occurrent it is fleeting, lasting only as long as the presentation (the experience)

† The foregoing appears in Castañeda 1989b, 36–37. —Eds.

lasts; (iii) the *I*-presentations, primarily, and the uses of 'I', derivatively, in-fallibly harpoon an existent beyond the representation, and (iv) they intrude as also infallible the very existence of the presenting representation, that is, the thought-of *I* itself. (The other types of indexical singular terms have properties similar to (i)-(iii). The only exception is demonstrative reference to experienced items, which lacks property (iii). Statements of the form "This is F" secure an internal referent, the subject *this*, but do not always harpoon an external target.)

[All the mentioned expressions in the uses under consideration share a se-mantic component, which is carried by the suffix '-*self*'. Hence, the locution '*oneself*' (like its substituends) in the contexts 'ONE refers to ONEself as *oneself*' depicts, is a proxy for, a first-person reference attributed to ONE (or the entity denoted by its substituends). Here '*oneself*' is what I have called a *quasi-indicator*, more precisely, a quasi-indexical variable.

Consequently, first-person quasi-indicators have a crucial internal, *de dicto* semantico-pragmatic strand: they depict the subjective internal self-reference peculiar to self-consciousness. They also have a most important external, *de re* syntactico-semantic dimension: through their connection to their antece-dents they express an intersubjective objectivity of first-person reference. (Here is another reason why I do not like the standard *de dicto/de re* contrast: it is supposed to be exclusive and exhaustive; thus conceived it makes it im-possible to understand the function of quasi-indicators.)

For perspicuity, let's append a star, '*', to an expression that functions quasi-indexically as a depiction of an indexical reference. The star in 'one*' or 'oneself*' ('he*' or 'himself*') thus replaces the underscoring in 'as *oneself* ('*himself*'). Recall that in 'ONEself' the suffix '-self' simply signals that 'ONEself' and 'ONE' are the selfsame variable. Thus, our formula (I*) has the sense of:

(I*.1)   In an episode of *self*-consciousness X refers to X as himself*.

As noted above, the quasi-indicator 'himself*' is composed of 'him-', which refers back to 'X', and the self-presentational content '-self*'. To signal this representational duality of quasi-indicators, we could put our formula of self-consciousness canonically as follows:

(I*.F)   In an episode of self-consciousness a thinker X refers to X as [X]*.

The bracketed component '[X]' represents the external anchoring of the quasi-indicator and of the depicted indexical reference; the brackets signal that this anchoring is external, a part of the speaker's location of X's *I* in his own world. The star '*' signals the internal depiction of a certain indexical reference. As remarked, the pseudo-internal 'X' in '[X]' has as antecedent the first occurrence of 'X', which denotes the referrer. Hence:

(I*R.1) The formula "Y refers to X as [X]*" is nonsensical, and so is the formula "X refers to [X]* as Y."

(I*R.2) The formula "X refers to X as [X]*" is an instantiation of the formula "X refers to Y as [X]*."

Obviously, (I*R.1) subsumes the impossibility of referring to another in the first-person. On the other hand, (I*R.2) records that one can attribute first-person references to somebody else whom one thinks to be the same as oneself*. The attribution of a first-person reference is a third-person quasi-indexical reference. Doubtless, rehearsing one's mis-self*-identification with another does require first-person reference—to oneself *not* to that other.

Recall that we are using the idealized term 'refers' with an existential commitment to the referrer. Hence:

(I*R.3) At t X refers to Y as [X]* $\longrightarrow$ X exists at t.

(I*R.4) At t X refers to Y as [X]* $\longrightarrow$ at t X assumes (knows) that [X]* exists at $[t]$*.

NOTE. The quasi-indicator 'at $[t]$*' is expressed in English as 'then'.

(I*R.5) At t X refers to Y as [X]* & X S= A & Y S= B $\longrightarrow$ at t A refers to B as [A]*.

(I*R.6) At t X refers to Y as X $\nrightarrow$ at t X refers to X as [X]*.

(I*R.7) At t X refers to Y as [X]* $\nrightarrow$ at t X refers to Y as X.

Principle (I*R.6) formulates in part the point, illustrated with example (2), that three-position reflexivity is inimical to self-consciousness. Both (I*R.6) and (I*R.7) are illustrated by (3) above and (4) below:

(4) The author of "Self-reference and Self-awareness" is thinking of the author of "Self-reference and Self-awareness" that the author of "Self-reference and Self-awareness" wrote *Self-Knowledge and Self-Identity*.

Clearly, (3) neither implies, nor is implied by, (4). This failure of implication holds not only for episodes of thinking, but also for dispositional states, e.g., believing. This is confirmed by a recent report that our author is in doubt about the existence of the book mentioned above, and has forgotten his ever having written an essay with the above title. (How the author of such great works can forget his writing them is not a conceptual matter, but an entirely different, biographical, question.)

In general, for any equation 'j S= the author of "Self-reference and Self-awareness," ' there is a pair of sentences (3.j)–(4.j) paralleling the pair (3)–(4). The author of the essay can think (even believe) that j wrote the book without thinking (or believing) that he* wrote it.

First-person reference is not just internal to a thinker's thought contents. It is unique even within the internal contents of a thinker's thoughts. Each one makes her own demonstrative (indexical) references to items in her experience. Yet one can think demonstratively of an entity X, which one encounters in a certain experience (for instance, by looking into a mirror), without thinking that X is *oneself*. Furthermore, a thinking entity, still without identifying what it sees with itself*, can address the entity it sees in the mirror, expressing thus some second-person thoughts: "You look terrible. You should not present yourself in public like that . . . " Therefore, "That (person) [she, he] is F" and "You are F" are entirely different thought contents from "I am F." Thus, the internality of third-person demonstrative reference, and also of second-person reference, may have a *de facto* external reflexivity.

First-person reference is necessarily reflexive. This feature is signaled by our formula 'ONE refers to ONEself as *oneself*'. The expression '*one-*' in '*oneself*' (and, canonically, 'X' in '[X]*') does co-refer with 'ONE' (that is, the first occurrence of 'X'). This reflexivity forces first-person reference to harpoon an external reality. This is partially captured by (I*R.3) and (I*R.4). By means of (GR.5.1) we have:

(I*R.8) At t X thinks (. . . I . . .) $\longrightarrow$ There exists an entity u such that u S= I<X,t>.

This principle is valid for every speaker. Therefore, it secures a referent of the first-person pronoun in the shared world, the real world. The speaker who uses 'I' is no exception. Hence, for each thinker the following hold:

(I*R.8.1) At t I think (. . . I . . .) $\longrightarrow$ There exists an entity u such that u S= I<I,t>.
(Id.I**) u S= I<I, now> $\longrightarrow$ u S= I.

(These postulates constitute the core of Descartes's *cogito*.)

Let us turn now to the particular *internal* content one thinks in self-reference. Doubtless, the external target of self-reference is ONEself. One always succeeds in harpooning it. But what is the presentational representation with which one harpoons ONEself? Evidently, it is what a use of the first-person pronoun presents to its user: an *I*. This is a unique and irreducible representation. Its irreducibility is precisely what (I*R.6) and (I*R.7) formulate, what the non-implication between (3) and (4) shows. The first-person pronoun has a general meaning that determines a framework within which, on each occasion of its use, a speaker confronts a unique and personal representation of the reality he or she is. Every one thinks of himself as an *I*. The others can represent that personal representation, not just the private presentational role it plays in the given episode of thinking, by means of a quasi-indicator. Consider:

(5) X thinks (out loud for our convenience): I love Elly.

A hearer asserts:

(6) X thinks that he* loves Elly.

By making statement (6) the speaker opens a window to her world. Again, this window reveals a window open to X's world. This time, however, we do not see an item Z in that part of X's world shared with the speaker. We see a faithful painting—*himself*—of a literally unshared item in X's world—what X calls "I." Clearly, 'himself' is internal to the construction (6), somehow presenting to the hearer the presentational representation X confronts. Nevertheless, it does so indirectly. Evidently, X does not use the third-person pronoun 'he himself' to refer to himself as himself: he uses the first-person pronoun 'I'. Only his uses of 'I' refer to him—as himself*, of course.

In brief, the indexical uses of the first-person pronoun have three central features: (i) they have an ineradicable privacy of presentational representation; (ii) they infallibly harpoon an existent beyond the representation; and (iii) they intrude as also infallible the very existence of the presenting representation, that is, the thought of I itself. (The other types of indexical have properties similar to (i)-(iii). The only exception is demonstrative reference to experienced items, which lacks property (ii). Statements of the form "This is F" secure an internal referent, the subject *this*, but do not always harpoon an external referent.)

The uses of the quasi-indicator depicting first-person reference have therefore five crucial properties: (i) they occur in internal, *de dicto* positions as depictions of I-reference; (ii) they are literally third-person representations of such references; (iii) they involve an internal, reflexive existential commitment: they present the presentational depictions as existing; (iv) they involve a trans-internal existential commitment to their depicted I's; (v) they carry an external existential commitment to the referents of their antecedents. I-presentations, like all other indexical representations, exist only in their presentational function. On the other hand, our quasi-indexical representations of others' I representation representations are interpersonal and lasting, and can have repeated presentations in diverse thinking episodes. This is the constant content signaled by our quasi-indexical star in 'himself*' and in '[X]*'. Consequently, indexical statements or propositions are different from the quasi-indexical propositions, or thought contents, that correspond to and depict them.[9]†

But what exactly is that I content one is presented to in episodes of self-consciousness? That it is so peculiar and unique is further brought home by the fact that there is no special characteristic that one has to think that one possesses in order to think of oneself as I. Certainly, one *qua* I does not classify oneself as a self, a person, or a thinker—let alone as a human being, female, or whatever is true of all entities capable of *self*-consciousness. To illustrate, a small child at about the age of two can make perfect first-person references fully lacking knowledge involving those categories. In general:

† The previous section is taken from Castañeda 1989b, 38–41. —Eds.

(I*R.9)   Where *being F* is not simply *being myself*, or *being thinking*, or *existing*, or their joint logical implicates, all propositions of the form *I am F* are synthetic *a posteriori* in Kant's sense, i.e., non-redundant (non-tautological).

There is just no criterion one can apply to determine whether one is an *I* or not. One simply is an I. This primitive fact is primitively and immediately apprehended by a thinker who is an *I*.

[Let us look at the situation from another direction. As noted at the beginning, the dominant standard approach in the study of language and mentality takes dialogues as basic data; this has led to the adoption of an external, hearer's perspective. Yet certainly in the case of self-reference we must adopt the position of the speaker and her thinking references.

The following is certainly a correct rule governing the use of the first-person pronoun:

(K-I)   In any statement in which an indexical, singular use of a token of the first-person pronoun occurs, that use (or that token) designates the speaker of the statement.

This is a marvelous rule for *communicating* self-consciousness, not for experiencing self-consciousness. We can ignore the fact that one often thinks without making statements. We may suppose that at some level in the language of the brain we have personal pronouns; we may understand 'speaking' broadly enough to mean the production of symbols, whether overtly in a public language or covertly in the language of the brain, which symbols embody thought content. On these assumptions, (as Plato said) speaking is thinking, and thinking is speaking. By these semantic stipulations we secure that a hearer who understands a used sentence containing the first-person pronoun understands, concerning this pronoun, no less than what (K-I) requires.

Nonetheless, a hearer has to understand *more* than what rule (K-I) prescribes. The hearer has to understand the internality of the references the first-person pronoun has been invented to express. Rule (K-I), if not in the pedagogical process, at least in the ontological order, rests on the following rule:

(I*.I)   A thinker who makes a statement with a token of a sentence containing one token T, or more, of the first-person pronoun, indexically *used*, refers with T to HIMself *as himself*.

Furthermore, if all thinking is speaking, a *speaker* cannot act from (the conception of) rule (K-I) or (I*.I). He will have to conceive *himself** as the author of a first-person statement not yet made, or made in the very act of thinking something in the first-person way. But then how can he identify *himself** with the maker of that statement? This identification would simply be embodied in a use of the first-person pronoun that precedes the application of the rule.

Moreover, language must be spoken, indeed, before it is understood by a hearer. If thinking is speaking to oneself, then to hear oneself one must sometimes speak without hearing oneself. The fact is that for a speaker, his* referring to the maker of a statement with the first-person pronoun cannot be a criterion for his use of the first-person pronoun.[10]

Still, what is the content one thinks as *I*? This is a serious question that requires a separate study. In part 3 is the briefest outline of the answer.]†

We must fasten to the fact that each *I* is a primitive and ephemeral internal representation of the thinker as the subject of occurrent internally, presentationally convergent experiences. Because of (I*R.9) this representation contains no description or attribution of a property. It is merely the brute unanalyzable presentation of the internal unity of those experiences with their successful harpooning of something in the real world otherwise unknown—whatever it may be. Hence:

(I**) An *I* is an ephemeral hypostasis that presents a thinker to HIMself as the theater of ongoing mental activity. At bottom an *I* ensues from, and is thus the opaque presentation of, an operational unification of a set of structures that unify the particular contents of a manifold of ongoing experiences. To think an *I* content (. . . I . . .) is to EXE-CUTE (unconsciously, of course) a unification of presented representations (. . .) and to be presented with that execution.

The rest of this essay is a preliminary investigation into the unifications underlying an *I*. First we consider the presenting representations constitutive of self-consciousness; then we take a glimpse into the schema of "physiological" processes that make viable those unifications.

[2.6 The Worldliness/Nonworldliness Tension of Self-Consciousness

1. The unworldliness of the I's The internality of what we think and refer to in indexical first-person reference is fundamental and absolute. Overwhelming; tantalizing. The content of the reflexivity of *self*-consciousness is wholly internal and peculiar to the thinker's thought contents. That is:

(I**R.1) An *I* exists subjectively only, within the contents of episodes of *self*-consciousness.

This conforms to Descartes's immediate hesitancy after confronting his Evil Demon (or Wilfrid Sellars's Mad Scientist[11]). He claims cautiously (where the capitals express my added emphasis) that:

† The foregoing section is taken from pages 42–43 of Castañeda 1989b. In that paper, part 3 (below) is referred to as 'IV'. —Eds.

De sorte qu'après y voir bien pensé, et voir soigneusement examiné toutes choses, enfin il faut conclure, et tenir pour constant que cette proposition: *je suis, j'existe*, est nécessairement vrai, TOUTES LES FOIS QUE JE la prononce, ou que JE la conçois en MON esprit.[12]

Yet there is an exegetical problem with this *dictum* of Descartes's. Cautiously, he acknowledges that *I exist* is true, indeed, necessarily true, WHENEVER the proposition is thought by him. This leaves open that it may be false when it is not thought. However, then there is no *I* to think that proposition. These would intimate that perhaps each time *I exist* is thought a fresh new *I* is thereby brought into existence. All of this is in accordance with the internality of the *I*'s. On the other hand, Descartes's *I exist* is true every time I (a capitalized translation of 'JE') think so. What about this I that thinks at different times? Descartes of course did not bother with this. He simply took the capitalized I to be what his argument establishes. The immediately following paragraph begins: "Mais je ne connais pas encore assez clairement ce que je suis, moi qui suis certain que je suis." These expressions 'je' and 'moi' simply denote the JE of the preceding citation.

Descartes seems to be urging principles that in a more general form can be put as follows:

(I**R.2) For every I-proposition: (. . . I . . .) $\longrightarrow$ I exist.

(I**R.3) For every I-proposition: (. . . I . . .) $\longrightarrow$ I am thinking or I have thought.

I submit that the necessity of the truth of *I exist* that Descartes proclaims is just the necessity of the above implications. These are necessary truths in the logic of *self*-consciousness, or, better yet, in the logic of the *I*'s. These Cartesian principles are, however, compatible with a non–Cartesian, but quasi-Humean view of the *I*'s. This is the view mentioned above: the *I*'s are merely subjective entities, whose existence is exhausted in episodes of *self*-consciousness. On this view the essence of an *I* is, as for Descartes, thinking (*cogitare*), but, anti-Cartesianly, an *I* is not a *res cogitans*.

2. *The requisite worldliness of the I's* The more internal the *I*'s are the more non-real they become. Now, the pinnacle of human living is to live an examined and carefully planned life: a life that consists of the unfolding of a system of intentions. These are however first-person thought contents.[13] Consider a somewhat revised example I have used before:[14]

The Quine Award to Be Given to Sellars in the Chisholm Auditorium

(7) The Plantinga-Grünbaum Society for the Philosophy of Mind has unanimously approved that its President present Wilfrid Sellars with a special band containing an appropriate gilt inscription, an elegant diploma, and a check for US $1,000,000, the three together embodying the Willard V. O. Quine Award for Philosophical Accomplishment. The ceremony is to

take place at the Roderick Chisholm Auditorium of Brown University on May 12, 1989.

In the situation under consideration in (7) for somebody to be in a position to attempt to act intentionally, it is necessary that he/she places the entities in question in his/her experience at the proper time. The agent must answer questions about the relevant ceremonial identifications. If an agent is to carry out the ceremony voluntarily and intentionally, that agent must endorse the following answers to such indexical questions:

(8) *Indexical identifications*
    (a) *I* am the President of the Plantinga-Gruünbaum Society.
    (b) *This here* is [*you* are] Wilfrid Sellars.
    (c) *This* is the Chisholm Auditorium of Brown University.
    (d) *That* is the P-G Society band of the Willard Quine Award.
    (e) *That* is the P-G Society diploma of the Willard Quine Award.
    (f) *Today* is May 12, 1989.
    (g) *Now* is the time of the Award conferral ceremony.
    (h) *Here* is the location where the ceremony is scheduled to take place.

With these propositions in his/her doxastic repertoire, a person can become the agent to bestow The Quine Award on Sellars. Indexical equations (8)(a)-(h) constitute the bridge on which the agent-to-be can move from endorsing the external singular proposition (7) to thinking endorsingly its corresponding *indexical deontic proposition*, to wit:

(7*) *I* ought to give to *this* man *this* band and *this* diploma *now*.

   The success of our intentions and our complying with our duties requires that we act in one and the same world as we cognize. Intentional and voluntary action hinges on there being indexical internal contents that the agent takes to be true of the world. This is what (7*) illustrates. The connection between (7) and (7*) needs the mixed indexical-nonindexical equations (8) that link our experiences to the world at large. The sameness proclaimed by the (8) equations is a transcategorial sameness between the indexical items present in experience and their harpooned targets in the world.
   In brief, such absolutely indispensable mixed equations like those in (8) have two obverse functions. From the side of subjectivity, they provide the indexical particulars—the *I*'s, the *this*'s and *that*'s, the *now*'s and *here*'s—with worldly anchors. They all have, therefore, their deep-grounded worldliness. From the side of objectivity, the mixed equations provide the external entities that are experienced—the agents, the presidents of societies, the buildings, the Sellarses, the Quines, the Chisholms, the times, and the places—with their appropriate distinct experiential handles. Obviously, the mixed character of those equations presupposes that the equated subjective and objective items

are different individuals: they certainly differ in ontological status. What sort of sameness is that?

3. *The social worldliness of the I's* The necessarily worldliness of the *I*'s is valid for an agent, even if he is a lone and solipsistic agent. Of course, example (7) is not solipsistic. Nevertheless, (7) considers the situation (almost) exclusively from the point of view of the one who presents the award to Sellars. The participants are also sentient and thinking beings. For them to cooperate with the agent they must ascribe intentions and beliefs to the agent and to one another. Hence they must place in the shared world the others' *I*'s (and *this*'s and *that*'s, *now*'s and *here*'s). Then for the benefit of others, which revolves into one's benefit, the logic of *self*-consciousness requires this postulate of *I*-embodiment:

(I**R.4) No *I* is an ontological island unto itself. There must be infinitely many unique intersubjective characterizations Fness such that: One is (the same as) the person F, e.g., I am (the same as) the person F.

4. *Major problem: One type of solution* One serious problem for any theory of *self*-consciousness is to provide and account of *I*hood that reconciles, assuages, or dissolves the deep-rooted tension between the non-worldliness and the worldliness of the *I*'s. Non-worldliness arises from the internality of *self**-reference; worldliness springs forth from the externality of SELF-reference, which necessitates the embodiment of each *I*.

It seems that the most economical solution to the worldly/nonworldly tension about *I*'s requires a theory of sameness that recognizes different sameness relations. One simplification is this: The way in which every *I* must be the same as a physical object others can identify is the same way in which the thinker HIMself is the same as each of his ephemeral *I*'s. Clearly, this sameness is contingent and MUST be carefully distinguished from necessary samenesses, especially strict identity. Guise Theory is an already available theory of samenesses.[15]]†

---

3. The Hierarchy of Internal Reflexivity in
Self-Consciousness

3.1 The network of structural negativities composing I-schemata

Once again, an *I* is a hypostatic individual one thinks by means of an indexical internal representation expressible through a token of the first-person pronoun. That individual is a device for successfully thinking of oneself. As such, we have seen, it has no objective properties. Since it reflexively represents the thinker, it is constituted by categorial contrasts that reveal fundamental struc-

† The foregoing is from pages 43–46 of Castañeda 1989b. —Eds.

tural properties of the thinker. Those are the *I*-structures that mold the contents of *self*-consciousness.

[Once again, an *I* is what one thinks as an individual with an indexically used token of the first-person pronoun. The categorization "as an individual" is meant to capture the common core across the different inflections of the pronoun. These inflections represent important distinctions. For instance, a token of 'me' used as a dative conveys information crucially different from that conveyed by an accusative token of 'me'. Both differ drastically from the information borne by a token of the genitive 'mine', and even more from that riding on a token of the possessive adjective 'my'. These are local semantic contrasts internal to our concept of the first-person. They represent subtle structures enveloping each *I*, within which a given *I* enters into particular relationships.

We face four related ontological questions:

First: Does each token of the first-person pronoun denote a unique *I*?
Second: If not, do all the tokens of the first-person pronoun issuing from one physical source denote one and the same *I* throughout the history of that source?
Third: If so, can the tokens of '*I*' emanating from different sources designate one and the same unifying *I*?
Fourth: If so, do *all* the tokens of the first-person pronoun designate one omni-comprehensive *I* that underlies the different utterances, regardless of the uttering source?

The answer to the first question must be a categorical and emphatic "No!" The tokens of the first-person pronoun in one piece of discourse expressing a unified train of thoughts, or experience, at least *normally* denote the same *I*. This *I* unifies the experience whose contents are deployed in that piece of discourse. Nevertheless, the unity of the experienced content is a logically necessary condition of, but not a sufficient condition for, the uniqueness and the unity of the experiencing *I*. In principle, the tight unification of a rich experienced content could be experienced by different *I*'s. We could have in such a case *psychological Siamese twins*. Given a physical or physiological basis for episodes of consciousness such twins do not seem entirely unfeasible. Two brains may for certain experiences be connected to one common source of the experience. Can, for example, two Siamese twins sharing one leg and one arm feel exactly the same pain on the shared leg? Or can two different personalities embodied in the same brain, or in different parts (for example, different hemispheres) of the same brain, share the same numerical experience? Of course here we move within an area where stipulations suitable for economic description of our stable world are available. Yet different meaning postulates may provide a better terminology for adequate theorizing. The problem is more for psychiatrists. They treat patients who together present an extraordinary diversity of experiences. Their problem is to make enough distinctions that could enable them to deal with all their cases. Short but thick terminologies that express narrow theories are often torn apart by scientific progress and technological developments.

The answer to the second question is generally affirmative.[16] I am one of those who prefer a negative answer. We shall consider this below.

Those who answer "Yes" to the second question should in general be flexible enough to answer "Yes" to the third question. In the less committal cases the answer to the third question depends on the adopted criteria of personal identity. To the extent that a person can alter its (her, his) physical embodiment, given a certain diachronic unity of experiences, the same lasting I might be said to underwrite that unity. On the other hand, an affirmative answer to the third question is a basis for an affirmative answer to the fourth question.

Let's return to the I-structures that mold the contents of *self*-consciousness. We seek further I-enveloping structures beyond the local ones carried by pronominal declension.]† They can be gleaned by charting the types of properties and relations characteristic of I's. Each such type is a domain of possibilities open in principle to all I's. Here we will not carry out this cartographical investigation. Our present concern is confined to the internal I-structures, bundles of which constitute *I-schemata*. These structures have certain independences; hence, they need not be present all at once. There is, thus, a hierarchy of I-schemata. Consequently, the I's can be partially ordered in accordance with the ordering of the I-schemata constituting them.

The I-schemata provide blueprints for egological development. Under a conception of normality, the I-schemata furnish also a master chart against which to check a person for possible I-disturbances.

The internal I-structures are I-strands hinging on contrasts between what one is *qua* oneself and something one is not. Alternatively phrased, an I-strand is the polar negation of something intrinsically non-I. Because of the polarity, the negation is dichotomous.[17] Thus, an I-schema is a complex of *negativities*. To gain a concept of I is to acquire the capacity to pick out immediately *instances* of one or more of those polar negations. This instantiation is of course confronted by thinking of ONEself *qua oneSELF*. Here is a fundamental ingredient in the peculiar reflexivity of *self*-consciousness.

To think of ONEself as *oneSELF* is to think of something *intimated* to be, *felt as it were*, the opposite of each of such and such N's—for the appropriate values of 'N'. I have chosen the words 'intimated' and 'felt' advisedly. We have already seen how to think contents of the form (. . . I . . .) is to have a primitive apprehension of the subject one calls "I," not mediated by any identification procedure. That basic truth remains unaltered. Hence, to apprehend one-SELF in the content (. . . I . . .) is to apprehend a manifold of polar negations of the different non-I's as one fully unified manifold of I-strands. Fur-

† The foregoing is taken from Castañeda 1989b, 46–48. —Eds.

thermore, it is to apprehend that manifoldness in a non-conceptual way, as a sensory content. Conceptually one apprehends only the unity. The apprehension of the manifoldness underlying the unitary *I* consists partly of feeling that sensory-like content. Intellectually, such an act of apprehension sets in readiness a hierarchical manifold of propensities to think, especially think believingly, appropriate ranges of propositions. These ranges are demarcated by the felt negativities. The elements of those ranges are determined by the personality of the thinker, the context of the thinking episode, including her surface purposes, and her preceding trains of thought.

Self-consciousness is, thus, erected on a reflexive sensory consciousness. This reflexivity is not reflective (in the sense of reflecting on something); it is of the ONEself type of reflexivity discussed in Part II above. We will see that *self*-consciousness is mounted on other forms of non-reflective consciousness. Also *self*-consciousness occurs on a *doxastic pedestal* composed of propensities to think or to rehearse belief. We elucidate the doxastic pedestal below. The empirical contents of episodes of self-consciousness fall, then, within one or more of the negativities composing the *I*-strands. The most pervasive of these are:

Chief *I*-strands
1. The contrast *I—this/that*
2. The contrast *I*—they [the external objects of the world]
3. The contrast *I—he/she* [this/that (thinker)]
4. The contrast *I*—they [the others]
5. The contrast *I* [believer/knower]—*I* [agent]
6. The contrast *I—he/she* [this/that (person: sentient-thinking-and-acting individual]
7. The contrast *I—you*
8. The contrast *I—we* [partners at a conversation]
9. The contrast *I*—they/we [the members of one's community]

REMARK 1. Here I have been inspired by Ferdinand de Saussure in conceiving a meaning of an expression as a contrast between a usage of the expression and the usages of other related expressions within a family.[18] Each contrast of usage is a semantic strand. To me Saussure's general thesis seems to be correct, but it is particularly suitable for the semantics of the first-person pronoun. Of course here the usages and meanings of words interest us only as avenues for approaching thought contents. The above nine contrasts are contrasts in thought content, in what we find in experience, and what we believe to be in the world.

REMARK 2. I have adopted the dash in between the contrasted expressions from Buber. He contrasted "the two meanings" of 'I': *I-It* and *I-Thou*.[19]

REMARK 3. The different *I*-strands listed above divide the full-fledged concept of *I* along different axes. The endpoints of these axes are: (i) what is being experienced vs. what perhaps although not experienced belongs nevertheless to the world at large; (ii) what is internal to the mind vs. what is external; (iii) being vs. not being a person or a mentally endowed individual; (iv) cognizing the world vs. acting on it, which rests on the axis believing vs. intending; (v) being a thinking-acting individual vs. being a member of a community. Undoubtedly other axes must be added for a full account of the *I*-schemata and their strands.

REMARK 4. The nine *I*-strands enumerated above intermingle in many different ways. This yields a spiralic process of steady enrichment of one's concept of *I*. The mingling principles are of different sorts. Some are required by the kind of world we find ourselves in, with its physical, chemical, and biological natures, but also with its social organizations and other cultural products. Some principles of mingling lie deeply seated in the thinker's ontologico-psychological make-up, which manifests itself in the thinker-agent's metaphysical postures. For example, animists mingle the *I*-strands in such a way that everything has its own internal *I*. Solipsists find the total world at large to be merely experiential content of the only accessible *I*. Deists promote the whole of reality to the veridical content of an all-embracing *I*. Pantheists are animist deists. Mystics do all sorts of things; some raise themselves up to the status of partial *I*'s within an all-encompassing one.

REMARK 5. The order in which the *I*-strands are listed is logical from the perspective of the experience of thinking. It is not meant to prejudge the philosophical disputes about the possibility, or viability, of solipsistic consciousness. It is not intended to cast any aspersion on, or endorse with its converse, the semantic socialism now fashionable.[20] It is not meant to decide in advance the outcome of controversies (philosophical, pedagogical, or otherwise) about the learning of language or the acquisition of concepts.

REMARK 6. The network of negativities is a network of structures. They have to be filled in with special contents. These are empirical and metaphysical beliefs, or even deep-seated takens-for-granted, at the foundation of the thinker's doxastic pedestal.

3.2 The Hierarchy of Modalities of Consciousness within Self-Consciousness

The existence of consciousness, hence, also the existence of *self*-consciousness, rests on a complex doxastic pedestal. This is a hierarchy of powers, dispositions, and propensities to think believingly that such-and-such, or disbelievingly of what contradicts what one believes, or skeptically of some other things. That pedestal in its turn pivots causally on, so to speak, an iceberg of unconscious processes. The contents of consciousness are not, however, a uniform monolith somehow above the line separating what is in the light of consciousness and what is submerged in the dark water of the unconscious. Those contents have, rather, a hierarchical structure. This is not just a hierarchical logical or epistemic order of those contents; it is also a hierarchy of modalities of mental attitude and of consciousness. The uppermost tiers are propensities to think, which may be also activated, appearing through propositions also present to consciousness; some propensities will manifest themselves in the penumbra of consciousness; others lurk behind perhaps as merely felt in sensory consciousness. Most of the tiers of the pedestal are utterly unconscious. The bottommost ones are metaphysical; yet they are not so much beliefs that can on occasion be brought to consciousness. They are, rather, deep-seated takens-for-granted, built in the hardware of the inferential or computational mechanisms that underlie the embodying of thinking episodes. These cannot (physically, or psychologically) be brought to consciousness. Some of them may be actually unformulable.

Consciousness is suffusive and subsumptive. It is suffusive in that, not only do thought of contents enter consciousness in networks, but the appearing of certain contents mobilize the doxastic hierarchy. This mobilization is, as noted, hierarchical: some propensities to think certain contents are triggered and placed in different degrees of thinking readiness. On the other hand, consciousness is subsumptive in that lower forms of consciousness are present in the higher forms, although in an altered nature. In brief:

(Cons*) The unitary structure of consciousness proceeds upwards, but its illumination flows downwards.

In this sense consciousness contains an internal hierarchy of reflexivity. Most important consequences are suggested by (Cons*) about the hierarchical integration of the underlying physiological processes.

Self-consciousness is the highest form of consciousness. It exhibits, therefore, the highest forms of suffusiveness and subsumptiveness. As indicated above, it subsumes all other modalities of consciousness. This is another dimension of the characteristic and peculiar internal reflexivity of *self*-consciousness.

Now, the subsumptive internal hierarchy of consciousness within *self*-consciousness includes the following levels:

1. sensory content, conceptually inarticulated:
       (a) bodily   (b) worldly
2. I-less articulated content pertaining to:
       (a) external objects
       (b) bodily content
       (c) occurring mental acts
3. I-less focal consciousness, the core of which is a complex of perceptual judgments
4. I-owned content articulating the contrast between Self and Object
5. I-owned content articulating intentional agency
6. I-owned content articulating the contrast between Self and others
7. I-owned content articulating an interaction between Self and *you* as well as absent persons.

The maximal degree of *self*-consciousness has an *I* as its focus and anchor. This fills in the *I*-schema in which all the relevant negativities intersect and have their proper empirical and metaphysical content.

The integration of a manifold of contents as the contents of a unitary *self*-consciousness proceeds from the lower levels up. That is, we cannot explain the unity of an episode of consciousness in terms of an *I* to whom that episode belongs. This can be established empirically: there are episodes of *I*-less consciousness. It is not just that there is a quiet *I* in the background, which can at any moment come into the open. At this point the positing of an enduring *I* as the underwriter of the experiences of one and the same person at different times becomes handy. This positing must, however, be grounded on some evidence or reasons. No matter. The consciousness of some lower animals obtains without being owned by any *I* that can come to the light of *self*-consciousness.

All consciousness is subsumptive and suffusive. Accordingly, I submit that in gaining full consciousness after a deep sleep we go through all the levels of consciousness as different stages of the process of waking up. As I see things, since each *I* exists only during and within an episode of *self*-consciousness, waking up is really a case of ontogeny recapitulating phylogeny. Anti-recapitulation occurs in cases of falling asleep slowly.

Level 1 is a theoretical posit. We assume that there is a manifold within sensory consciousness, which includes no awareness of objects or events. The primary consciousness is perceptual. We may assume that the sensory manifold is, underneath consciousness, partitioned into masses belonging to the different types of perception.

At *level 2* there is conceptualization of some sort. The minimal sort is what I have called *zero-consciousness*.[21] This is the confrontation of a perceptual field that contains as distinct points some perceptual states of affairs (or propositions) as unanalyzed units, with no logical structure, not even a subject-predicate one. I theorize that this is the kind of consciousness exemplified by animals that respond to differences in color, shape, distance, without any consciousness of objects as such. However, I know so little about animals that I cannot offer a well studied example.

In higher degrees of *level 2* some of the presented states of affairs (propositions) receive some structural analysis. The subject-predicate structure enters the scene. This consciousness is *I*-less and not focal.

A very interesting case of *level-2* consciousness is so-called BLINDSIGHT. Some persons who have lost part of their cerebral cortex connected to vision illustrate what to many specialists seems to be a paradoxical situation. While declaring that they do not see, such persons are nonetheless able to respond correctly to questions that seem to require clear visual perception. A certain patient named D. B. in the literature is particularly interesting. He had part of his brain removed but had lost only his left visual field. In the experiments items were placed in his visual field. He insisted that he* (himself) did not see anything in his left field. He engaged in "guessing," as he called it. He had a perfect score in thirty "guesses." D. B. sometimes reported having a "feeling" that certain figures he said he* did not see had certain properties, which they in fact had.[22] Similar studies have been carried out with monkeys. Apparently monkeys and men with blindsight can improve the strength of those "feelings" and also their powers of discrimination of "unseen" objects.

Some philosophers prefer to interpret the cases of blindsight as cases of no perception at all. To them they are evidence that consciousness is a well-entrenched fiction, which science will eventually vanish.[23] Others see blindsight as cases of vision, that is, visual consciousness without *self*-consciousness.[24] This is the view I have adopted.

As I see it, in blindsight the integration of the visual contents is, first, incomplete. Then only the fully integrated part of those contents acquires an owning *I*. The contents of blindsight remain at *level 2*. Now, the patient learns to link the I-less contents of his left field to those of his I-owned contents of his right field. This produces a partial lopsided integration of his *level-2* contents. There is now an *I* that owns the new structured experience. This, however, remains mixed because of the partial integration. The contents in D. B.'s left field become accessible to him as if they were seen, but they continue being as if they were not seen *by him*.

Consciousness is subsumptive. Hence, *level 2* is present in the higher levels. Most of what we see surrounds the part of the visual field where we focus, and we see it within consciousness of *level 2*. Sometimes we store such contents in memory in the form of mechanisms for producing visual images. These mechanisms can be turned on by using the memory of the focal contents of the original field, so to say, as handles, or push-buttons. Then the produced image can be inspected by changing the focus. This way one can *ex post facto* promote contents of consciousness from *level 2* to *level 3*. This posthumous promotion is feasible because of the integration of the contents of these two levels within a consciousness of *level 4*. This provides the stage. The promotion itself, executed by a voluntary action, occurs within consciousness of *level 5*.

An external reflexivity with a crude internal pointing operates in consciousness of *level 2*. At this level what appears in a perceptual field is determined in part by the perceptual powers of the perceiver. The contents of the field reflect to HIM what he is, but of course he does not find himself* reflected in them. By hypothesis there is no *I* that could find anything.

Consciousness of *level 3* is a modification of consciousness of *level 2*. A central nucleus appears. It brings perspectival organization into the contents of the perceptual field. This perspective is a mixed, albeit blind, external-internal reflexivity. The perspective quietly reflects an orientation of the perceptual contents with respect to the perceiver. This orientation is certainly physical, especially in the case of visual perception. It is also psychological because the nucleus of the perceptual field exists thanks to the perceiver's attention. What is attended to reflects the attender's attention. Yet in the absence of *self*-consciousness the perspective is not apprehended as such.

Perceptual experience is primarily a phenomenon at *level 3*. One faces not merely a uniform perceptual field, but a focal and perspectival one. The perceptual judgments in which a perceptual experience culminates are judgments about the focal contents. These are demonstrative judgments about *this*'s or *that*'s, or *here*'s or *there*'s in the perceptual field in the *now* of the perceiving. Palpably, all of these items have an implicit reference to a potential, or actual, perceiving I.[25] The reference is implicit. As noted, it evinces a blind mixed external-internal reflexivity.

At *level 4* an explicit reflexivity enters the stage. As this level has been described, the *I* here is just a blend of the reflexive sides of the contrasts *I-this/that* and *I*-it [external object of the world]. This *I* is a crude solipsistic one, which rounds up all the present experiences and unifies them as an *I* exhausted by them. This *I* collects and formalizes the internal/external axis.[26]

As characterized here, *level 5* is a solipsistic consciousness. On the chart offered, it is the last solipsistic level. As remarked above, the chart is merely a distillation of consciousness of *I*-strands; it says nothing about the causal independence, or dependence, or the chronological order, of the strands. For all we know at this moment, perhaps solipsistic episodes of consciousness occur as the extreme cases within a non-solipsistic experience, or life. Be this as it may, the execution of an act of will presupposes a consciousness in which an intended content of the form *I to do A [here] now* is brought into the causal process. This consciousness must not at the time of execution be concerned with other persons or objects. Its topic and concern are its effective causation. To be sure, other persons may still be involved in action A, as accusatives, beneficiaries, or circumstantial factors. However, action A need not involve any relation to any other: A may be a purely personal action for the exclusive benefit of the agent with no involvement of others. Hence, the consciousness of will, the acme of *level 5*, must always be not non-solipsistic. The *I* of deliberation is broader. The reasons for doing action A may involve all kinds of relationships to all sorts of persons. In principle, however, the deliberating *I* may believe that there exist no other *I*'s or persons. This belief may, of course, be a symptom of mental illness.

Level 5 necessitates a special internal reflexivity. In deliberation the agent seeks to ascertain the range of his/her causal powers. Nonetheless, the search is not an intellectual aiming at a description of those powers. The search is a practical aiming at locating them, however blindly, in order to activate them. Hence, the agent's causal powers need be present in a *level 1* of consciousness.[27] Everything else is supernumerary.

At *level 6* the internality of *self*-reference becomes enhanced. Here a non-solipsistic *I*-strand appears. Yet the *I*'s with this *I*-strand as their social limit are isolated. They observe each other, but do not converse with one another. They can just contemplate their sharing of mental properties.

At *level 7* the internality of the reflexivity of *self*-reference grows by big strides. The full panoply of negativities determine the one instance that is apprehended in its total individuality. To reach this level of consciousness a person must have resources for basking in personal relationships, for enjoying cooperative plans, for experiencing personal conflicts.

Living requires that one raises to higher levels of consciousness when one encounters problems, and has to deliberate and then adopt plans of action. However, when one is engaged in carrying out those plans, one better not squander one's *self*-consciousness. Yet one need be attentive to the drift of events and be ready to make new decisions when obstacles turn up. Hence, the central level of consciousness for human living is *suffused level 3*, that is, suffused with the higher *I*-strands as potentialities for appropriate response.

3.3 Upwards Integration of Self-Consciousness on Converging I's

Given the subsumptive nature of consciousness, the lower levels of consciousness can exist independently of the higher levels. *A fortiori*:

(C.—SC)   NOT all consciousness is *self*-consciousness.

This thesis is the exact contradictory of one of the fundamental presuppositions of Fichte's idealism. The naturalization of consciousness requires not only the anti-Fichtean thesis (C.—SC), but also our whole subsumptive thesis. The ontological dependence of higher forms of consciousness together with their greater epistemic scope is accounted for better, under the thesis of their incorporating the lower forms on which they are grounded and which they illuminate.

From (C.—SC) it follows that:

(UC.—S)   The unity of an episode of consciousness is not explicable by virtue of that consciousness belonging to a self, or *I*.

The unity of content of an episode of consciousness has to be understood in its own terms. In fact, the unity of each content of consciousness is presupposed by the unity of experience under an *I*. That is:

(UC.+S)   If an episode of consciousness is internally owned by an *I*, then the unity of that consciousness is an element in the constitution of that ownership, hence, it is an internal presupposition of the existence of the *I*.

Yet the Fichtean assumption is still widespread, even in contemporary philosophers decidedly anti-Cartesian.[28]

To elucidate the integration of self-consciousness from below let us consider a slightly revised version of an example discussed in "Egos, Persons, and *I*'s":

Friedrich's Bee Watching. At a park Friedrich is fully absorbed watching the birds and the bees carrying on their usual affairs. He is then having an *I*-less experience, of the sort of thing Sartre made a big fuss as irreflexive consciousness. He even feels some pressure on his bent knees, and without jumping to an I-owned experience he simply stands up and then sits on the grass. Then he becomes aware of himself. A thought that the experience was pleasant made him think that he himSELF was enjoying it. He continues watching some bees descend on some flowers, pick up some pollen, and then fly away— in full awareness of himself. Then his whole experience is present to him under a diachronic *I*-unity. This unity is in fact a diachronically fusive succession of overlapping *I*'s existing alongside a succession of overlapping specious presents. Friedrich is enjoying several sub-experiences. He is attending to one big yellow jacket. He sees it move from a red flower to a yellow one. This seeing occupies a specious present: "From here to here." There is thus the subject of that seeing. During that interval he hears several drones from different bees. Each hearing has its own subject, an *I* that lasts less than the seeing *I*. Similarly, during the same interval he throws off several ants crawling up his legs. Each one of these seeing and throwing episodes has its own subject, again very short-lived. Also about the middle of Friedrich's seeing his favorite yellow jacket he feels an itching on his head; he scratches. An itching *I*, a scratching *I*, and an itching-and-scratching *I* come into existence and quickly vanish.

The itching-and-scratching *I* overlaps the other two *I*'s. During the first moment of just itching the itching *I* coincides with the itching-and-scratching *I*. Then this *I* is the subject of the integrated experiences of itching and scratching. Likewise, Friedrich's whole experience of seeing the yellow jacket fly from one flower to another pivots on one *I*. This ensues from the integration of the different sub-experiences into one comprehensive reflexive consciousness. That *I* is a unit built up from the subjects of the sub-experiences. The specious present determined by a succession of overlapping of co-consciousness determines in the normal human cases the short-lived *I* of the interval.

Because of the suffusiveness of consciousness, there is in Friedrich's normal case a total *I* of the totally integrated experience. Here the law of fusion that governs the phenomena is this:

(SC.I*) A real *I* of an episode of self-consciousness at a given time T is the reflexive subject of the maximal co-conscious integration of experiences at T.

REMARK 1. So far nothing precludes that there be one *I* unifying experiences across different persons or bodies. There must be, however, a suitable underlying "physiology" connecting the bodies.

REMARK 2. The sub-experiences of a person at a given time may fail to unify into one subject of experience. In principle, for instance, Friedrich may have been mentally disorganized. Some of the experiences mentioned above may have failed to integrate at all, or may have integrated only partially. These are empirically matters that may appear in many different degrees. Psychiatric practice may have already established many types and families of such failures of *I*-integration.

3.4 Major Integrating Internal Relations

The integrated contents of an experience of self-consciousness involves, internally as framing the experience, a good number of primitive relations. These relations are structural emergents upon the physical-physiological mechanisms upon which consciousness accrues. At the second level a primitive relation of CO-CONSCIOUSNESS links the contents of a simple experience (or sub-experience) as the contents of *one* (sub-)experience. Each experience (or sub-experience) has its own *now-here*[*there*] spatio-temporal framework. More or less simultaneous experiences normally combine into more comprehensive experiences. This requires an intimate organization of the different synchronous experiential spaces and times. Let's call CO-INTEGRATION the network of structural relations through which a unified total experience is built. Thus, the unity of a person's normal, fully organized total experience at a given time T is wrought out by a system of low-level instantiations of CO-CONSCIOUSNESS, and by a thorough system of instances of CO-INTEGRATION. Let's call META-INTEGRATION the relations that structure unowned reflexive experiences. Let's call SUBJECTIONS those structural relations that subordinate an experience to a subject, that is, relations through which an *I* is posited, or hypostatized.

In the normal case every mechanism runs perfectly and all run in marvelous unison. In the normal case of self-consciousness all the contents of the experience are unified into sub-experiences, and these into a fully unified experience, each sub-experience is experienced as a strand of consciousness that forms part of a unified experience and is owned by an *I*. In such cases the *I* referred to is the maximally integrated and unified *I*—the *I* subsuming all the *I*'s of the unified sub-experiences. Likewise, the *now* of the total experience is the hierarchical cumulation of the *now*'s of the sub-experiences.

In an abnormal case a single mechanism by itself or a combination of such mechanisms fails to work properly. Abnormal cases are data about the distinctness of strands in reality that normally go together. The closer the togetherness in question, the more informative is the abnormality that breaks it. For instance, a person whose mechanisms eliciting the CO-CONSCIOUSNESS, CO-INTEGRATION, and META-INTEGRATION relations work well may yet suffer from disruption of a SUBJECTION mechanism. He may experience a sub-experience as if it were not his.

In the case of blindsight, the "unseen" contents are present and even connected by the appropriate CO-CONSCIOUSNESS relations. These include the relations of VISUAL CO-CONSCIOUSNESS, which prepare the visual manifold for CO-INTEGRATION as a unitary visual field. The visual data of the person suffering from blind sight has a visual field containing the blind data. These are, thus CO-INTEGRATED with the remaining data he sees. The visual field fails, however, to be META-INTEGRATED as an undividedly presented field. This crucial gap in META-INTEGRATION precludes the whole visual field to be structured under SUBJECTION to one masterful *I*. Nevertheless, the whole field is there under the surface of consciousness. The patient learns to posit an abstract SUBJECTION of the not-META-INTEGRATED data. Because of the deficiency in META-INTEGRATION the posited extended SUBJECTION must remain hypothetical: the postulated extended *I* is not a visual *I*, although by (SC.I*) it comprehends suffusively a concurrent visual *I*.

The preceding list is of types of internally integrating relations. Their respective species must be charted in order to achieve a useful profile of consciousness. Such a profile could be of help to psychiatry. Conversely, psychopathology, by furnishing detailed descriptions of cases in which some integration relation is missing, must contribute the criteria for differentiating such relations from one another.

3.5 Naturalization of Self-Consciousness

The internal hierarchy of an episode of consciousness sits on top of an underlying hierarchy of physical-physiological mechanisms. Mere sensory consciousness is underwritten by, accrues on, complicated networks of physiological mechanisms. At bottom these are simple stimulus-response patterns. They combine into simple thermostatic-like feedback subsystems. These in their turn bundle up in systems containing fine tuning in the adjustment of response to stimulus. In complex cases such fine-tuned adjustment amounts to a physical, blind *monitoring*. This monitoring involves something like representations of degrees of stimuli which cause the corresponding degree of response. This brute reflexivity of such systems underlies the internal reflexivity of episodes of self-consciousness supervening on them.

Clearly, the physical-physiological monitoring of stimulus-response patterns may provide the basis for the emergence of presentations of stimuli, without the emergence of a presentational representation of the monitoring itself. Then there would be consciousness without self-consciousness. Of course, each monitorial subsystem may be enlarged into a system that *records* the monitorial activity. This "recording" is meta-monitorial activity. Then there would be a representation of the subsystem. Something like this recording underlies the self-consciousness; of course, such a physical-physiological recording is not identical with self-consciousness, nor is it by itself sufficient to yield self-consciousness.

Patently, a network of monitorial subsystems *cum* self-recording meta-compartments can all operate in unison. Unison operations of that sort provide the physical basis of an *I*-owned experience. Here we can see the basis for each local *I*—as in Friedrich's many *I*'s, e.g., his itching, his scratching, and his itching-scratching *I*'s. Evidently, some of those physical-physiological mechanisms may be out of tune, delivering then no *I* at all or a separate, non-integrated *I*. Such are the physical bases of the different types of *I*-disturbances. In any case, survival value accrues to the following psycho-physical connection:

(Ps-Ph.I*) In a well functioning system S endowed with mentality, S's *I* at time T is the fusion of the different *I*'s that emerge from the meta-activities of the distinct monitorial mechanisms underwriting episodes of consciousness at T.

Obviously we must investigate very carefully the bodily structures needed for the realization of the diverse *I*-strands. However, the preceding little glimpse into the appropriate structural properties of a body endowed with self-consciousness is all we can do here.

4. Summary

This partial study of the nature of self-consciousness focuses on the twofold hierarchical reflexivity of self-consciousness. It can be reasonably described as follows:

(R-SC) In episodes of *self*-consciousness ONE is conscious of ONEself *qua oneSELF*.

Fundamental is the *external* reflexivity of ONE referring to ONEself. As such it has nothing to do with consciousness. It is the reflexivity of a reflexive relation: Rxx, whether R is an action or not. One is, for example, as tall as ONEself; a sleepwalker may wound HIMself accidentally and fully unawares by stepping on a shaving blade. Acts of referring are of course the cores of episodes of consciousness. As such they have an internal referent. Nevertheless, self-reference, the backbone of self-consciousness, is built up on the external reference of a thinker's referring to HIMself. Patently, a thinker may think, believingly, that the such-and-such is this or that, without having any idea that he is in fact the such-and-such in question. In this case: *the such-and-such refers to the such-and-such as the such-and-such*—yet there is no self-reference. What is missing is the *internal* reflexivity of ONE referring to something, whatever it may be, as *oneSELF*. This internal reflexivity is the peculiar core of *self*-consciousness. That self-consciousness rests so firmly on its external reflexivity is brought home by one linguistic fact. The expression 'x refers to x as himself' is redundant. It is part of the logic, or semantics, of the expression 'x refers to y as herself' that this entails that y is the same as x.

We can, then, concentrate on the internal reflexivity of *self*-consciousness without loss. This internal reflexivity, constitutive of the moment *qua* one-

SELF, is expressed in natural language by means of singular-referring uses of the first-person pronoun. It is the reflexivity of the appearing of the thinker to HIMself as himSELF, that is, as an *I*. Self-consciousness is *I*-consciousness not because we identify *I*-consciousness with the use of the pronoun 'I', but because the uses of 'I'-sentences reveal the speaker's thinking *I*-contents, and, consequently, his having a brain *I*-representation. A thinking episode is not an event of uttering. It is embodied in—indeed, in some *appropriate* sense of 'sameness', a thinking episode is the same as—an event or process in the thinker's brain, or thinking box, whatever this may be.

The preceding reflection suggests that *I*'s may exist only as internal referents in episodes of self-consciousness. This suggestion is strongly supported by further data. These additional data include an ontologico-epistemological analysis of the so-called *de dicto/de re* contrast in attributions of psychological states to others. In the formula (R-SC), as well as in the general schema 'x refers to y as z', the component 'to y' is *de re*, whereas the component 'as z' is *de dicto*. Internal, *de dicto* expressions are depictions of representations the speaker exhibits as SHARED by him and the person he speaks of. *De re* expressions just vent the speaker's references. *De dicto* indirect speech has a Chinese-box structure, each box revealing the presented representations constituting thinking content—regardless of the physical existence of what is thought of.

A psychological statement that has as its core an attribution of the form 'X refers to Y as Z' discloses to the hearer that the speaker is presented with thinker X as thinker X, with item Y as Y, with item Z as Z. It reveals that the speaker takes Z to be an *intersubjective* thinkable. The *de dicto* occurrence of Z in 'X refers to Y as Z' is thus cumulative and shared. It manifests an accessible *intersubjective subjectivity* of Z. However, intersubjectivity is not always objectivity. By equating Z with Y the speaker reveals, besides, that Z has at least a vicarious objective status in her world. This status need not be existence. Even if X in fact refers to the speaker's Y as Z, Y may be only an intersubjective thought of item. In short, the externality of the moment *to Y as Z* consists of the speaker's positing the *perhaps vicarious objective intersubjectivity* of Z through Y. The genuine objectivity of Z consists of Z being as such, as Z, an autonomous part of the shared world. Now, when X refers to HIMself [that is, to X] as himSELF, he is presented with what he calls "I"—but this cannot be present in anybody else's experience. Hence, the vicarious objective intersubjectivity of the *I*'s captured by the quasi-indexical mechanism 'he himSELF' or 'oneSELF' does not evolve into their genuine objectivity. The *I*'s are not as such parts of the world; they are only vicariously in the world by means of the persons they are the same as, when such persons enjoy episodes of self-consciousness.

If *I*'s exist only within episodes of self-consciousness, then different episodes have different *I*'s. Since, as noted above, consciousness does not presuppose, or require, self-consciousness, the contents of self-consciousness must be built up from the contents of self-less consciousness. These contents must be, hence, integrated prior to the appearance of a subordinating self. Further, the self-less contents and their unity impose constraints on the type of *I*-unity they can be subordinated to. Thus, we must distinguish different *I*-strands that characterize the different types of integration of the contents of episodes of self-consciousness. We engage in a very preliminary investigation of the most important *I*-strands, and their combinations into *I*-schemata.

The basic *I*-less contents of consciousness are themselves hierarchical. They are built of the integrated contents of many different sub-experiences. Each of these is the content of a potential *I* under which it can be subordinated. The *I* of a comprehensive reflexive consciousness is a unit built up from the subjects of the sub-experiences. The specious present determined by a succession of overlapping of co-consciousness determines in the normal human cases the short-lived *I* of the interval. He may, as in the case of *blindsight*, fail to experience a sub-experience as his own altogether.†

The ruptures of the internal, *de dicto* structurings is what the psychiatrist investigates directly through the study of the logical connections between the patient's speeches, and between practical speech and behavior.‡

Patently, a network of monitorial subsystems *cum* self-recording meta-compartments can all operate at unison. Unison operations of that sort provide the physical basis of an *I*-owned experience. Evidently, some of those physical-physiological mechanisms may be out of tune, delivering no *I* at all or separate, non-integrated *I*s. Such are, schematically, the physical bases of the different types of *I*-disturbances.

[5. Taking Stock

In Parts 2–3 we have gone through a preliminary phenomeno-logical reflection on the reflexivity and self-reference of *self*-consciousness. This was in partial keeping with the promises made in Part I. We have to say more about the doxastic pedestal of episodes of thinking. We need to explain in detail how indexicality is the categorial structure of subjectivity. This includes the thesis that the *I*'s are evanescent subjective particulars existing only within and during episodes of *self*-consciousness. (See Note 8.)

We have seen over and over again how the contents of thought involve a contingent sameness, which must be thoroughly distinguished from strict identity. We have also seen that the worldliness/nonworldliness of the *I*'s and the other indexical particulars pivots on a contrast between sameness and strict identity. Hence, the results of our phenomeno-logical investigation need

† In Castañeda 1990a, 142–143, the opening three paragraphs of Section 3.4 above are repeated at this point. We have deleted them here. —Eds.
‡ The next two paragraphs of the paper, on page 143 of Castañeda 1990a, repeat the opening two paragraphs of section 3.5. We have deleted them here. —Eds.

to be grounded on a theory of sameness. This theory must include an account of the contents of episodes thinking as contrasted with doxastic attitudes. One theory that can do the job is Guise Theory. This is a comprehensive ontological account of the semantics of thinking. (See Note 1.)

The analysis of the *I*-schemata so far developed is only a preliminary one. It needs to be enriched drastically before it can provide some guidance in the systematic study of *I*-disturbances.

Well, there is so much more to be done!]†

Notes

1. For a theory of the sameness family of relations see Hector-Neri Castañeda 1974, 1975b, both in Castañeda 1982a, and the former in both Castañeda 1989a and Jacobi and Pape 1990. On my view the identity between mental and physical states is the sameness called in those papers *consubstantiation*. On the other hand, the basic sameness between veridical thought content and what makes it veridical hinges on a sameness called *consociation*. Consubstantiation is also the sameness between the morning star and the evening star. Thus I seem to be endorsing a version of the Contingent-Identity Theory. See, for example, Place 1956, Smart 1959, and Lewis 1966. My version of the contingent identity of mental events and processes to physical ones is not reductionist. See Note 2 below. Furthermore, the theory is mounted on a general theory of contingent identity or sameness.

2. Many different types of mental fact constitute serious hurdles and tasks for reductionist programs. Here I mention just one fact seldom noticed. To me it has for the last thirty years seemed to be, not a mere hurdle, but a stumbling block for the reduction of episodes of consciousness to physical events. That fact is normal veridical, partially illusory visual experience. Not to generalize unduly, let me put the fact concretely. I am looking at the sky and see a triangle having as vertices the moon, the North Star, and the chimney on my house. This is a veridical perception of the objects in question. The triangle is not a physical, but an illusory, one. Because of the time needed for light to travel, the position of the moon I see is one it occupied minutes before, whereas the position of the North Star is years older. My visual experience is precisely the visual presentation of what I see, that is, the mere existence of my visual field. My visual experience consists of the visual field containing the triangle just described. It does not occur in my brain (or whatever my thinking box may be). Of course, events in my brain have caused the existence of the presented visual field. My experience, however, occurs before my eyes, spread about in the piece of physical space containing the objects I see. My visual experience is *not* reductionally equivalent, let alone identical, to events in my brain (or thinking gadget). Because my veridical visual experience is partly illusory, the contents of my visual consciousness are not identical with the sub-domain of physical entities I see. (I say "entities" to include not so much physical objects in their fullness, but only their seen parts or surfaces.) My veridical visual displays occupy visual spaces which at least overlap with physical space. But even if such overlappings exhausted my visual spaces, there would be in visual space

† This section appears as the final section of Castañeda 1989b, 55. —Eds.

non-physical content. The physics and physiology of vision may causally explain why my visual spaces have certain non-physical, illusory contents. Nonetheless, causal explanation is not reduction. To cause is to bring into existence. (This is a basic truth often forgotten in defenses of reductionist causal claims.) Clearly, episodes of thinking, as well as dispositional states of believing, are individuated by their contents. In brief, my episodes of veridical visual consciousness are not reducible to complexes of physical events, including those within and those without my body. Patently, no theory of the world or of the mind, or of consciousness, can be satisfactory if it leaves my visual experience out of account. There is, however, a reductionism I have adopted: the economical view that reduces visual consciousness to the occurrence of visual content. For more data for and details of these theses see Castañeda 1977a.

3. We have here no difficulties with Wittgenstein's arguments against private languages. See Wittgenstein 1952. We accept that our mature thinker has learned her language exactly as Wittgensteinians say: by having been engaged in social practices. We may also grant Wittgenstein's tenets that to follow a rule presupposes a community of rule-followers, and that internal psychological states must have external criteria.

4. Processes in the brain (or whatever) are the embodiments of thinking. Such processes must be sequences of events that embody representations of what is thought in a train of thinking episodes. The linguistic expressions of such thoughts have a characteristic grammatical form. Yet the embodying brain events need not be in a one-one correspondence with the spoken sentences or their components. What matters is that there be brain mechanisms that unfold those grammatical structures at the proper source of speech on the basis of the thinking-embodying events. Furthermore, the brain has to store mechanisms of representation, that is, mechanisms that have as outputs those thinking-embodying brain events. Likewise, the brain states or particulars that store such mechanisms need not involve the storing of items with the syntactic structure of the output sentences. In brief, whatever layers the hierarchy of brain mechanisms may have, at none of them is there a domain of brain items that is isomorphic to the sentences of the person's spoken language. The *syntacticism-connectionism* dispute is indifferent to our concerns here. These focus on the internal contents of the representations characteristic of, and peculiar to, self-consciousness.

5. Some distinguished philosophers hold this. See, for example, Pollock 1988, Chisholm 1981, and Shoemaker 1968.

6. Plato's life examination is not merely a quest for determining what one ought everything considered to do. He assumes that this *ought* is also a moral *ought*. He grounds his assumption on the view that human nature is such that immoral action is a manifestation of a sort of mental illness. The *Republic* is a sustained, ambitious, and brilliant, yet bound to fail, effort at executing that grounding project.

7. The idea that what one thinks exists and what does not exist cannot have *any* properties at all is at least traceable to Parmenides's poem. Against him, Plato argued in the *Sophist* that non-existents are thinkable and can have some properties. Since then this issue has divided philosophers into antagonic camps. For instance, William of Sherwood seemed to have adopted a Parmenidean position, very much like Bertrand Russell's. (See Jacobi 1980, 318ff.) In this century Alexius Meinong and Bertrand Russell argued about the Parmenidean issue. Their focus was Meinong's existing round square. (For references and appraisal of this debate see Castañeda 1985/1986, reprinted in Jacobi and Pape 1990. It contains references to recent discussions of non-existing objects and of fiction.)

8. For an extensive study of indexical and quasi-indexical reference see Castañeda 1989a, chapters 1, 4, and 12, or Castañeda 1982a, chapters II.2, II.5, and II.6.

9. On the difference and connections between indexical and corresponding quasi-indexical propositions see "Knowledge and Self: A Correspondence between Robert M. Adams and Hector-Neri Castañeda," in Tomberlin 1983, and reprinted in Castañeda 1989a.

10. For more on the thinker's use of the first-person pronoun see Castañeda 1983b.

11. Wilfrid Sellars's class lectures, 1950.

12. Descartes 1641, 167.

13. Castañeda 1975a, chapter 6; Castañeda 1989a, chapter 7; and Perry 1979.

14. In Castañeda 1989b.

15. See Note 1. Guise Theory is essentially a theory of individuation and predication that distinguishes a rich family of sameness relations and conceives them as forms of predication. For discussion and developments of Guise Theory see the exchanges with Romane Clark and Alvin Plantinga in Tomberlin 1983, the exchanges with Jay Rosenberg, David W. Smith, Esa Saarinen, and Jeffrey Sicha in Tomberlin 1986, and the exchanges with Frank Düring, Heinz-Dieter Heckmann, Klaus Jacobi, Tomis Kapitan, Guido Küng, Wolfgang Künne, Anton Koch, Paolo Leonardi, Harald Pilot, Gerold Prauss, Friedrich Rapp, Richard Schantz, in Jacobi and Pape 1990.

16. See, for example, Chisholm 1976.

17. For a study of the family of the different types of negation and its contrasts with the family of colors properties, see Castañeda 1988b.

18. See de Saussure 1915, e.g. his view of plural as the whole network of contrasts, for instance, 'girl'/'girls', 'potato'/'potatoes', 'ox'/'oxen', etc.

19. Buber 1923.

20. See, for example, Wittgenstein 1952; Putnam 1975b, 1987; and Burge 1979. I am not convinced. I explain why in Castañeda 1989d.

21. In Castañeda 1977a.

22. Weiskrantz et al. 1974, Weiskrantz 1977, 1980.

23. Churchland 1980.

24. John Pollock, in paper cited in Note 5.

25. Chisholm attempts in *The First Person* (Chisholm 1981) to define 'this' and all other indicators in terms of 'I'. I argue for crucial differences between 'this' and 'I' in Castañeda 1987c.

26. Castañeda 1967d.

27. For a discussion of this see Castañeda 1975a, chapter 10.

28. See, for instance, Fichte 1794. On page 41 we read: "Without self-consciousness there is no consciousness whatever." For contemporary echoes of this, see, for example, Pollock 1988, Chisholm 1981, Shoemaker 1968. Kant seemed to have allowed for some forms of egoless consciousness in his famous slogan: "The *I think* must be able to accompany all of my representations." Yet in his transcendental deduction of the categories in his *Critique of Pure Reason* he adopts a Fichtean position. The result is that his conclusion is weaker than it should have been, namely: the categories apply to objects thought of in experience subordinate to self-consciousness. He needs a stronger conclusion: consciousness of objects, whether subsumed under self-consciousness or not, involves the application of the categories. He did not know about blindsight—discussed above—; nevertheless his remark that if the *I think* does not accompany my representations these would be

"nothing to me" is applicable to blindsight. Note, firstly, that for this he must move up from "is able to accompany my representations" to "accompanies my representation." Note, secondly, that my representations, whether they mean anything to me or not, must nevertheless involve the application of the categories—as in the case of blindsight. Hence, rather than, as Kant claims, the application of the categories and the unity of consciousness hinging on a transcendental apperception, it is the apperception that pivots on the lower levels of consciousness, which already involve the application of the categories.

References

The items listed in this bibliography include (i) each of the articles by Hector-Neri Castañeda published in this volume; (ii) each of the references made by Castañeda within these articles; and (iii) references made by the editors in their introductions.

Adams, Robert M. 1983. "Knowledge and Self: A Correspondence between Robert M. Adams and Hector-Neri Castañeda." In Tomberlin 1983, 293–309.

Almog, Joseph, et al., eds. 1989. *Themes from Kaplan*. Oxford: Oxford University Press.

Ameriks, Karl, and Dieter Sturma, eds. 1995. *The Modern Subject: Conceptions of the Self in Classical German Philosophy*. Albany: State University of New York Press.

Austin, David, ed. 1988. *Philosophical Analysis: A Defense by Example*. Dordrecht: Reidel.

Austin, John L. 1956. "Ifs and Cans." *Proceedings of the British Academy,* 42: 109–132.

———. 1962. *Sense and Sensibilia*. Clarendon: Oxford University Press.

Baker, Lynne Rudder. 1979. "Indexical Reference and 'De Re' Belief." *Philosophical Studies* 36: 31–32.

———. 1981a. "On Making and Attributing Demonstrative Reference." *Synthese* 49: 245–273.

———. 1981b. "Why Computers Can't Act." *American Philosophical Quarterly* 18, 2: 157–164.

Beck, Lewis White. 1988. "Two Ways of Reading Kant's Letter to Herz: Comments on Carl." In Förster 1989.

Belnap, Nuel D. 1960. Review of J. Hintikka, "Towards a Theory of Definite Descriptions." *Journal of Symbolic Logic* 25: 88–89.

Bergmann, Gustav. 1964. *Logic and Reality*. Madison: The University of Wisconsin Press.

Bezuidenhout, A. 1996. "Pragmatics and Singular Reference." *Mind & Language* 11: 133–159.

Blackburn, Simon. 1975. "The Identity of Propositions." In Simon Blackburn, ed., *Meaning, Reference, and Necessity*. Cambridge: Cambridge University Press.

Boër, Stephen E., and William G. Lycan. 1975. "Knowing Who." *Philosophical Studies* 28: 299–344.

——. 1980. "Who, Me?" *The Philosophical Review* 89: 427–466.

——. 1986a. *Knowing Who*. Cambridge: MIT Press.

——. 1986b. "Castañeda's Theory of Knowing." In Tomberlin 1986, 215–236.

Brand, Myles. 1983. "Intending and Believing." In Tomberlin 1983.

——. 1984. *Intending and Acting*. Cambridge: MIT Press.

Breazeale, Daniel. 1995. "Check or Checkmate? On the Finitude of the Fichtean Self." In Ameriks and Sturma 1995.

Buber, Martin. 1923. *I and Thou*. Trans. Walter Kaufman. New York: Charles Scribner's Sons, 1970.

Burge, Tyler. 1977. "Belief *de Re*." *The Journal of Philosophy* 74: 338–362.

——. 1979. "Individualism and the Mental." *Midwest Studies in Philosophy: Metaphysics* 12: 73–121.

Burkhardt, H., and C. Dufour. 1989. "Zwei Prädikationsarten und ihre ontologischen Implikationen." In Jacobi and Pape 1990.

Carl, Wolfgang. 1989. "Kant's First Drafts of the Deduction." In Förster 1989.

Carnap, Rudolf. 1947. *Meaning and Necessity*. Chicago: University of Chicago Press.

Cartwright, Richard. 1962. "Propositions." In R. J. Butler, ed., *Analytic Philosophy*. Oxford: Blackwell.

——. 1968. "Propositions Again." *Nous* 2: 199–246.

Castañeda, Hector-Neri. 1960a. *La Dialèctica de la Conseiencia de Si Mismo*. Guatemala: University of San Carlos Press.

——. 1960b. "Lenguaje, Pensamiento, y Realidad." *Humanitas* (University of Nuevo Leon Yearbook, Monterrey, Mexico) 3: 199–217.

——. 1963a. "The Private Language Argument." In Rollins 1963. Reprinted in E. D. Klemke, ed., *Essays on Wittgenstein*. Chicago and London: University of Chicago, 1971; also in O. R. Jones, ed., *The Private Language Argument*. London: Macmillan Ltd. St. Martin Press, 1971.

——. 1963b. "Rejoinders" to Mr. Chappell and Mr. Thomson. In C. D. Rollins 1963, 125–132.

——. 1964a. "A Note on S5." *The Journal of Symbolic Logic* 29: 191–192.

——. 1964b. Review of J. Hintikka, *Knowledge and Belief*. In *Journal of Symbolic Logic* 3: 132–134.

——. 1966. " 'He:' " On the Logic of Self-Consciousness." *Ratio* 8: 130–157.

——. 1967a. "Indicators and Quasi-Indicators." *American Philosophical Quarterly* 4: 85–100.

——. 1967b. "Omniscience and Indexical Reference." *Journal of Philosophy* 64: 203–209.

——. 1967c. "On the Logic of Self-Knowledge." *Nous* 1: 9–22.

——. 1967d. "Consciousness and Behavior: Their Basic Connections." In H.-N. Castañeda, ed., *Intentionality, Minds, and Perception*. Detroit: Wayne State University Press. 1967.

——. 1967e. "The Private Language Problem." In Paul Edwards, ed., *Encyclopedia of Philosophy*. Glencoe, Ill.: Free Press.

——. 1968a. "On the Logic of Self-Attribution of Self-Knowledge to Others." *Journal of Philosophy* 65: 439–456.

——. 1968b. "On the Phenomeno-logic of the I." *Proceedings of the XIVth International Congress of Philosophy* 3: 260–266.

——. 1970. "On Knowing (or Believing) That One Knows (or Believes)." *Synthese* 21: 187–203.

——. 1974. "Thinking and the Structure of the World." *Philosophia* 4: 4–40.

——. 1975a. *Thinking and Doing*. Dordrecht: Reidel.

——. 1975b. "Identity and Sameness." *Philosophia* 5: 121–150.

——. 1975c. "Individuation and Non-identity: A New Look." *American Philosophical Quarterly* 12 (1975): 131–140.

——. 1976. "Rejoinder to Professor Michael Loux." 109–116. *Critica* 5: 105–108.

——. 1977a. "Perception, Belief, and the Structure of Physical Objects and Consciousness." *Synthese* 35: 285–351.

——. 1977b. "On the Philosophical Foundations of the Theory of Communication: I. Reference." In *Midwest Studies in Philosophy 2*: 165–186.

——. 1978a. "Philosophical Method and the Theory of Predication and Identity." *Nous* 12: 189–210.

——. 1978b. "Leibniz's Meditation on April 15, 1676 about Existence, Dreams, and Space." In G. W. Leibniz-Gesellschaft (Hanover) and Centre National de la Recherche Scientifique (Paris) *La Philosophie de Leibniz*, Vol. II of *Leibniz à Paris (1672–1676)*. Wiesbaden: Franz Steiner Verlag, 91–94.

——. 1979a. "Philosophical Method and Direct Awareness of the Self." *Grazer philosophische Studien* 7/8: 1–58.

——. 1979b. "The Causal and the Epistemic Roles of Proper Names in Our Thinking of Particulars." In French, Uehling, and Wettstein 1979.

——. 1980a. *On Philosophical Method*. Bloomington: Nous Publications.

——. 1980b. "Reference, Reality, and Perceptual Fields." Presidential Address. *Proceedings and Addresses of the American Philosophical Association* 50: 763–823.

——. 1981. "The Semiotic Profile of Indexical (Experiential) Reference." *Synthese* 49: 275–316.

——. 1982a. *Sprache und Erfahrung: Texte zu einer neuen Ontologie*, Trans. Helmut Pape. Frankfurt am Main: Suhrkamp.

——. 1982b. "Intentional Actions, Conditional Intentions, and Aristotelian Practical Syllogisms." *Erkenntnis* 18: 239–260.

——. 1983a. "Knowledge and Self: A Correspondence between Robert M. Adams and Hector-Neri Castañeda." In Tomberlin 1983, 293–309.

——. 1983b. "Reply to John Perry: Meaning, Belief, and Reference." In Tomberlin 1983, 313–328.

——. 1983c. "Reply to Alvin Plantinga: Method, Individuals, and Guise Theory." In Tomberlin 1983, 329–354.

——. 1983d. "Reply to Romane Clark: Belief, Sameness, and Cambridge Changes." In Tomberlin 1983, 373–384.

——. 1983e. "Reply to Ernest Sosa: Self-Reference and Propositions." In Tomberlin 1983, 385–392.

——. 1983f. "Reply to Michael Bratman: Deontic Truth, Intentions, and Weakness of Will." In Tomberlin 1983, 395–410.

——. 1983g. "Reply to Myles Brand: Intentions, Properties, and Propositions." In Tomberlin 1983, 411–418.

——. 1983h. "Reply to Carl Ginet: The Private Language Argument." In Tomberlin 1983, 459–462.

——. 1983i. "Reply to Roderick M. Chisholm: Indefeasible Evidence." In Tomberlin 1983, 463–464.

——. 1984a. "The Semiotics of Indicators." In Oehler 1984, 189–210.

——. 1984b. "Self-Consciousness and Indexicals (Rejoinder to Harald Pilot)." In Oehler 1984, 225–231.

——. 1984c. "Philosophical Refutations." In James H. Fetzer, ed. *Principles of Philosophical Reasoning*. New Jersey: Rowman and Allanheld.

——. 1985/1986. "Objects, Existence, and Reference: A Prolegomenon to Guise Theory." *Grazer philosphische Studien* 25/26: 31–66; reprinted in Jacobi and Pape 1990.

——. 1986a. "*De Dicto*. My Philosophical Search" (Part II of Hector-Neri Castañeda, "Self-Profile"). In Tomberlin 1983, 77–140.

——. 1986b. "Replies" to Jay Rosenberg, David Woodruff Smith, Esa Saarinen, Stephen Boër and William Lycan, and Jeffrey Sicha. In Tomberlin 1986.

——. 1987a. "Practical Reasons, Reasons for Doing, and Intentional Action (The Thinking of Doing and the Doing of Thinking)." *Theoria II*, 2 (1986–87): 69–96.

——. 1987b. "The Self and the I-Guises, Empirical and Transcendental." In Konrad Cramer et al. 1987, 105–140.

——. 1987c. "Self-Consciousness, Demonstrative Reference, and the Self-Ascription View of Believing." In Tomberlin, J. E. (ed.), 1987. *Philosophical Perspectives: 1. Metaphysics*. Atascadero, Calif.: Ridgeview, 405–450.

——. 1987d. "Metaphysical Internalism, Selves, and the Indivisible Noumenon (A Frego-Kantian Reflection on Descartes's *Cogito*)." *Midwest Studies in Philosophy* 12: 129–144.

——. 1988a. "Persons, Egos, and I's: Their Sameness Relations." In Manfred Spitzer, Friedrich Uehlein, and Godehard Oepen, eds. 1988. *Psychopathology and Philosophy*. Berlin: Springer, 210–234.

——. 1988b. "Negations, Imperatives, Colors, Indexical Properties, Non-Existence, and Russell's Paradox." In Austin 1988, 169–205.

——. 1989a. *Thinking, Language, and Experience*. Minneapolis: University of Minnesota Press.

——. 1989b. "The Reflexivity of Self-Consciousness: Sameness/Identity, Data for Artificial Intelligence." *Philosophical Topics* 17: 27–58.

——. 1989c. "Direct Reference, Realism, and Guise Theory: Constructive Reflections on David Kaplan's Theory of Reference." In Almog et al. 1989.

——. 1989d. "Semantic Holism without Semantic Socialism: Twin Earths, Thinking, Language, Bodies, and the World." *Midwest Studies in Philosophy: Philosophy of Language* XIV: 101–126.

——. 1990a. "Self-Consciousness, I-Structures and Physiology." In Manfred Spitzer and Brenden A. Maher, eds. *Philosophy and Psychopathology*. Berlin, Heidelberg, New York: Springer Verlag, 118–145.

——. 1990b. "The Role of Apperception in Kant's Transcendental Deduction of the Categories." *Nous* 24: 147–157.

———. 1990c. *Erwiderung* [to Wolfgang Künne]: "Fiction, Perception, and Forms of Predication." In Jacobi and Pape 1990, 268–284.

———. 1990d. *Erwiderung* [to Harold Pilot]: "Indexical Thinking and Indexical Guises." In Jacobi and Pape 1990, 299–307.

———. 1990e. *Erwiderung* [to Gerold Praus]: "Demonstrative Reference, and Kant's Copernican Revolution." In Jacobi and Pape 1990, 312–319.

———. 1990f. *Erwiderung* [to Guido Küng]: "Individual Guises, Spatiality, and Reality." In Jacobi and Pape 1990, 409–415.

———. 1990g. *Erwiderung* [to Heinz-Dieter Heckmann]: "Intentionality, Perception, and Guise Theory." In Jacobi and Pape 1990, 425–437.

———. 1990h. *Erwiderung* [to Tomis Kapitan]: "Individuals, Reference, and Existence." In Jacobi and Pape 1990, 459–472.

———. 1990i. *Erwiderung* [to Friedrich Rapp]: "Ontological Perspectivity and Guise Theory." In Jacobi and Pape 1990, 477–481.

———. 1990j. *Erwiderung*: [to Hans Burkhardt and Carolos Dufour]: "Forms of Predication." In Jacobi and Pape 1990, 491–494.

———. 1990k. *Erwiderung* [to Klaus Jacobi]: "Individuals, Idealism, and the Realism of Thinking." In Jacobi and Pape 1990, 523–546.

———. 1990l. "Objects, Existence, and Reference: A Prolegomenon to Guise Theory." In Jacobi and Pape 1990, 94–141.

———. 1991a. "Die Reflexivität des Selbstbewusstseins: Eine phänomeno-logische Untersuchung." In Kienzle and Pape 1991, 85–136. This is a translation by Christel Fricke of 1989b.

———. 1991b. "Über die Möglichkeit der mit dem Selbstbewusstsein verbundenen Gewissheit." Response to Christel Fricke's Commentary on 1991a. In Kienzle and Pape 1991, 147–151.

Chisholm, Roderick. 1957. *Perceiving*. Ithaca: Cornell University Press.

———. 1976. *Person and Object: A Metaphysical Study*, LaSale, Ill.: Open Court.

———. 1977. *Theory of Knowledge*. 2nd ed. Englewood Cliffs: Prentice Hall.

———. 1979. "Review of *Thinking and Doing*." *Nous* 12: 385–396.

———. 1981. *The First Person*. Minneapolis: University of Minnesota Press.

———. 1986. *Revisions of the First Person* (unpublished).

Churchland, P. S., 1980. "A Perspective on Mind-Brain Research." *Journal of Philosophy* 77: 185–207.

Clark, Romane. 1978. "Not Every Object of Thought Has Being: A Paradox in Naive Predication Theory." *Nous* 12: 181–188.

———. 1983. "Predication Theory: Guised and Disguise." In Tomberlin 1983, 111–130.

Cornman, James. 1975. *Perception, Common Sense, and Science*. New Haven: Yale University Press.

Cramer, Konrad, et al., eds. 1987. *Theorie der Subjektivität: Festschrift für Dieter Henrich*. Frankfurt am Main: Suhrkamp.

Davidson, Donald. 1969. "On Saying That." In D. Davidson and K. J. J. Hintikka, eds., *Words and Objections: Essays on the Work of W. V. Quine*. Dordrecht: Reidel.

Descartes, René. 1641. *Meditations*.

———. 1941. ed. André Bridoux. *Oeuvres et lettres*. Paris: Bibliotheque de la Pleade.

Donnellan, Keith. 1966. "Reference and Definite Descriptions." *The Philosophical Review* 75: 281–304.

Dumas, Alexandre. 1952. *Fils, La Dame aux Camèlias*. In Stephen S. Stanton, ed., *Camille and Other Plays*, trans. Edith Reynolds and Nigel Playfair. New York: Hill and Wang.

Dunn, Michael, and Nuel Belnap. 1968. "The Substitution Interpretation of the Quantifiers." *Nous* 2: 177–185.

Evans, Gareth. 1977. "Pronouns, Quantifiers, and Relative Clauses." *Canadian Journal of Philosophy* 17: 467–536.

———. 1982. *The Varieties of Reference*. Oxford: Oxford University Press.

———. 1985. *Collected Papers*. Oxford: Oxford University Press.

Falk, Hans-Peter. 1985. "Neuere analytische Literatur zur Theorie des Selbstbewusstseins." *Philosophische Rundschau* 32: 117–134.

Fetzer, James, ed. 1984. *Principles of Philosophical Reasoning*. New Jersey: Rowman and Allanheld.

Fichte, Johann Gottlieb. 1794. *Science of Knowledge*. Trans. Peter Heath and John Lachs. New York: Appleton-Century-Crofts, 1970.

Fine, Kit. 1984. "Critical Review of Parson's *Non-Existent Objects*." *Philosophical Studies* 45: 95–142.

Förster, Eckert, ed. 1989. *Kant's Transcendental Deductions: The Three "Critiques" and the "Opus Posthumum*." Stanford: Stanford University Press.

Frank, Manfred. 1988. *What Is Neostructuralism?*. Trans. Sabine Wilke and Richard Gray. Minneapolis: University of Minnesota Press.

———. 1990. *Zeitbewusstsein*. Tübingen: Neske.

———. 1991a. *Selbstbewusstsein und Selbsterkenntnis*. Stuttgart: Reclam.

———. 1991b. "Fragmente einer Geschichte der Selbstbewusstseinstheorien von Kant bis Sartre." In *Selbstbewusstseinstheorien von Fichte bis Sartre*, ed. Manfred Frank. Frankfurt am Main: Suhrkamp, 413–599.

———. 1994. *Analytische Theorien des Selbstbewusstseins und Selbsterkenntnis*. Stuttgart: Reclam.

———. 1995. "On Some Difficulties in Naturalistic Reductions of Self-Consciousness." In *The Modern Subject: Conceptions of the Self in Classical German Philosophy*, ed. Karl Ameriks and Dieter Sturma. Albany: State University of New York Press.

Frege, Gottlob. 1892. *Translations from the Philosophical Writings of Gottlob Frege*, ed. Peter Geach and Max Black. Oxford: Basil Blackwell.

———. 1918. "The Thought: A Logical Enquiry." Trans. A. and M. Quinton. *Mind* 65 (1956): 289–311.

French, Peter, Ted Uewhling, and Howard Wettstein, eds. 1977. *Contemporary Perspectives in the Philosophy of Language*. Minneapolis: University of Minnesota Press.

Freud, Sigmund. 1900/1938. *The Interpretation of Dreams*. In *The Basic Writings of Sigmund Freud*. Trans. and ed. A. A. Brill. New York: The Modern Library.

Fricke, Christel. 1991. "Über die externe und interne Reflexivität von Akten geistiger Bezugnahme: Correferat zu Hector-Neri Castañeda." In Kienzle and Pape, 137–146.

Geach, Peter T. 1956. *Mental Acts*. London: Routledge and Kegan Paul.

———. 1957. "On Beliefs about Oneself." *Analysis* 18: 23–24.

———. 1962. *Reference and Generality*. Ithaca: Cornell University Press.

Goodman, Nelson. 1951. *The Structure of Appearance*. Cambridge: Harvard University Press.

Grim, Patrick. 1985. "Against Omniscience: The Case from Essential Indexicals." *Nous* 19: 151–180.

———. 1988. "Logic and the Limits of Knowledge and Truth." *Nous* 22: 341–367.

Grossmann, Reinhardt. 1965. *The Structure of Mind*. Madison: University of Wisconsin Press.

———. 1976. Review of Cornman 1975. In *International Studies in Philosophy* 8 (1976): 210–213.

Grundmann, Thomas. 1994. "*Einleitung*" to Castañeda 1987c. In Frank 1994, 321–334.

Gunderson, Keith, ed. 1975. *Language, Mind, and Knowledge*. Minneapolis: University of Minnesota Press.

Guyer, Paul. 1980. "Kant on Apperception and A Priori Synthesis." *American Journal of Philosophy* 17.

———. 1989. "Psychology and the Transcendental Deduction." In Förster 1989.

Hahn, Lewis Edwin, ed. 1997. *The Philosophy of Roderick M. Chisholm*. Chicago and LaSalle: Open Court.

Hart, James G. 1992. "Being's Mindfulness." In *The Phenomenology of the Noema*, ed. John Drummond and Lester Embree. Dordrecht: Kluwer, 122–126.

———. 1998. "Intentionality, Phenomenality, and Light." In Zahavi 1998.

Heckmann, Heinz-Dieter. 1990. "Guise-Theory and the Riddle of Intentionality (of Thinking about Particulars)." In Jacobi and Pape 1990.

Henrich, Dieter. 1966. "Fichtes' ursprüngliche Einsicht"; trans. "Fichte's Original Insight." In *Contemporary German Philosophy*, Vol. I. University Park and London: Pennsylvania State University Press, 1982, 15–53.

———. 1971. "Self-Consciousness: A Critical Introduction to a Theory." *Man and World* IV: 3–28.

———. 1982a. *Fluchtlinien*. Frankfurt am Main: Suhrkamp, 99ff.

———. 1982b. *Selbstverhältnisse*. Stuttgart: Reclam, 57–130.

———. 1989. "Kant's Notion of a Deduction and the Methodological Background of the First *Critique*." In Förster 1989.

Henry, Michel. 1973. *The Essence of Manifestation*. Trans. Girard Etzkorn. The Hague: Martinus Nijhoff; reissue, Dordrecht: Kluwer.

Hintikka, Jaakko. 1958. "Towards a Theory of Definite Descriptions." *Analysis* 19: 78–95.

———. 1962. *Knowledge and Belief: An Introduction to the Logic of the Two Notions*. Ithaca: Cornell University Press.

———. 1966. "Knowing Oneself and Other Problems in Epistemic Logic." *Theoria* 32: 1–13.

———. 1967. "Individuals, Possible Worlds, and Epistemic Logic." *Nous* 1: 33–62.

———. 1970a. "On Attributions of Self-Knowledge." *The Journal of Philosophy* 67, No. 3: 73–87.

———. 1970b. "'Knowing That One Knows' Reviewed." *Synthese* 21: 141–162.

Husserl, Edmund. 1991. *On the Phenomenology of the Consciousness of Internal Time (1893–1917)*. Trans. John Barnett Brough. Dordrecht: Kluwer, 1991.

———. 1996. *Analysen zur passiven Synthesis (1918–1926)*. The Hague: Martinus Nijhoff.

Jackson, Frank. 1975. "On the Adverbial Analysis of Visual Experience." *Metaphilosophy* 6: 127–135.

Jacobi, Klaus. 1980. *Die Modalbegriffe in den logischen Schriften des Wilhelm von Shyreswood*. Leiden: Brill.

———. 1990. "Individuation—Prädikation: Bermerkungen zu Castañeda's 'Theorie der individuellen Gestaltungen.'" In Jacobi and Pape 1990, 495–522.

Jacobi, Klaus, and Helmut Pape. 1990. *Thinking and the Structure of the World/ Das Denken und die Struktur der Welt*. Berlin and New York: Walter de Gruyter.

Jaeger, Robert. 1977. "Am I in the World?" *American Philosophical Quarterly* 14: 239–245.

Johnstone, Henry, Jr. 1970. *The Problem of the Self*. University Park: Pennsylvania State University Press.

Kant, Immanuel. 1781, 1787. *Critique of Pure Reason*. Trans. Norman Kemp Smith. London: Macmillan, 1963.

Kapitan, Tomis. 1990a. "Preserving a Robust Sense of Reality." In Jacobi and Pape 1990, 449–458.

———. 1990b. Review of Tomberlin 1986. *Nous* 24: 473–486.

———. 1998a. "The Ubiquity of Self-Awareness." In *Grazer philosophische Studien* (forthcoming).

———. 1998b. "On Depicting Indexical Reference." In William Rapaport and Francesco Orilia, *Thought, Language, and Ontology: Essays in Memory of Hector-Neri Castañeda*. Dordrecht: Kluwer, 1988, 183–215.

Kaplan, David. 1975. "How to Russell a Frege-Church." *The Journal of Philosophy* 72: 716–729.

———. 1977. "Demonstratives: An Essay on the Semantics, Logic, Metaphysics, and Epistemology of Demonstratives and Other Indexicals." Widely circulated manuscript eventually published in Almog et al. 1989, 481–564.

———. 1989. "Afterthoughts." In Almog et al. 1989, 565–614.

Kienzle, Bertram, and Helmut Pape, eds. 1991. *Dimensionen des Selbst*. Frankfurt am Main: Suhrkamp.

King-Farlow, John. 1978. *Self-Knowledge and Social Relations*. New York: Science History Publications.

Kraut, Robert. 1982. "Sensory States and Sensory Objects." *Nous* 16: 277–293.

Kretzmann, Norman. 1966. "Omniscience and Immutability." *The Journal of Philosophy*. 63: 409–421.

Kripke, Saul. 1972. "Naming and Necessity." In Donald Davidson and Gilbert Harman, eds., *Semantics of Natural Language*. 1972. Dordrecht: Reidel.

Küng, Guido. 1990. "'Guises' and Noemata." In Jacobi and Pape 1990, 409–415.

Künne, Wolfgang. 1990. "Perception, Fiction, and Elliptical Speech." In Jacobi and Pape 1990, 259–267.

Lee, Jig-chuen. 1984. "Frege's Paradox and Castañeda's Guise Theory." *Philosophical Studies* 46: 403–415.

Leibniz, Gottfried Wilhelm. 1690. "On the Method of Distinguishing Real from Imaginary Phenomena." In Loemker 1976, 363–366.

Lewis, David. 1966. "An Argument for Identity Theory." *Journal of Philosophy* 63:

17–25. Reprinted in his *Philosophical Papers*, Vol. 1. Oxford: Oxford University Press, 1983.

———. 1979. "Attitudes *De Dicto* and *De Se*." *The Philosophical Review* 88: 513–543.

Loemker, Leroy E., ed. 1976. *Philosophical Papers and Letters*. Dordrecht: Reidel.

Loux, Michael. 1976. "Comments on 'Individuation and Non-Identity': A Reply to Hector-Neri Castañeda." *Critica* V: 105–108.

Lycan, William. 1996. *Consciousness and Experience*. Cambridge: MIT Press.

Mazoue, James. 1986. "Self-Synthesis and Self-Knowledge" (unpublished ms).

Millikan, Ruth. 1993. *White Queen Psychology and Other Essays for Alice*. Cambridge: MIT Press.

Moore, George Edward. 1922. *Philosophical Studies*. London: Kegan Paul, Trench, Trubner & Co.; New York: Harcourt, Brace & Co.

———. 1959. "Wittgenstein's Lectures in 1930–33." Reprinted in G. E. Moore, *Philosophical Papers*. London: George Allen & Unwin; New York: Macmillan, 1959.

Nozick, Robert. 1981. *Philosophical Explanations*. Cambridge: Harvard University Press.

Oehler, Klaus, ed. 1984. *Zeichen und Realität*. Tübingen: Stauffenburg Verlag.

Orilia, Francesco. 1986. *Natural Language Semantics and Guise Theory*. Doctoral Dissertation. Indiana University, Bloomington.

———. 1987. "Review of Zalta's *Abstract Objects: An Introduction to Axiomatic Metaphysics*." *Nous* 21, 2: 270–276.

———. 1989. "Identity across Frames." *Topoi*, Supplement 4.

Pape, Helmut. 1984. "Comment on Castañeda." In Oehler 1984, 219–223.

———. 1994. "*Einleitung*" to Castañeda 1966 and Castañeda 1990a. In Frank 1994, 155–171.

Parsons, Terence. 1980. *Nonexistent Objects*. New Haven and London: Yale University Press.

Pasquerella, Lynn. 1986. "*De Re* Reference and the Problem of the 'He, Himself' Locution" (unpublished).

Perry, John, ed. 1975. *Personal Identity*. Berkeley: University of California Press.

———. 1977. "Frege on Demonstratives." *The Philosophical Review* 86: 464–497.

———. 1979. "The Problem of the Essential Indexical." *Nous* 13: 3–21.

———. 1983. "Castañeda on *He* and *I*." In Tomberlin 1983, 15–42.

Pilot, Harald. 1984. "Comment on Castañeda." In Oehler 1984, 211–218.

———. 1990. "The Executional Role of Indexical Thinking and How to Account for It: Castañeda on Indexical Expressions." In Jacobi and Pape, 285–298.

Place, U. T. 1956. "Is Consciousness a Brain Process?" *British Journal of Psychology* 47: 44–50.

Plantinga, Alvin. 1974. *The Nature of Necessity*. Oxford: Clarendon Press.

———. 1983. "Guise Theory." In Tomberlin 1983, 43–78.

Pollock, John. 1988. "My Bother, the Machine." *Nous* 22: 173–211.

Prauss, Gerold. 1990. "Ptolemaic and Copernican Theories of Reference." In Jacobi and Pape 1990, 308–311.

Prufer, Thomas. 1993. *Recapitulations*. Washington: Catholic University of America Press.

Putnam, Hilary. 1975a. *Mind, Language, and Reality*, Vol. II. Cambridge: Cambridge University Press.

——. 1975b. "The Meaning of 'Meaning.'" In Gunderson 1975.

——. 1987. "Meaning Holism and Epistemic Holism." In Konrad Cramer et al., 1987.

Quine, Willard Van Orman. 1953. *From a Logical Point of View*. Cambridge: Harvard University Press.

——. 1960. *Word and Object*. Cambridge: MIT Press.

Rapaport, William. 1978. "Meinongian Theories and a Russellian Paradox." *Nous* 12: 153–180.

——. 1979a. "How to Make the World Fit Our Language: An Essay in Meinongian Semantics." *Grazer philosophische Studien* 14: 1–21.

——. 1979b. "Adverbial Theories and Meinongian Theories." *Analysis* 39, 2: 75–81.

——. 1982. "Meinong, Defective Objects, and (Psycho-)Logical Paradox." *Grazer philosophische Studien* 18: 17–39.

——. 1985. "Meinongian Semantics for Propositional Attitude Networks." *Proceedings of the Association for Computational Linguistics*, Vol. 23.

——. 1985/1986. "Non-Existent Objects and Epistemological Ontology." *Grazer philosophische Studien*, 25/26.

Rapp, Friedrich. "Conceptualization, the Unity of the World, and Perspectivity." In Jacobi and Pape 1990, 473–476.

Recanati, François. 1993. *Direct Reference*. Oxford: Blackwell.

Reichenbach, Hans. 1947. *Elements of Symbolic Logic*. New York: Macmillan.

Richards, William. 1984. "Self-Consciousness and Agency." *Synthese* 61: 149–172.

Rollins, C. D., ed. 1963. *Knowledge and Experience*. Pittsburgh: Pittsburgh University Press.

Rorty, Amelie O., ed. 1976. *The Identities of Persons*. Berkeley: University of California Press.

Rosenberg, Jay F. 1974. *Linguistic Representation*. Dordrecht: Reidel.

——. 1981. "Apperception and Sartre's 'Pre-Reflective Cogito.'" *American Philosophical Quarterly* 18, 3: 255–260.

——. 1986a. "Castañeda's Ontology." In Tomberlin 1986, 141–166.

——. 1986b. *The Thinking Self*. Philadelphia: Temple University Press.

Rovane, Carol. 1987. "The Epistemology of First-Person Reference." *The Journal of Philosophy* 84: 147–167.

Russell, Bertrand. 1903. *The Principles of Mathematics*. Cambridge: Cambridge University Press.

——. 1905. "On Denoting." *Mind* 14: 479–493.

Saarinen, Esa. 1982. "How to Frege a Russell-Kaplan." *Nous* 16: 253–276.

——. 1986. "Castañeda's Philosophy of Language." In Tomberlin 1986, 187–214.

Sartre, Jean-Paul. 1943. *Being and Nothingness: An Essay on Phenomenological Ontology*. Trans. Hazel Barnes. New York: Philosophical Library, 1956.

——. 1948. "Conscience de soi et la connaissance de soi." *Bulletin de la Société française philosophie* 42; reprinted in Frank 1991b.

——. 1957. *The Transcendence of the Ego*. New York: Noonday Press.

Saussure, Ferdinand de. 1915. *Curso de Lingüística General*. Trans. Amado Alonso. Buenos Aires, 1945.

Searle, John R. 1958. "Proper Names." *Mind*, n.s. 67: 166–173.

Sellars, Wilfrid. 1950. Unpublished Class Lectures.

——. 1956. "Empiricism and the Philosophy of Mind." *Minnesota Studies in the Philosophy of Science* I: 305–328; also in Sellars 1963.

——. 1957. "Time and World Order." In H. Feigl, M. Scriven, and G. Maxwell, eds. *Minnesota Studies in the Philosophy of Science*. Minneapolis: University of Minnesota Press.

——. 1960. "Grammar and Existence: A Preface to Ontology." *Mind* 69: 499–533.

——. 1963. *Science, Perception, and Reality*. London: Routledge & Kegan Paul.

——. 1969. *Science and Metaphysics: Variations on Kantian Themes*. New York: Humanities Press.

——. 1972. " . . . this I or he or it (the thing) which thinks. . . . " *Proceedings of the American Philosophical Association* 44 (1972).

——. 1975. "The Adverbial Theory of Objects of Sensation." *Metaphilosophy* 6: 144–160.

Shirley, Edward. 1987. "Chisholm's Noncomparative Predicates." *Erkenntnis* 27, 3: 371–378.

Shoemaker, Sydney. 1963. *Self-Knowledge and Self-Identity*. Ithaca: Cornell University Press.

——. 1968. "Self-Reference and Self-Awareness." *Journal of Philosophy* 65: 555–578.

Sicha, Jeffrey. 1986. "Castañeda on Plato, Leibniz, and Kant." In Tomberlin 1986, 309–332.

Sleigh, Robert C., Jr. 1965. "On Quantifying into Epistemic Contexts." *Nous* 1: 23–31.

Smart, J. J. C. 1959. "Sensations and Brain Processes." *Philosophical Review* 68: 141–156.

Smith, David Woodruff. 1982. "What's the Meaning of 'This'?" *Nous* 16: 181–208.

——. 1986. "Mind and Guise." In Tomberlin 1986, 167–186.

Smith, Quentin. 1991. "Castañeda's Quasi-Indicators and the Tensed Theory of Time." *Critica: Revista Hispanoamericana de Filosofia* 23: 59–73.

Sokolowski, Robert. 1974. *Husserlian Meditations*. Evanston: Northwestern University Press.

——. 1976. *Presence and Absence*. Bloomington: Indiana University Press.

Soldati, Gianfranco. 1994. "*Einleitung*" to Perry 1979, Perry 1983, and Castañeda 1983b. In Frank 1994, 393–401.

Sosa, Ernest. 1983. "Consciousness of the Self and of the Present." In Tomberlin 1983, 131–146.

Spitzer, Manfred, Friedrich Uehlein, and Godehard Oepen, eds. 1988. *Psychopathology and Philosophy*. Berlin: Springer.

Spitzer, Manfred, and Brendan Maher, eds. 1989. *Philosophy and Psychopathology*. Berlin: Springer.

Strawson, Peter Frederick. 1950. "On Referring." *Mind* 59: 320–344.

——. 1952. *Introduction to Logical Theory*. London: Methuen; New York: John Wiley.

——. 1959. *Individuals: An Essay in Descriptive Metaphysics*. London: Methuen.

——. 1964. "Identifying Reference and Truth-Values." *Theoria* 30: 96–118.

——. 1989. "Sensibility, Understanding, and the Doctrine of Synthesis; Comments on Henrich and Guyer." In Förster 1989.

Thompson, Manley. 1959. "On the Elimination of Singular Terms." *Mind* 6: 361–376.

Tomberlin, James E., ed. 1983. *Agent, Language, and the Structure of the World*. Indianapolis: Hackett.

——. 1984. "Identity, Intensionality, and Intentionality." *Synthese* 61: 111–131.

———. 1985. "Critical Review of Ernest Sosa, ed., *Essays on the Philosophy of Roderick M. Chisholm.*" *Nous* 19: 136–144.

———. 1986. *Hector-Neri Castañeda.* Dordrecht: Reidel.

———. 1987. "Critical Review of Myles Brand's *Intending and Acting.*" *Nous* 21: 45–55.

———. 1988a. "Semantics, Psychological Attitudes, and Conceptual Role." *Philosophical Studies* 53, No. 2: 205–226.

———. 1988b. "Critical Review of William Lycan's *Logical Form in Natural Language.*" *Nous* 22, 1: 133–142.

———. 1989. "Critical Review of David Lewis's *On the Plurality of Worlds.*" *Nous* 23, 1: 117–125.

Tye, Michael. 1975. "The Adverbial Theory: A Defence of Sellars against Jackson." *Metaphilosophy* 6: 136–143.

Weiskrantz, L. 1977. "Trying to Bridge Some Neurophysiological Gaps between Monkey and Man." *British Journal of Psychology* 68: 431–455.

———. 1980. "Varieties of Residual Experience." *Quarterly Journal of Experimental Psychology* 32: 365–386.

Weiskrantz, L.; Warrington, E. K.; Sanders, M. D.; and Marshall, J. 1974. "Visual capacity in the hemianopic field followed by restricted occipital ablation." *Brain* 97: 709–728.

Whitehead, Alfred North. 1929. *Process and Reality.* London and New York: Macmillan.

Wittgenstein, Ludwig. 1952. *Philosophical Investigation.* Trans. Elizabeth M. Anscombe. Oxford: Blackwell.

Zahavi, Dan. 1999. *Self-Awareness and Alterity* (forthcoming, Northwestern University Press).

———, ed. 1998. *Self-Awareness, Temporality, and Alterity.* Dordrecht: Kluwer.

Zalta, E. N. 1983. *Abstract Objects: An Introduction to Axiomatic Metaphysics.* Dordrecht: Reidel.

Zemach, Eddy M. 1985. "*De Se* and Descartes: A New Semantics for Indexicals." *Nous* 19: 181–204.

Index

Index

James G. Hart is Professor of Religious Studies at Indiana University.

Tomis Kapitan is Professor of Philosophy at Northern Illinois University.